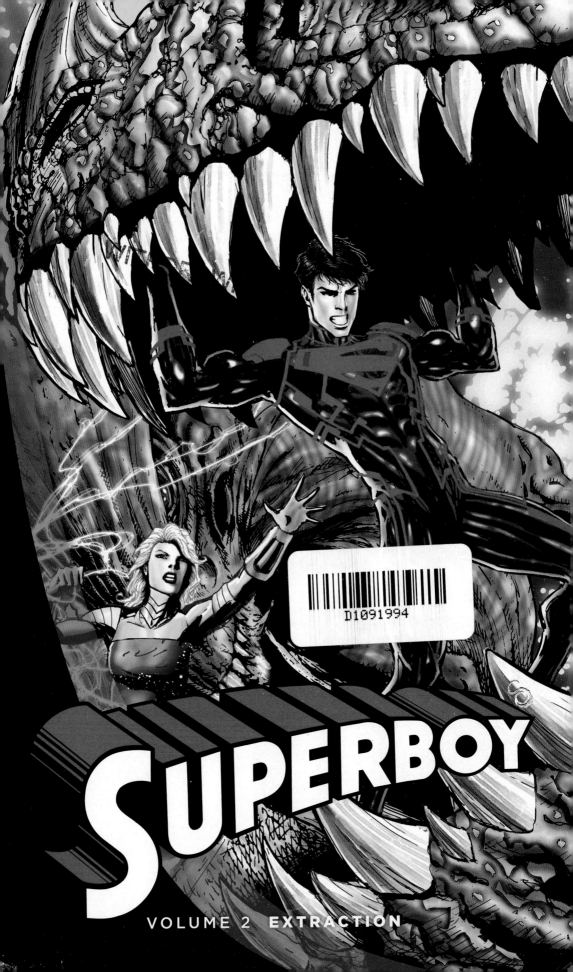

SUPERBOY

VOLUME 2 EXTRACTION

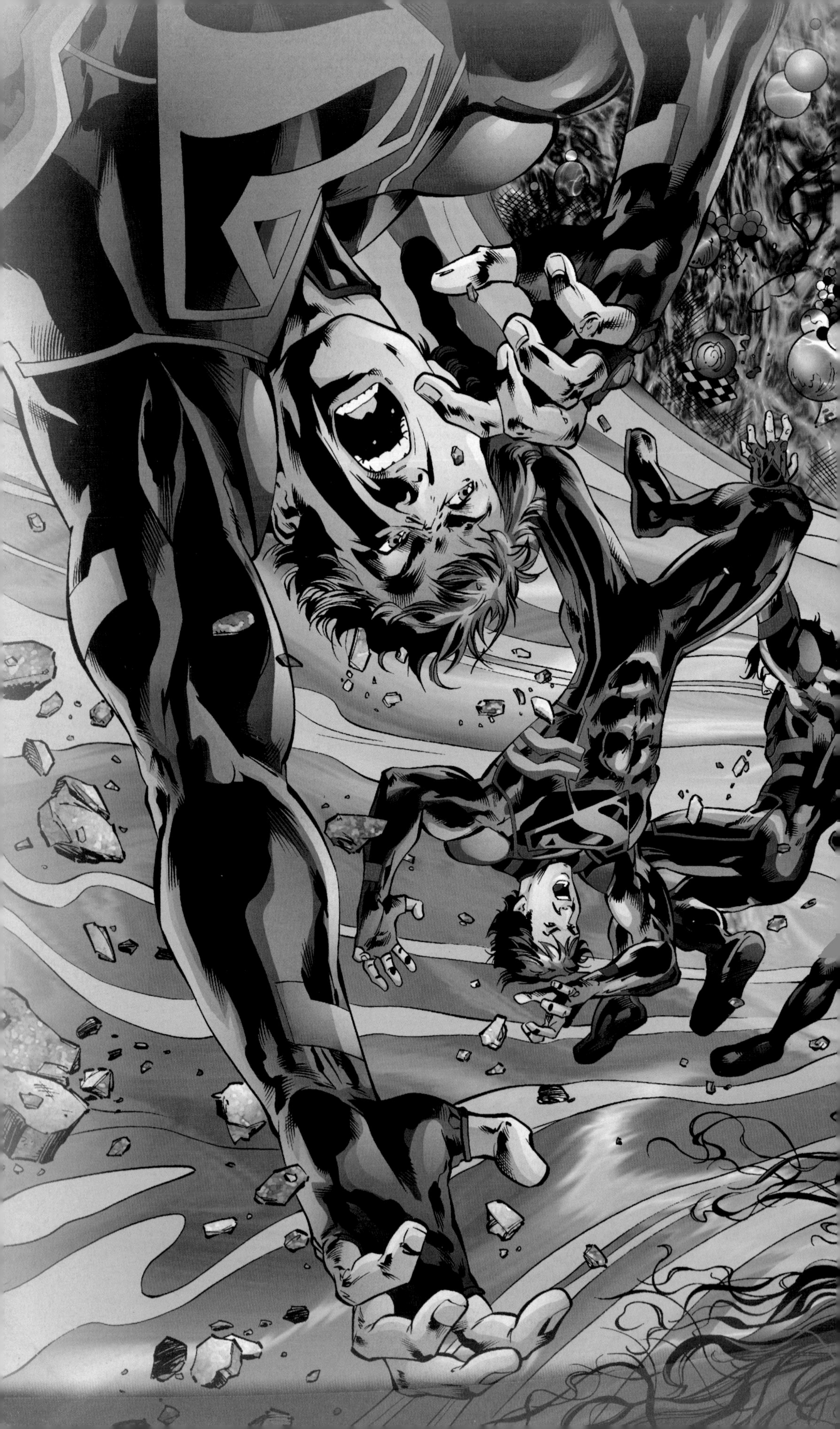

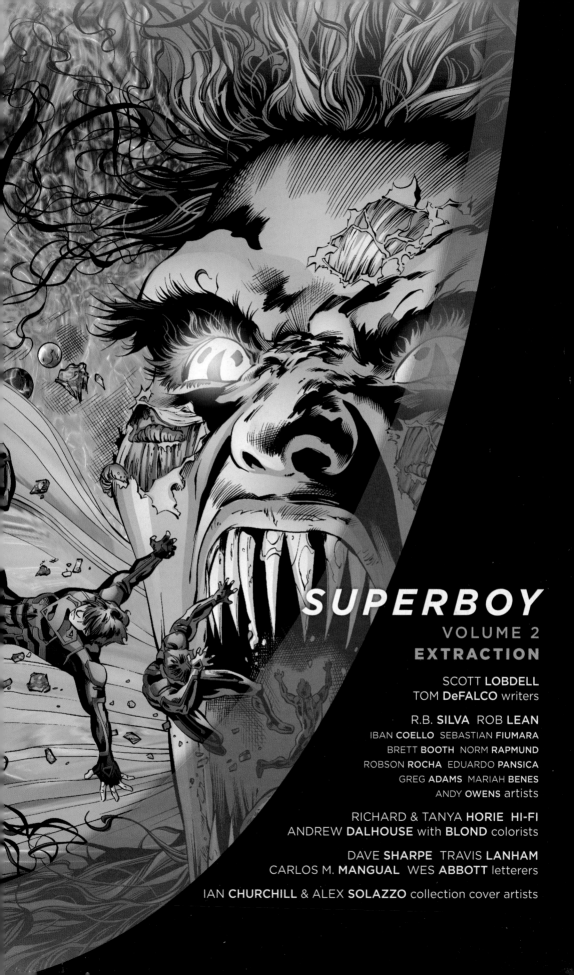

SUPERBOY

VOLUME 2
EXTRACTION

SCOTT **LOBDELL**
TOM **DeFALCO** writers

R.B. **SILVA**   ROB **LEAN**
IBAN **COELLO**   SEBASTIAN **FIUMARA**
BRETT **BOOTH**   NORM **RAPMUND**
ROBSON **ROCHA**   EDUARDO **PANSICA**
GREG **ADAMS**   MARIAH **BENES**
ANDY **OWENS** artists

RICHARD & TANYA **HORIE**   **HI-FI**
ANDREW **DALHOUSE** with **BLOND** colorists

DAVE **SHARPE**   TRAVIS **LANHAM**
CARLOS M. **MANGUAL**   WES **ABBOTT** letterers

IAN **CHURCHILL** & ALEX **SOLAZZO** collection cover artists

CHRIS CONROY EDDIE BERGANZA Editors – Original Series DARREN SHAN Assistant Editor – Original Series
ROWENA YOW Editor ROBBIN BROSTERMAN Design Director – Books ROBBIE BIEDERMAN Publication Design

BOB HARRAS VP – Editor-in-Chief

DIANE NELSON President DAN DIDIO and JIM LEE Co-Publishers GEOFF JOHNS Chief Creative Officer
JOHN ROOD Executive VP – Sales, Marketing and Business Development AMY GENKINS Senior VP – Business and Legal Affairs
NAIRI GARDINER Senior VP – Finance JEFF BOISON VP – Publishing Operations
MARK CHIARELLO VP – Art Direction and Design JOHN CUNNINGHAM VP – Marketing
TERRI CUNNINGHAM VP – Talent Relations and Services ALISON GILL Senior VP – Manufacturing and Operations
HANK KANALZ Senior VP – Digital JAY KOGAN VP – Business and Legal Affairs, Publishing
JACK MAHAN VP – Business Affairs, Talent NICK NAPOLITANO VP – Manufacturing Administration
SUE POHJA VP – Book Sales COURTNEY SIMMONS Senior VP – Publicity BOB WAYNE Senior VP – Sales

SUPERBOY VOLUME 2: EXTRACTION

DC Comics, 1700 Broadway, New York, NY 10019
A Warner Bros. Entertainment Company.
Printed by RR Donnelley, Salem, VA, USA. 5/29/13. First Printing.

ISBN: 978-1-4012-4049-3

Library of Congress Cataloging-in-Publication Data

Lobdell, Scott, author.
Superboy. Volume 2, Extraction / Scott Lobdell, R.B. Silva, Tom DeFalco.
pages cm
"Originally published in single magazine form in Superboy 8-12, 0; Teen Titans 10."
ISBN 978-1-4012-4049-3
1. Graphic novels. I. Silva, R. B., 1985- illustrator. II. DeFalco, Tom, author. III. Title. IV. Title: Extraction.
PN6728.S87L64 2013
741.5'973—dc23
                                2012050772

SUSTAINABLE Certified Chain of Custody
FORESTRY   At Least 20% Certified Forest Content
INITIATIVE www.sfiprogram.org
SFI-01042
APPLIES TO TEXT STOCK ONLY

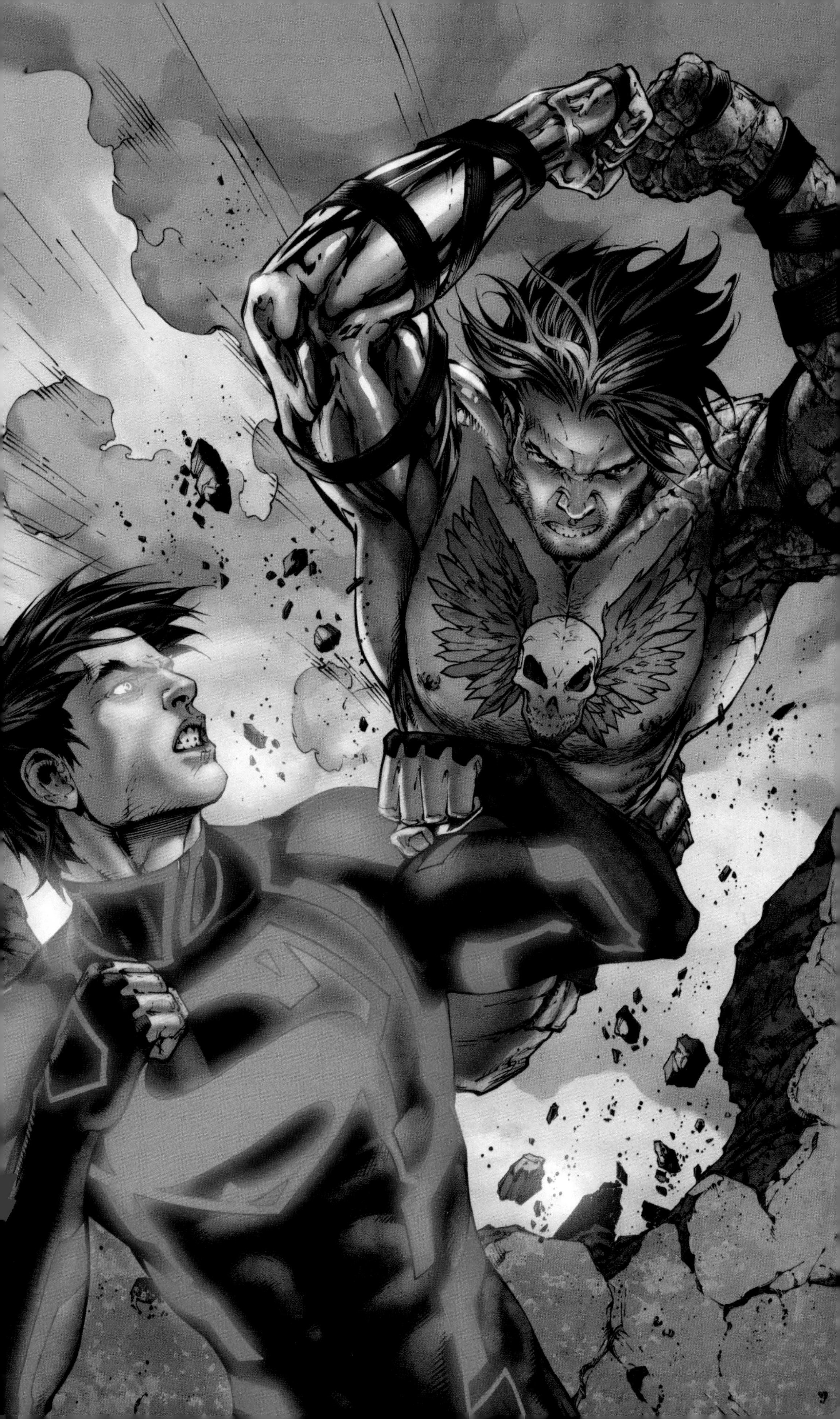

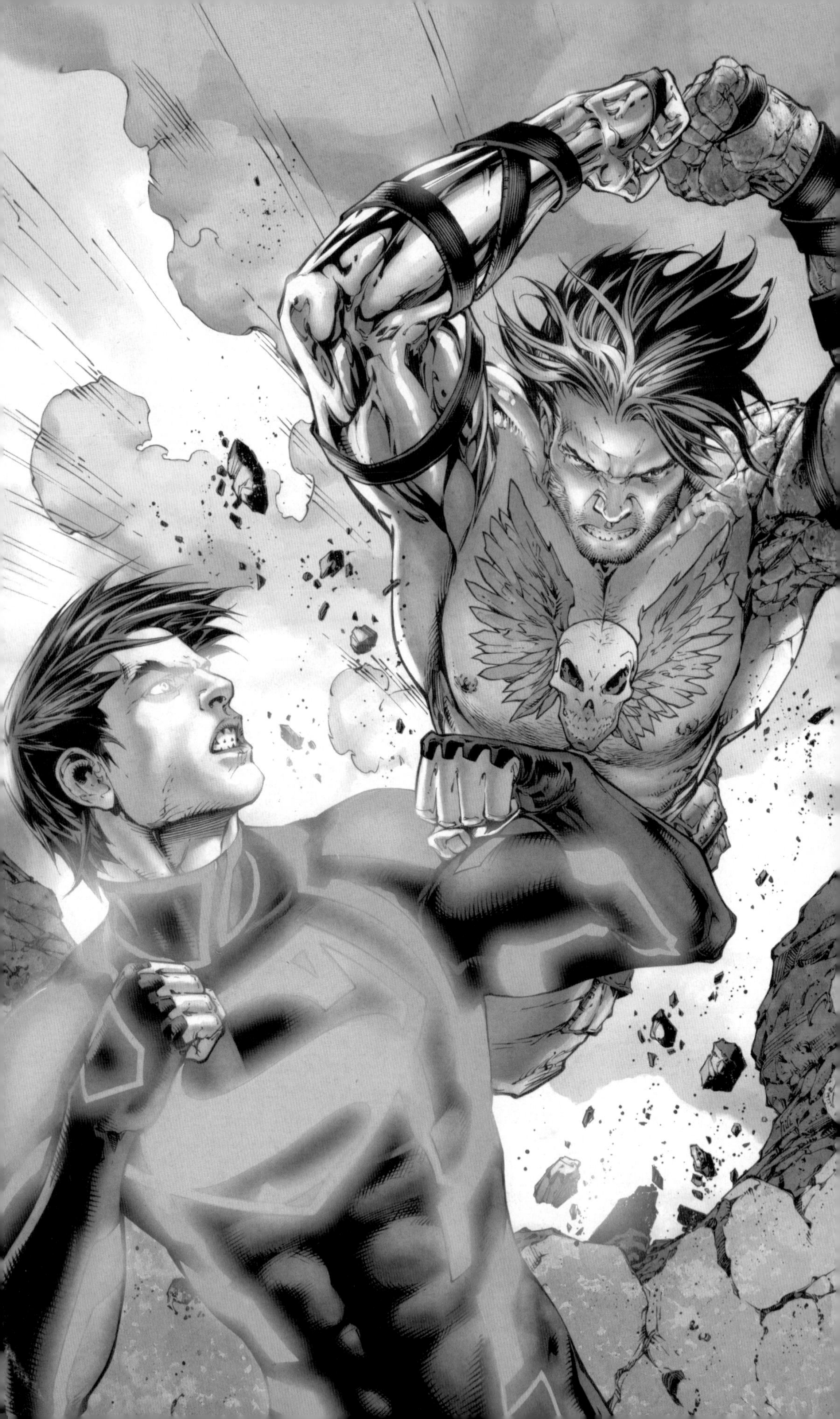

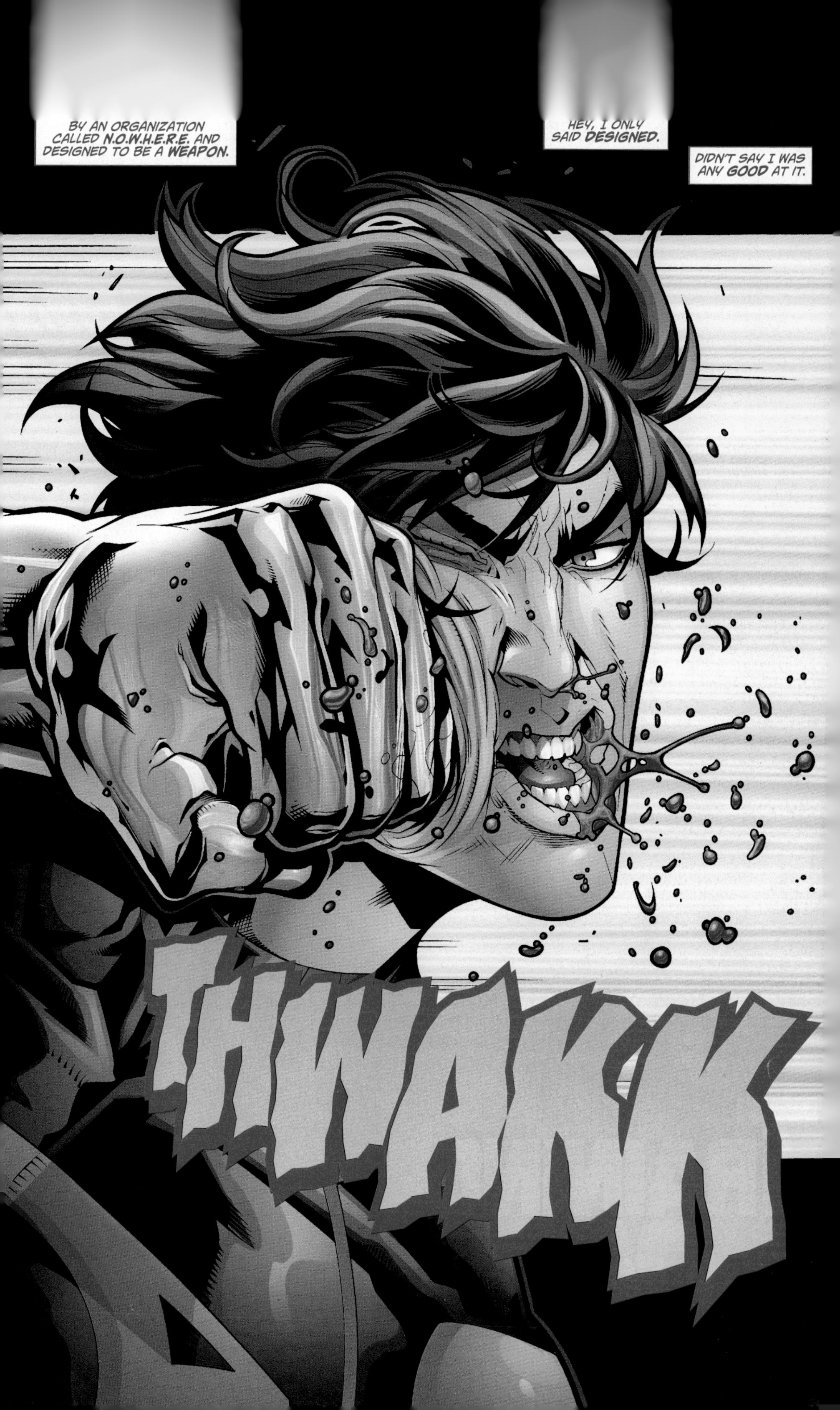

BY AN ORGANIZATION CALLED N.O.W.H.E.R.E. AND DESIGNED TO BE A WEAPON.
HEY, I ONLY SAID DESIGNED.
DIDN'T SAY I WAS ANY GOOD AT IT.
THWAKK

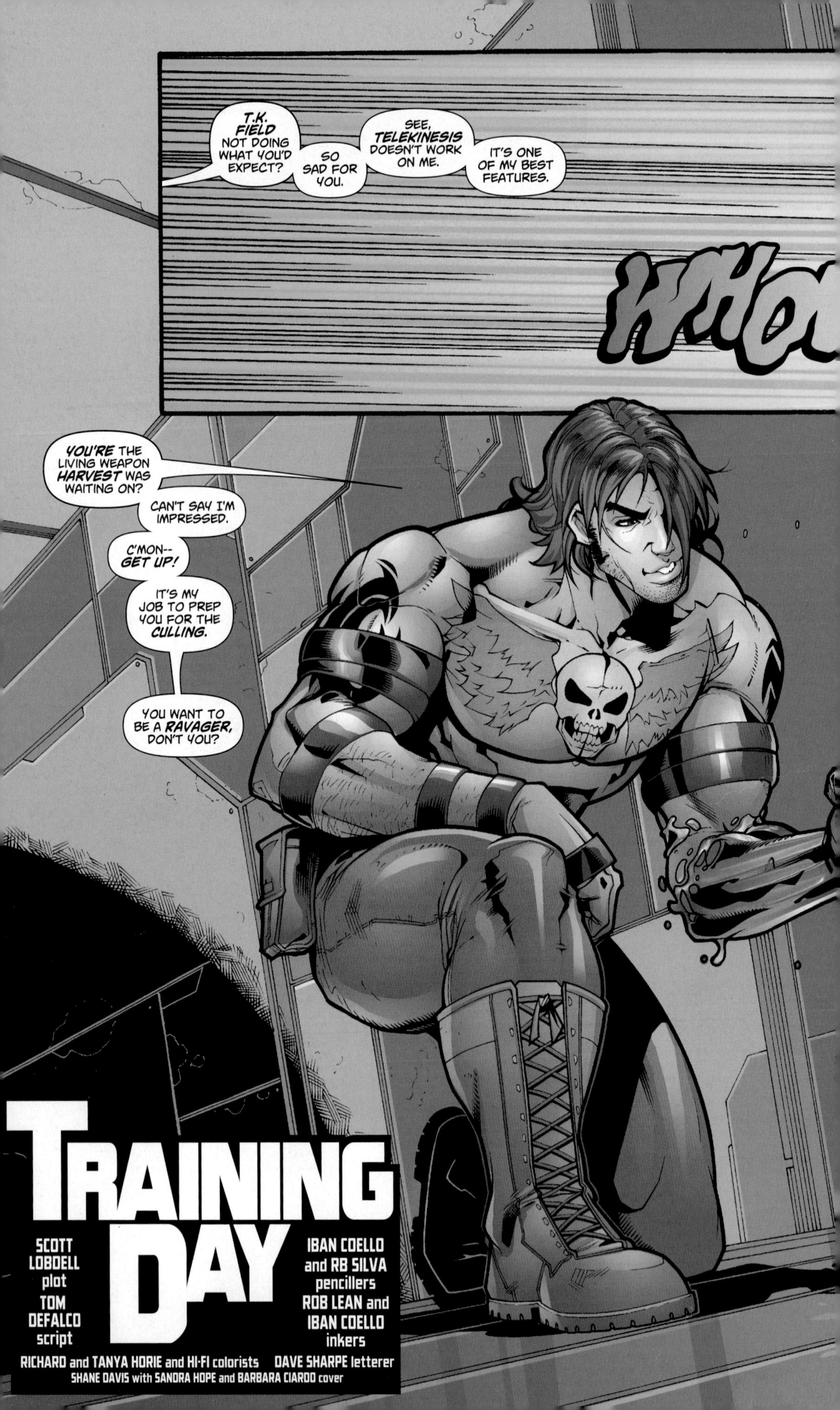
T.K. FIELD NOT DOING WHAT YOU'D EXPECT?
SO SAD FOR YOU.
SEE, TELEKINESIS DOESN'T WORK ON ME.
IT'S ONE OF MY BEST FEATURES.
YOU'RE THE LIVING WEAPON HARVEST WAS WAITING ON?
CAN'T SAY I'M IMPRESSED.
C'MON-- GET UP!
IT'S MY JOB TO PREP YOU FOR THE CULLING.
YOU WANT TO BE A RAVAGER, DON'T YOU?
TRAINING DAY
SCOTT LOBDELL plot
TOM DEFALCO script
IBAN COELLO and RB SILVA pencillers
ROB LEAN and IBAN COELLO inkers
RICHARD and TANYA HORIE and HI-FI colorists
DAVE SHARPE letterer
SHANE DAVIS with SANDRA HOPE and BARBARA CIARDO cover

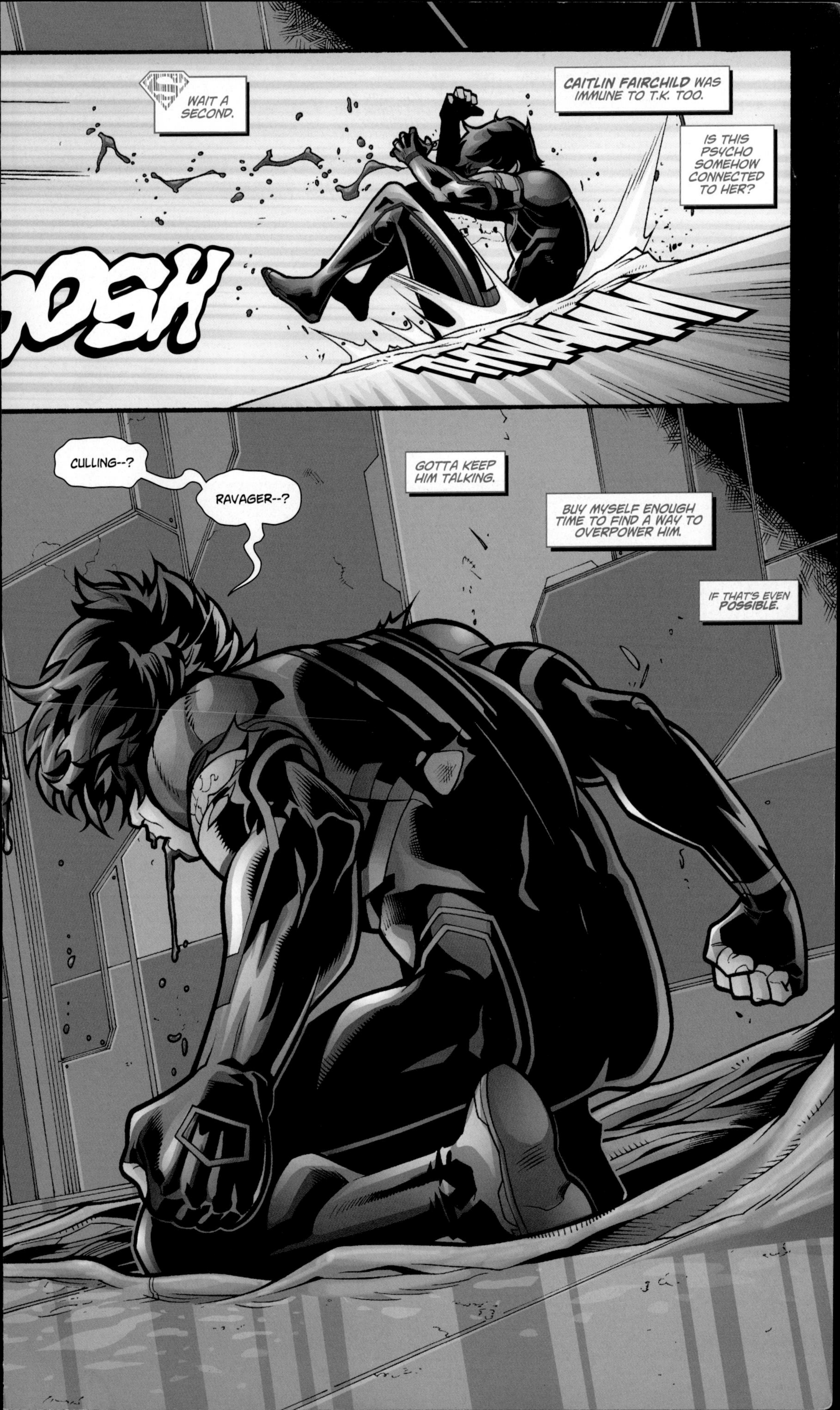

WAIT A SECOND.
CAITLIN FAIRCHILD WAS IMMUNE TO T.K. TOO.
IS THIS PSYCHO SOMEHOW CONNECTED TO HER?
OSH
CULLING--?
RAVAGER--?
GOTTA KEEP HIM TALKING.
BUY MYSELF ENOUGH TIME TO FIND A WAY TO OVERPOWER HIM.
IF THAT'S EVEN POSSIBLE.

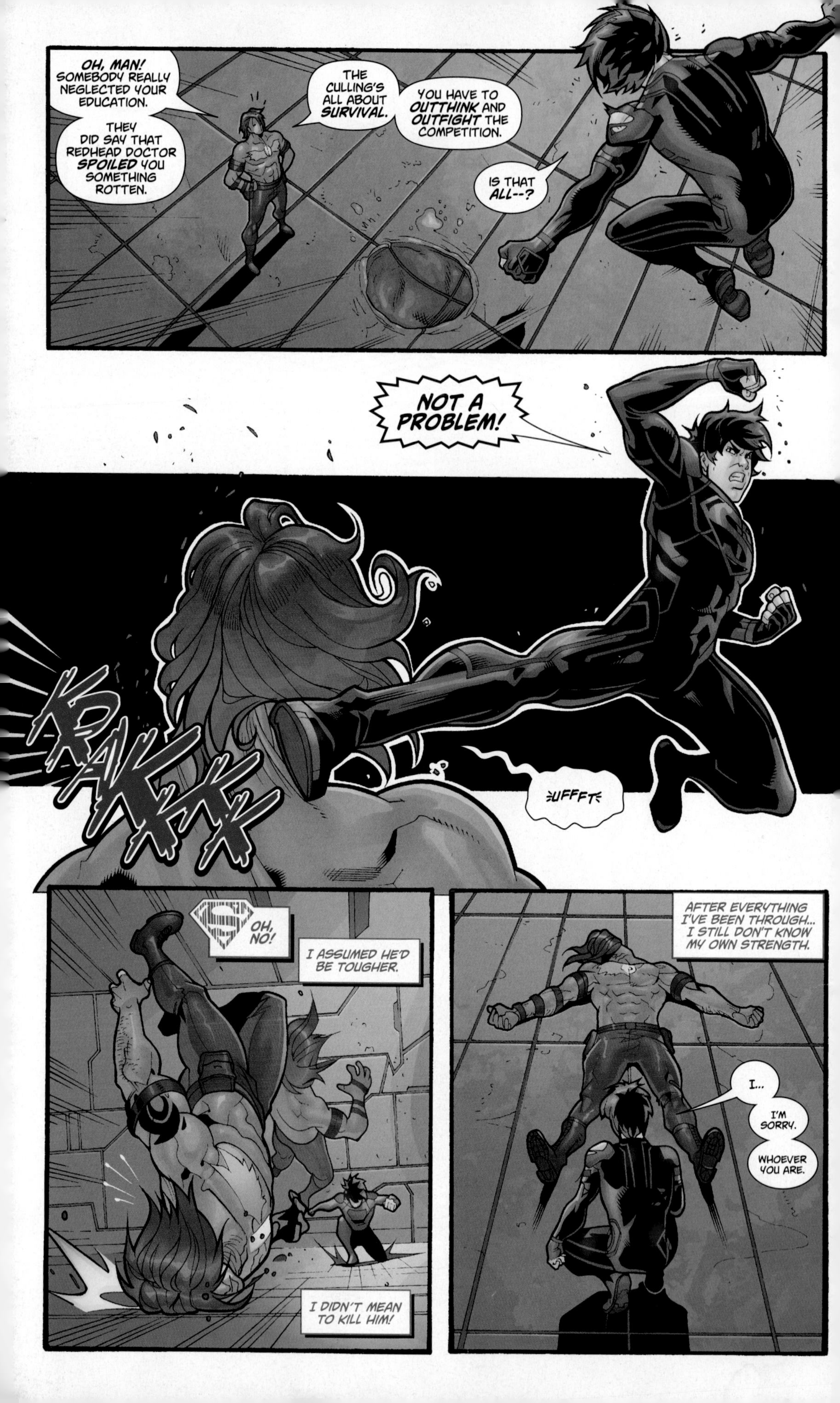
OH, MAN! SOMEBODY REALLY NEGLECTED YOUR EDUCATION.
THEY DID SAY THAT REDHEAD DOCTOR SPOILED YOU SOMETHING ROTTEN.
THE CULLING'S ALL ABOUT SURVIVAL.
YOU HAVE TO OUTTHINK AND OUTFIGHT THE COMPETITION.
IS THAT ALL--?
NOT A PROBLEM!
KRAKKKK
UFFFT
OH, NO!
I ASSUMED HE'D BE TOUGHER.
I DIDN'T MEAN TO KILL HIM!
AFTER EVERYTHING I'VE BEEN THROUGH... I STILL DON'T KNOW MY OWN STRENGTH.
I...
I'M SORRY.
WHOEVER YOU ARE.

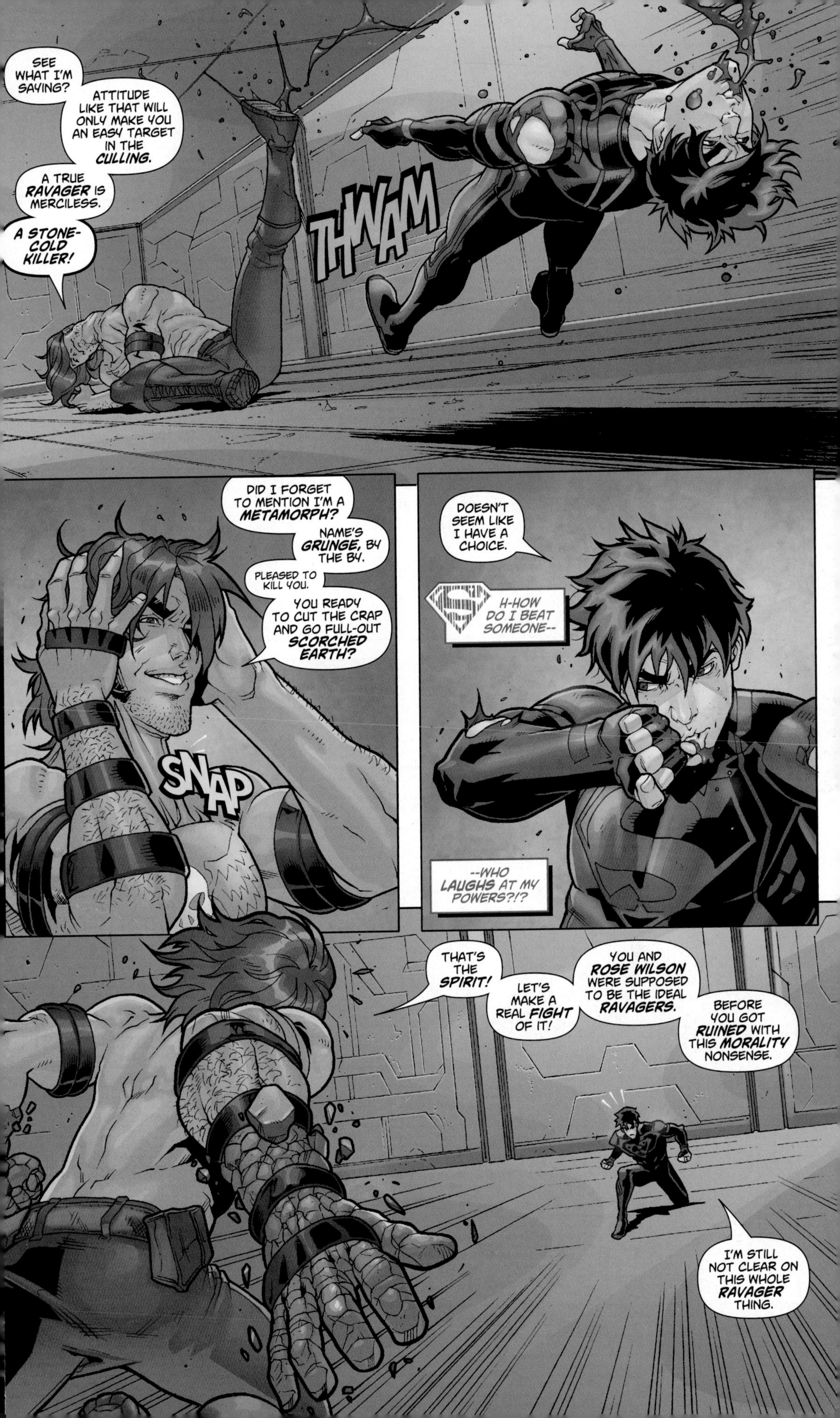
SEE WHAT I'M SAYING?
ATTITUDE LIKE THAT WILL ONLY MAKE YOU AN EASY TARGET IN THE CULLING.
A TRUE RAVAGER IS MERCILESS.
A STONE-COLD KILLER!
THWAM
DID I FORGET TO MENTION I'M A METAMORPH?
NAME'S GRUNGE, BY THE BY.
PLEASED TO KILL YOU.
YOU READY TO CUT THE CRAP AND GO FULL-OUT SCORCHED EARTH?
SNAP
DOESN'T SEEM LIKE I HAVE A CHOICE.
H-HOW DO I BEAT SOMEONE--
--WHO LAUGHS AT MY POWERS?!?
THAT'S THE SPIRIT!
LET'S MAKE A REAL FIGHT OF IT!
YOU AND ROSE WILSON WERE SUPPOSED TO BE THE IDEAL RAVAGERS.
BEFORE YOU GOT RUINED WITH THIS MORALITY NONSENSE.
I'M STILL NOT CLEAR ON THIS WHOLE RAVAGER THING.

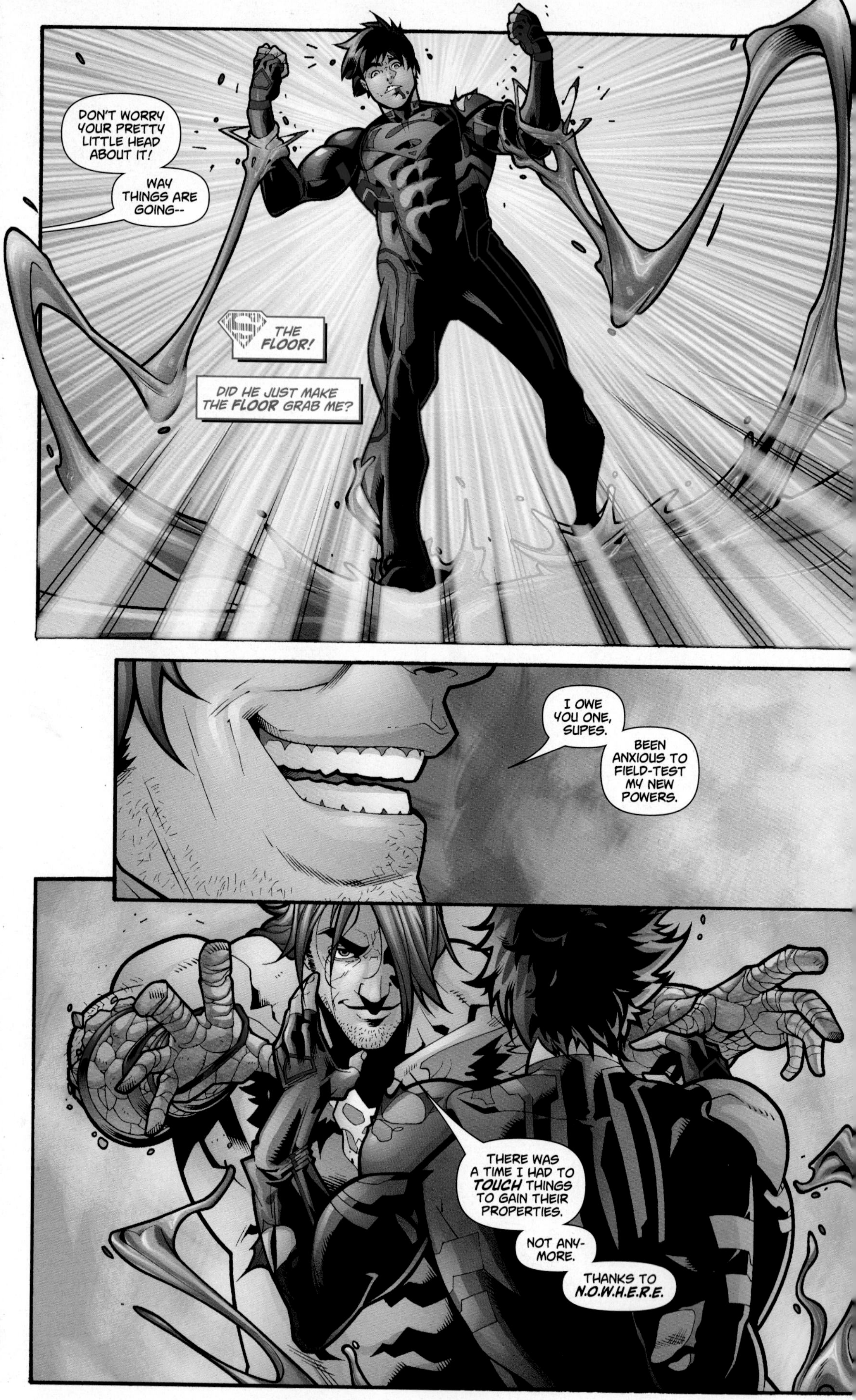
DON'T WORRY YOUR PRETTY LITTLE HEAD ABOUT IT!
WAY THINGS ARE GOING--
THE FLOOR!
DID HE JUST MAKE THE FLOOR GRAB ME?
I OWE YOU ONE, SUPES.
BEEN ANXIOUS TO FIELD-TEST MY NEW POWERS.
THERE WAS A TIME I HAD TO TOUCH THINGS TO GAIN THEIR PROPERTIES.
NOT ANY-MORE.
THANKS TO N.O.W.H.E.R.E.

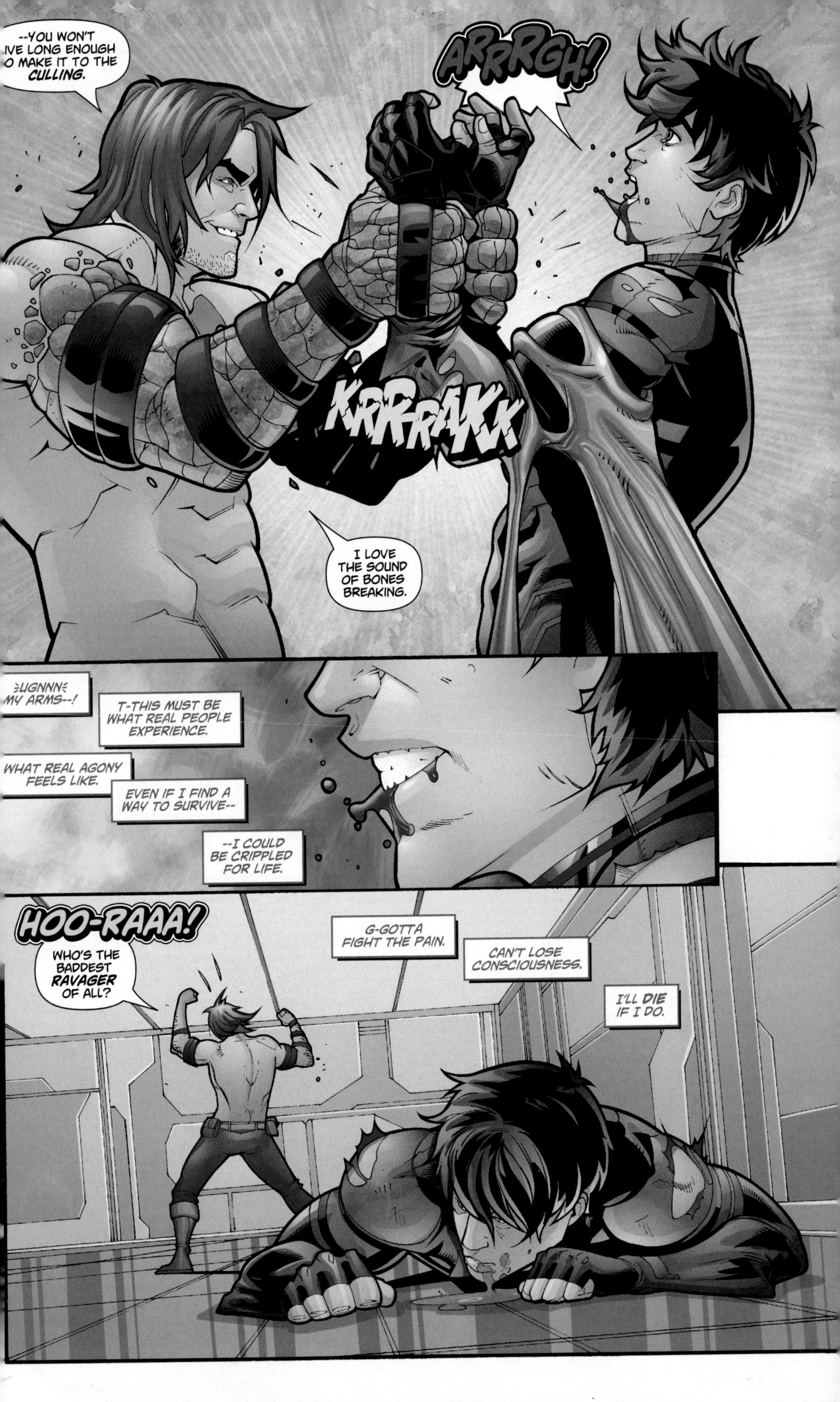
--YOU WON'T LIVE LONG ENOUGH TO MAKE IT TO THE CULLING.
ARRRGH!
KRRRRAKKK
I LOVE THE SOUND OF BONES BREAKING.
UGNNN MY ARMS--!
T-THIS MUST BE WHAT REAL PEOPLE EXPERIENCE.
WHAT REAL AGONY FEELS LIKE.
EVEN IF I FIND A WAY TO SURVIVE--
--I COULD BE CRIPPLED FOR LIFE.
HOO-RAAA!
WHO'S THE BADDEST RAVAGER OF ALL?
G-GOTTA FIGHT THE PAIN.
CAN'T LOSE CONSCIOUSNESS.
I'LL DIE IF I DO.

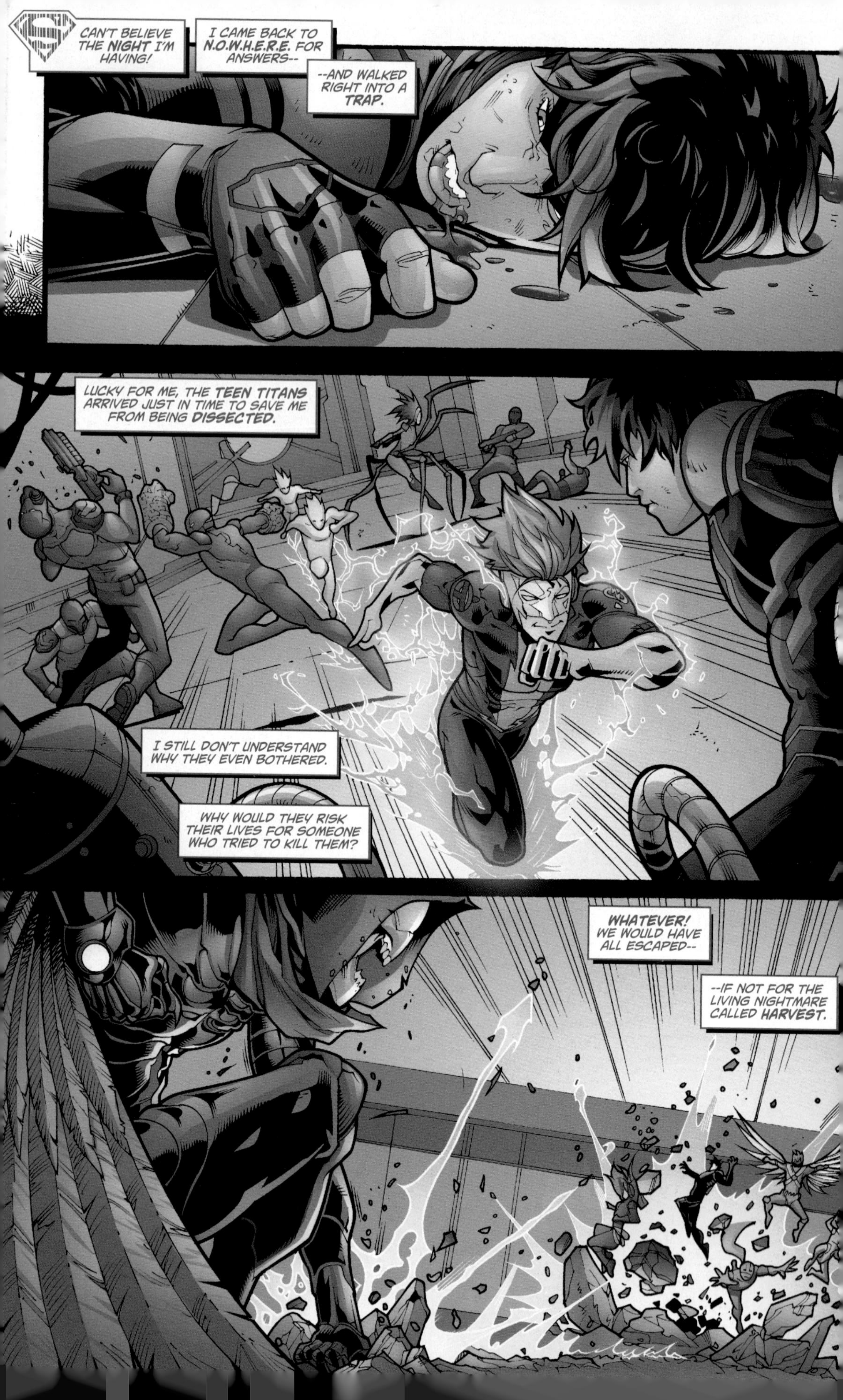
CAN'T BELIEVE THE NIGHT I'M HAVING!
I CAME BACK TO N.O.W.H.E.R.E. FOR ANSWERS--
--AND WALKED RIGHT INTO A TRAP.
LUCKY FOR ME, THE TEEN TITANS ARRIVED JUST IN TIME TO SAVE ME FROM BEING DISSECTED.
I STILL DON'T UNDERSTAND WHY THEY EVEN BOTHERED.
WHY WOULD THEY RISK THEIR LIVES FOR SOMEONE WHO TRIED TO KILL THEM?
WHATEVER! WE WOULD HAVE ALL ESCAPED--
--IF NOT FOR THE LIVING NIGHTMARE CALLED HARVEST.

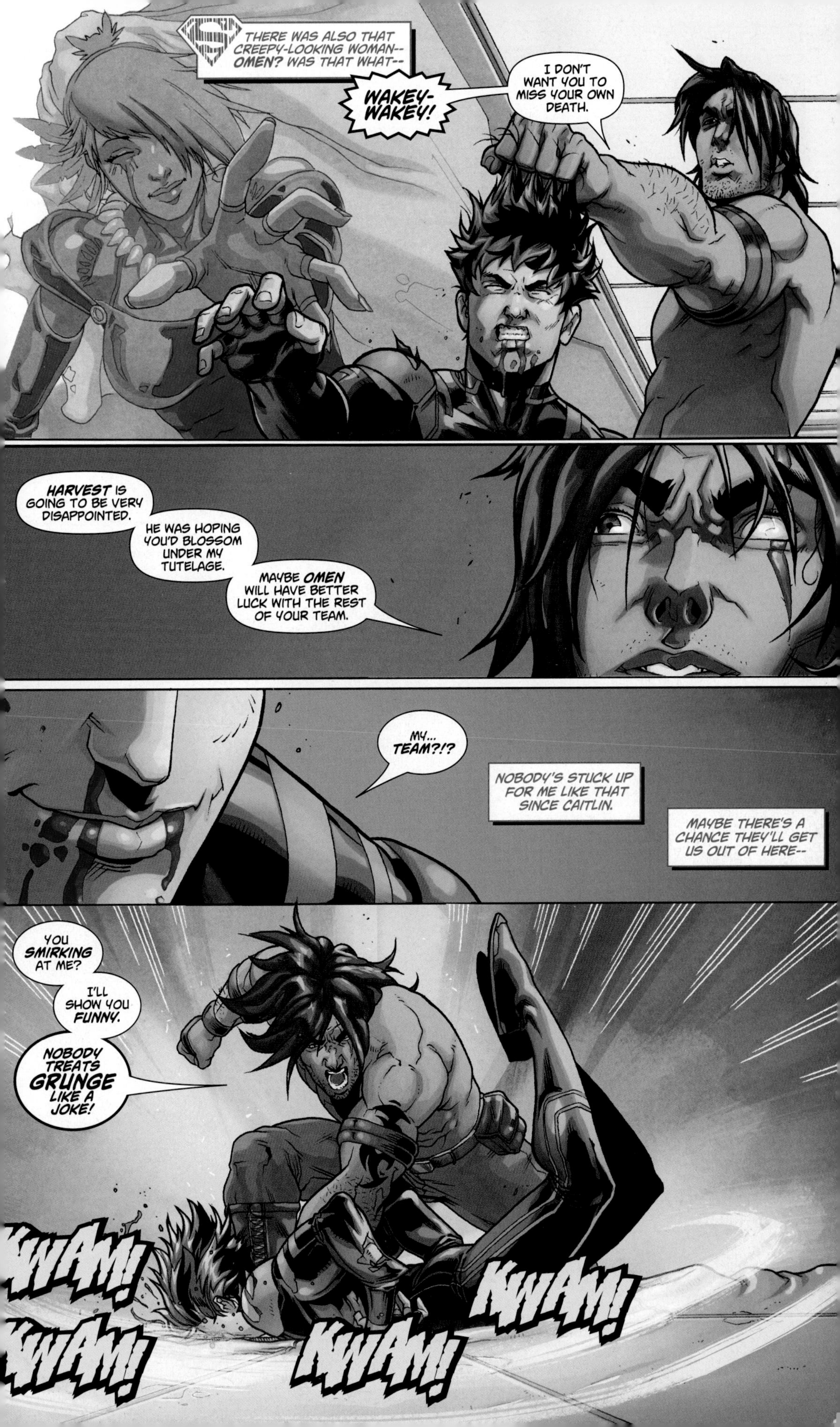
THERE WAS ALSO THAT CREEPY-LOOKING WOMAN-- OMEN? WAS THAT WHAT--
WAKEY-WAKEY!
I DON'T WANT YOU TO MISS YOUR OWN DEATH.
HARVEST IS GOING TO BE VERY DISAPPOINTED.
HE WAS HOPING YOU'D BLOSSOM UNDER MY TUTELAGE.
MAYBE OMEN WILL HAVE BETTER LUCK WITH THE REST OF YOUR TEAM.
MY... TEAM?!?
NOBODY'S STUCK UP FOR ME LIKE THAT SINCE CAITLIN.
MAYBE THERE'S A CHANCE THEY'LL GET US OUT OF HERE--
YOU SMIRKING AT ME?
I'LL SHOW YOU FUNNY.
NOBODY TREATS GRUNGE LIKE A JOKE!
KWAM!
KWAM!
KWAM!
KWAM!

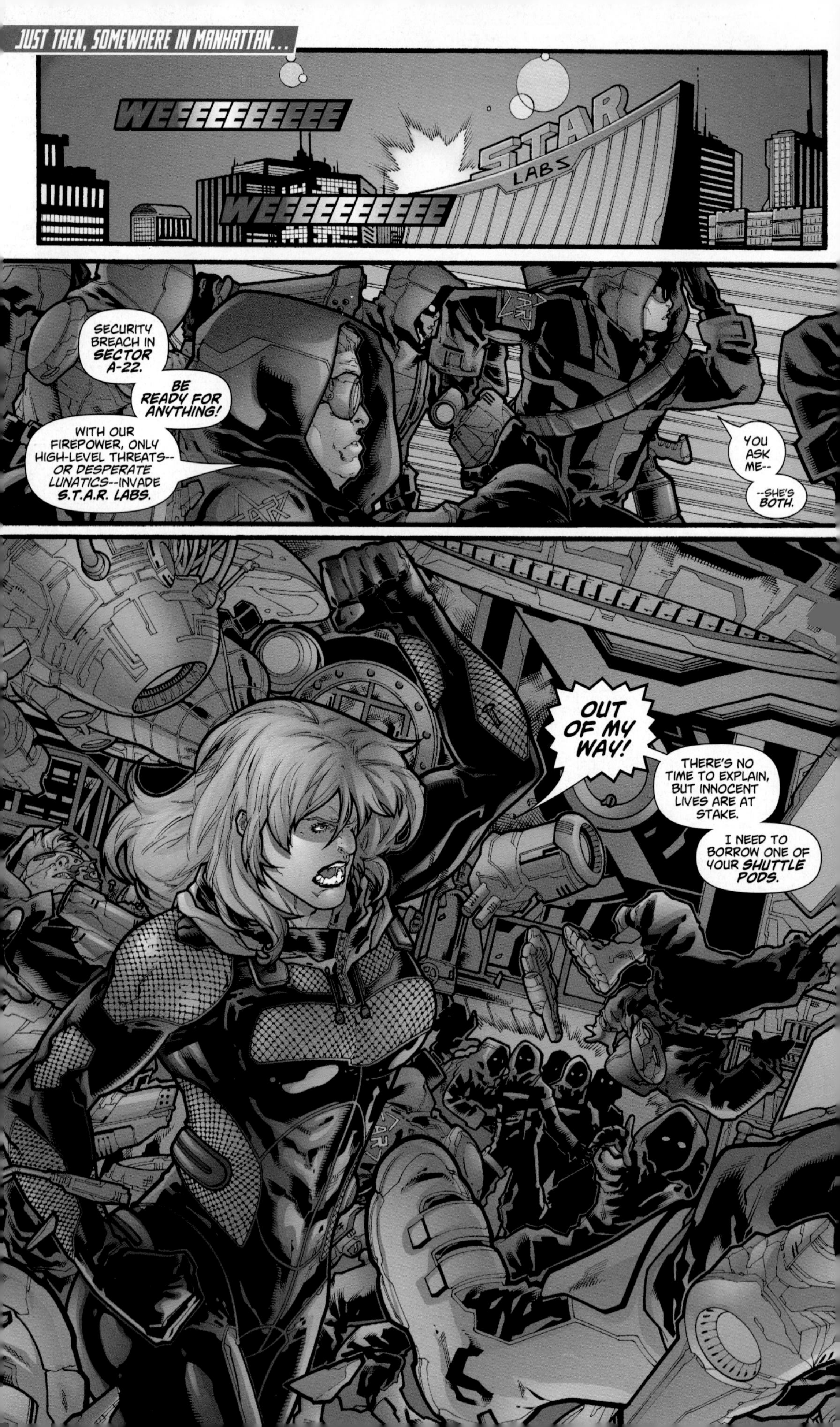
JUST THEN, SOMEWHERE IN MANHATTAN...
WEEEEEEEEEE
S.T.A.R. LABS
WEEEEEEEEEEE
SECURITY BREACH IN SECTOR A-22.
BE READY FOR ANYTHING!
WITH OUR FIREPOWER, ONLY HIGH-LEVEL THREATS--OR DESPERATE LUNATICS--INVADE S.T.A.R. LABS.
YOU ASK ME--
--SHE'S BOTH.
OUT OF MY WAY!
THERE'S NO TIME TO EXPLAIN, BUT INNOCENT LIVES ARE AT STAKE.
I NEED TO BORROW ONE OF YOUR SHUTTLE PODS.

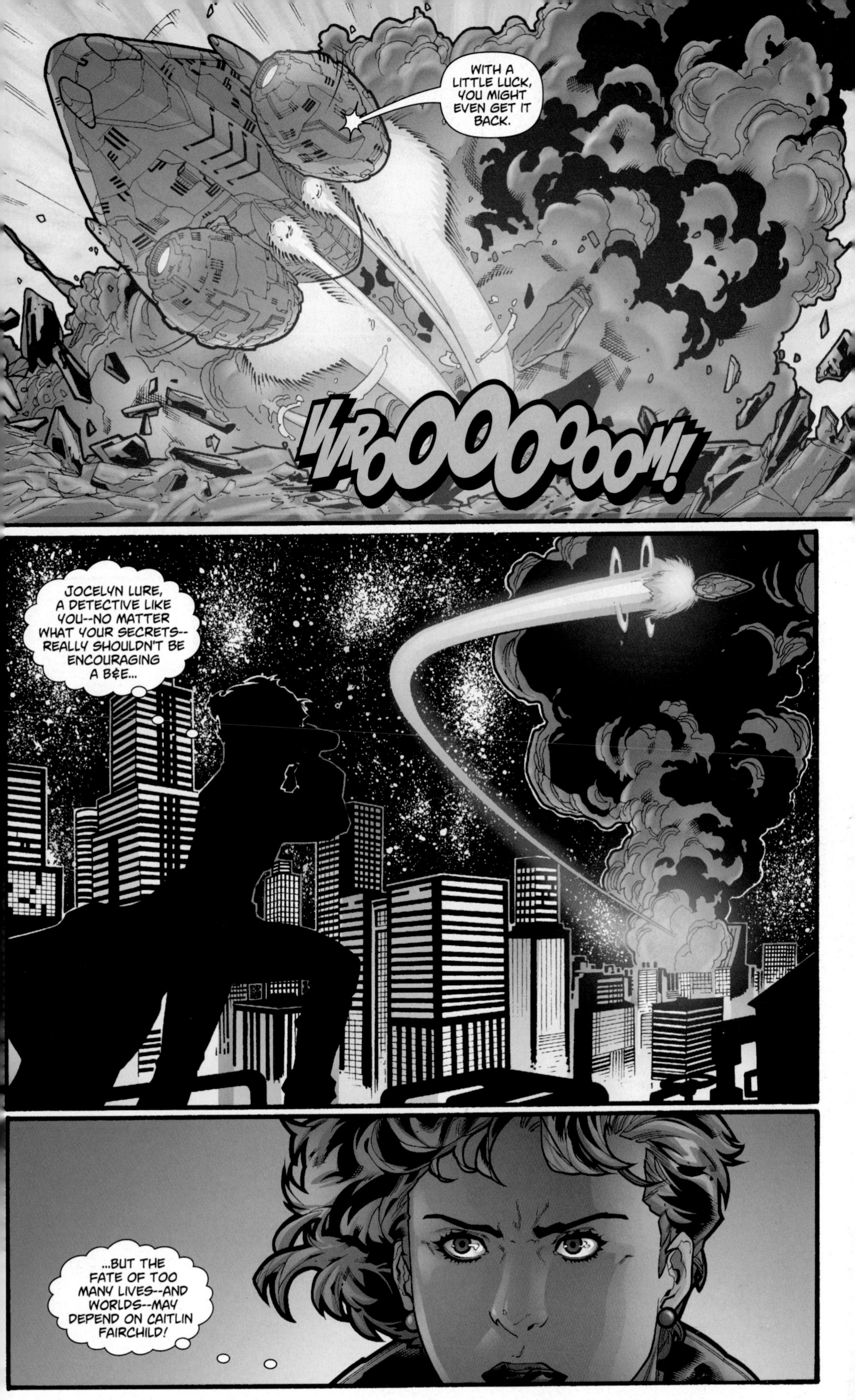
WITH A LITTLE LUCK, YOU MIGHT EVEN GET IT BACK.
VVROOOOOOOOOM!
JOCELYN LURE, A DETECTIVE LIKE YOU--NO MATTER WHAT YOUR SECRETS--REALLY SHOULDN'T BE ENCOURAGING A B&E...
...BUT THE FATE OF TOO MANY LIVES--AND WORLDS--MAY DEPEND ON CAITLIN FAIRCHILD!

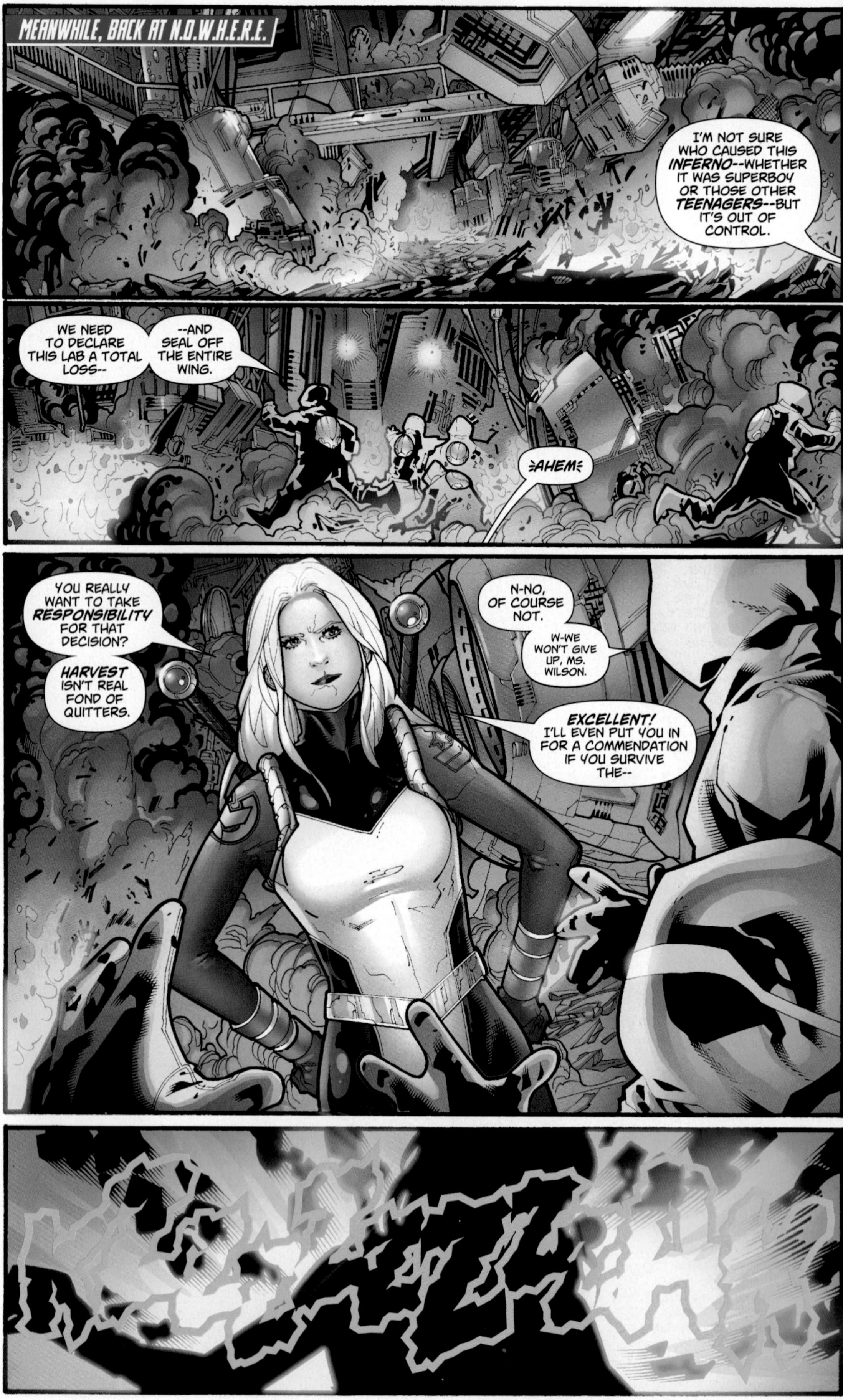

MEANWHILE, BACK AT N.O.W.H.E.R.E.
I'M NOT SURE WHO CAUSED THIS INFERNO--WHETHER IT WAS SUPERBOY OR THOSE OTHER TEENAGERS--BUT IT'S OUT OF CONTROL.
WE NEED TO DECLARE THIS LAB A TOTAL LOSS--
--AND SEAL OFF THE ENTIRE WING.
AHEM
YOU REALLY WANT TO TAKE RESPONSIBILITY FOR THAT DECISION?
HARVEST ISN'T REAL FOND OF QUITTERS.
N-NO, OF COURSE NOT.
W-WE WON'T GIVE UP, MS. WILSON.
EXCELLENT! I'LL EVEN PUT YOU IN FOR A COMMENDATION IF YOU SURVIVE THE--

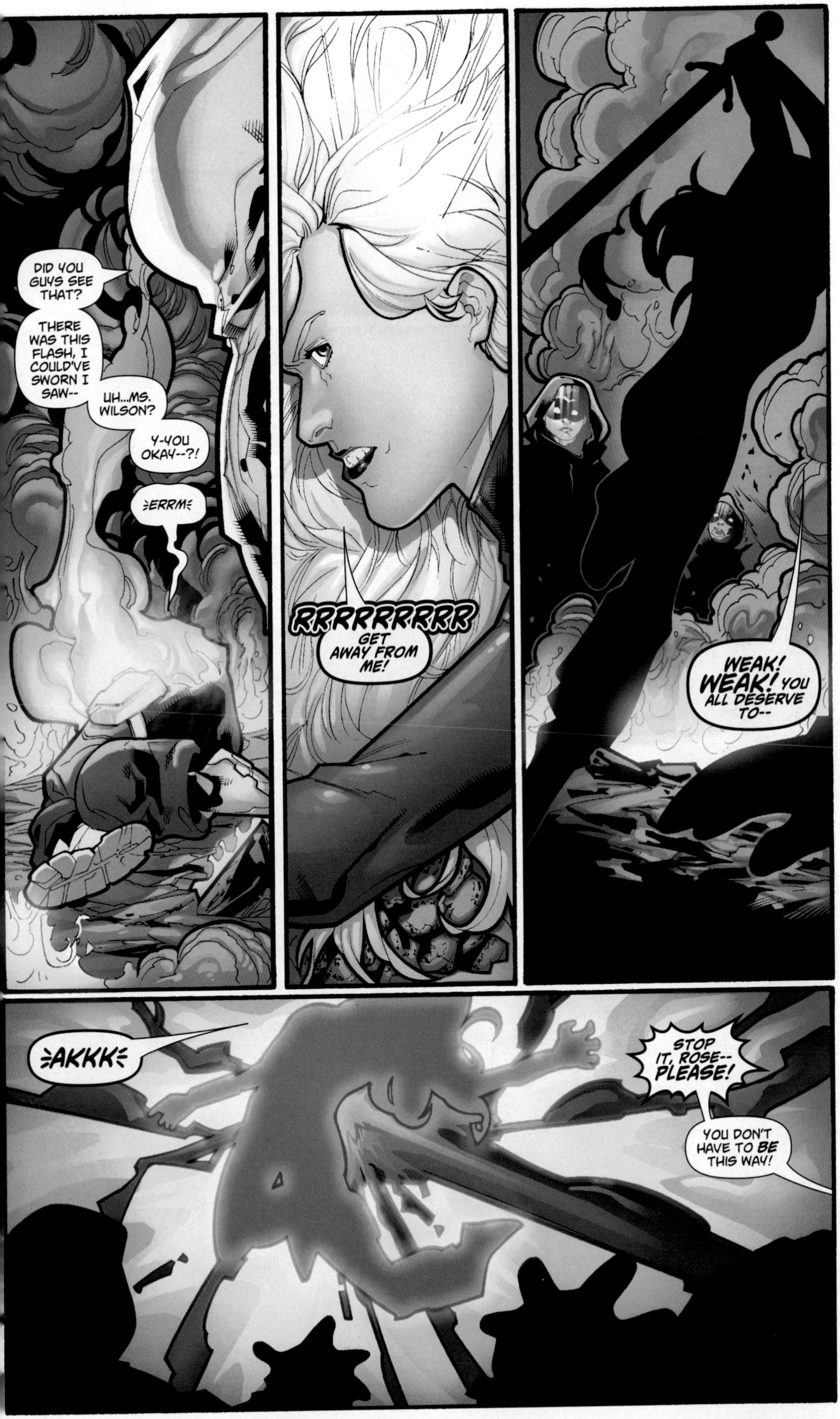
DID YOU GUYS SEE THAT?
THERE WAS THIS FLASH, I COULD'VE SWORN I SAW--
UH...MS. WILSON?
Y-YOU OKAY--?!
ERRM
RRRRRRRRR GET AWAY FROM ME!
WEAK! WEAK! YOU ALL DESERVE TO--
AKKK
STOP IT, ROSE-- PLEASE!
YOU DON'T HAVE TO BE THIS WAY!

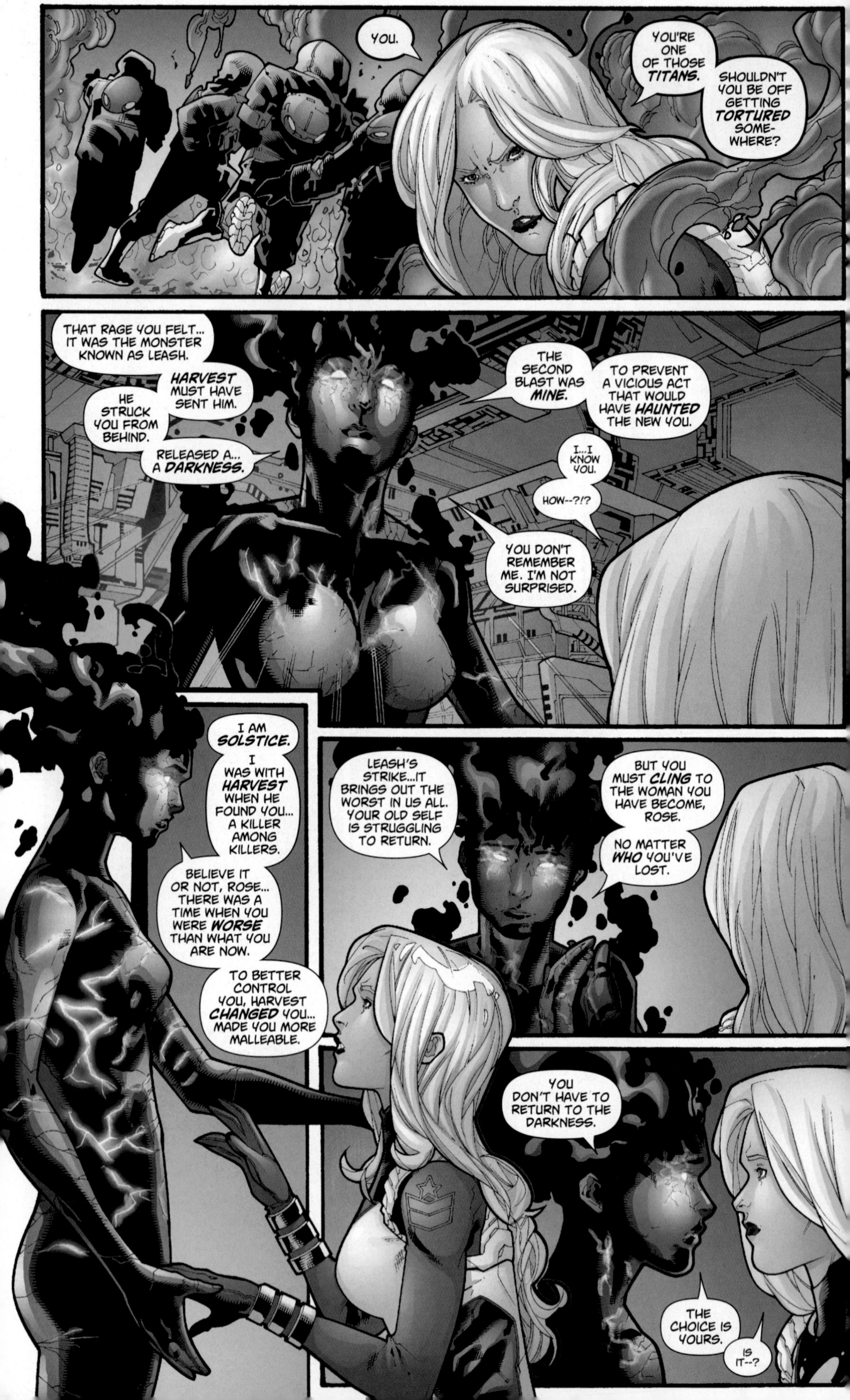

YOU.
YOU'RE ONE OF THOSE TITANS.
SHOULDN'T YOU BE OFF GETTING TORTURED SOME-WHERE?
THAT RAGE YOU FELT... IT WAS THE MONSTER KNOWN AS LEASH.
HARVEST MUST HAVE SENT HIM.
HE STRUCK YOU FROM BEHIND.
RELEASED A... A DARKNESS.
THE SECOND BLAST WAS MINE.
TO PREVENT A VICIOUS ACT THAT WOULD HAVE HAUNTED THE NEW YOU.
I...I KNOW YOU.
HOW--?!?
YOU DON'T REMEMBER ME. I'M NOT SURPRISED.
I AM SOLSTICE.
I WAS WITH HARVEST WHEN HE FOUND YOU... A KILLER AMONG KILLERS.
BELIEVE IT OR NOT, ROSE... THERE WAS A TIME WHEN YOU WERE WORSE THAN WHAT YOU ARE NOW.
TO BETTER CONTROL YOU, HARVEST CHANGED YOU... MADE YOU MORE MALLEABLE.
LEASH'S STRIKE...IT BRINGS OUT THE WORST IN US ALL. YOUR OLD SELF IS STRUGGLING TO RETURN.
BUT YOU MUST CLING TO THE WOMAN YOU HAVE BECOME, ROSE.
NO MATTER WHO YOU'VE LOST.
YOU DON'T HAVE TO RETURN TO THE DARKNESS.
THE CHOICE IS YOURS.
IS IT--?

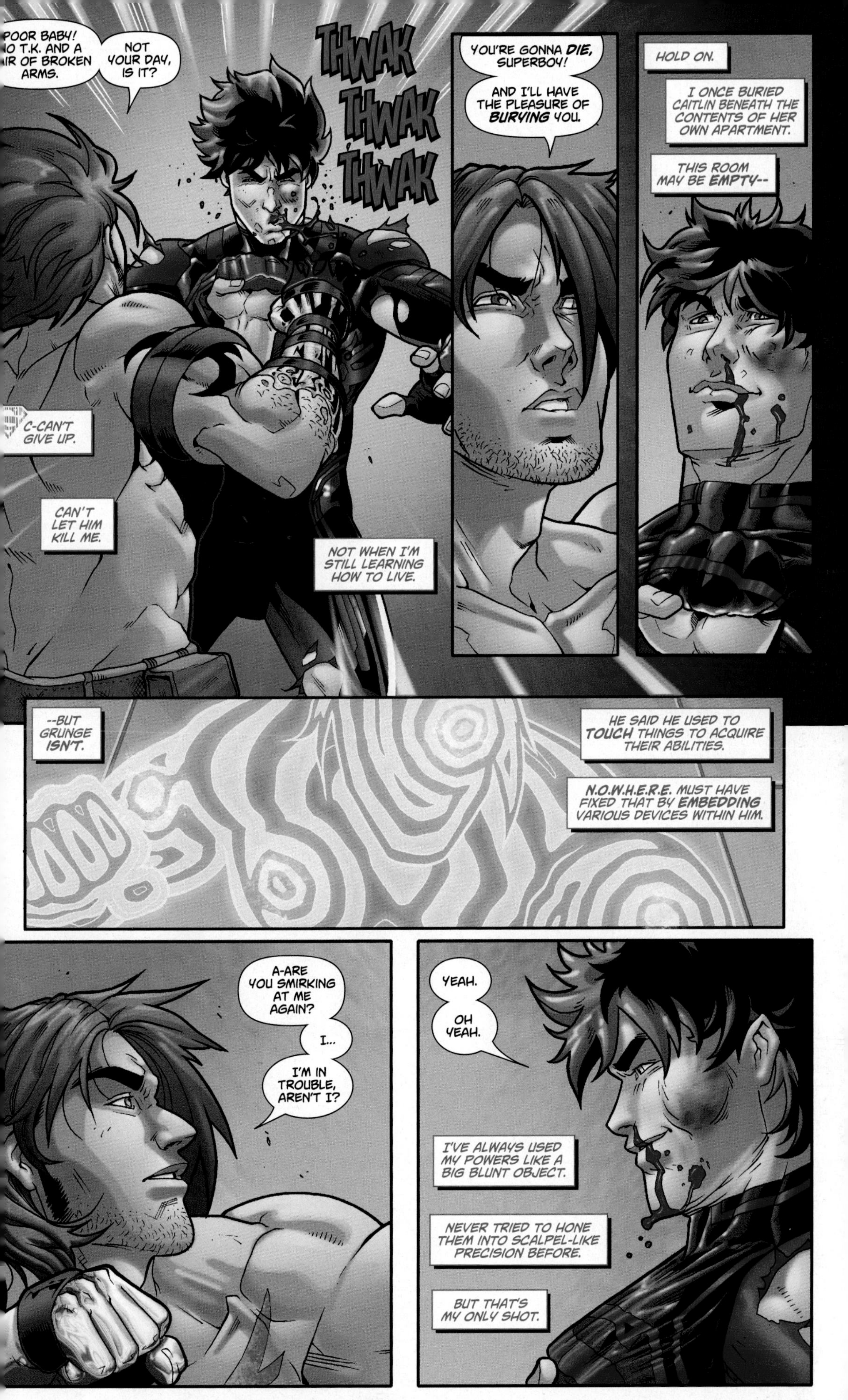
POOR BABY! NO T.K. AND A PAIR OF BROKEN ARMS.
NOT YOUR DAY, IS IT?
THWAK THWAK THWAK
C-CAN'T GIVE UP.
CAN'T LET HIM KILL ME.
NOT WHEN I'M STILL LEARNING HOW TO LIVE.
YOU'RE GONNA DIE, SUPERBOY!
AND I'LL HAVE THE PLEASURE OF BURYING YOU.
HOLD ON.
I ONCE BURIED CAITLIN BENEATH THE CONTENTS OF HER OWN APARTMENT.
THIS ROOM MAY BE EMPTY--
--BUT GRUNGE ISN'T.
HE SAID HE USED TO TOUCH THINGS TO ACQUIRE THEIR ABILITIES.
N.O.W.H.E.R.E. MUST HAVE FIXED THAT BY EMBEDDING VARIOUS DEVICES WITHIN HIM.
A-ARE YOU SMIRKING AT ME AGAIN?
I...
I'M IN TROUBLE, AREN'T I?
YEAH.
OH YEAH.
I'VE ALWAYS USED MY POWERS LIKE A BIG BLUNT OBJECT.
NEVER TRIED TO HONE THEM INTO SCALPEL-LIKE PRECISION BEFORE.
BUT THAT'S MY ONLY SHOT.

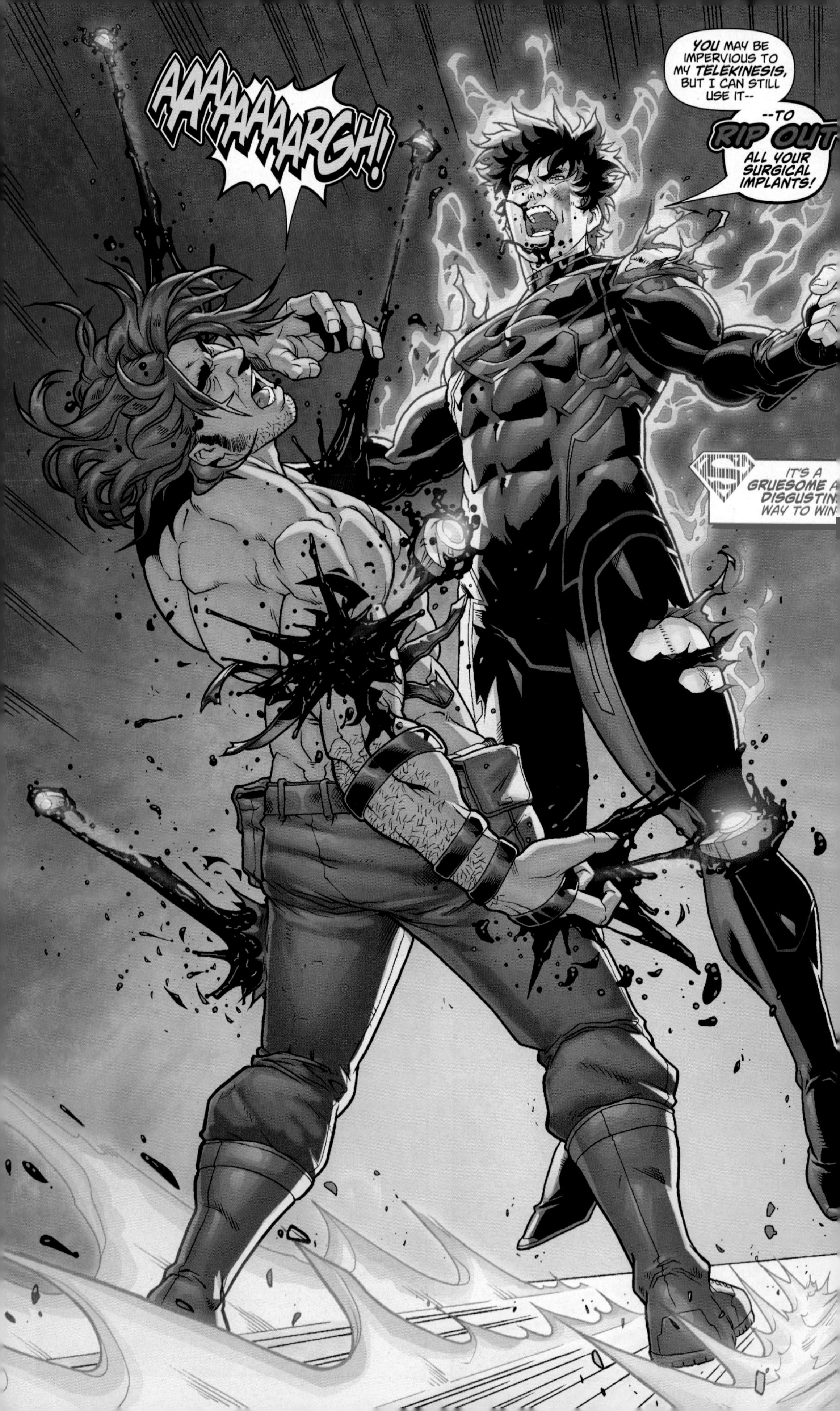
AAAAAAAARGH!
YOU MAY BE IMPERVIOUS TO MY TELEKINESIS, BUT I CAN STILL USE IT--
--TO RIP OUT ALL YOUR SURGICAL IMPLANTS!
IT'S A GRUESOME A
DISGUSTIN
WAY TO WIN

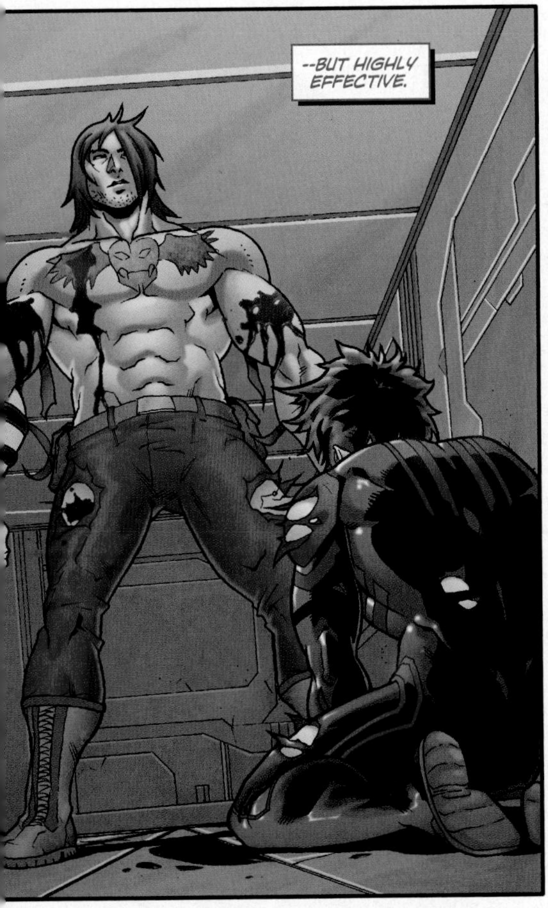
--BUT HIGHLY EFFECTIVE.

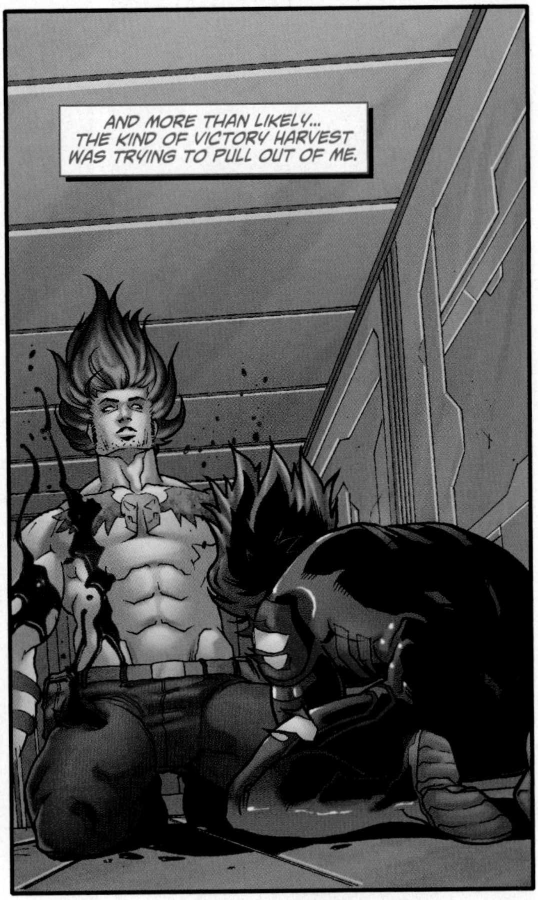
AND MORE THAN LIKELY... THE KIND OF VICTORY HARVEST WAS TRYING TO PULL OUT OF ME.

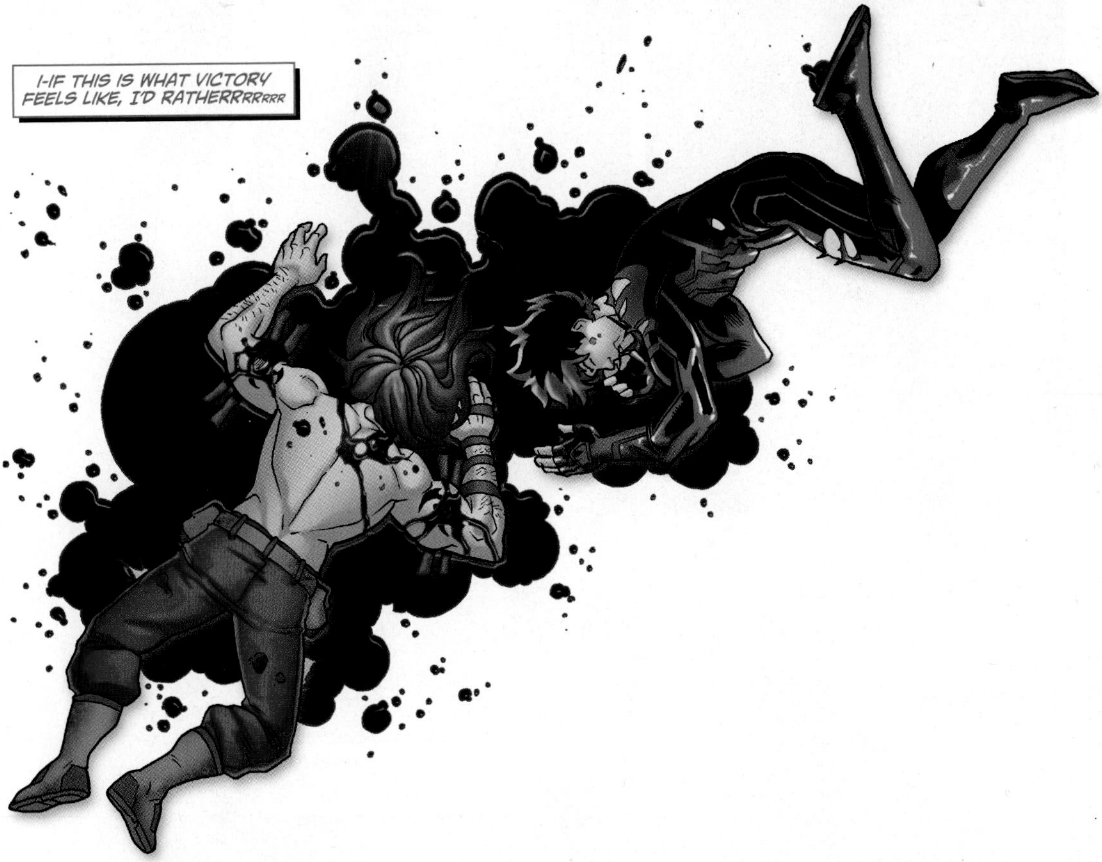
I-IF THIS IS WHAT VICTORY FEELS LIKE, I'D RATHERRrrrrr

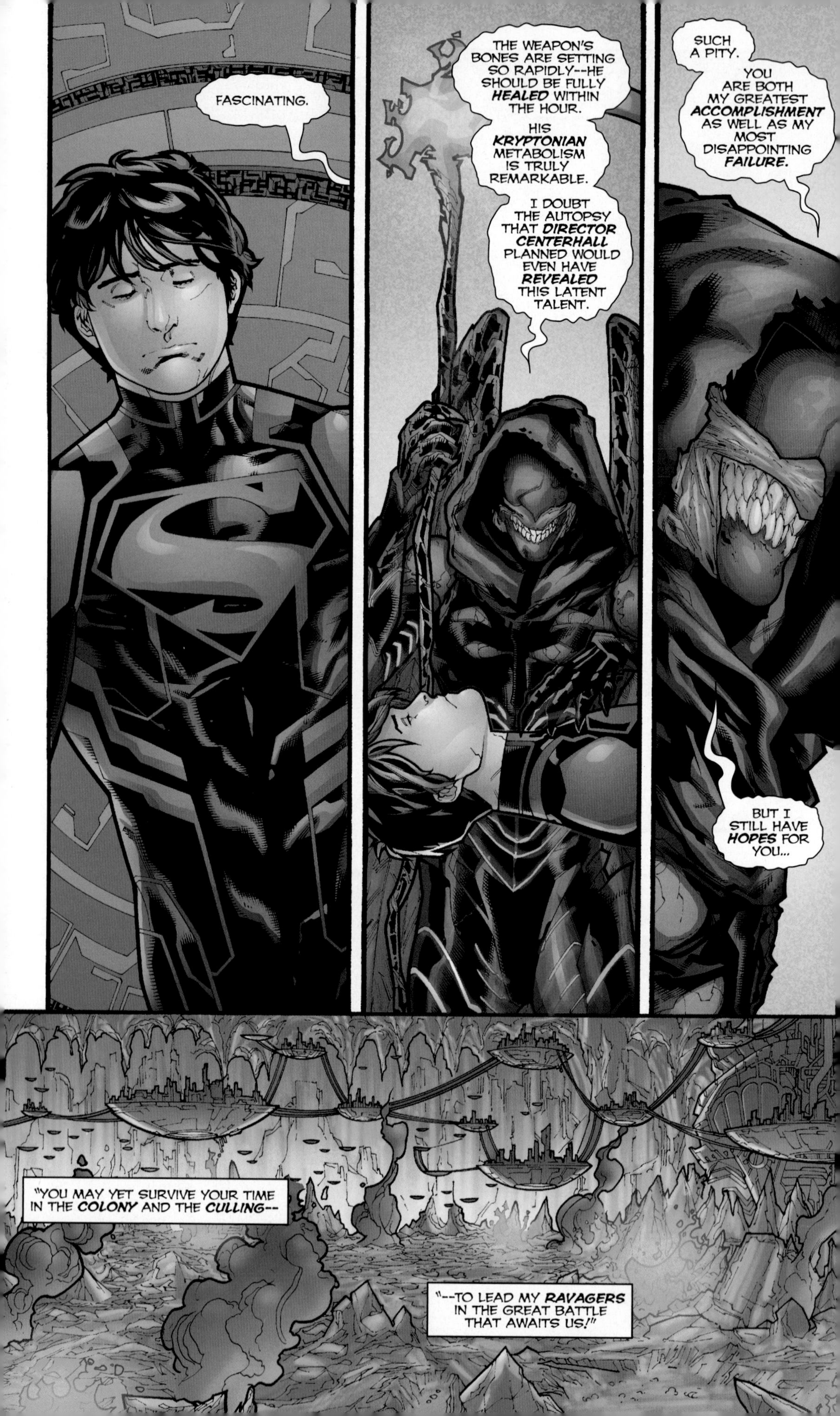
FASCINATING.
THE WEAPON'S BONES ARE SETTING SO RAPIDLY--HE SHOULD BE FULLY HEALED WITHIN THE HOUR.
HIS KRYPTONIAN METABOLISM IS TRULY REMARKABLE.
I DOUBT THE AUTOPSY THAT DIRECTOR CENTERHALL PLANNED WOULD EVEN HAVE REVEALED THIS LATENT TALENT.
SUCH A PITY.
YOU ARE BOTH MY GREATEST ACCOMPLISHMENT AS WELL AS MY MOST DISAPPOINTING FAILURE.
BUT I STILL HAVE HOPES FOR YOU...
"YOU MAY YET SURVIVE YOUR TIME IN THE COLONY AND THE CULLING--
"--TO LEAD MY RAVAGERS IN THE GREAT BATTLE THAT AWAITS US!"

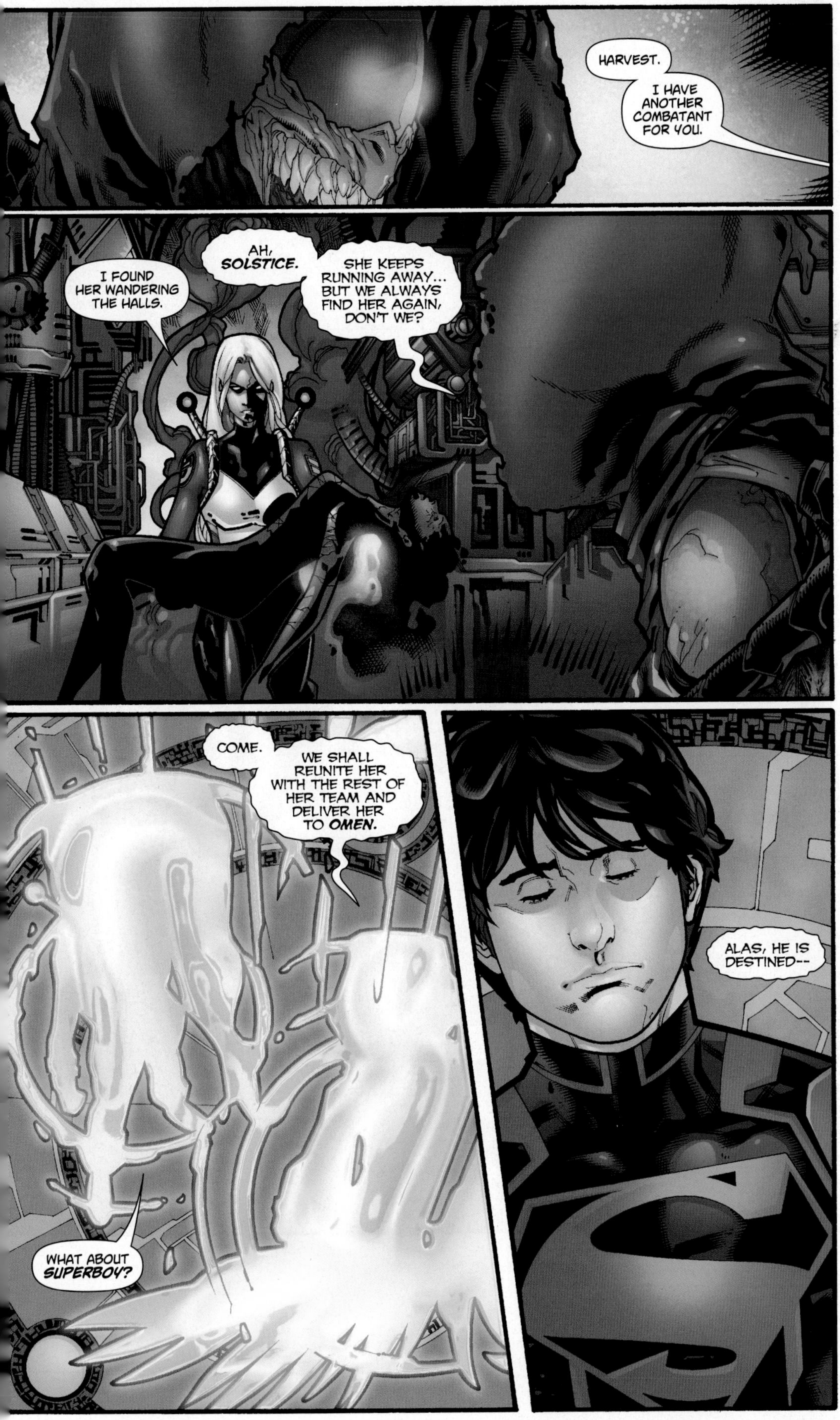
HARVEST.
I HAVE ANOTHER COMBATANT FOR YOU.
I FOUND HER WANDERING THE HALLS.
AH, *SOLSTICE.*
SHE KEEPS RUNNING AWAY... BUT WE ALWAYS FIND HER AGAIN, DON'T WE?
COME.
WE SHALL REUNITE HER WITH THE REST OF HER TEAM AND DELIVER HER TO *OMEN.*
WHAT ABOUT *SUPERBOY?*
ALAS, HE IS DESTINED--

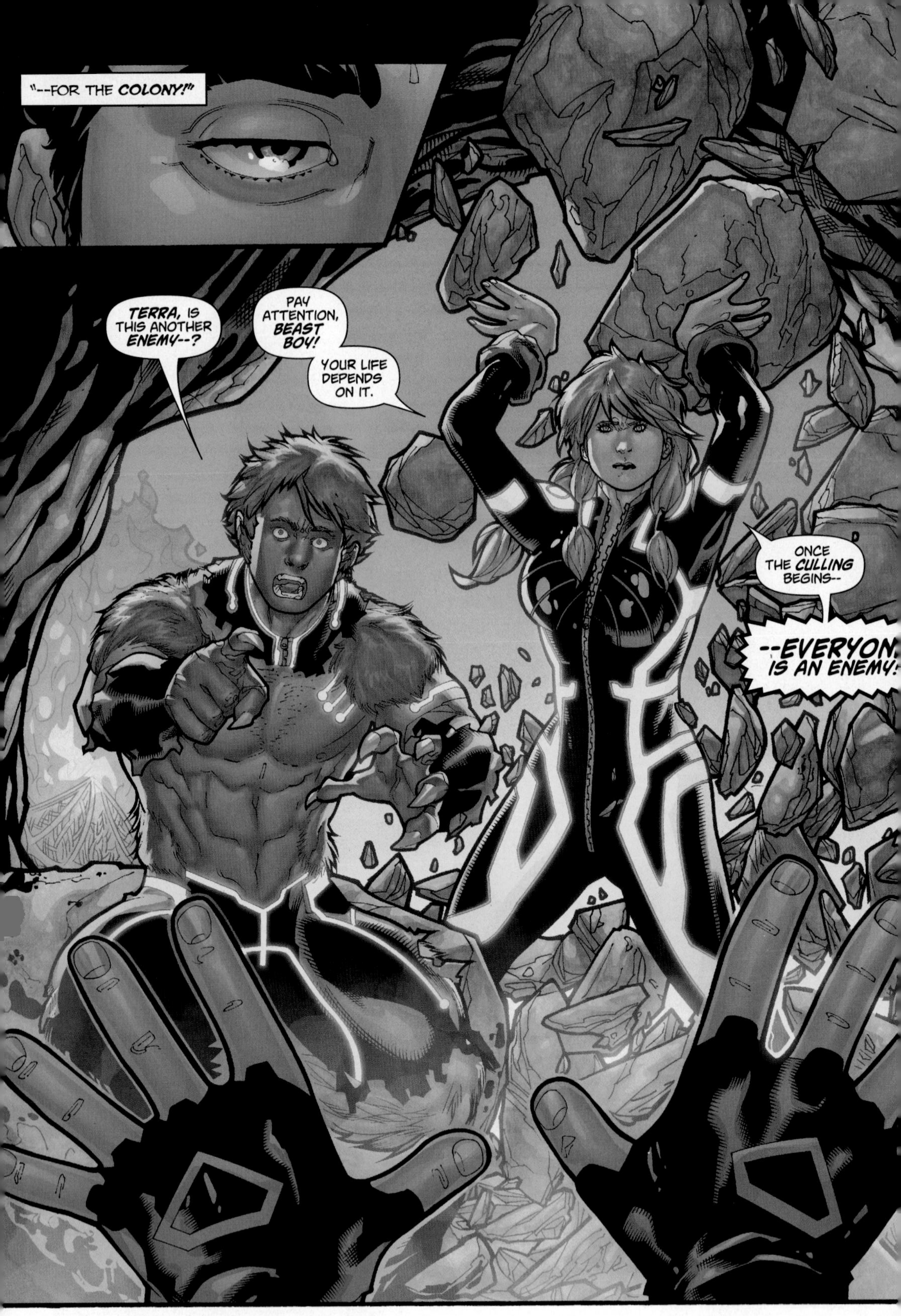
"--FOR THE COLONY!"
TERRA, IS THIS ANOTHER ENEMY--?
PAY ATTENTION, BEAST BOY!
YOUR LIFE DEPENDS ON IT.
ONCE THE CULLING BEGINS--
--EVERYON IS AN ENEMY!

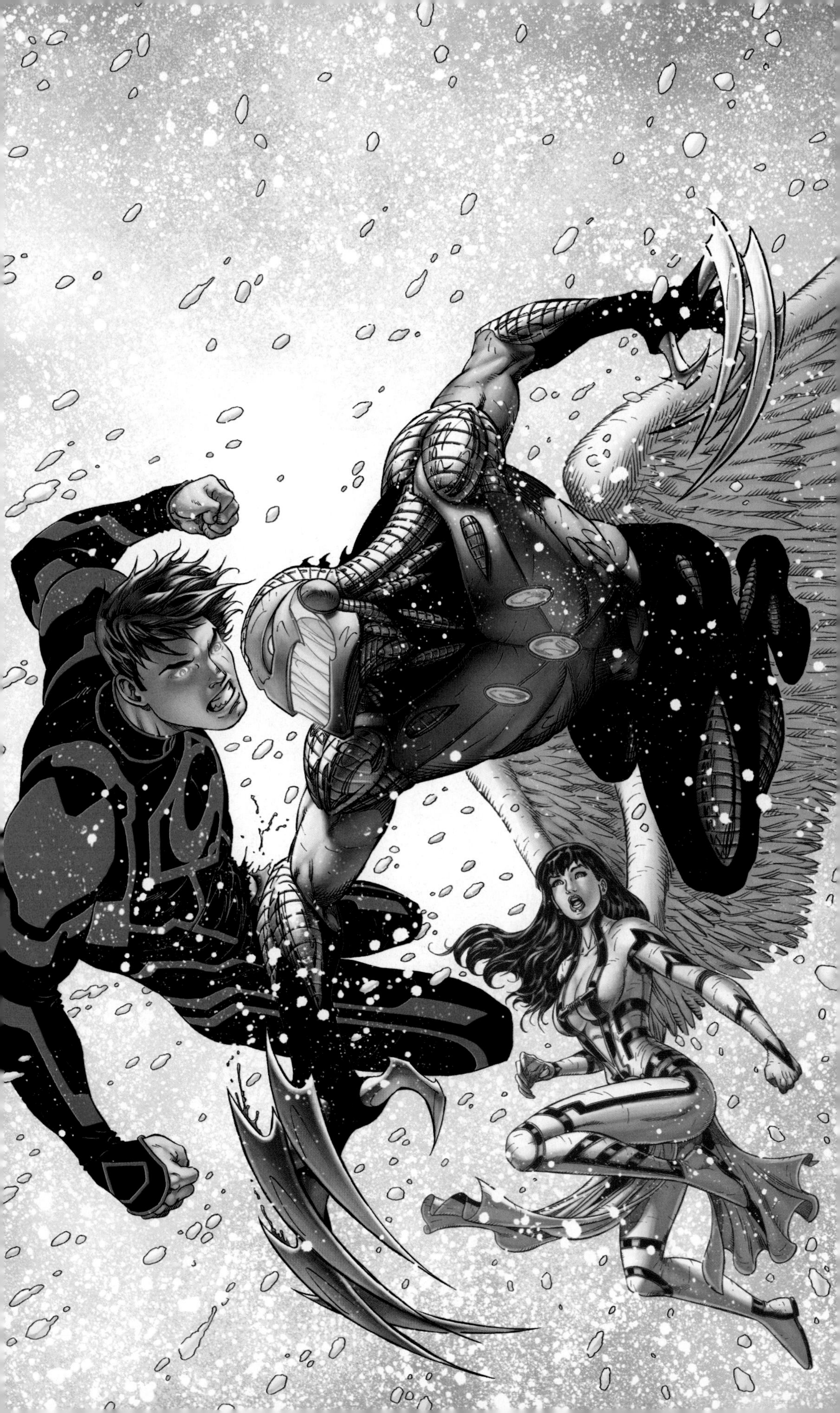

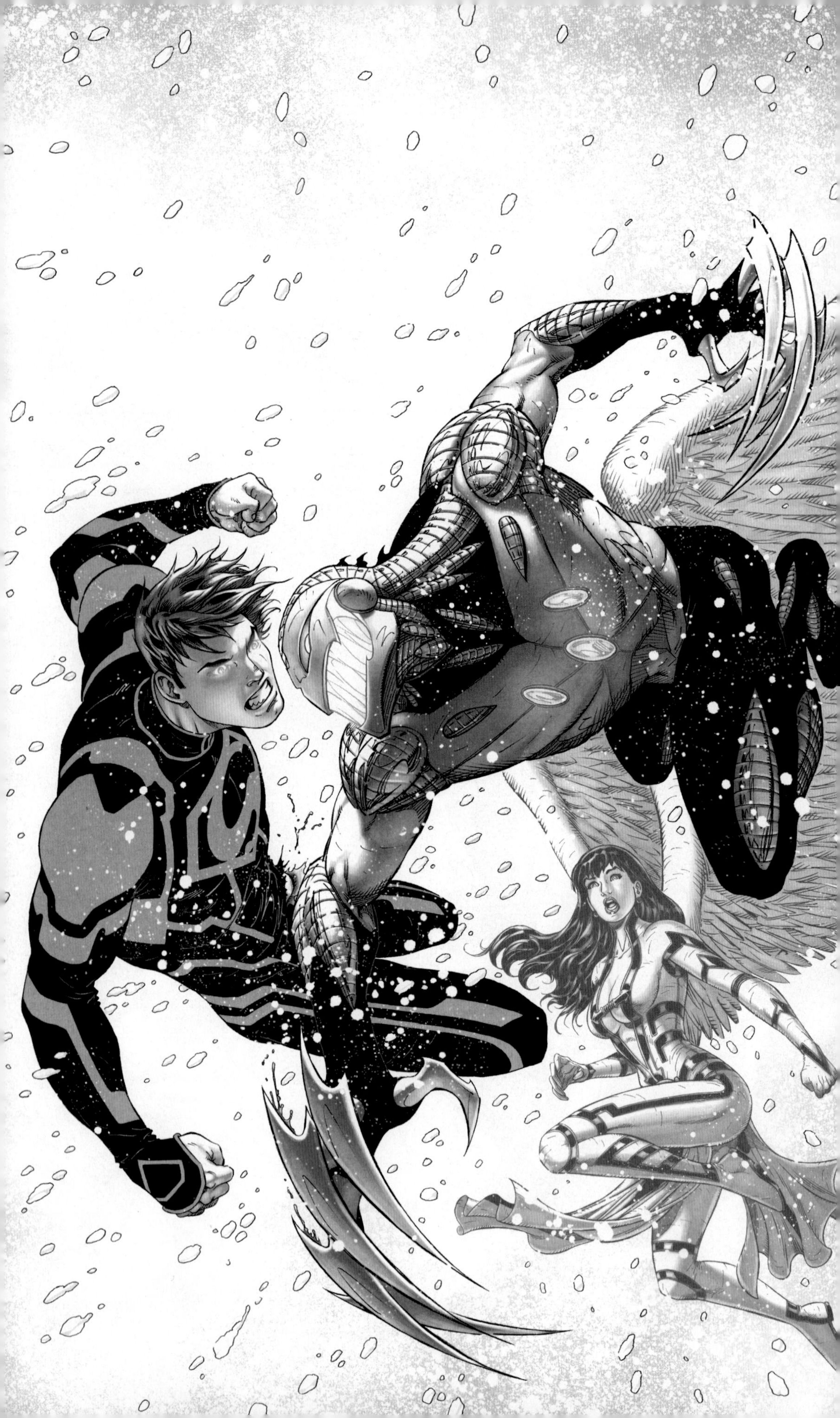

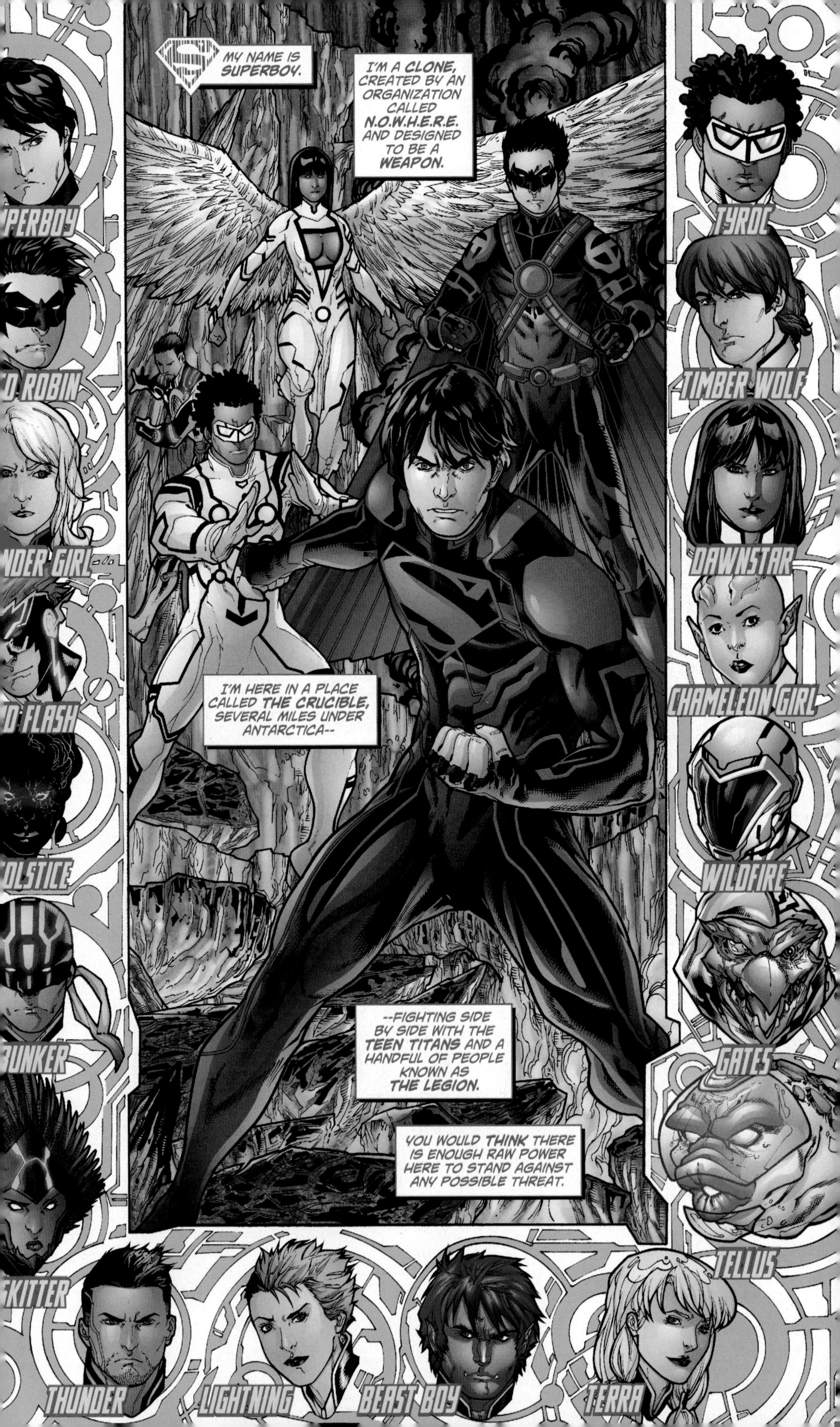
MY NAME IS SUPERBOY.
I'M A CLONE, CREATED BY AN ORGANIZATION CALLED N.O.W.H.E.R.E. AND DESIGNED TO BE A WEAPON.
I'M HERE IN A PLACE CALLED THE CRUCIBLE, SEVERAL MILES UNDER ANTARCTICA--
--FIGHTING SIDE BY SIDE WITH THE TEEN TITANS AND A HANDFUL OF PEOPLE KNOWN AS THE LEGION.
YOU WOULD THINK THERE IS ENOUGH RAW POWER HERE TO STAND AGAINST ANY POSSIBLE THREAT.
TYROC
TIMBER WOLF
DAWNSTAR
CHAMELEON GIRL
WILDFIRE
GATES
TELLUS
THUNDER
LIGHTNING
BEAST BOY
TERRA

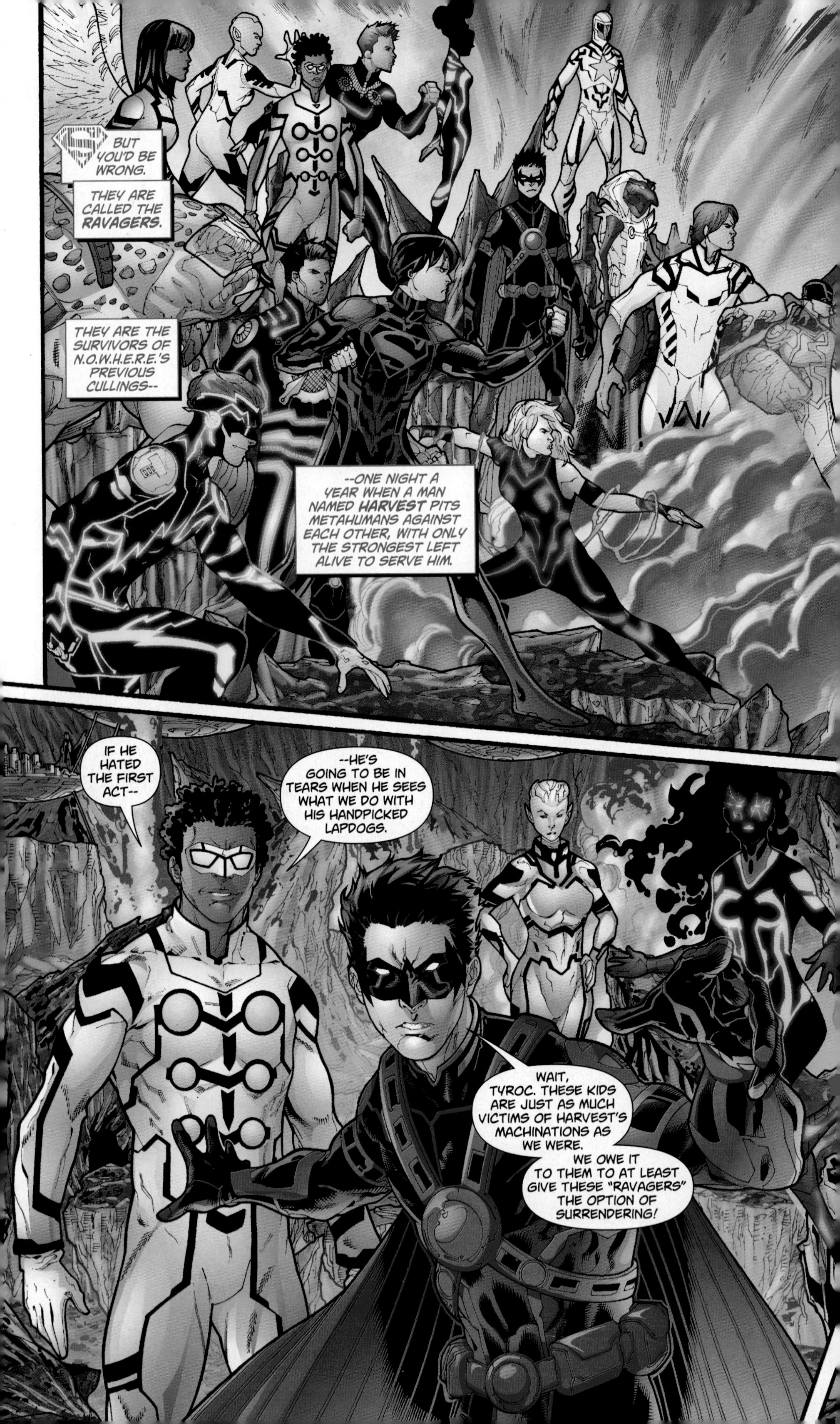
BUT YOU'D BE WRONG.
THEY ARE CALLED THE RAVAGERS.
THEY ARE THE SURVIVORS OF N.O.W.H.E.R.E.'S PREVIOUS CULLINGS--
--ONE NIGHT A YEAR WHEN A MAN NAMED HARVEST PITS METAHUMANS AGAINST EACH OTHER, WITH ONLY THE STRONGEST LEFT ALIVE TO SERVE HIM.
IF HE HATED THE FIRST ACT--
--HE'S GOING TO BE IN TEARS WHEN HE SEES WHAT WE DO WITH HIS HANDPICKED LAPDOGS.
WAIT, TYROC. THESE KIDS ARE JUST AS MUCH VICTIMS OF HARVEST'S MACHINATIONS AS WE WERE.
WE OWE IT TO THEM TO AT LEAST GIVE THESE "RAVAGERS" THE OPTION OF SURRENDERING!

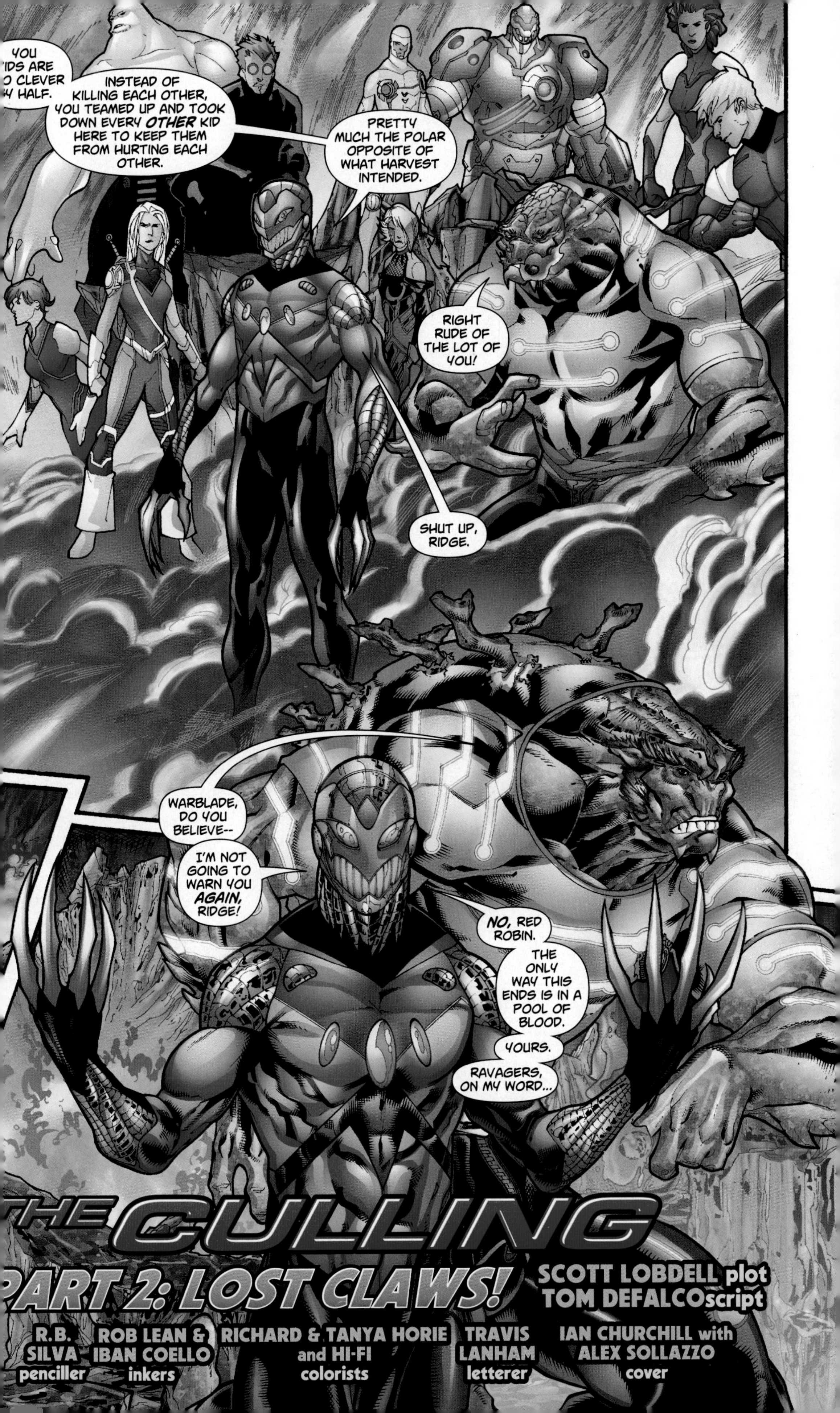
YOU KIDS ARE TOO CLEVER BY HALF.
INSTEAD OF KILLING EACH OTHER, YOU TEAMED UP AND TOOK DOWN EVERY OTHER KID HERE TO KEEP THEM FROM HURTING EACH OTHER.
PRETTY MUCH THE POLAR OPPOSITE OF WHAT HARVEST INTENDED.
RIGHT RUDE OF THE LOT OF YOU!
SHUT UP, RIDGE.
WARBLADE, DO YOU BELIEVE--
I'M NOT GOING TO WARN YOU AGAIN, RIDGE!
NO, RED ROBIN.
THE ONLY WAY THIS ENDS IS IN A POOL OF BLOOD.
YOURS.
RAVAGERS, ON MY WORD...
THE CULLING
PART 2: LOST CLAWS!
SCOTT LOBDELL plot
TOM DEFALCO script
R.B. SILVA penciller
ROB LEAN & IBAN COELLO inkers
RICHARD & TANYA HORIE and HI-FI colorists
TRAVIS LANHAM letterer
IAN CHURCHILL with ALEX SOLLAZZO cover

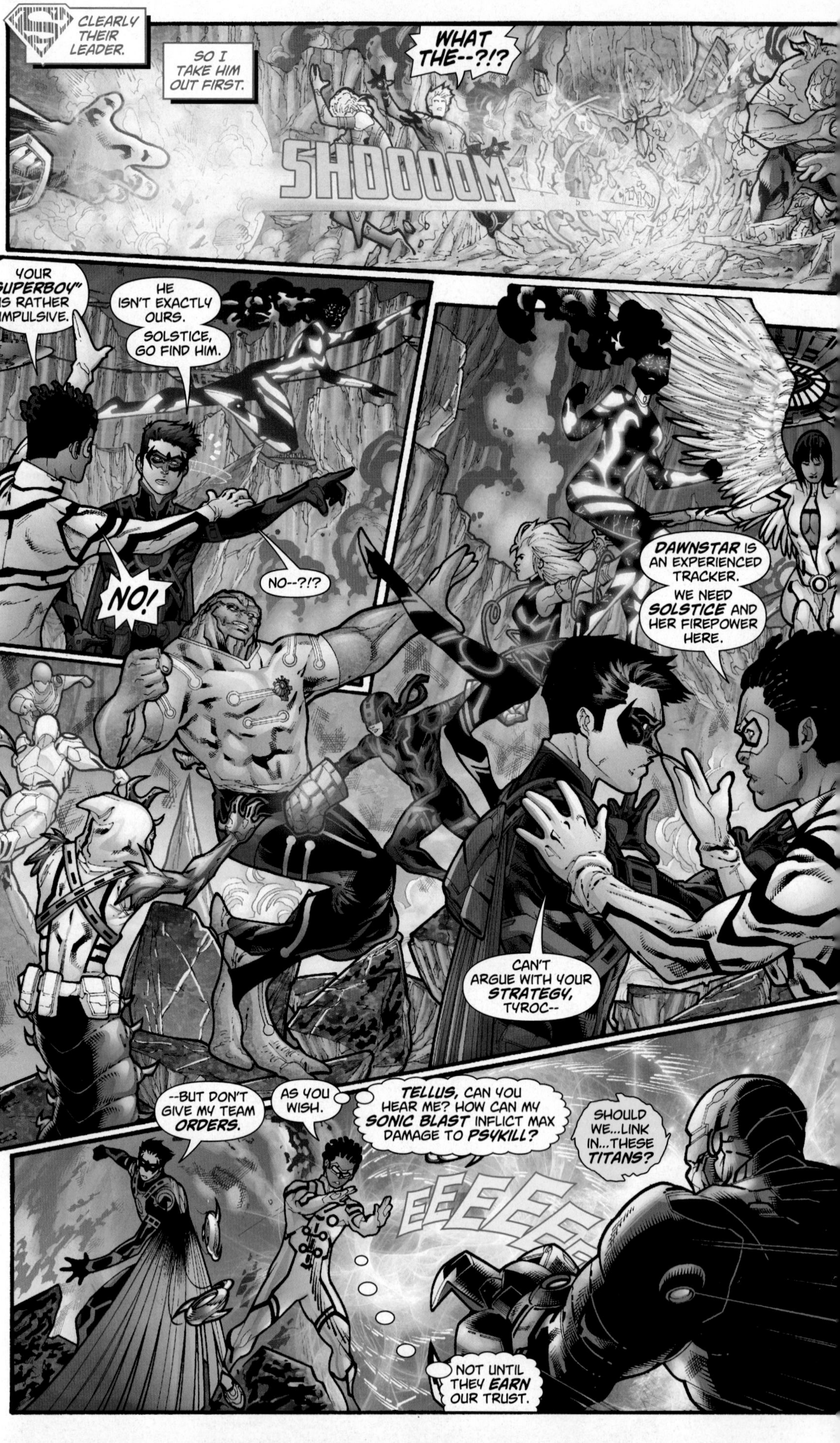
CLEARLY THEIR LEADER.
SO I TAKE HIM OUT FIRST.
WHAT THE--?!?
SHOOOOM
YOUR "SUPERBOY" IS RATHER IMPULSIVE.
HE ISN'T EXACTLY OURS.
SOLSTICE, GO FIND HIM.
NO!
NO--?!?
DAWNSTAR IS AN EXPERIENCED TRACKER.
WE NEED SOLSTICE AND HER FIREPOWER HERE.
CAN'T ARGUE WITH YOUR STRATEGY, TYROC--
--BUT DON'T GIVE MY TEAM ORDERS.
AS YOU WISH.
TELLUS, CAN YOU HEAR ME? HOW CAN MY SONIC BLAST INFLICT MAX DAMAGE TO PSYKILL?
SHOULD WE...LINK IN...THESE TITANS?
EEEEE
NOT UNTIL THEY EARN OUR TRUST.

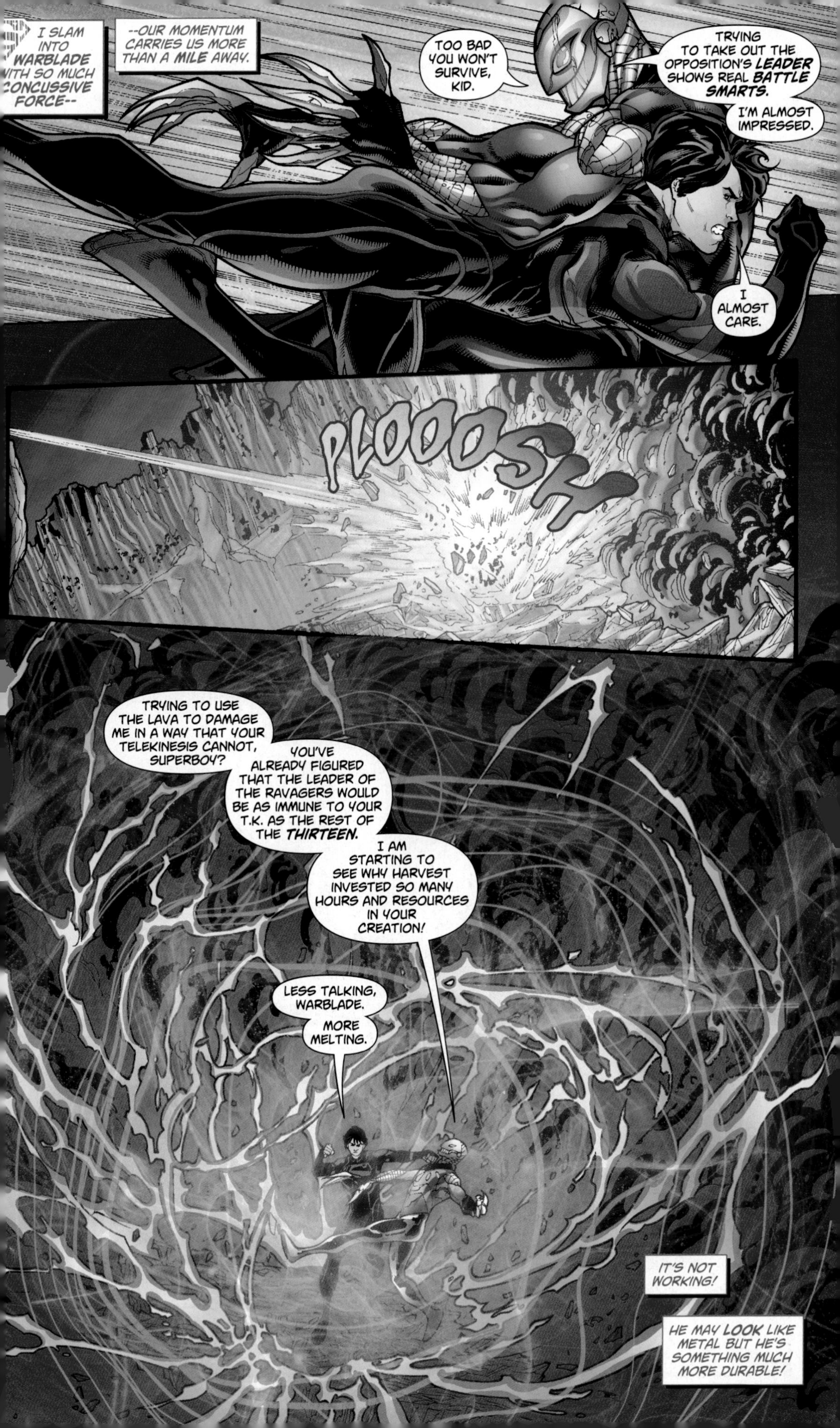
I SLAM INTO WARBLADE WITH SO MUCH CONCUSSIVE FORCE--
--OUR MOMENTUM CARRIES US MORE THAN A MILE AWAY.
TOO BAD YOU WON'T SURVIVE, KID.
TRYING TO TAKE OUT THE OPPOSITION'S LEADER SHOWS REAL BATTLE SMARTS.
I'M ALMOST IMPRESSED.
I ALMOST CARE.
PLOOOSH
TRYING TO USE THE LAVA TO DAMAGE ME IN A WAY THAT YOUR TELEKINESIS CANNOT, SUPERBOY?
YOU'VE ALREADY FIGURED THAT THE LEADER OF THE RAVAGERS WOULD BE AS IMMUNE TO YOUR T.K. AS THE REST OF THE THIRTEEN.
I AM STARTING TO SEE WHY HARVEST INVESTED SO MANY HOURS AND RESOURCES IN YOUR CREATION!
LESS TALKING, WARBLADE.
MORE MELTING.
IT'S NOT WORKING!
HE MAY LOOK LIKE METAL BUT HE'S SOMETHING MUCH MORE DURABLE!

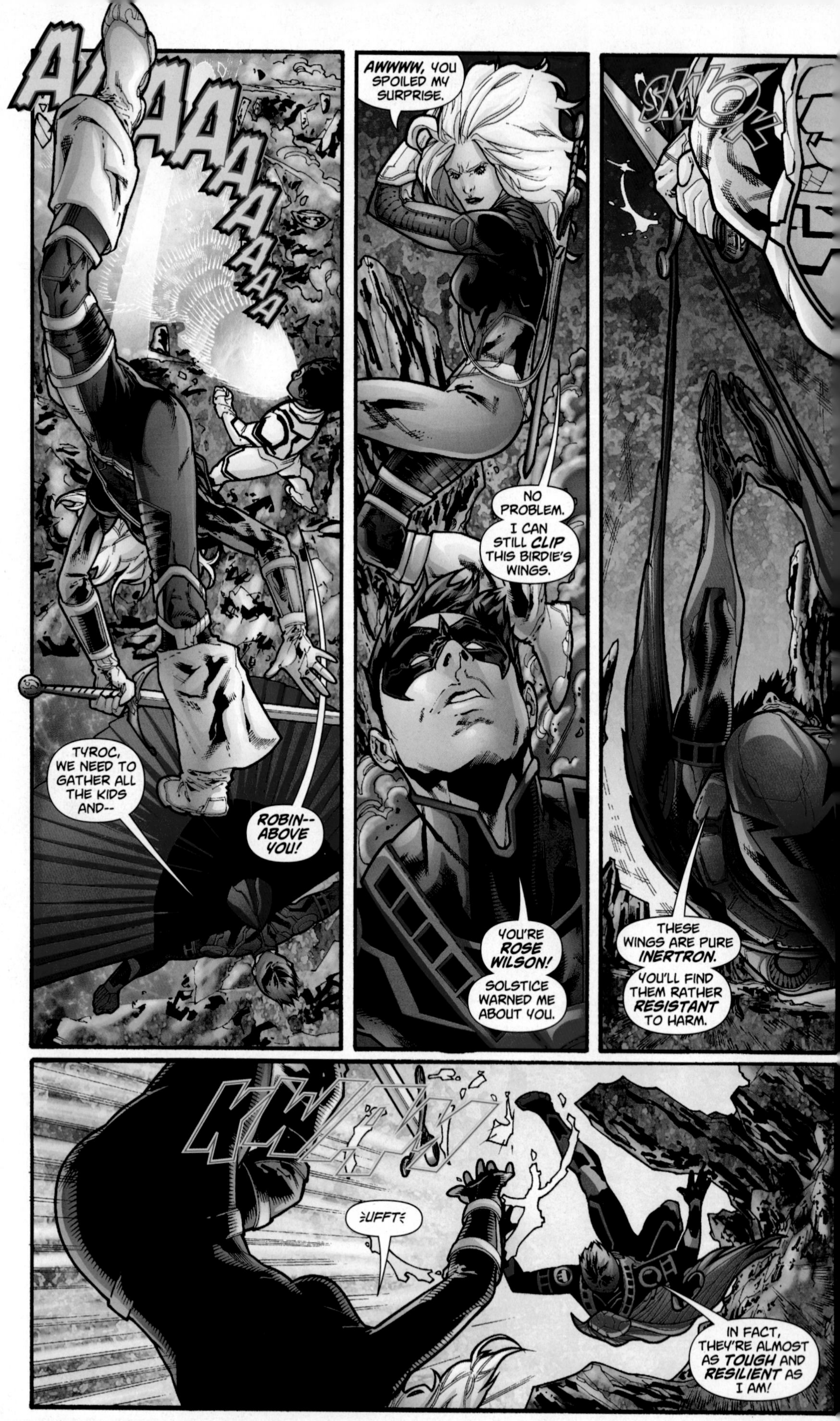
AAAAAAAAAAA
TYROC, WE NEED TO GATHER ALL THE KIDS AND--
ROBIN-- ABOVE YOU!
AWWWW, YOU SPOILED MY SURPRISE.
NO PROBLEM. I CAN STILL CLIP THIS BIRDIE'S WINGS.
YOU'RE ROSE WILSON!
SOLSTICE WARNED ME ABOUT YOU.
SHOOK
THESE WINGS ARE PURE INERTRON.
YOU'LL FIND THEM RATHER RESISTANT TO HARM.
KWAKK
UFFT
IN FACT, THEY'RE ALMOST AS TOUGH AND RESILIENT AS I AM!

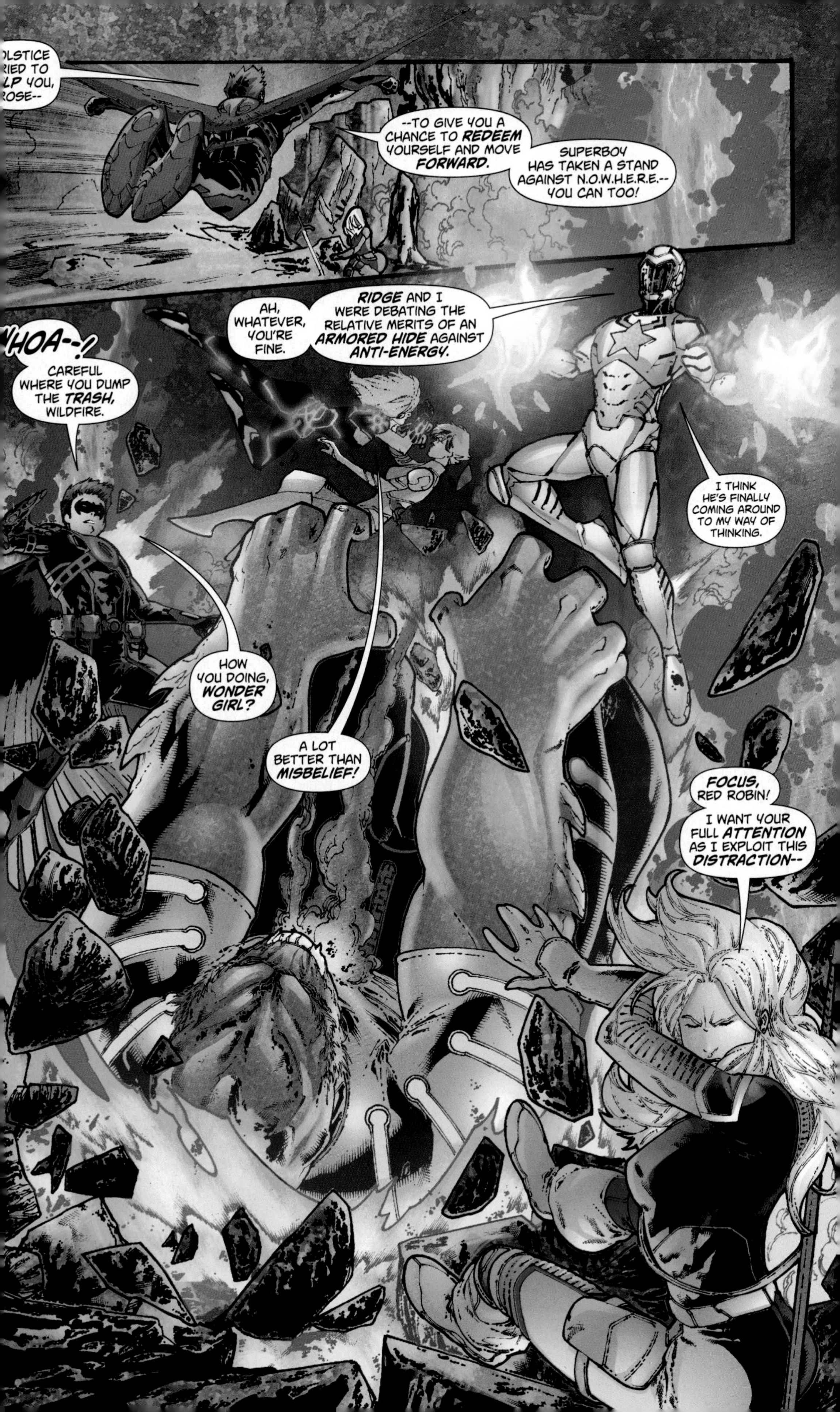

OLSTICE RIED TO LP YOU, ROSE--
--TO GIVE YOU A CHANCE TO REDEEM YOURSELF AND MOVE FORWARD.
SUPERBOY HAS TAKEN A STAND AGAINST N.O.W.H.E.R.E.-- YOU CAN TOO!
HOA--!
CAREFUL WHERE YOU DUMP THE TRASH, WILDFIRE.
AH, WHATEVER, YOU'RE FINE.
RIDGE AND I WERE DEBATING THE RELATIVE MERITS OF AN ARMORED HIDE AGAINST ANTI-ENERGY.
I THINK HE'S FINALLY COMING AROUND TO MY WAY OF THINKING.
HOW YOU DOING, WONDER GIRL?
A LOT BETTER THAN MISBELIEF!
FOCUS, RED ROBIN!
I WANT YOUR FULL ATTENTION AS I EXPLOIT THIS DISTRACTION--

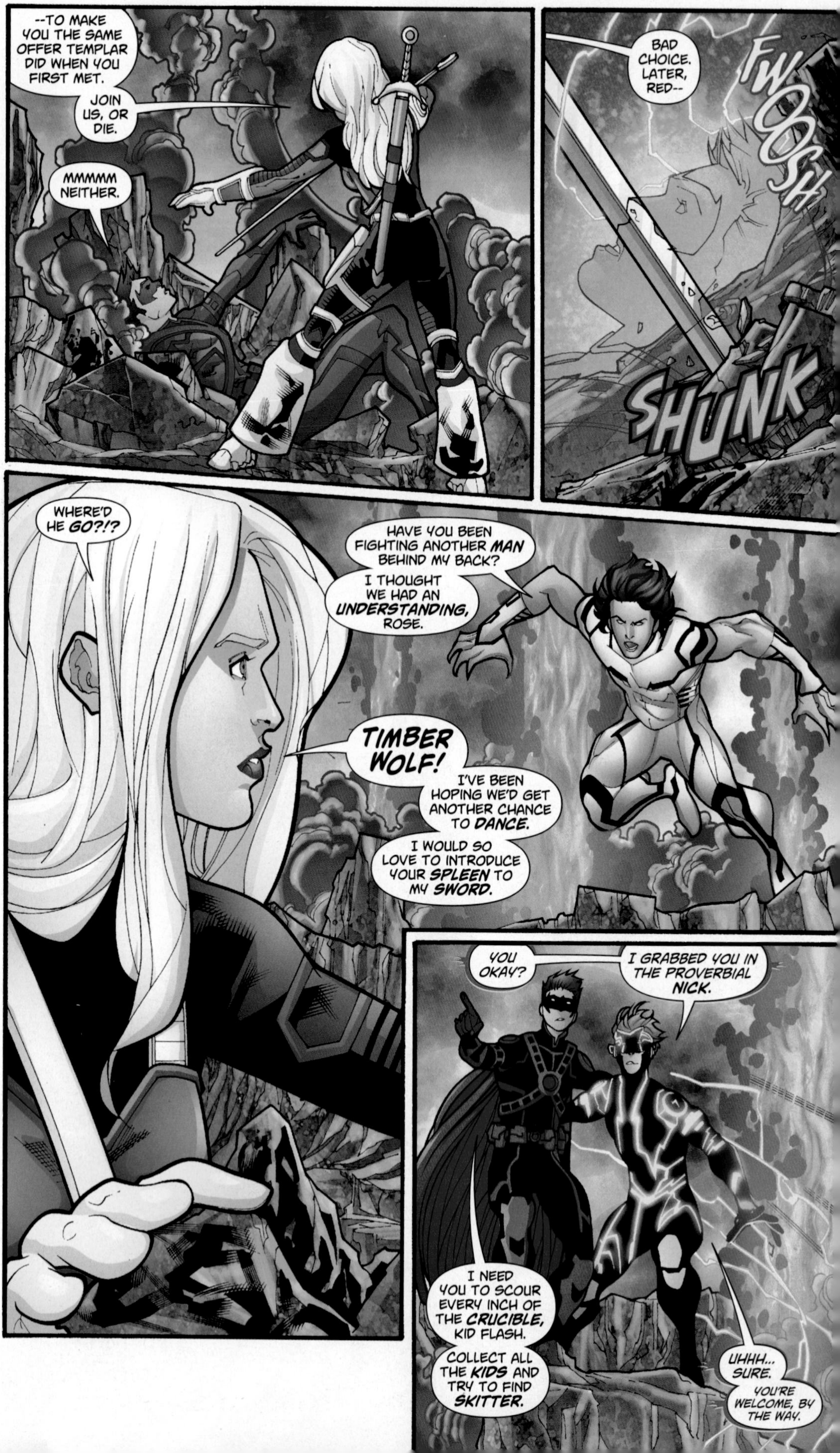
--TO MAKE YOU THE SAME OFFER TEMPLAR DID WHEN YOU FIRST MET.
JOIN US, OR DIE.
MMMMM NEITHER.
BAD CHOICE. LATER, RED--
FWOOSH
SHUNK
WHERE'D HE GO?!?
HAVE YOU BEEN FIGHTING ANOTHER MAN BEHIND MY BACK?
I THOUGHT WE HAD AN UNDERSTANDING, ROSE.
TIMBER WOLF!
I'VE BEEN HOPING WE'D GET ANOTHER CHANCE TO DANCE.
I WOULD SO LOVE TO INTRODUCE YOUR SPLEEN TO MY SWORD.
YOU OKAY?
I GRABBED YOU IN THE PROVERBIAL NICK.
I NEED YOU TO SCOUR EVERY INCH OF THE CRUCIBLE, KID FLASH.
COLLECT ALL THE KIDS AND TRY TO FIND SKITTER.
UHHH... SURE.
YOU'RE WELCOME, BY THE WAY.

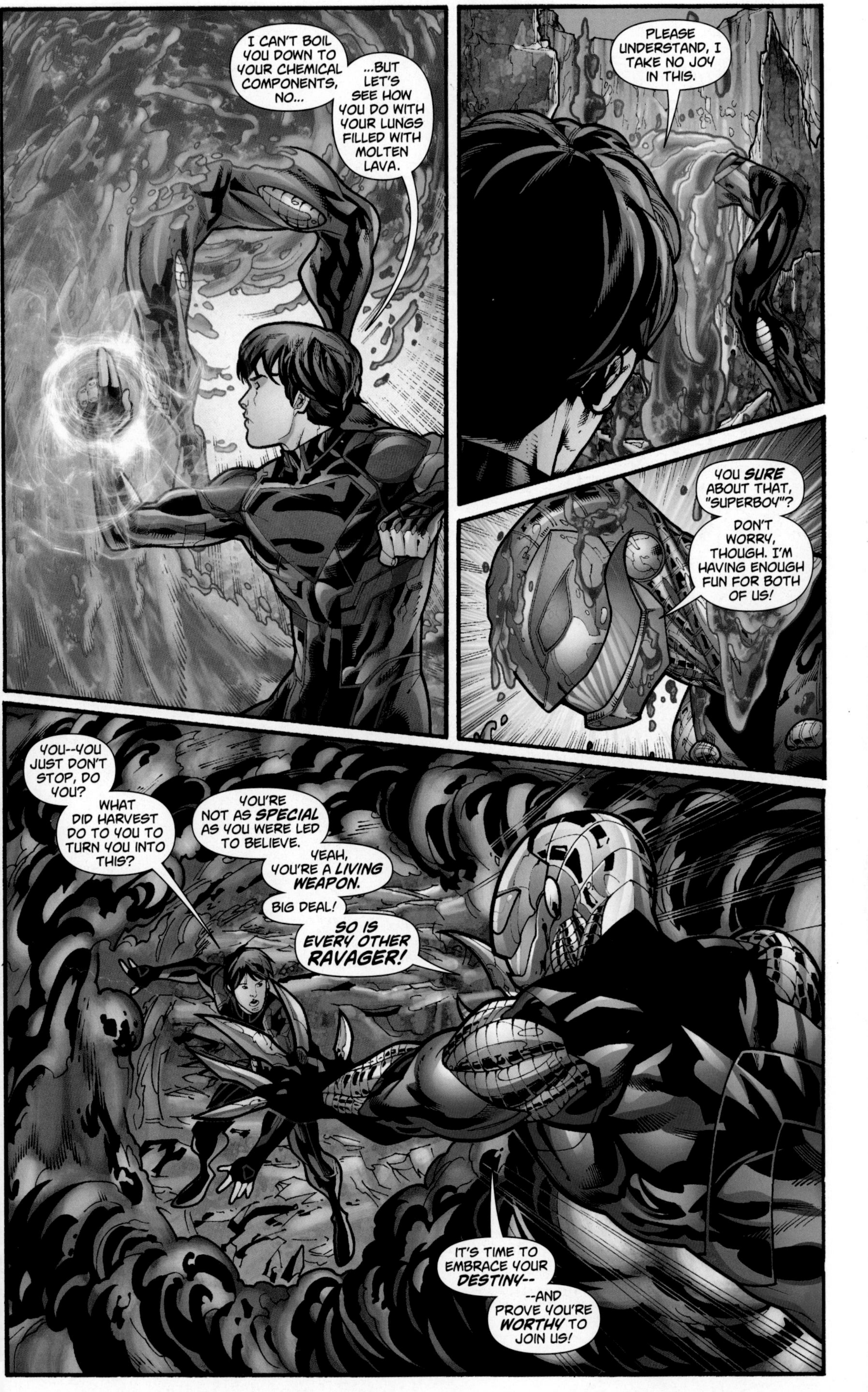

I CAN'T BOIL YOU DOWN TO YOUR CHEMICAL COMPONENTS, NO...
...BUT LET'S SEE HOW YOU DO WITH YOUR LUNGS FILLED WITH MOLTEN LAVA.
PLEASE UNDERSTAND, I TAKE NO JOY IN THIS.
YOU SURE ABOUT THAT, "SUPERBOY"?
DON'T WORRY, THOUGH. I'M HAVING ENOUGH FUN FOR BOTH OF US!
YOU--YOU JUST DON'T STOP, DO YOU?
WHAT DID HARVEST DO TO YOU TO TURN YOU INTO THIS?
YOU'RE NOT AS SPECIAL AS YOU WERE LED TO BELIEVE.
YEAH, YOU'RE A LIVING WEAPON.
BIG DEAL!
SO IS EVERY OTHER RAVAGER!
IT'S TIME TO EMBRACE YOUR DESTINY--
--AND PROVE YOU'RE WORTHY TO JOIN US!

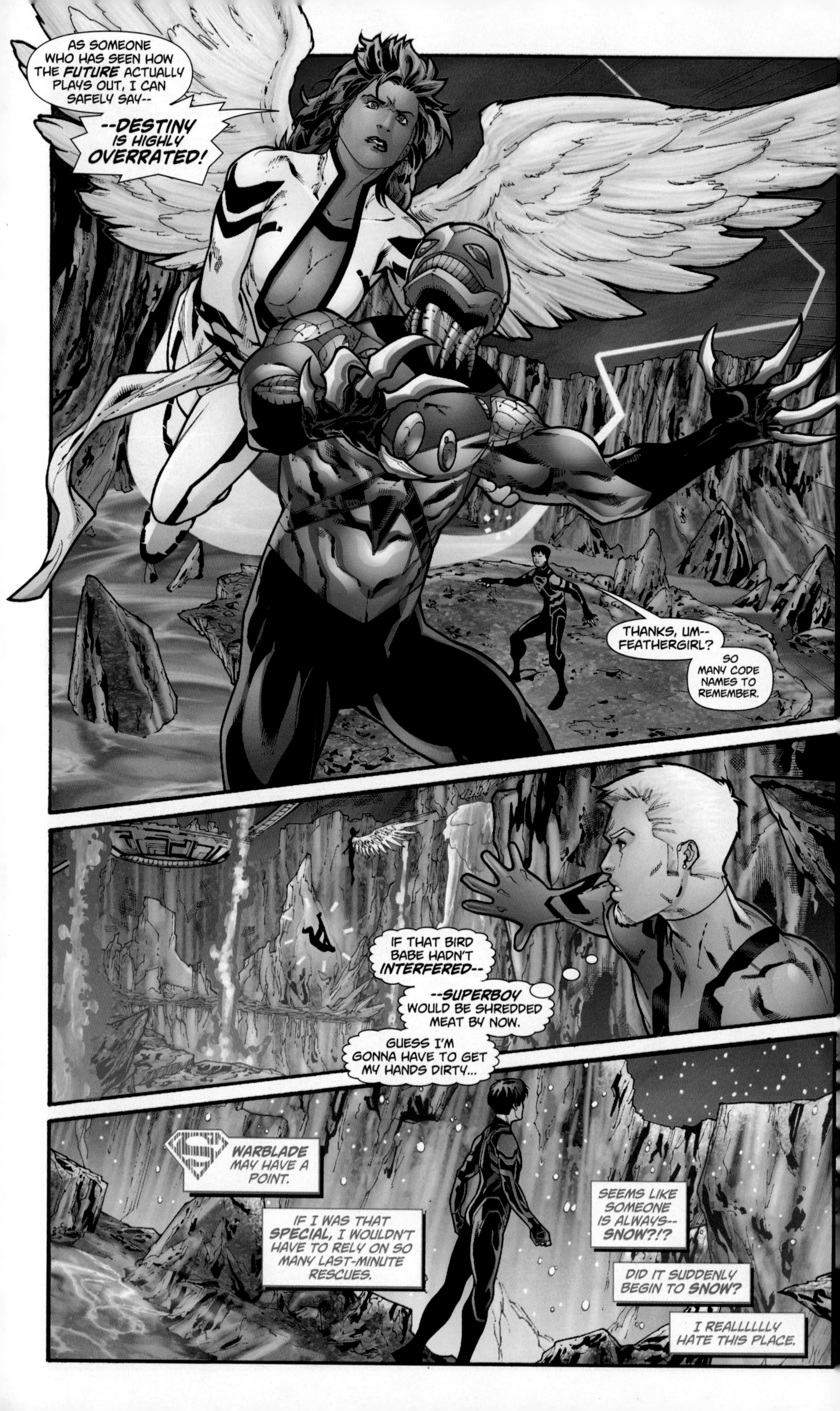
AS SOMEONE WHO HAS SEEN HOW THE FUTURE ACTUALLY PLAYS OUT, I CAN SAFELY SAY--
--DESTINY IS HIGHLY OVERRATED!
THANKS, UM-- FEATHERGIRL?
SO MANY CODE NAMES TO REMEMBER.
IF THAT BIRD BABE HADN'T INTERFERED--
--SUPERBOY WOULD BE SHREDDED MEAT BY NOW.
GUESS I'M GONNA HAVE TO GET MY HANDS DIRTY...
WARBLADE MAY HAVE A POINT.
IF I WAS THAT SPECIAL, I WOULDN'T HAVE TO RELY ON SO MANY LAST-MINUTE RESCUES.
SEEMS LIKE SOMEONE IS ALWAYS-- SNOW?!?
DID IT SUDDENLY BEGIN TO SNOW?
I REALLLLLLY HATE THIS PLACE.

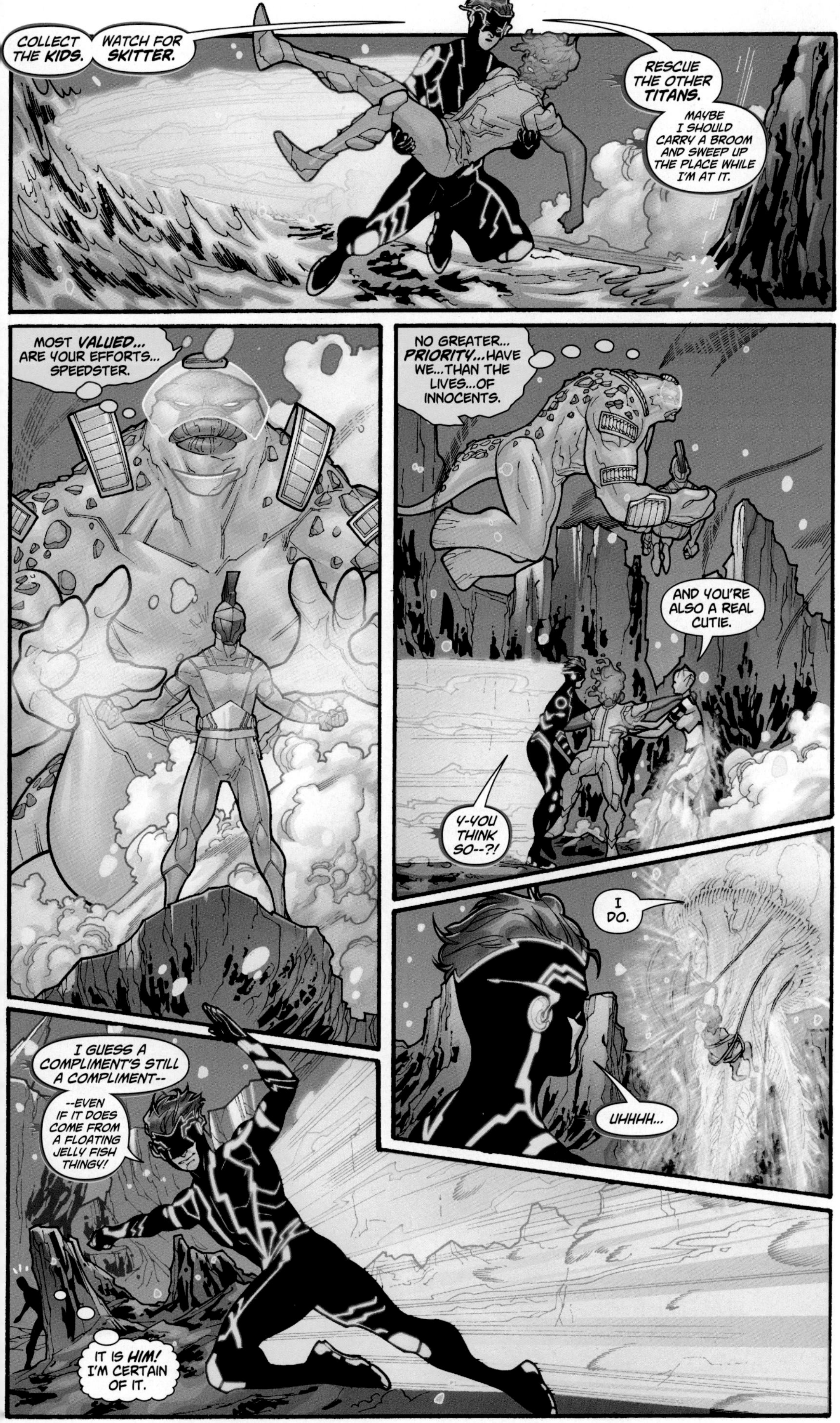

COLLECT THE KIDS.
WATCH FOR SKITTER.
RESCUE THE OTHER TITANS.
MAYBE I SHOULD CARRY A BROOM AND SWEEP UP THE PLACE WHILE I'M AT IT.
MOST VALUED... ARE YOUR EFFORTS... SPEEDSTER.
NO GREATER... PRIORITY...HAVE WE...THAN THE LIVES...OF INNOCENTS.
AND YOU'RE ALSO A REAL CUTIE.
Y-YOU THINK SO--?!
I DO.
UHHHH...
I GUESS A COMPLIMENT'S STILL A COMPLIMENT--
--EVEN IF IT DOES COME FROM A FLOATING JELLY FISH THINGY!
IT IS HIM! I'M CERTAIN OF IT.

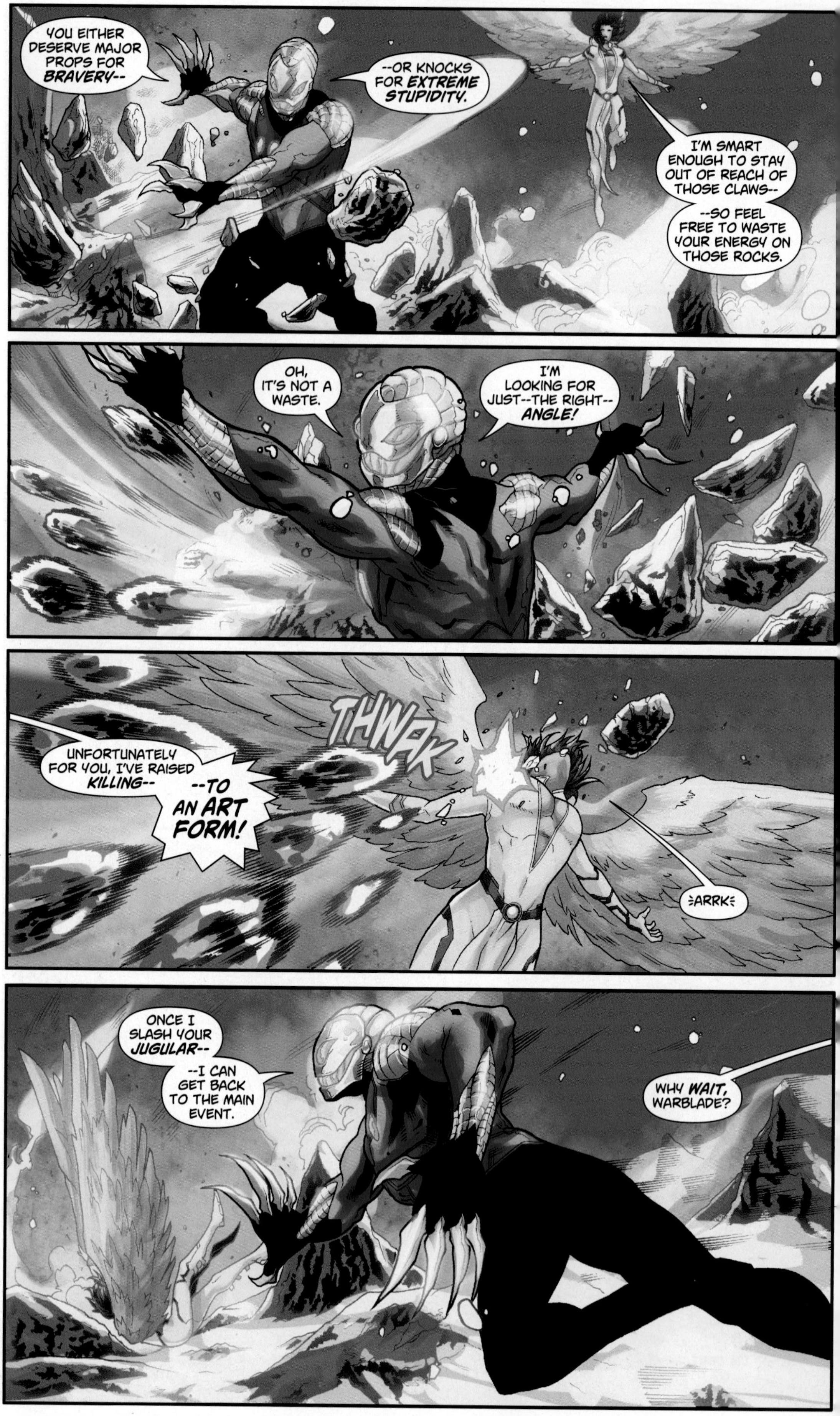
YOU EITHER DESERVE MAJOR PROPS FOR BRAVERY--
--OR KNOCKS FOR EXTREME STUPIDITY.
I'M SMART ENOUGH TO STAY OUT OF REACH OF THOSE CLAWS--
--SO FEEL FREE TO WASTE YOUR ENERGY ON THOSE ROCKS.
OH, IT'S NOT A WASTE.
I'M LOOKING FOR JUST--THE RIGHT--ANGLE!
THWAK
UNFORTUNATELY FOR YOU, I'VE RAISED KILLING--
--TO AN ART FORM!
ARRK
ONCE I SLASH YOUR JUGULAR--
--I CAN GET BACK TO THE MAIN EVENT.
WHY WAIT, WARBLADE?

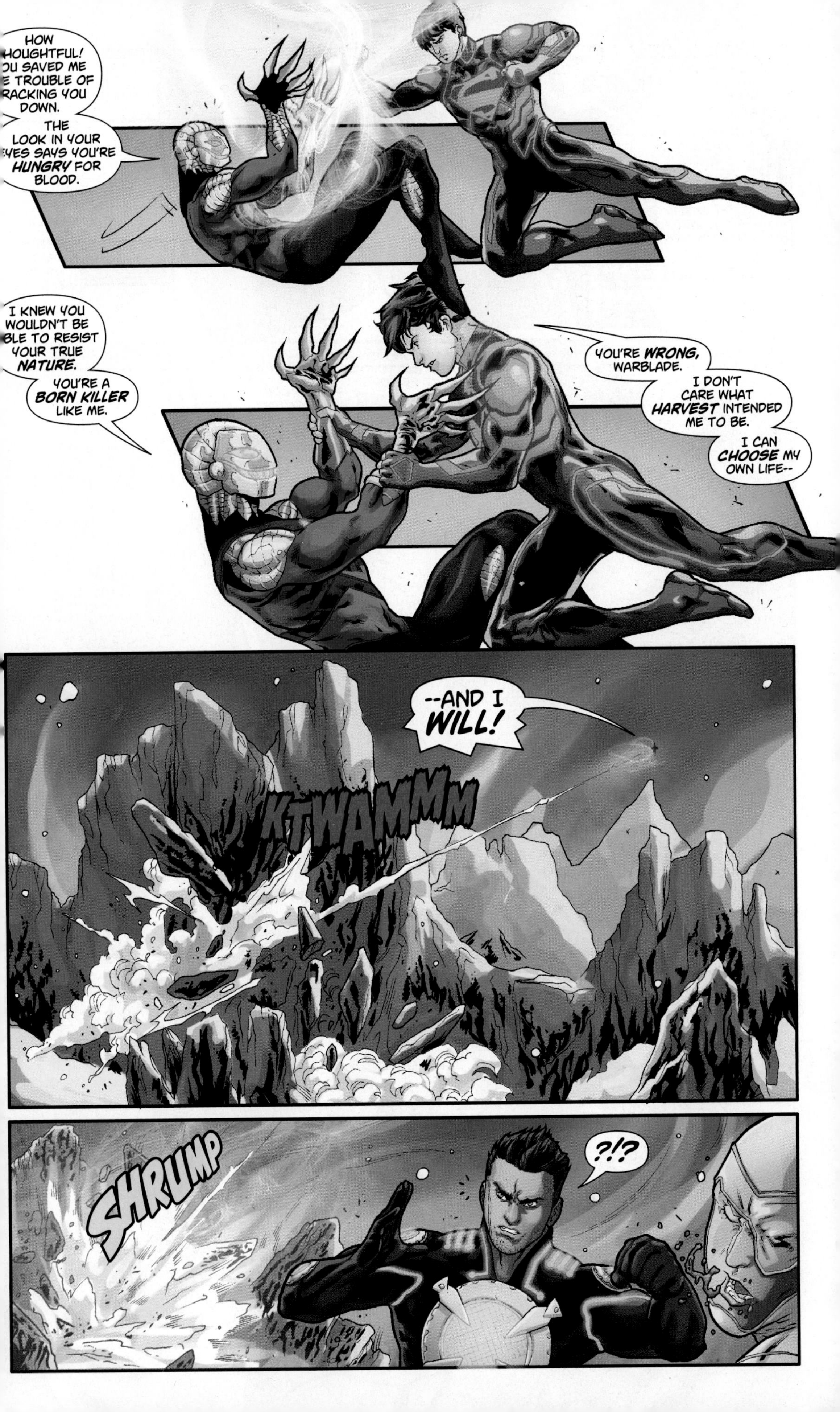
HOW
HOUGHTFUL!
OU SAVED ME
E TROUBLE OF
RACKING YOU
DOWN.
THE
LOOK IN YOUR
EYES SAYS YOU'RE
HUNGRY FOR
BLOOD.
I KNEW YOU
WOULDN'T BE
BLE TO RESIST
YOUR TRUE
NATURE.
YOU'RE A
BORN KILLER
LIKE ME.
YOU'RE WRONG,
WARBLADE.
I DON'T
CARE WHAT
HARVEST INTENDED
ME TO BE.
I CAN
CHOOSE MY
OWN LIFE--
--AND I
WILL!
KTWAMMM
SHRUMP
?!?

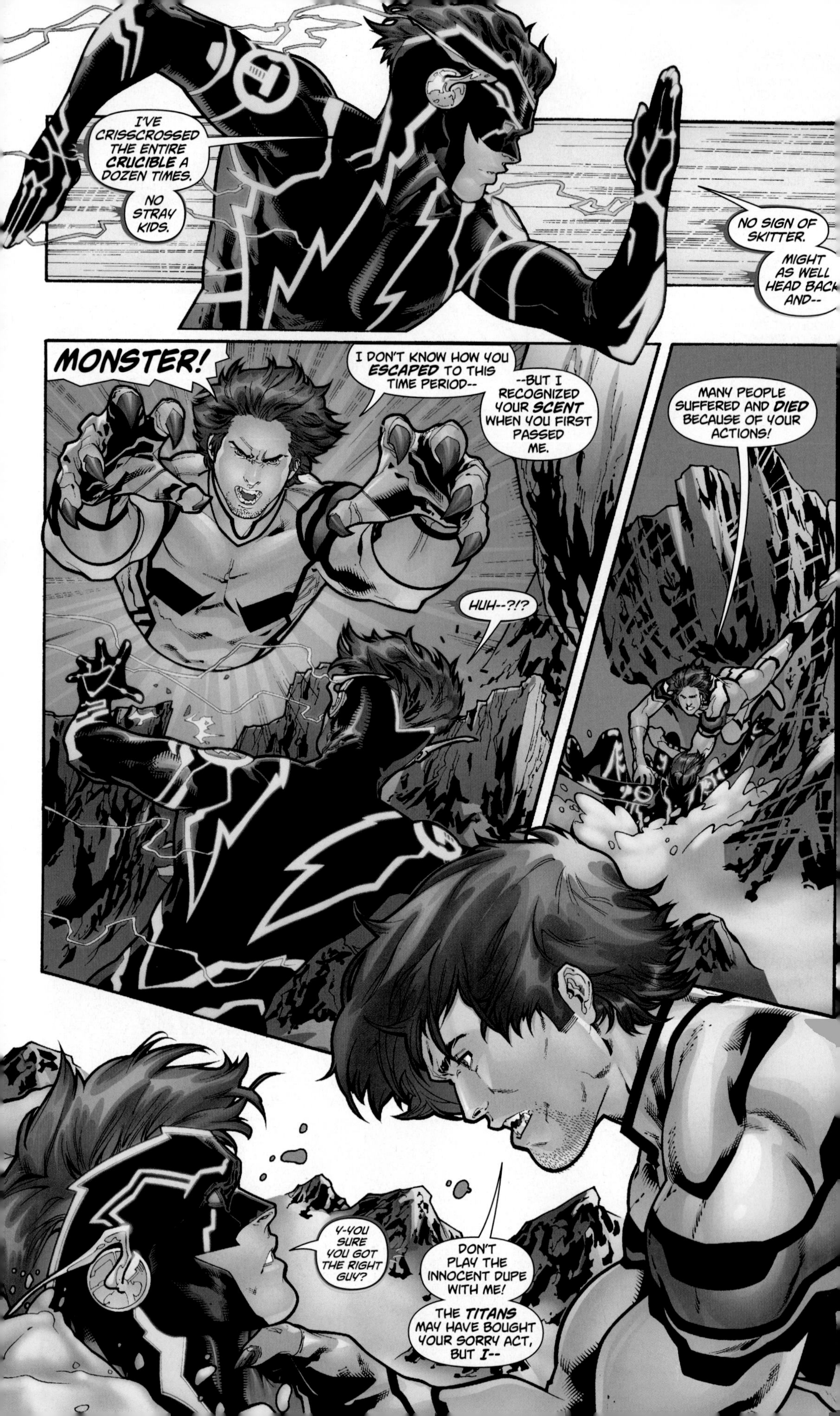

I'VE CRISSCROSSED THE ENTIRE CRUCIBLE A DOZEN TIMES.
NO STRAY KIDS.
NO SIGN OF SKITTER.
MIGHT AS WELL HEAD BACK AND--
MONSTER!
I DON'T KNOW HOW YOU ESCAPED TO THIS TIME PERIOD--
--BUT I RECOGNIZED YOUR SCENT WHEN YOU FIRST PASSED ME.
HUH--?!?
MANY PEOPLE SUFFERED AND DIED BECAUSE OF YOUR ACTIONS!
Y-YOU SURE YOU GOT THE RIGHT GUY?
DON'T PLAY THE INNOCENT DUPE WITH ME!
THE TITANS MAY HAVE BOUGHT YOUR SORRY ACT, BUT I--

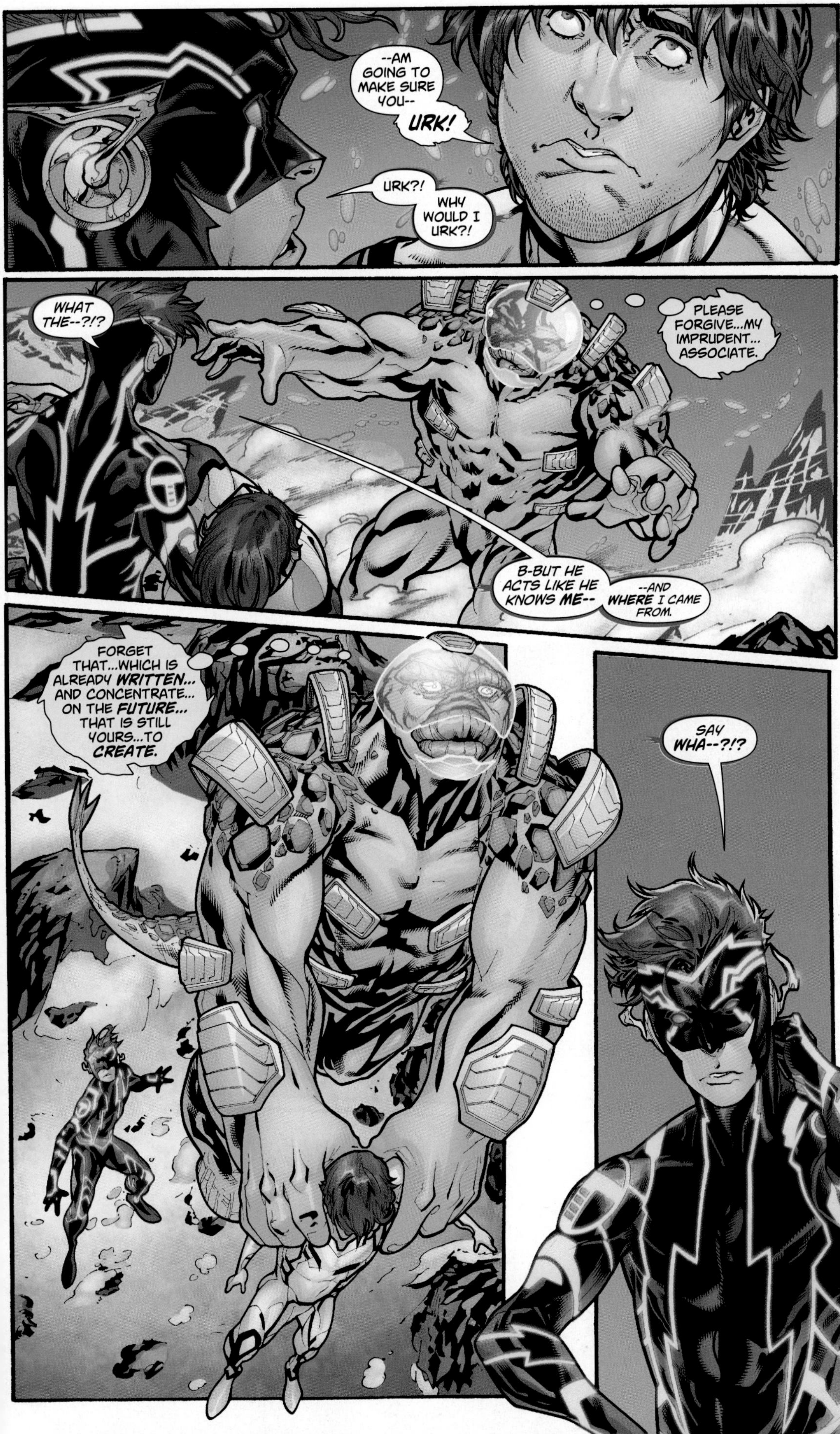
--AM GOING TO MAKE SURE YOU-- URK!
URK?! WHY WOULD I URK?!
WHAT THE--?!?
PLEASE FORGIVE...MY IMPRUDENT... ASSOCIATE.
B-BUT HE ACTS LIKE HE KNOWS ME--
--AND WHERE I CAME FROM.
FORGET THAT...WHICH IS ALREADY WRITTEN... AND CONCENTRATE... ON THE FUTURE... THAT IS STILL YOURS...TO CREATE.
SAY WHA--?!?

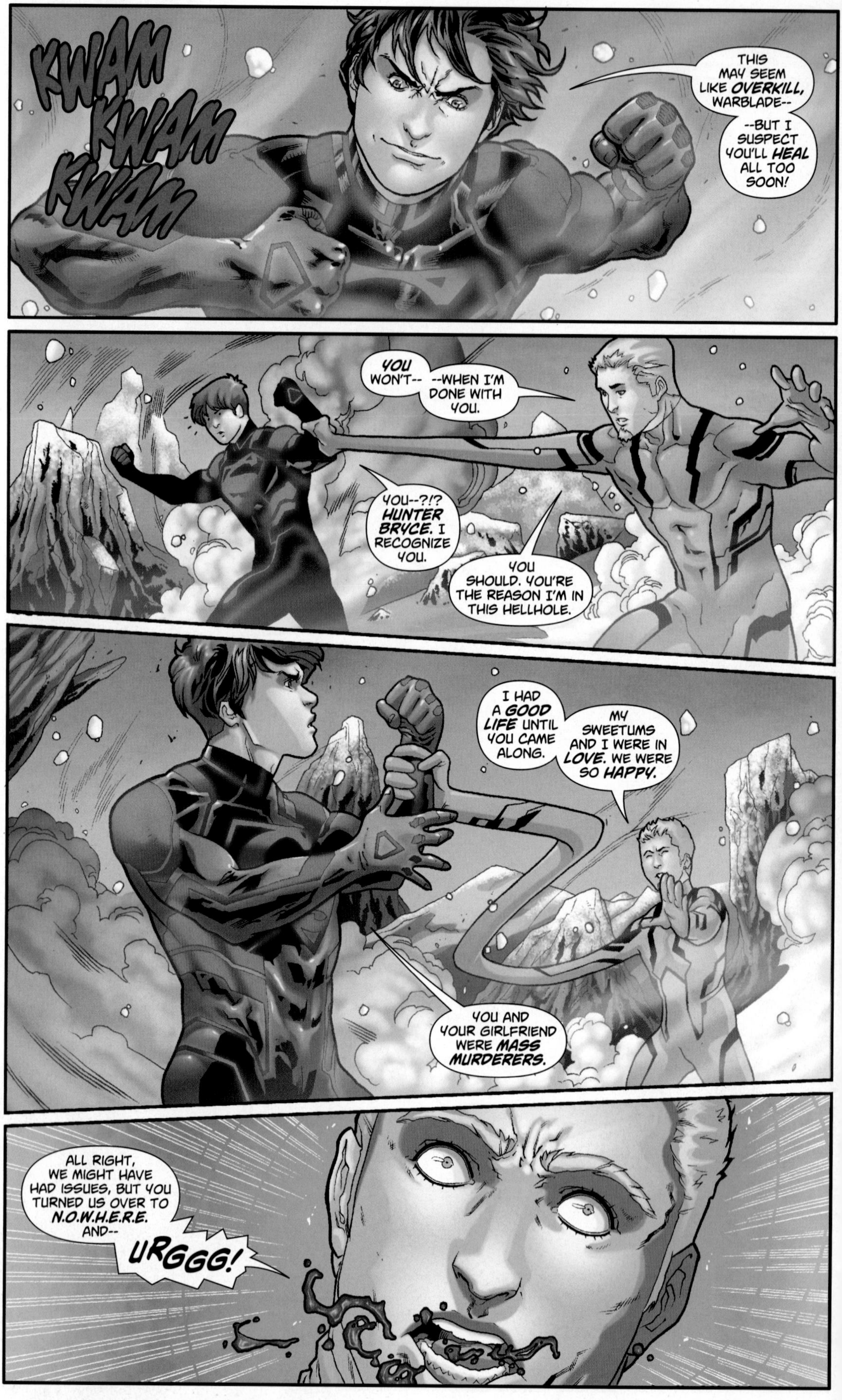
KWAM KWAM KWAM
THIS MAY SEEM LIKE OVERKILL, WARBLADE--
--BUT I SUSPECT YOU'LL HEAL ALL TOO SOON!
YOU WON'T--
--WHEN I'M DONE WITH YOU.
YOU--?!? HUNTER BRYCE. I RECOGNIZE YOU.
YOU SHOULD. YOU'RE THE REASON I'M IN THIS HELLHOLE.
I HAD A GOOD LIFE UNTIL YOU CAME ALONG.
MY SWEETUMS AND I WERE IN LOVE. WE WERE SO HAPPY.
YOU AND YOUR GIRLFRIEND WERE MASS MURDERERS.
ALL RIGHT, WE MIGHT HAVE HAD ISSUES, BUT YOU TURNED US OVER TO N.O.W.H.E.R.E. AND--
URGGG!

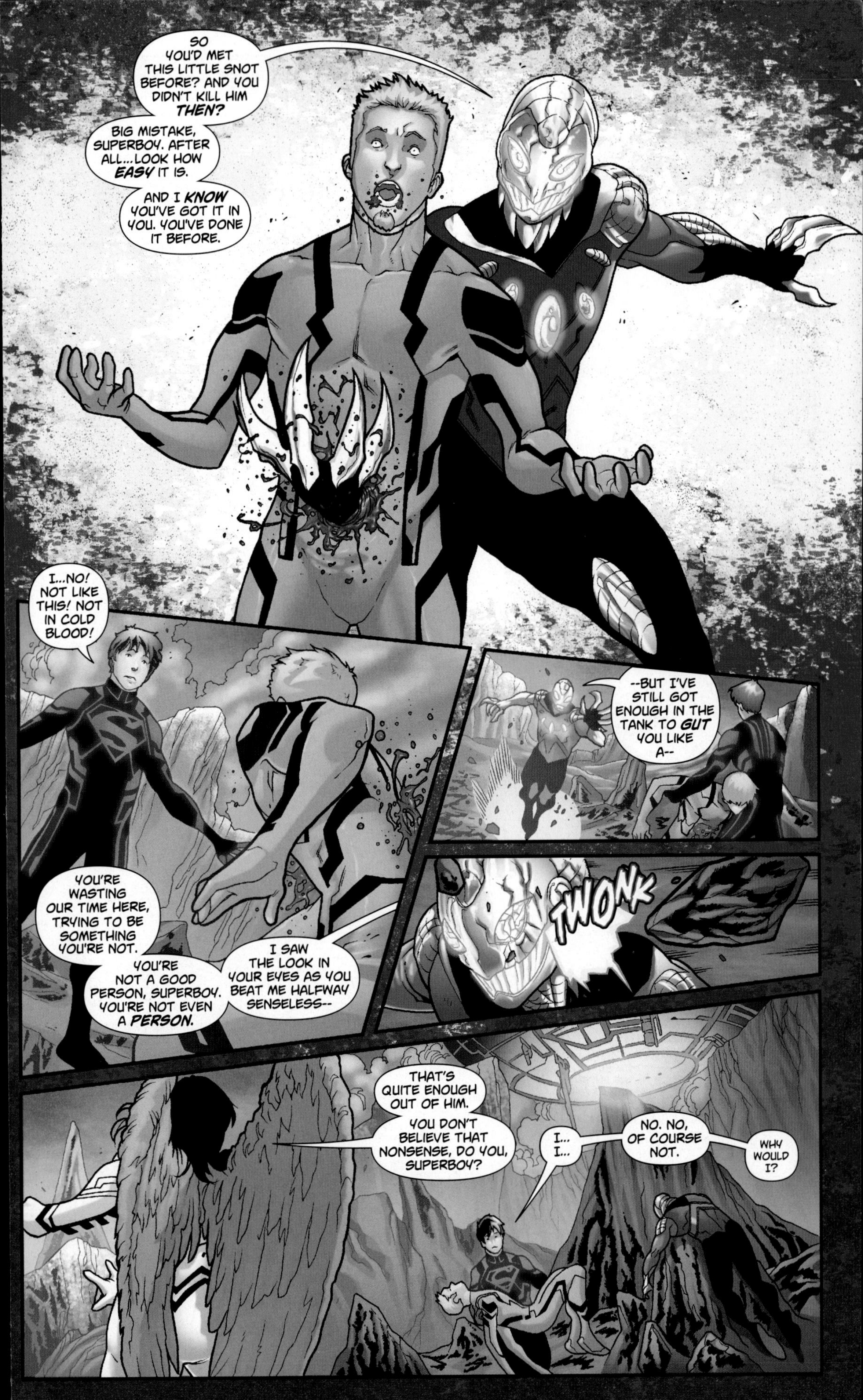

SO YOU'D MET THIS LITTLE SNOT BEFORE? AND YOU DIDN'T KILL HIM THEN?
BIG MISTAKE, SUPERBOY. AFTER ALL...LOOK HOW EASY IT IS.
AND I KNOW YOU'VE GOT IT IN YOU. YOU'VE DONE IT BEFORE.
I...NO! NOT LIKE THIS! NOT IN COLD BLOOD!
YOU'RE WASTING OUR TIME HERE, TRYING TO BE SOMETHING YOU'RE NOT.
YOU'RE NOT A GOOD PERSON, SUPERBOY. YOU'RE NOT EVEN A PERSON.
I SAW THE LOOK IN YOUR EYES AS YOU BEAT ME HALFWAY SENSELESS--
--BUT I'VE STILL GOT ENOUGH IN THE TANK TO GUT YOU LIKE A--
TWONK
THAT'S QUITE ENOUGH OUT OF HIM.
YOU DON'T BELIEVE THAT NONSENSE, DO YOU, SUPERBOY?
I... I...
NO. NO, OF COURSE NOT.
WHY WOULD I?

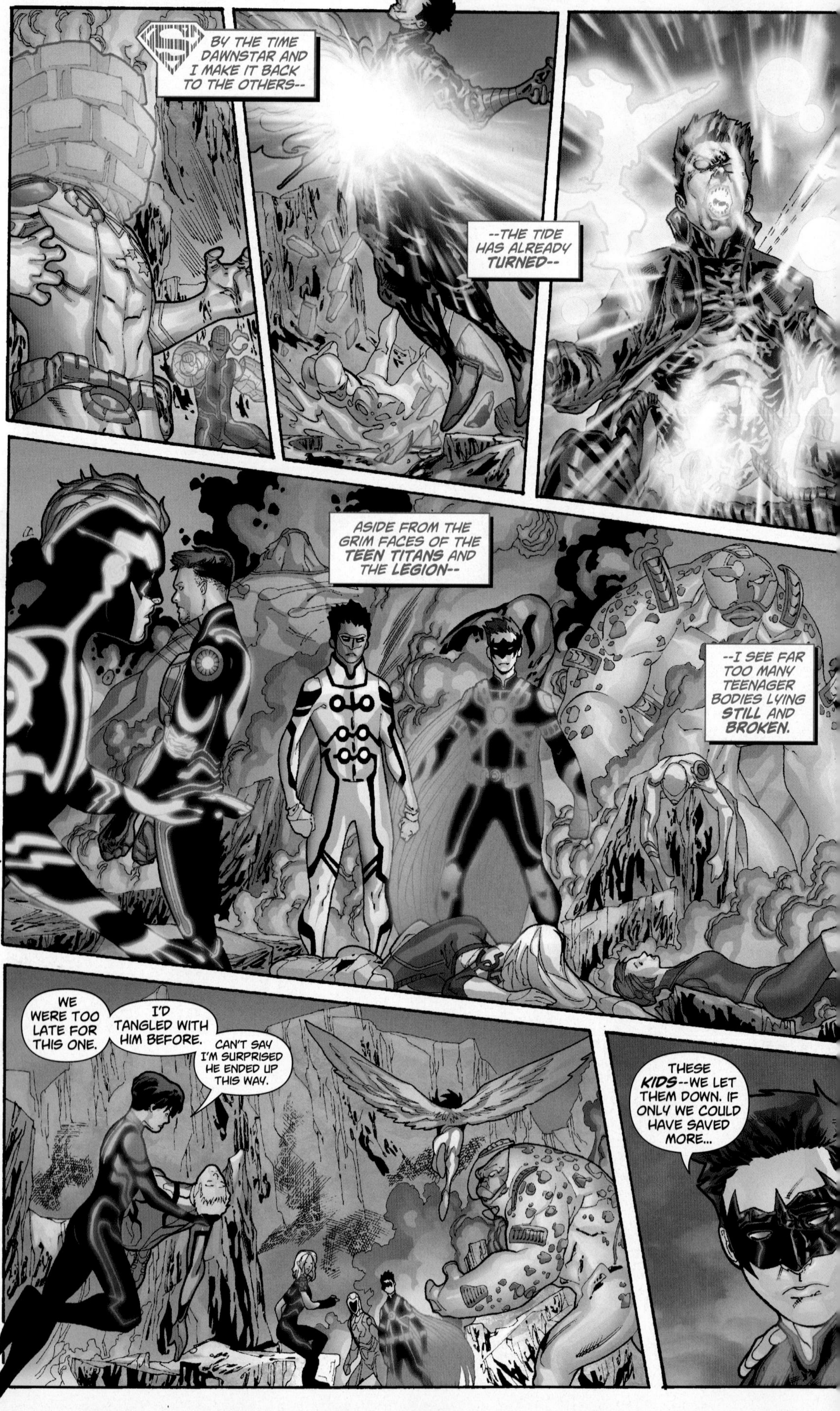
BY THE TIME DAWNSTAR AND I MAKE IT BACK TO THE OTHERS--
--THE TIDE HAS ALREADY TURNED--
ASIDE FROM THE GRIM FACES OF THE TEEN TITANS AND THE LEGION--
--I SEE FAR TOO MANY TEENAGER BODIES LYING STILL AND BROKEN.
WE WERE TOO LATE FOR THIS ONE.
I'D TANGLED WITH HIM BEFORE.
CAN'T SAY I'M SURPRISED HE ENDED UP THIS WAY.
THESE KIDS--WE LET THEM DOWN. IF ONLY WE COULD HAVE SAVED MORE...

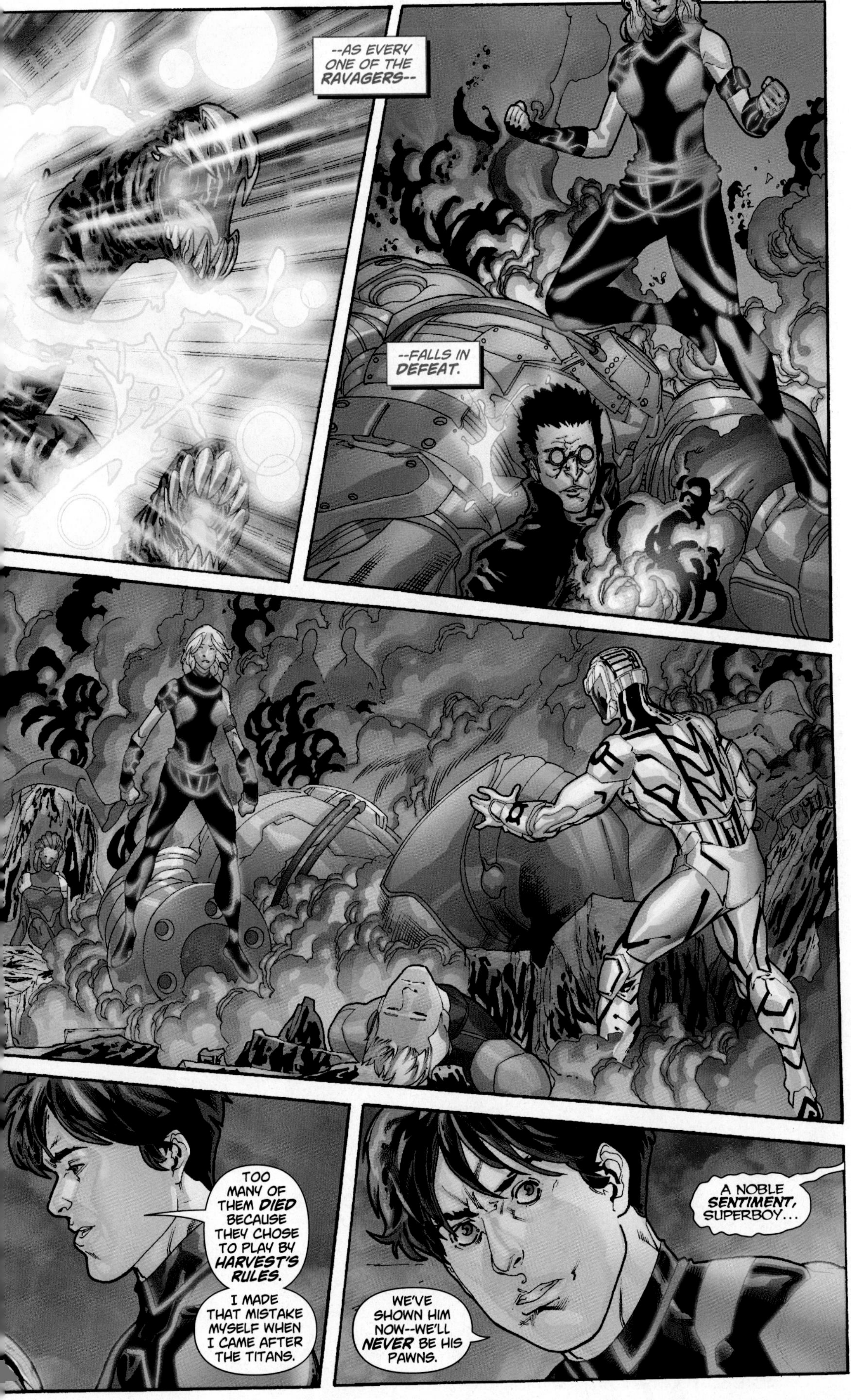
--AS EVERY ONE OF THE RAVAGERS--
--FALLS IN DEFEAT.
TOO MANY OF THEM DIED BECAUSE THEY CHOSE TO PLAY BY HARVEST'S RULES.
I MADE THAT MISTAKE MYSELF WHEN I CAME AFTER THE TITANS.
A NOBLE SENTIMENT, SUPERBOY...
WE'VE SHOWN HIM NOW--WE'LL NEVER BE HIS PAWNS.

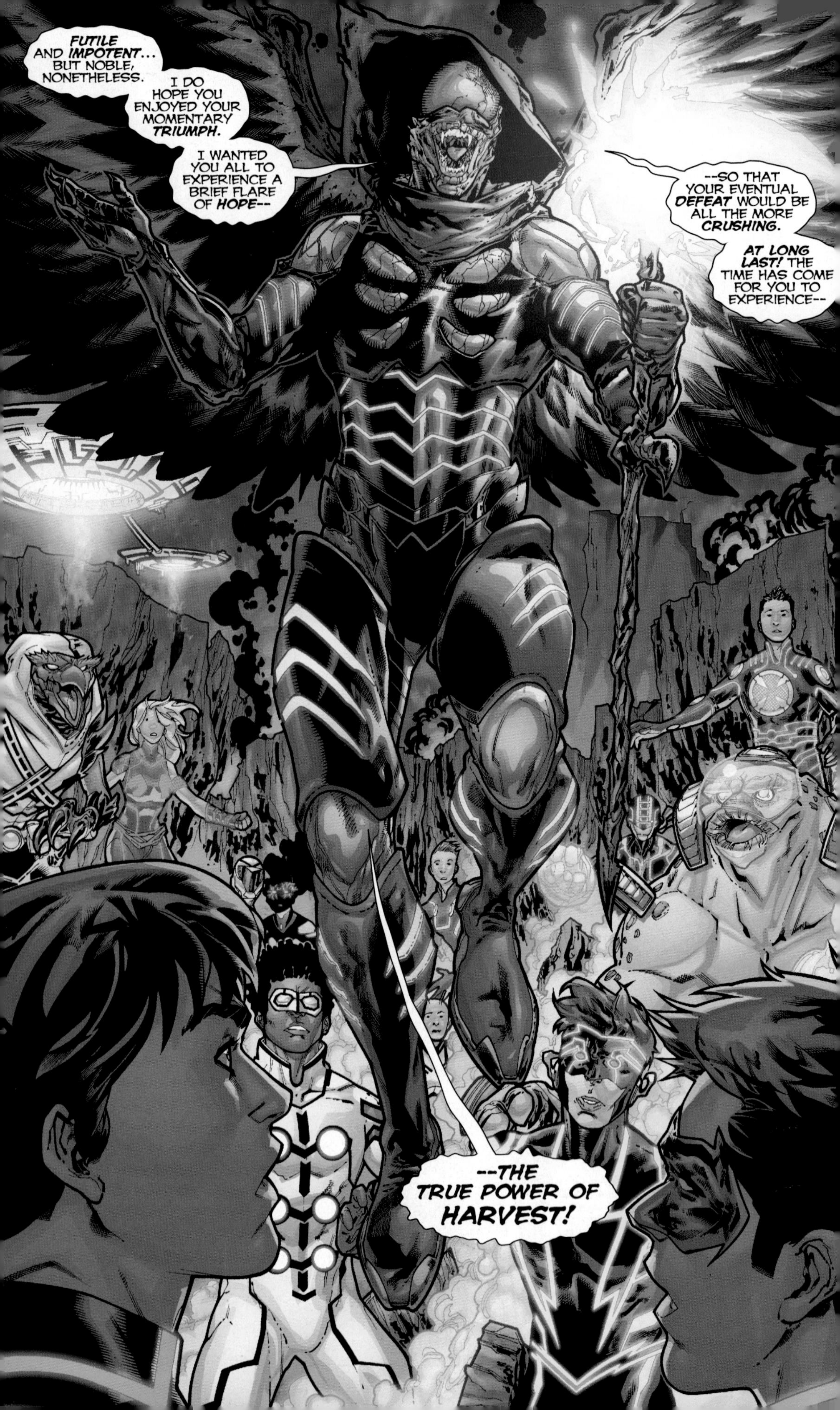
FUTILE AND IMPOTENT... BUT NOBLE, NONETHELESS.
I DO HOPE YOU ENJOYED YOUR MOMENTARY TRIUMPH.
I WANTED YOU ALL TO EXPERIENCE A BRIEF FLARE OF HOPE--
--SO THAT YOUR EVENTUAL DEFEAT WOULD BE ALL THE MORE CRUSHING.
AT LONG LAST! THE TIME HAS COME FOR YOU TO EXPERIENCE--
--THE TRUE POWER OF HARVEST!

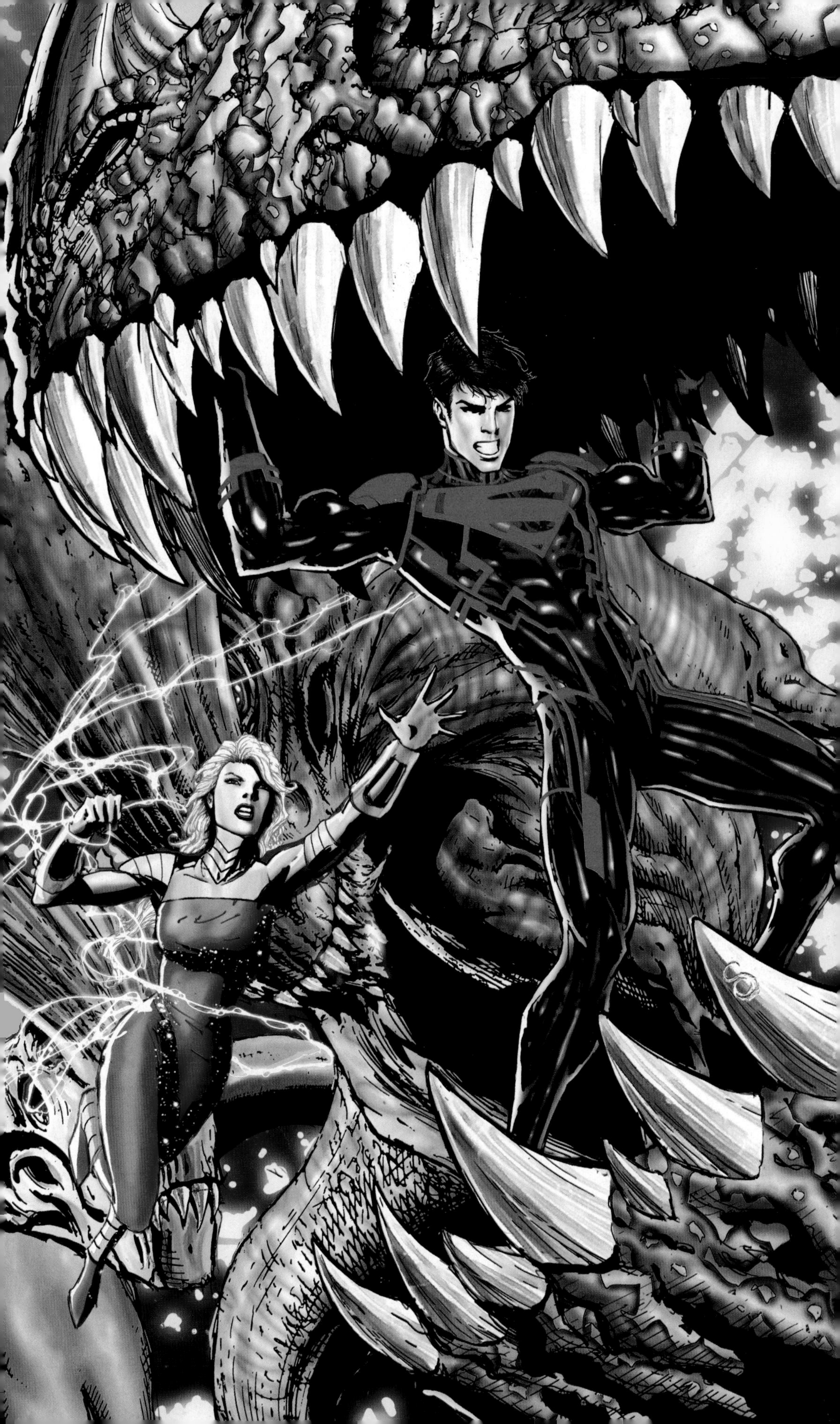

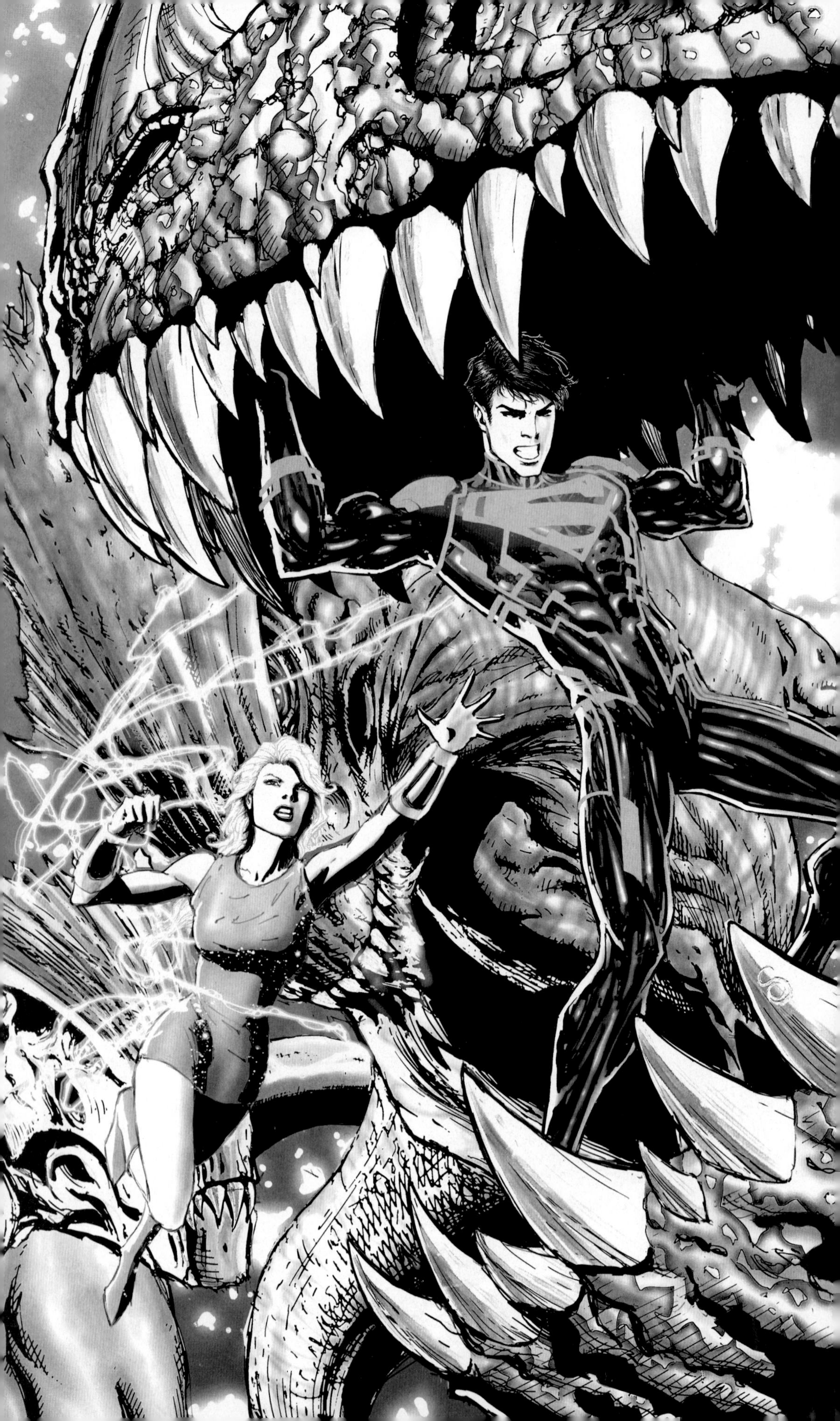

HER NAME IS CASSIE SANDSMARK.

(DON'T CALL HER WONDER GIRL.)

SHE IS VERY STRONG AND THROWS A MEAN RIGHT HOOK.

SHE'S ALSO GORGEOUS.

SELF-POSSESSED.

DETERMINED.

AND, JUST THIS MOMENT, SHE'S WAKING UP...

...ATOP A GUY WHO SHE RECENTLY CONSIDERED HER MORTAL ENEMY.

?!

THAT WOULD BE ME. SUPERBOY.

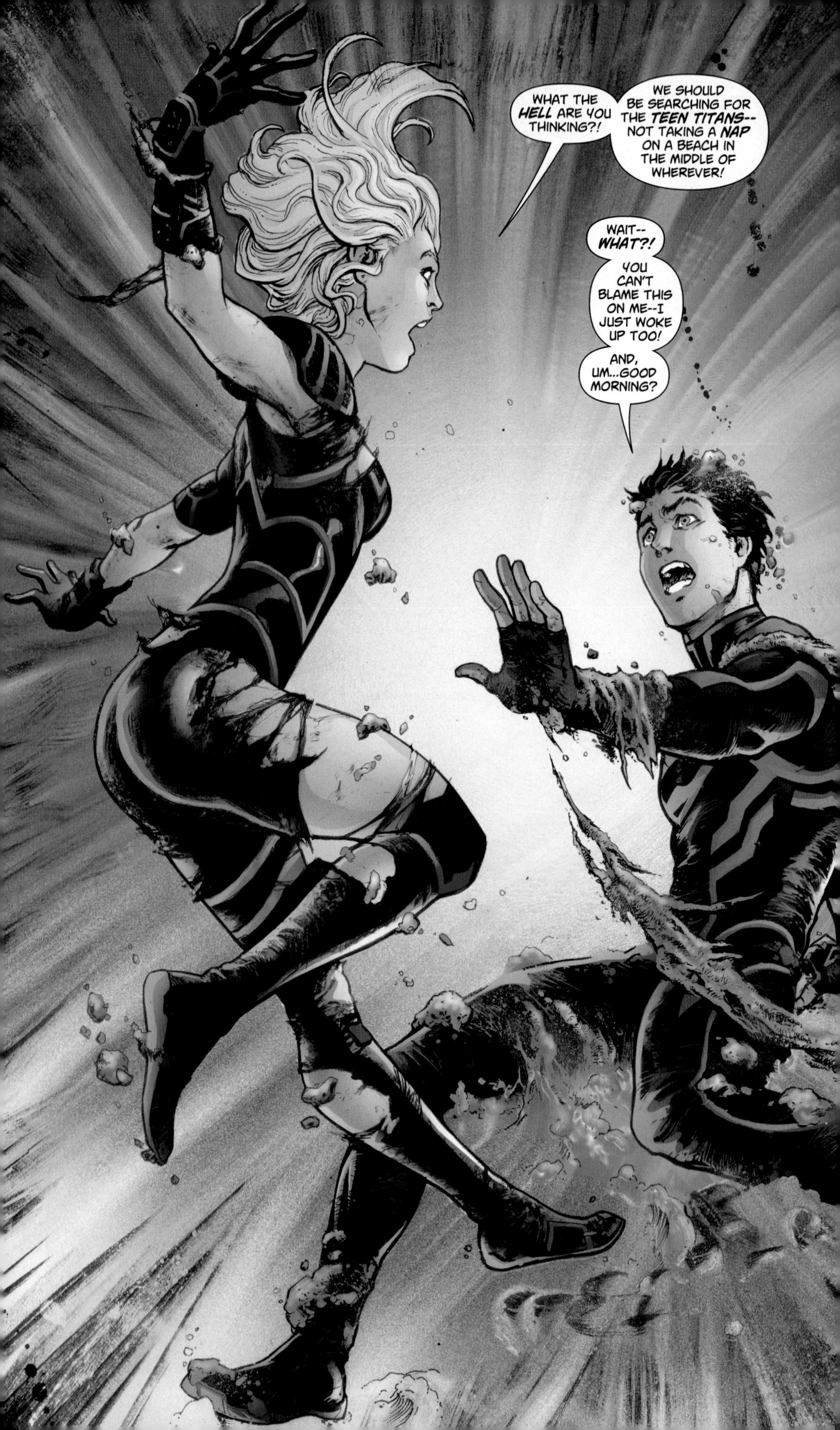
WHAT THE HELL ARE YOU THINKING?!
WE SHOULD BE SEARCHING FOR THE TEEN TITANS--NOT TAKING A NAP ON A BEACH IN THE MIDDLE OF WHEREVER!
WAIT--WHAT?!
YOU CAN'T BLAME THIS ON ME--I JUST WOKE UP TOO!
AND, UM...GOOD MORNING?

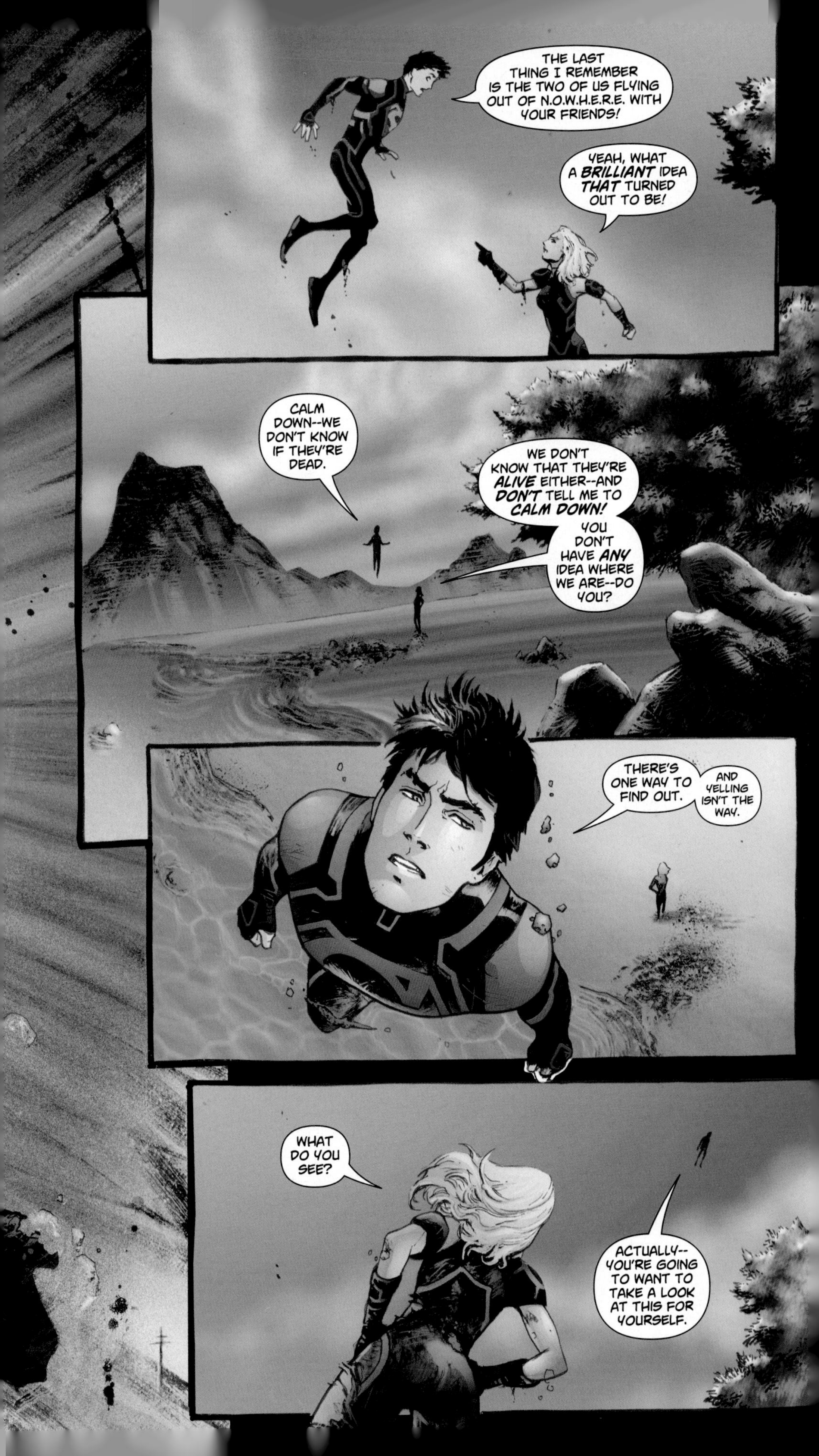
THE LAST THING I REMEMBER IS THE TWO OF US FLYING OUT OF N.O.W.H.E.R.E. WITH YOUR FRIENDS!
YEAH, WHAT A BRILLIANT IDEA THAT TURNED OUT TO BE!
CALM DOWN--WE DON'T KNOW IF THEY'RE DEAD.
WE DON'T KNOW THAT THEY'RE ALIVE EITHER--AND DON'T TELL ME TO CALM DOWN!
YOU DON'T HAVE ANY IDEA WHERE WE ARE--DO YOU?
THERE'S ONE WAY TO FIND OUT.
AND YELLING ISN'T THE WAY.
WHAT DO YOU SEE?
ACTUALLY--YOU'RE GOING TO WANT TO TAKE A LOOK AT THIS FOR YOURSELF.

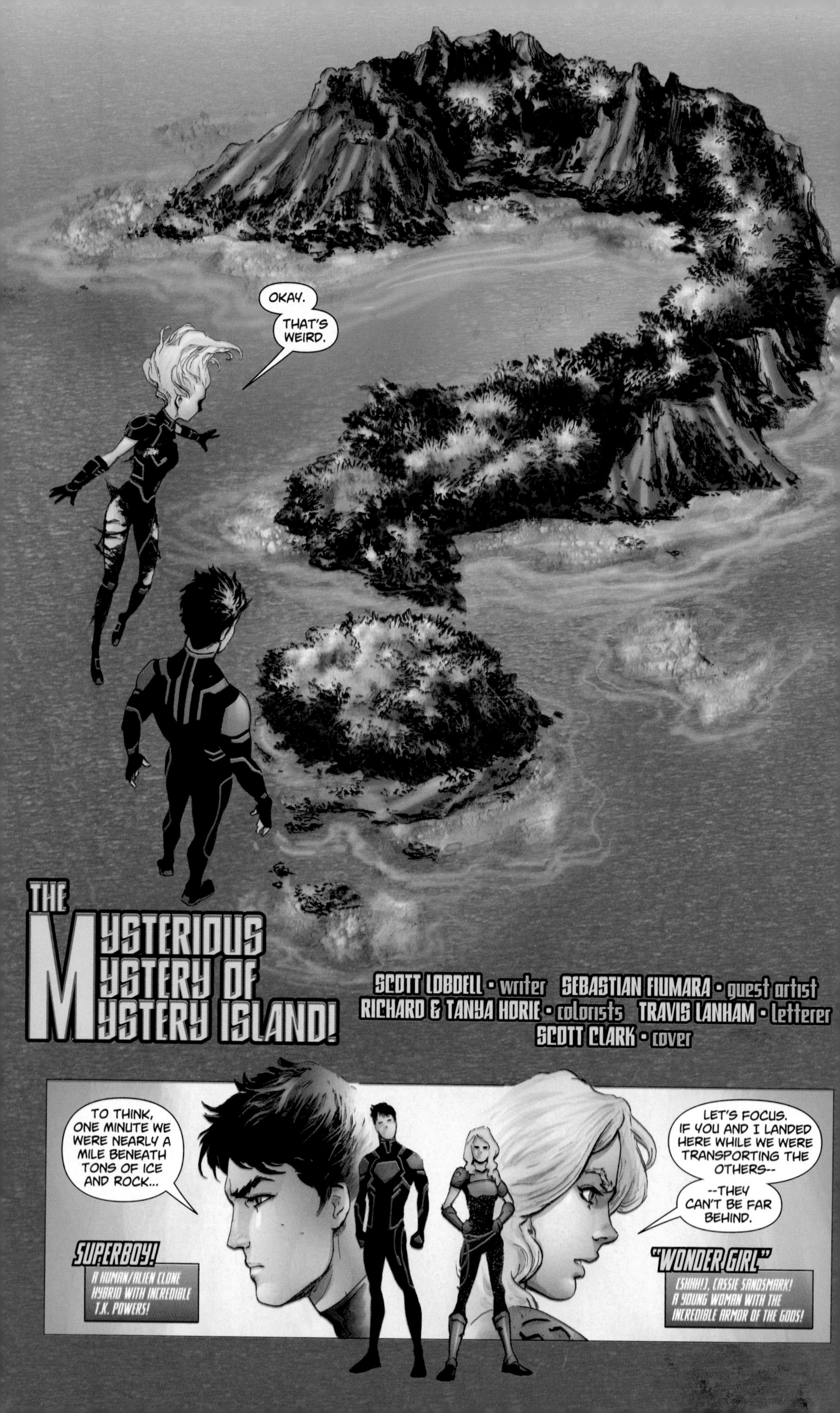
OKAY.
THAT'S WEIRD.
THE MYSTERIOUS MYSTERY OF MYSTERY ISLAND!
SCOTT LOBDELL • writer SEBASTIAN FIUMARA • guest artist
RICHARD & TANYA HORIE • colorists TRAVIS LANHAM • letterer
SCOTT CLARK • cover
TO THINK, ONE MINUTE WE WERE NEARLY A MILE BENEATH TONS OF ICE AND ROCK...
SUPERBOY!
A HUMAN/ALIEN CLONE HYBRID WITH INCREDIBLE T.K. POWERS!
LET'S FOCUS. IF YOU AND I LANDED HERE WHILE WE WERE TRANSPORTING THE OTHERS--
--THEY CAN'T BE FAR BEHIND.
"WONDER GIRL"
(SHHH!), CASSIE SANDSMARK! A YOUNG WOMAN WITH THE INCREDIBLE ARMOR OF THE GODS!

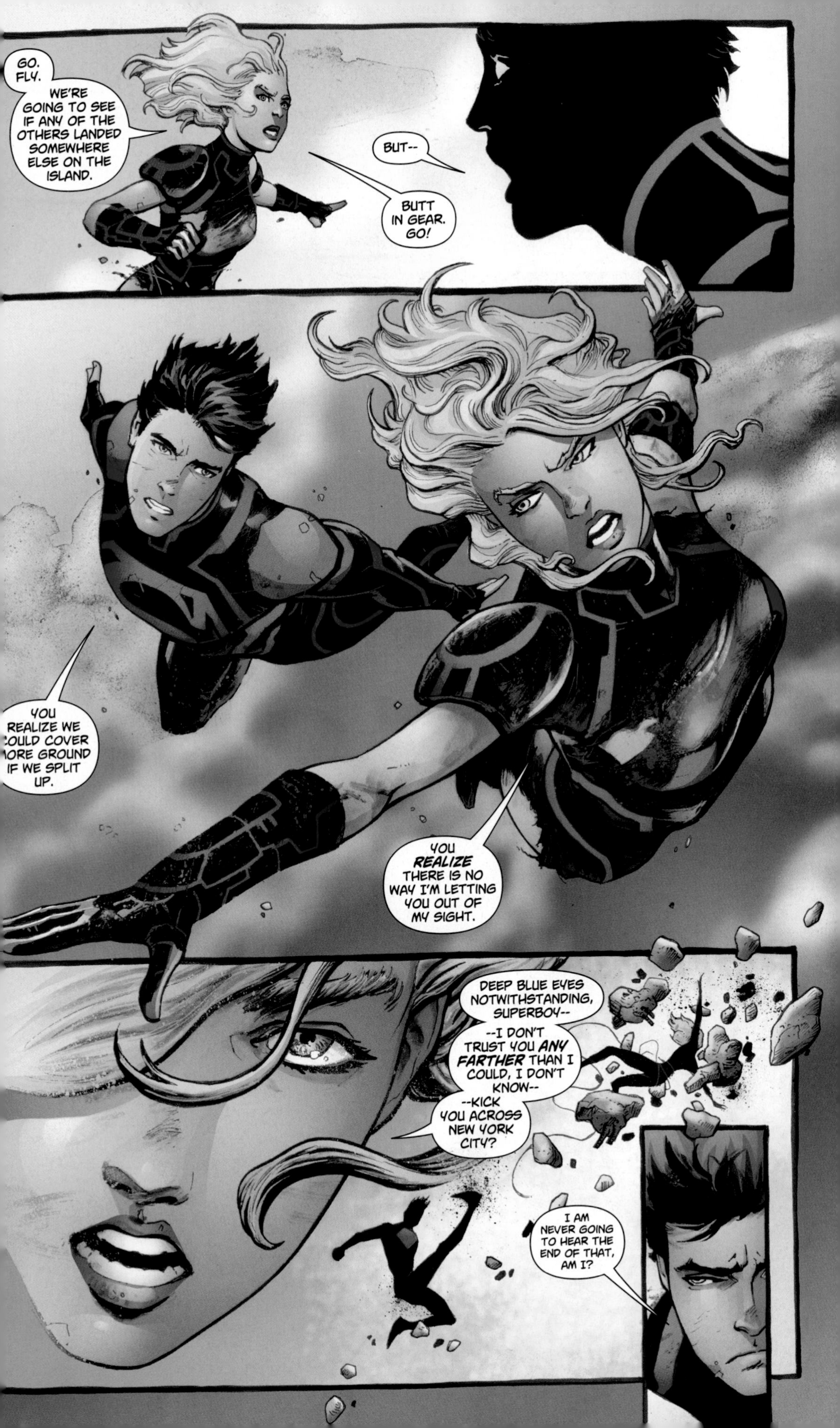
GO. FLY.
WE'RE GOING TO SEE IF ANY OF THE OTHERS LANDED SOMEWHERE ELSE ON THE ISLAND.
BUT--
BUTT IN GEAR. GO!
YOU REALIZE WE COULD COVER MORE GROUND IF WE SPLIT UP.
YOU *REALIZE* THERE IS NO WAY I'M LETTING YOU OUT OF MY SIGHT.
DEEP BLUE EYES NOTWITHSTANDING, SUPERBOY--
--I DON'T TRUST YOU *ANY FARTHER* THAN I COULD, I DON'T KNOW--
--KICK YOU ACROSS NEW YORK CITY?
I AM NEVER GOING TO HEAR THE END OF THAT, AM I?

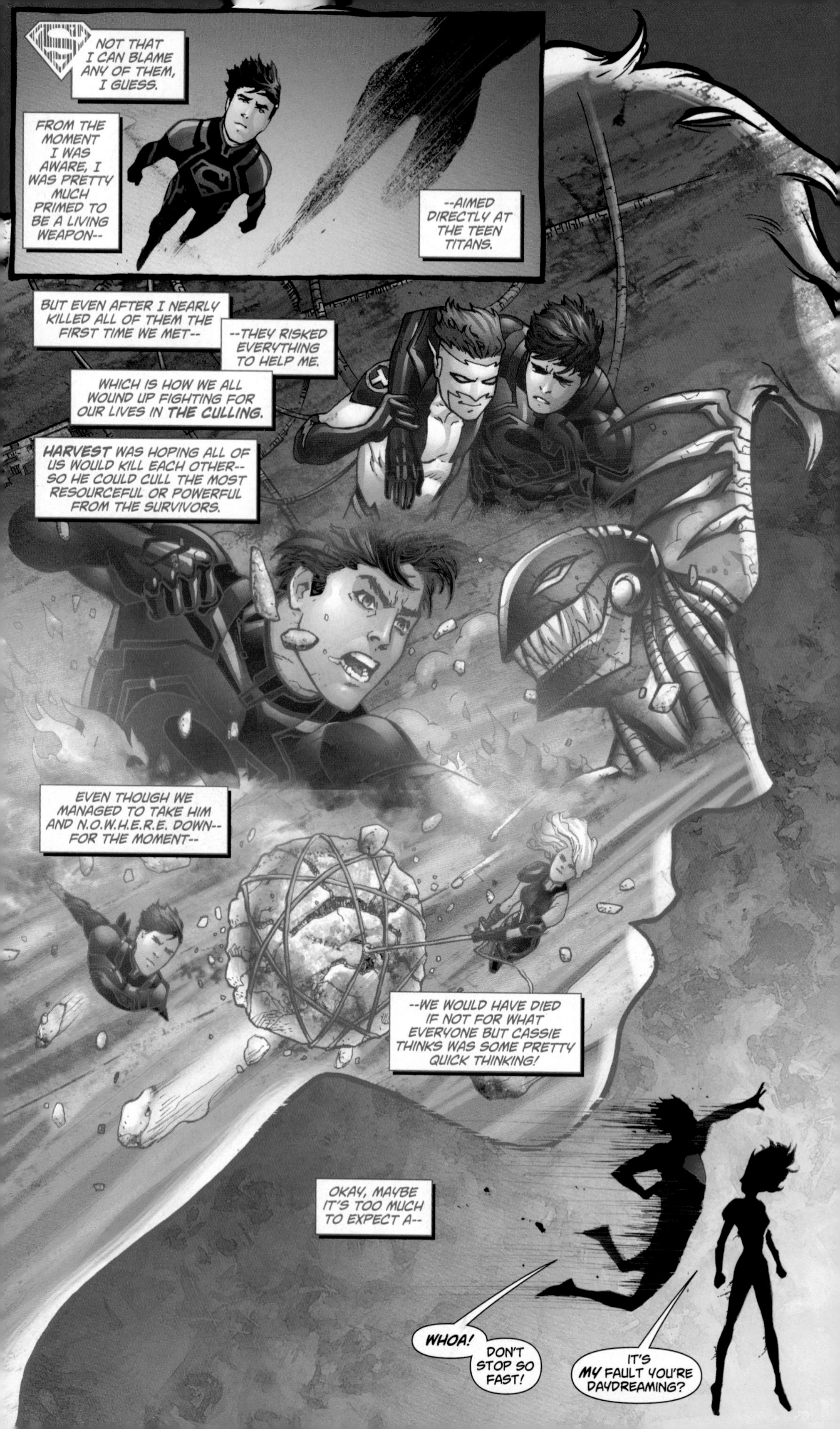
NOT THAT I CAN BLAME ANY OF THEM, I GUESS.
FROM THE MOMENT I WAS AWARE, I WAS PRETTY MUCH PRIMED TO BE A LIVING WEAPON--
--AIMED DIRECTLY AT THE TEEN TITANS.
BUT EVEN AFTER I NEARLY KILLED ALL OF THEM THE FIRST TIME WE MET--
--THEY RISKED EVERYTHING TO HELP ME.
WHICH IS HOW WE ALL WOUND UP FIGHTING FOR OUR LIVES IN THE CULLING.
HARVEST WAS HOPING ALL OF US WOULD KILL EACH OTHER--SO HE COULD CULL THE MOST RESOURCEFUL OR POWERFUL FROM THE SURVIVORS.
EVEN THOUGH WE MANAGED TO TAKE HIM AND N.O.W.H.E.R.E. DOWN--FOR THE MOMENT--
--WE WOULD HAVE DIED IF NOT FOR WHAT EVERYONE BUT CASSIE THINKS WAS SOME PRETTY QUICK THINKING!
OKAY, MAYBE IT'S TOO MUCH TO EXPECT A--
WHOA! DON'T STOP SO FAST!
IT'S MY FAULT YOU'RE DAYDREAMING?

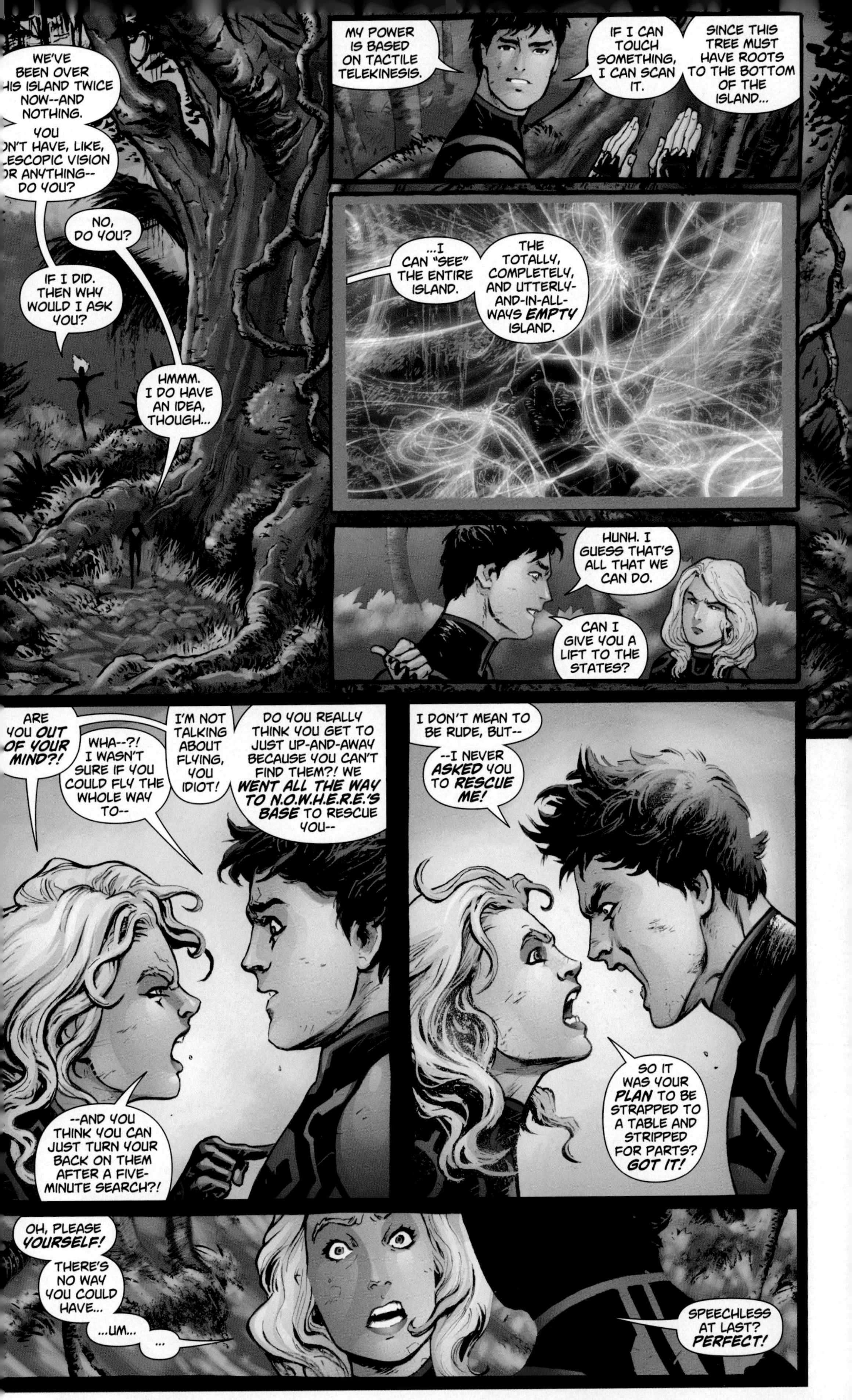

WE'VE BEEN OVER HIS ISLAND TWICE NOW--AND NOTHING.
YOU N'T HAVE, LIKE, LESCOPIC VISION R ANYTHING-- DO YOU?
NO, DO YOU?
IF I DID. THEN WHY WOULD I ASK YOU?
HMMM. I DO HAVE AN IDEA, THOUGH...
MY POWER IS BASED ON TACTILE TELEKINESIS.
IF I CAN TOUCH SOMETHING, I CAN SCAN IT.
SINCE THIS TREE MUST HAVE ROOTS TO THE BOTTOM OF THE ISLAND...
...I CAN "SEE" THE ENTIRE ISLAND.
THE TOTALLY, COMPLETELY, AND UTTERLY-AND-IN-ALL-WAYS EMPTY ISLAND.
HUNH. I GUESS THAT'S ALL THAT WE CAN DO.
CAN I GIVE YOU A LIFT TO THE STATES?
ARE YOU OUT OF YOUR MIND?!
WHA--?! I WASN'T SURE IF YOU COULD FLY THE WHOLE WAY TO--
I'M NOT TALKING ABOUT FLYING, YOU IDIOT!
DO YOU REALLY THINK YOU GET TO JUST UP-AND-AWAY BECAUSE YOU CAN'T FIND THEM?! WE WENT ALL THE WAY TO N.O.W.H.E.R.E.'S BASE TO RESCUE YOU--
--AND YOU THINK YOU CAN JUST TURN YOUR BACK ON THEM AFTER A FIVE-MINUTE SEARCH?!
I DON'T MEAN TO BE RUDE, BUT--
--I NEVER ASKED YOU TO RESCUE ME!
SO IT WAS YOUR PLAN TO BE STRAPPED TO A TABLE AND STRIPPED FOR PARTS? GOT IT!
OH, PLEASE YOURSELF!
THERE'S NO WAY YOU COULD HAVE...
...UM...
...
SPEECHLESS AT LAST? PERFECT!

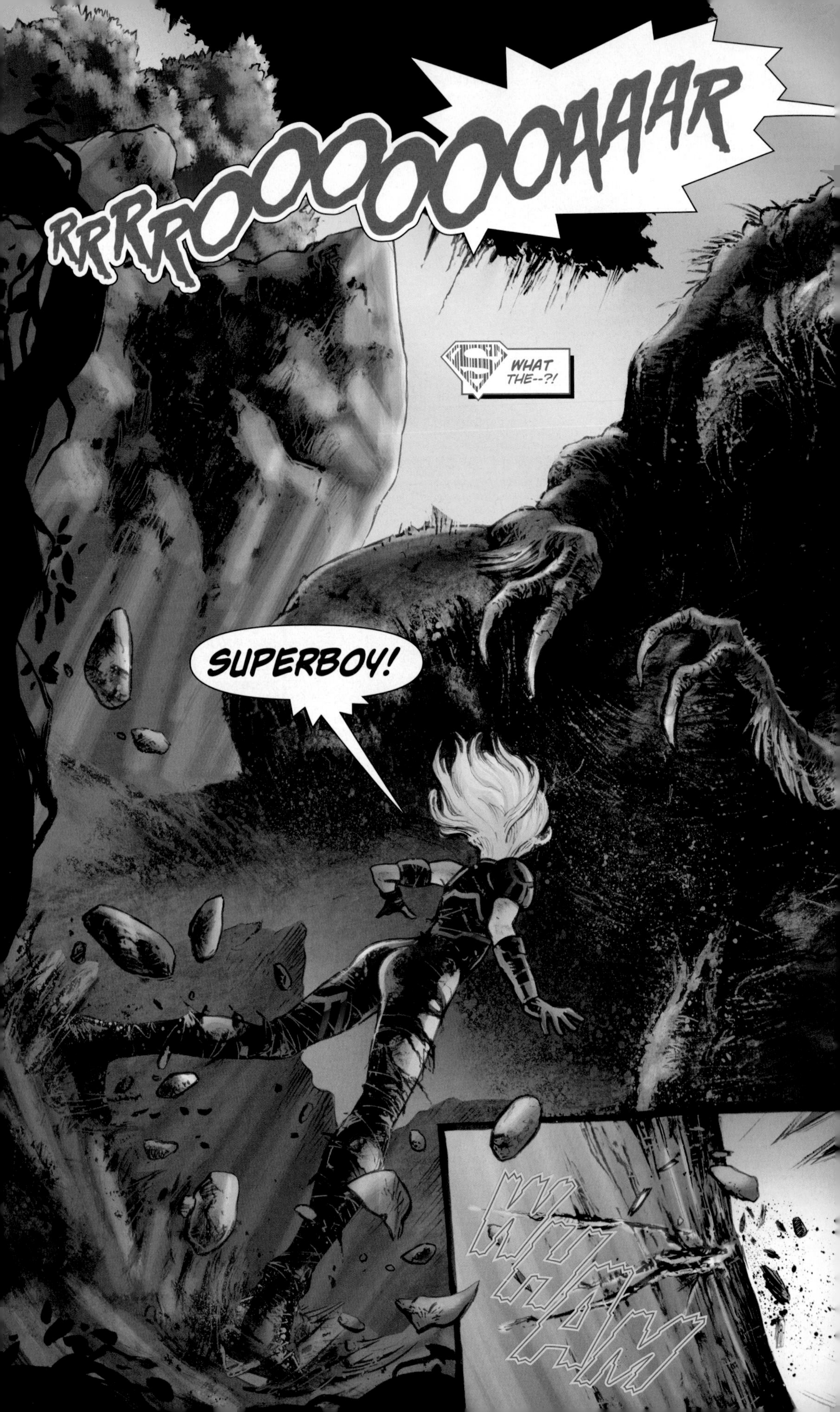
RRRROOOOOOOAAAAR
WHAT THE--?!
SUPERBOY!
KRRAKK

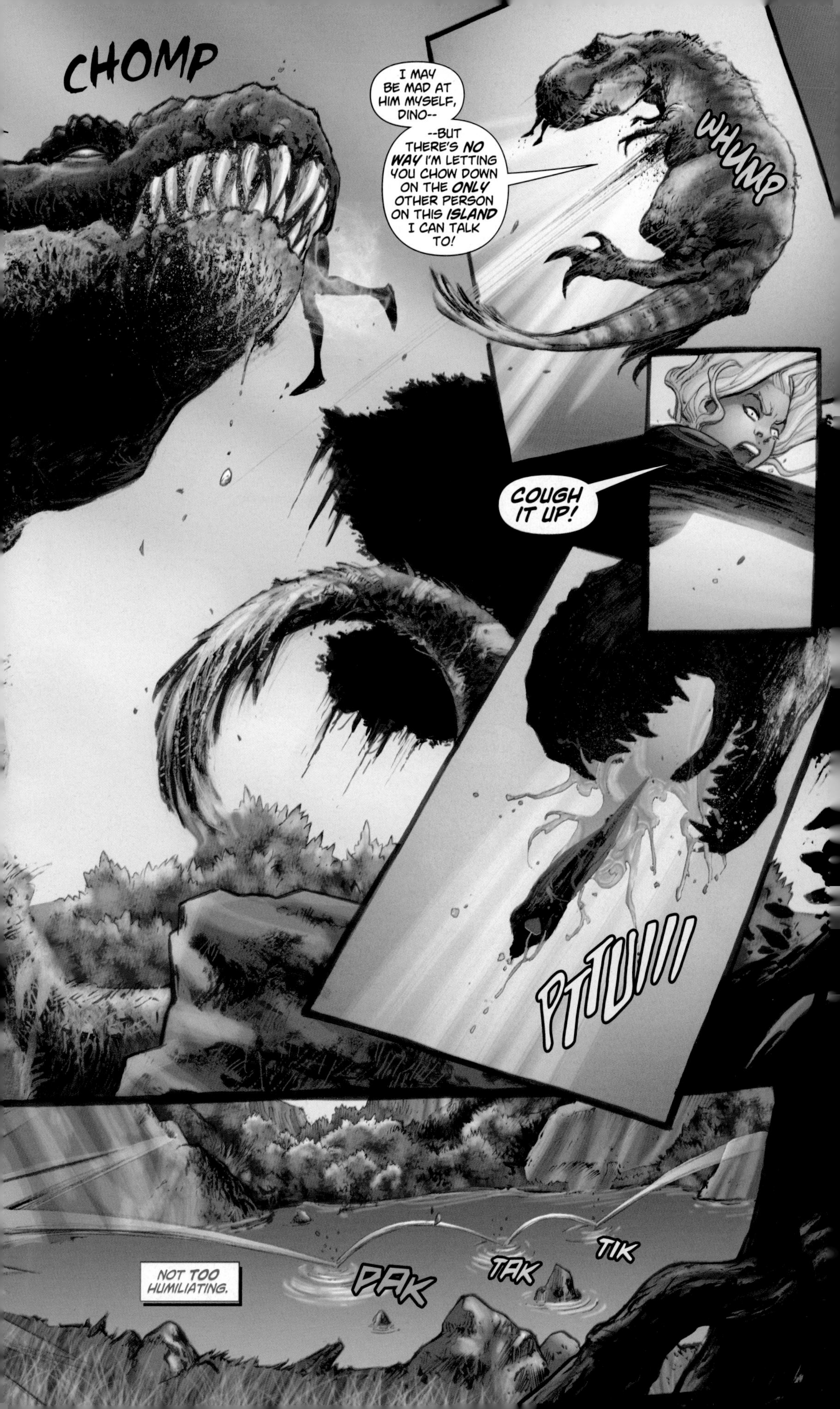
CHOMP
I MAY BE MAD AT HIM MYSELF, DINO--
--BUT THERE'S NO WAY I'M LETTING YOU CHOW DOWN ON THE ONLY OTHER PERSON ON THIS ISLAND I CAN TALK TO!
WHUMP
COUGH IT UP!
PTTUIII
NOT TOO HUMILIATING.
PAK
TAK
TIK

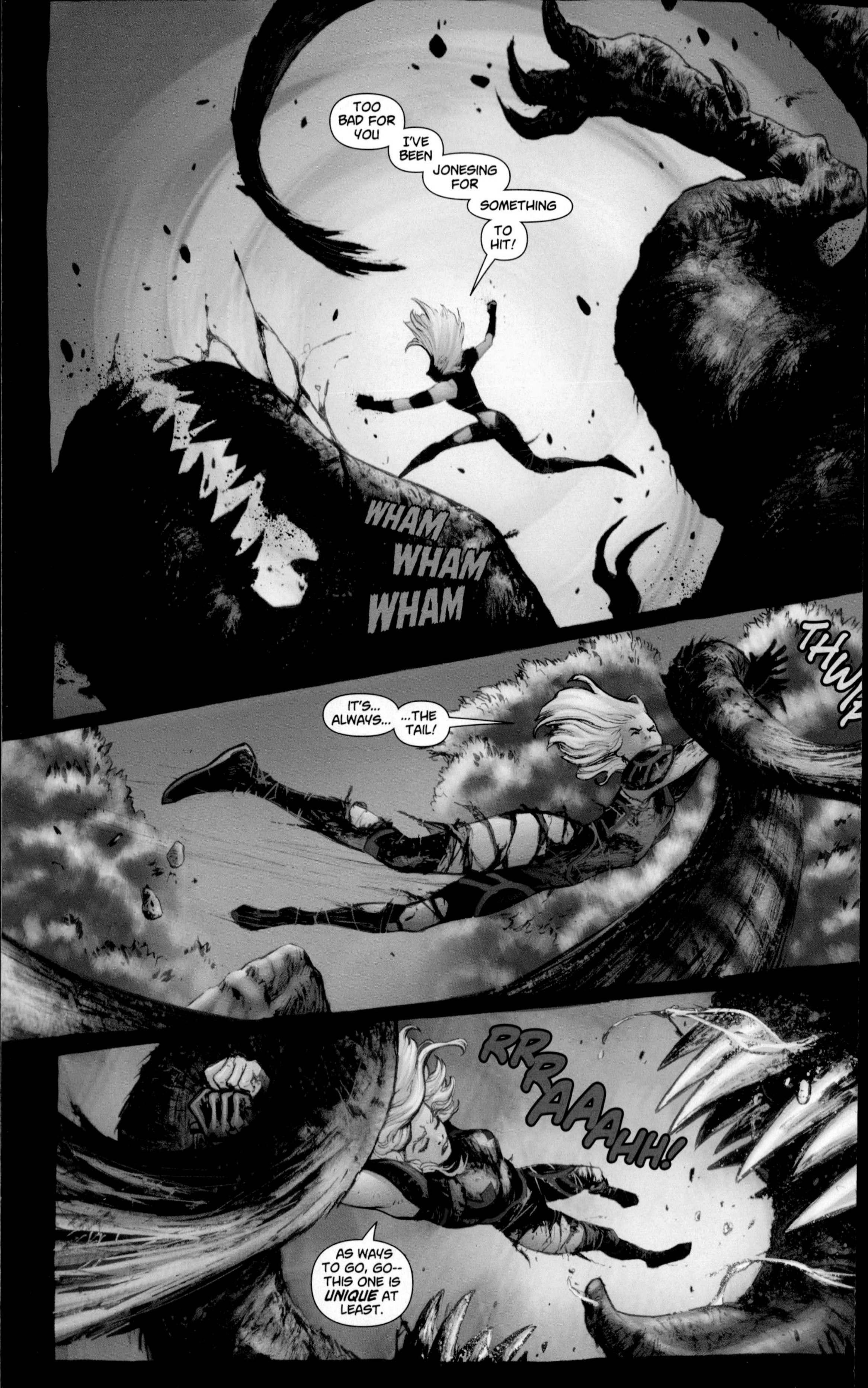
TOO BAD FOR YOU I'VE BEEN JONESING FOR SOMETHING TO HIT!
WHAM WHAM WHAM
THWIP
IT'S... ALWAYS... ...THE TAIL!
RRRAAAHH!
AS WAYS TO GO, GO-- THIS ONE IS ***UNIQUE*** AT LEAST.

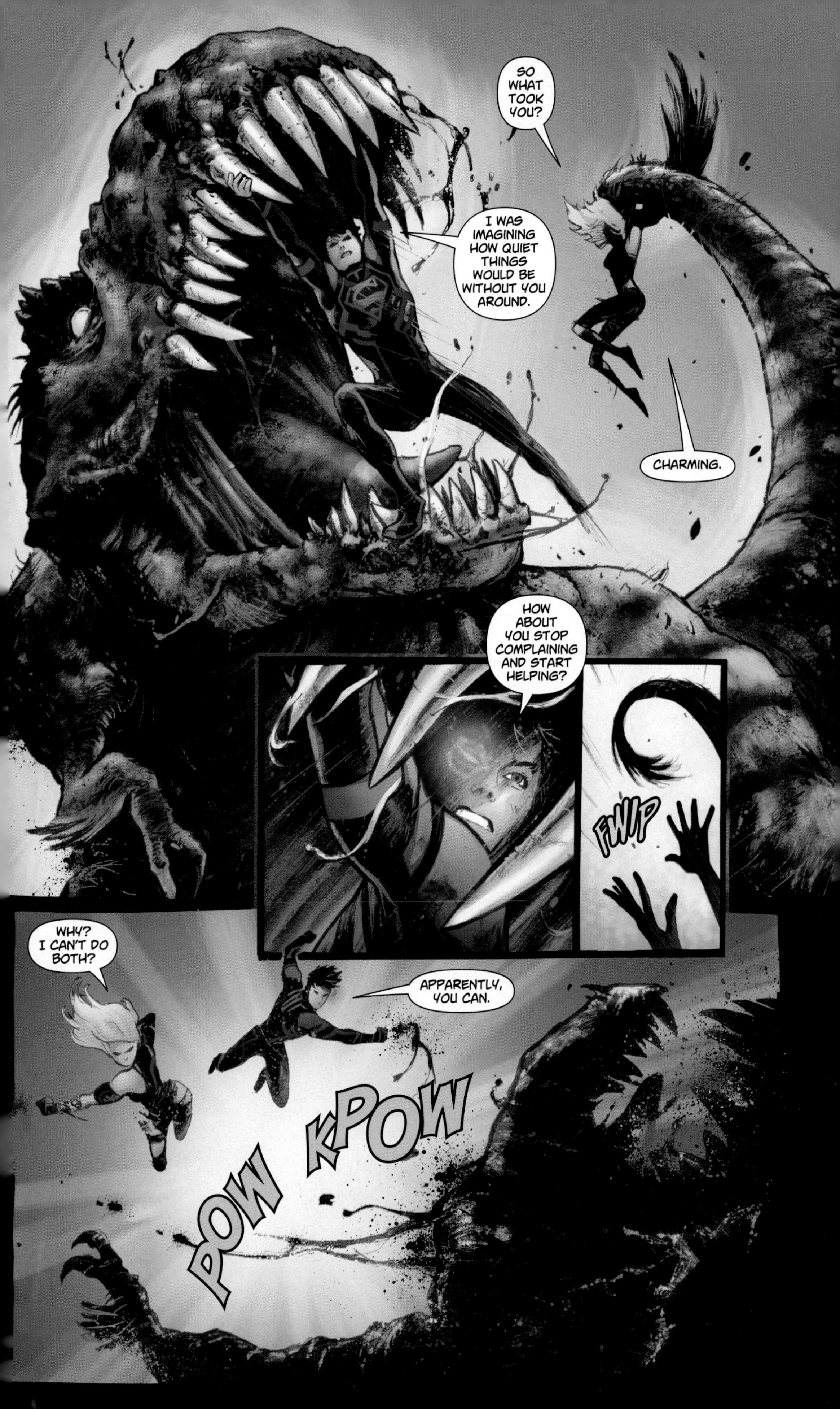
SO WHAT TOOK YOU?
I WAS IMAGINING HOW QUIET THINGS WOULD BE WITHOUT YOU AROUND.
CHARMING.
HOW ABOUT YOU STOP COMPLAINING AND START HELPING?
FWIP
WHY? I CAN'T DO BOTH?
APPARENTLY, YOU CAN.
POW KPOW

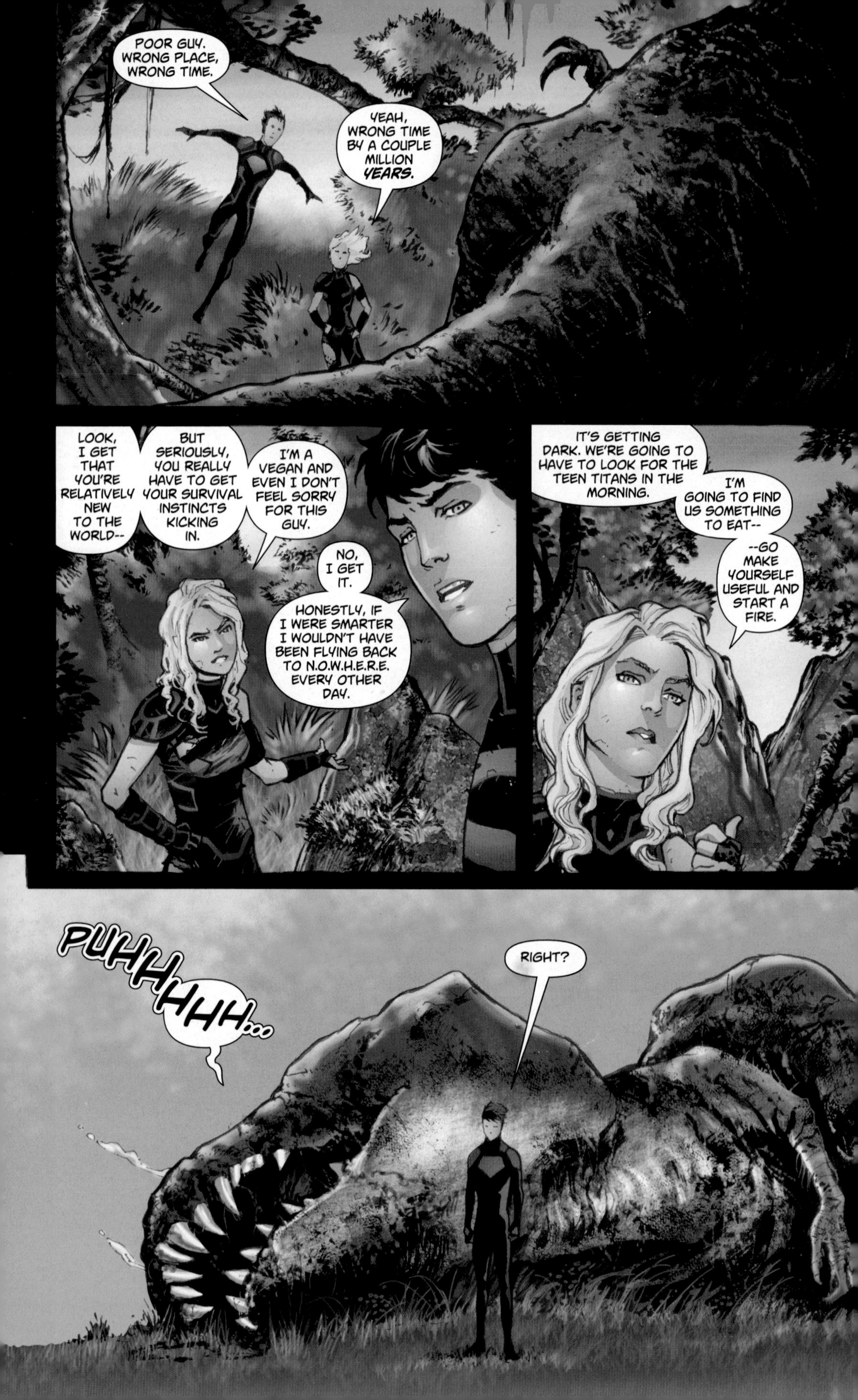
POOR GUY. WRONG PLACE, WRONG TIME.
YEAH, WRONG TIME BY A COUPLE MILLION *YEARS.*
LOOK, I GET THAT YOU'RE RELATIVELY NEW TO THE WORLD--
BUT SERIOUSLY, YOU REALLY HAVE TO GET YOUR SURVIVAL INSTINCTS KICKING IN.
I'M A VEGAN AND EVEN I DON'T FEEL SORRY FOR THIS GUY.
NO, I GET IT.
HONESTLY, IF I WERE SMARTER I WOULDN'T HAVE BEEN FLYING BACK TO N.O.W.H.E.R.E. EVERY OTHER DAY.
IT'S GETTING DARK. WE'RE GOING TO HAVE TO LOOK FOR THE TEEN TITANS IN THE MORNING.
I'M GOING TO FIND US SOMETHING TO EAT--
--GO MAKE YOURSELF USEFUL AND START A FIRE.
PUHHHHHH...
RIGHT?

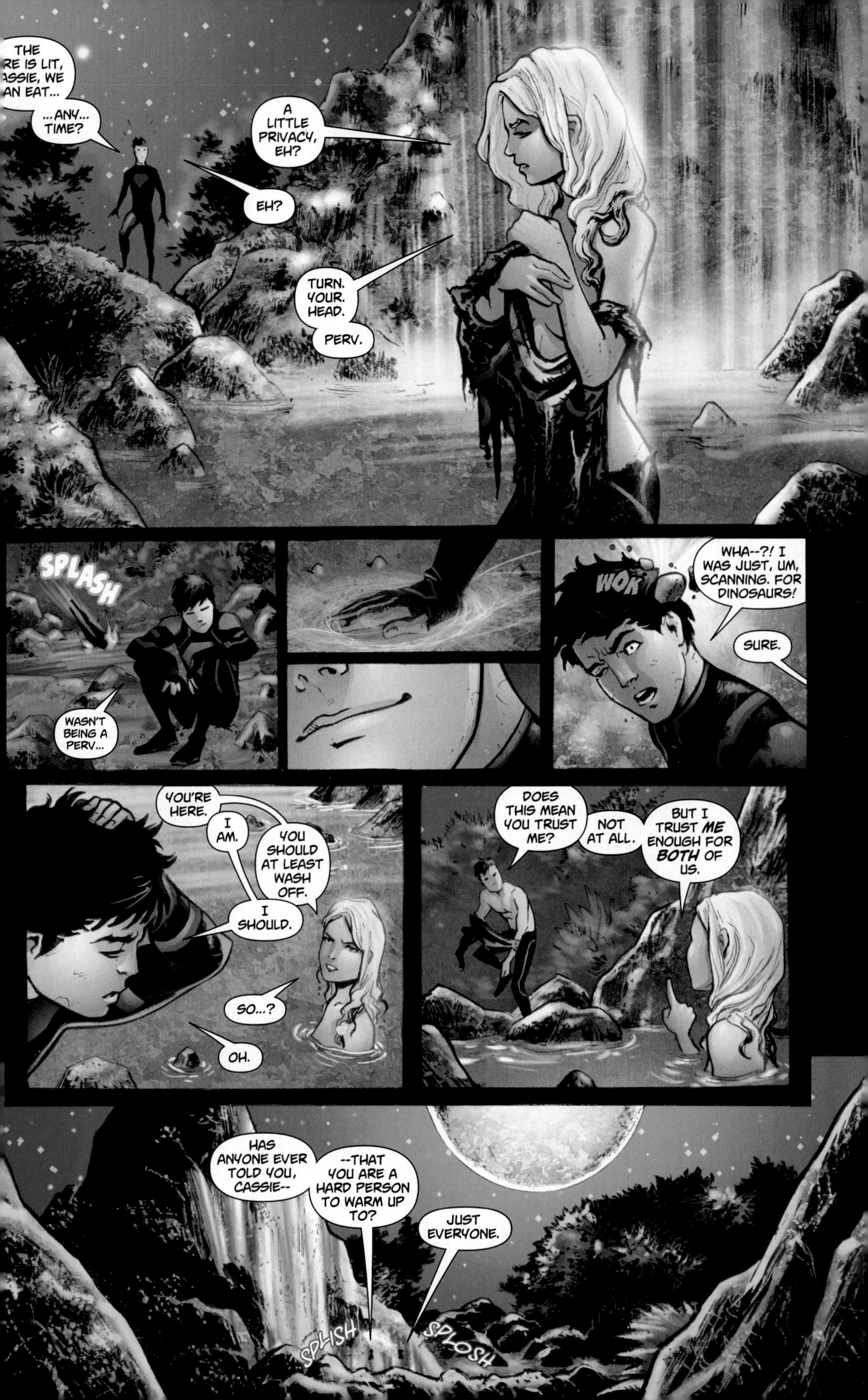

THE RE IS LIT, ASSIE, WE AN EAT...
...ANY... TIME?
A LITTLE PRIVACY, EH?
EH?
TURN. YOUR. HEAD.
PERV.
SPLASH
WASN'T BEING A PERV...
WOK
WHA--?! I WAS JUST, UM, SCANNING. FOR DINOSAURS!
SURE.
YOU'RE HERE.
I AM.
YOU SHOULD AT LEAST WASH OFF.
I SHOULD.
SO...?
OH.
DOES THIS MEAN YOU TRUST ME?
NOT AT ALL.
BUT I TRUST ME ENOUGH FOR BOTH OF US.
HAS ANYONE EVER TOLD YOU, CASSIE--
--THAT YOU ARE A HARD PERSON TO WARM UP TO?
JUST EVERYONE.
SPLISH
SPLOSH

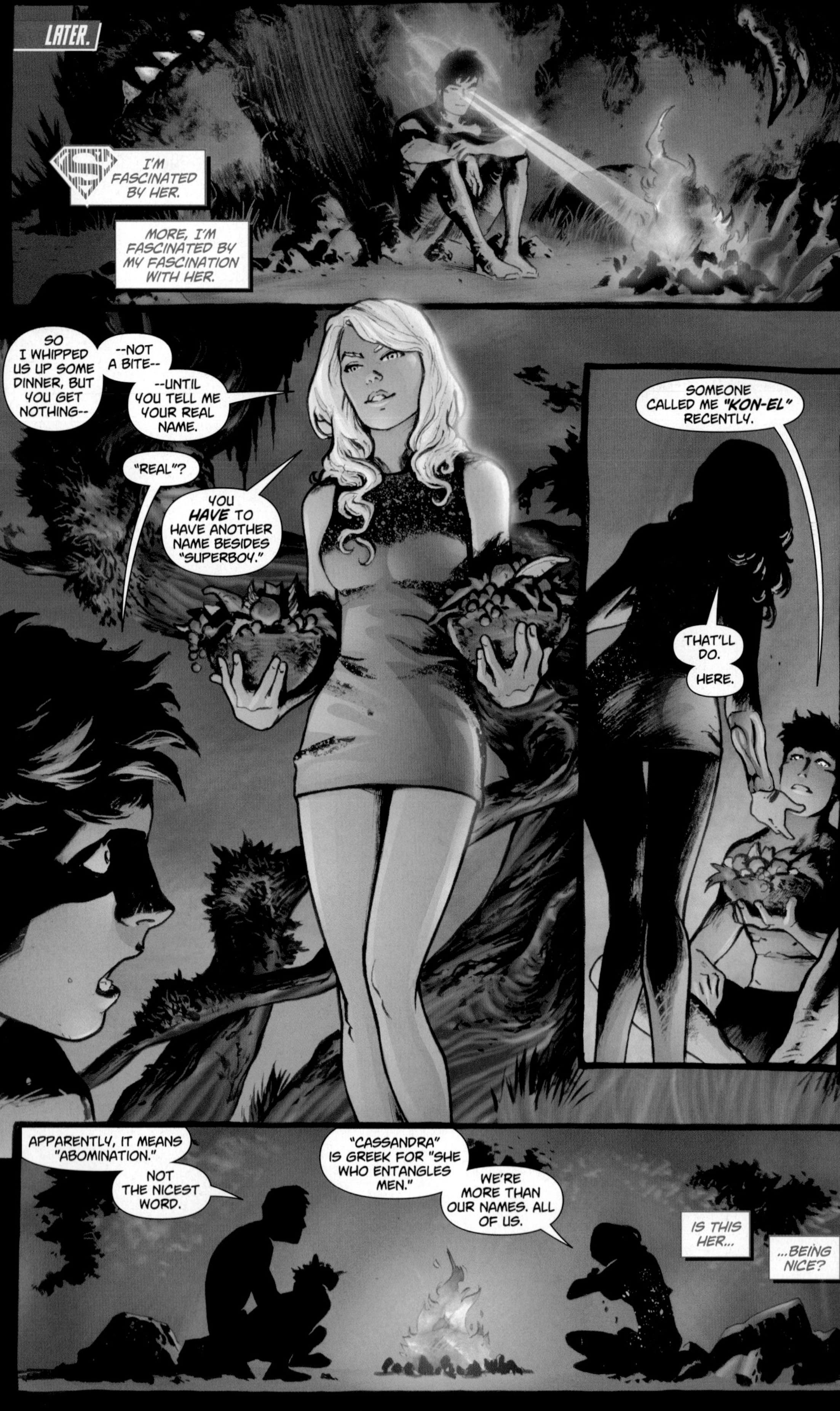
LATER.
I'M FASCINATED BY HER.
MORE, I'M FASCINATED BY MY FASCINATION WITH HER.
SO I WHIPPED US UP SOME DINNER, BUT YOU GET NOTHING--
--NOT A BITE--
--UNTIL YOU TELL ME YOUR REAL NAME.
"REAL"?
YOU HAVE TO HAVE ANOTHER NAME BESIDES "SUPERBOY."
SOMEONE CALLED ME "KON-EL" RECENTLY.
THAT'LL DO.
HERE.
APPARENTLY, IT MEANS "ABOMINATION."
NOT THE NICEST WORD.
"CASSANDRA" IS GREEK FOR "SHE WHO ENTANGLES MEN."
WE'RE MORE THAN OUR NAMES. ALL OF US.
IS THIS HER...
...BEING NICE?

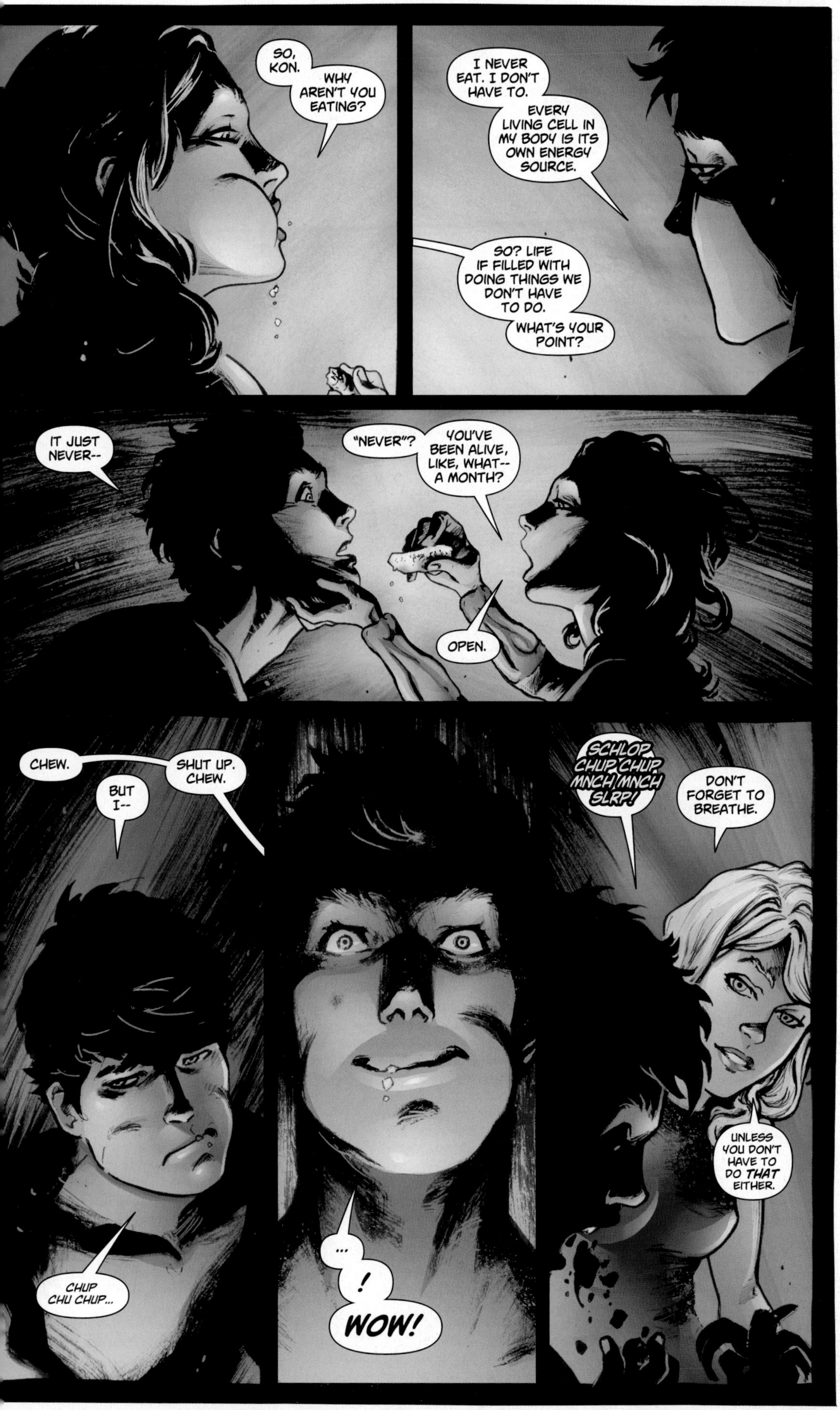
SO, KON.
WHY AREN'T YOU EATING?
I NEVER EAT. I DON'T HAVE TO.
EVERY LIVING CELL IN MY BODY IS ITS OWN ENERGY SOURCE.
SO? LIFE IF FILLED WITH DOING THINGS WE DON'T HAVE TO DO.
WHAT'S YOUR POINT?
IT JUST NEVER--
"NEVER"?
YOU'VE BEEN ALIVE, LIKE, WHAT--A MONTH?
OPEN.
CHEW.
BUT I--
SHUT UP. CHEW.
CHUP CHU CHUP...
...
!
WOW!
SCHLOP CHUP CHUP MNCH MNCH SLRP!
DON'T FORGET TO BREATHE.
UNLESS YOU DON'T HAVE TO DO *THAT* EITHER.

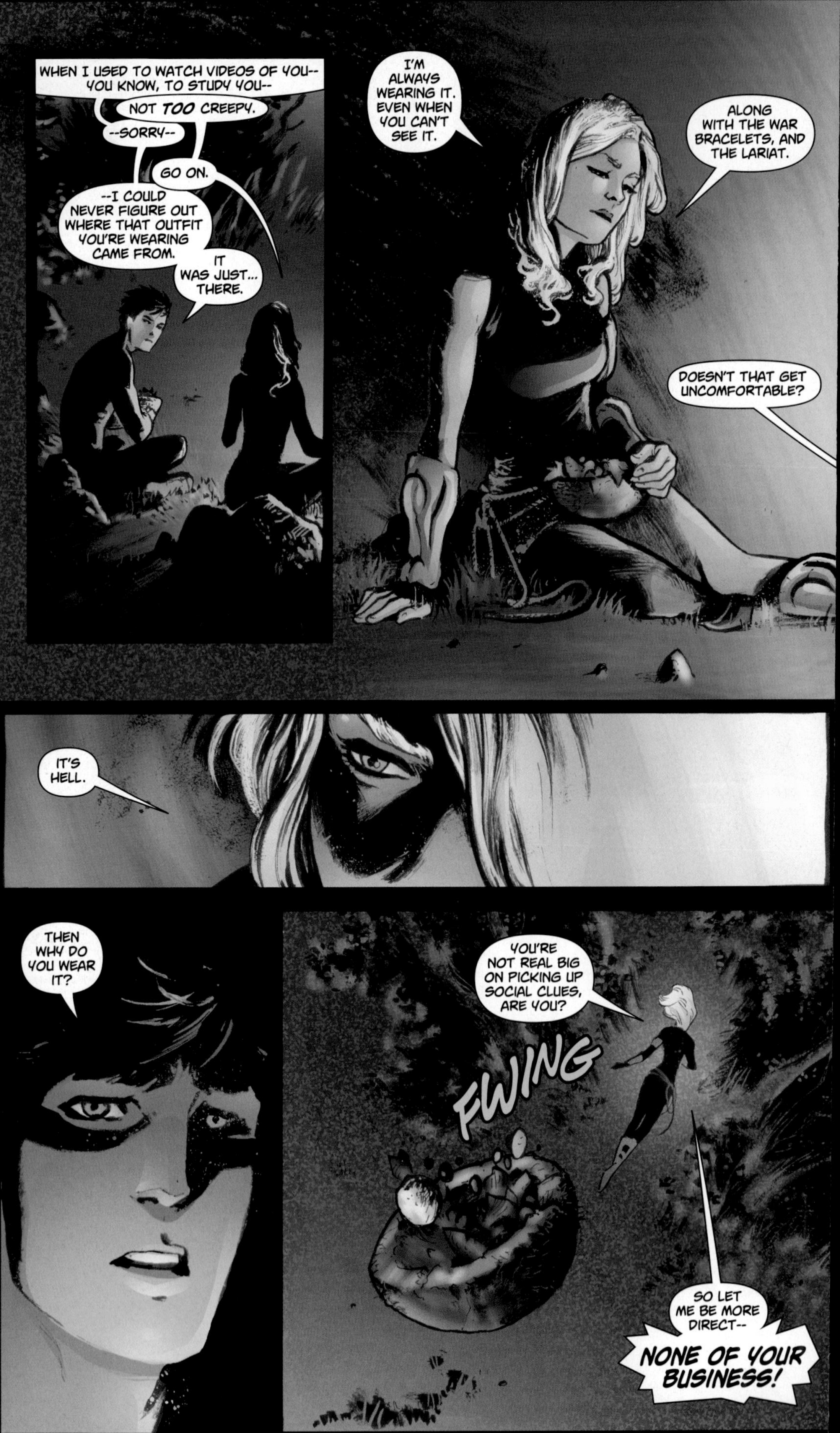

WHEN I USED TO WATCH VIDEOS OF YOU-- YOU KNOW, TO STUDY YOU--
NOT *TOO* CREEPY.
--SORRY--
GO ON.
--I COULD NEVER FIGURE OUT WHERE THAT OUTFIT YOU'RE WEARING CAME FROM.
IT WAS JUST... THERE.
I'M ALWAYS WEARING IT. EVEN WHEN YOU CAN'T SEE IT.
ALONG WITH THE WAR BRACELETS, AND THE LARIAT.
DOESN'T THAT GET UNCOMFORTABLE?
IT'S HELL.
THEN WHY DO YOU WEAR IT?
YOU'RE NOT REAL BIG ON PICKING UP SOCIAL CLUES, ARE YOU?
FWING
SO LET ME BE MORE DIRECT--
NONE OF YOUR BUSINESS!

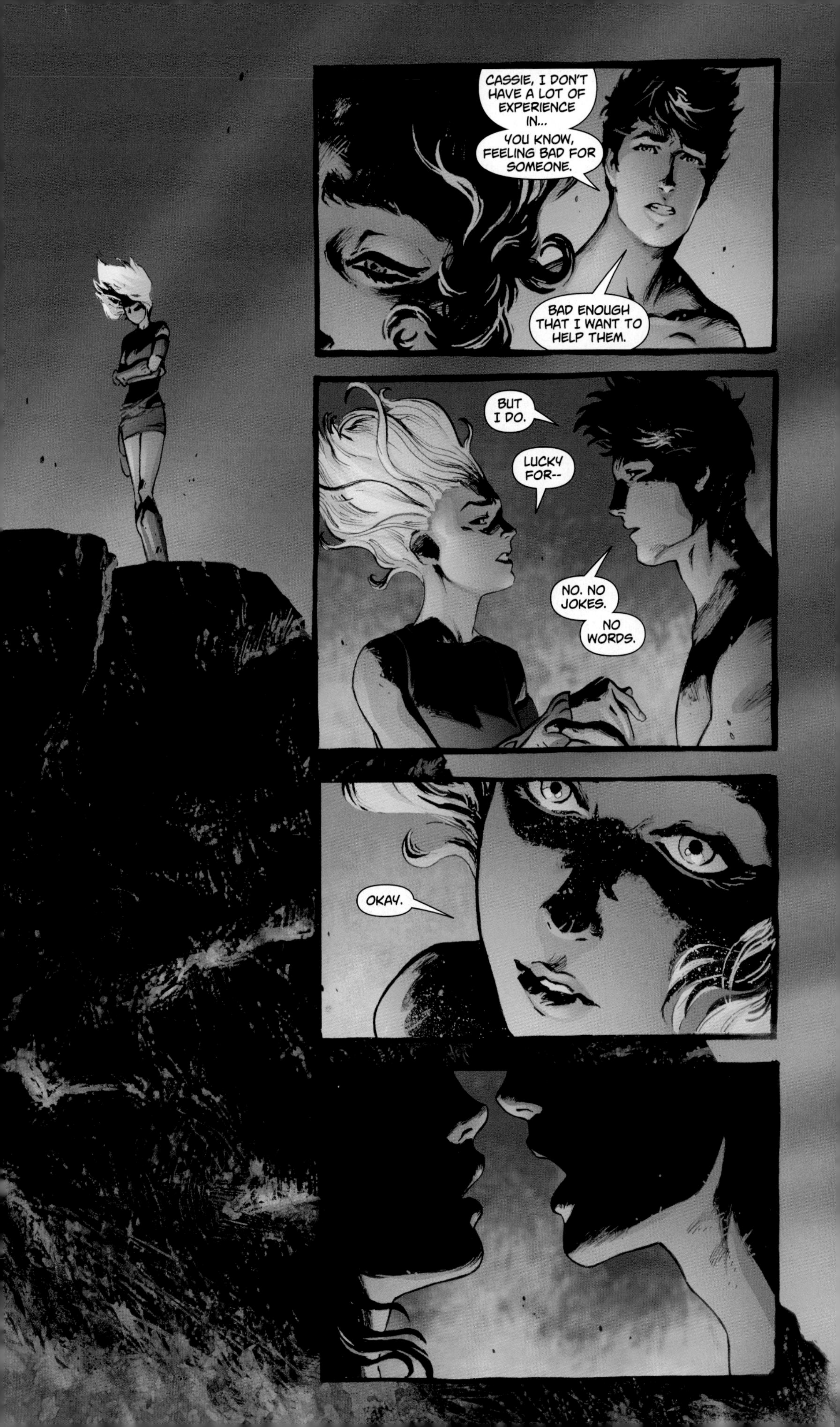
CASSIE, I DON'T HAVE A LOT OF EXPERIENCE IN...
YOU KNOW, FEELING BAD FOR SOMEONE.
BAD ENOUGH THAT I WANT TO HELP THEM.
BUT I DO.
LUCKY FOR--
NO. NO JOKES.
NO WORDS.
OKAY.

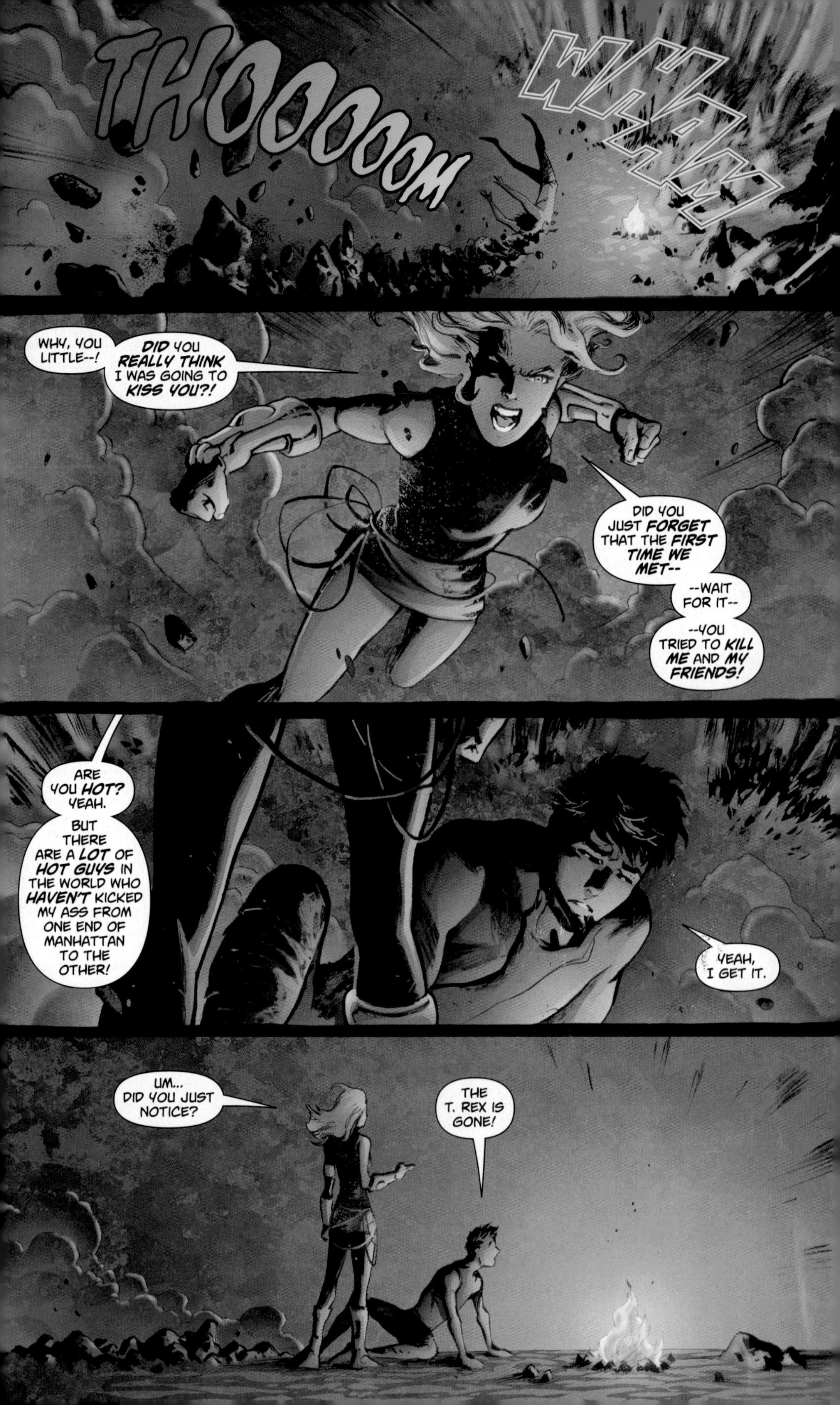
THOOOOOM
WHAM
WHY, YOU LITTLE--!
DID YOU REALLY THINK I WAS GOING TO KISS YOU?!
DID YOU JUST FORGET THAT THE FIRST TIME WE MET--
--WAIT FOR IT--
--YOU TRIED TO KILL ME AND MY FRIENDS!
ARE YOU HOT? YEAH.
BUT THERE ARE A LOT OF HOT GUYS IN THE WORLD WHO HAVEN'T KICKED MY ASS FROM ONE END OF MANHATTAN TO THE OTHER!
YEAH, I GET IT.
UM... DID YOU JUST NOTICE?
THE T. REX IS GONE!

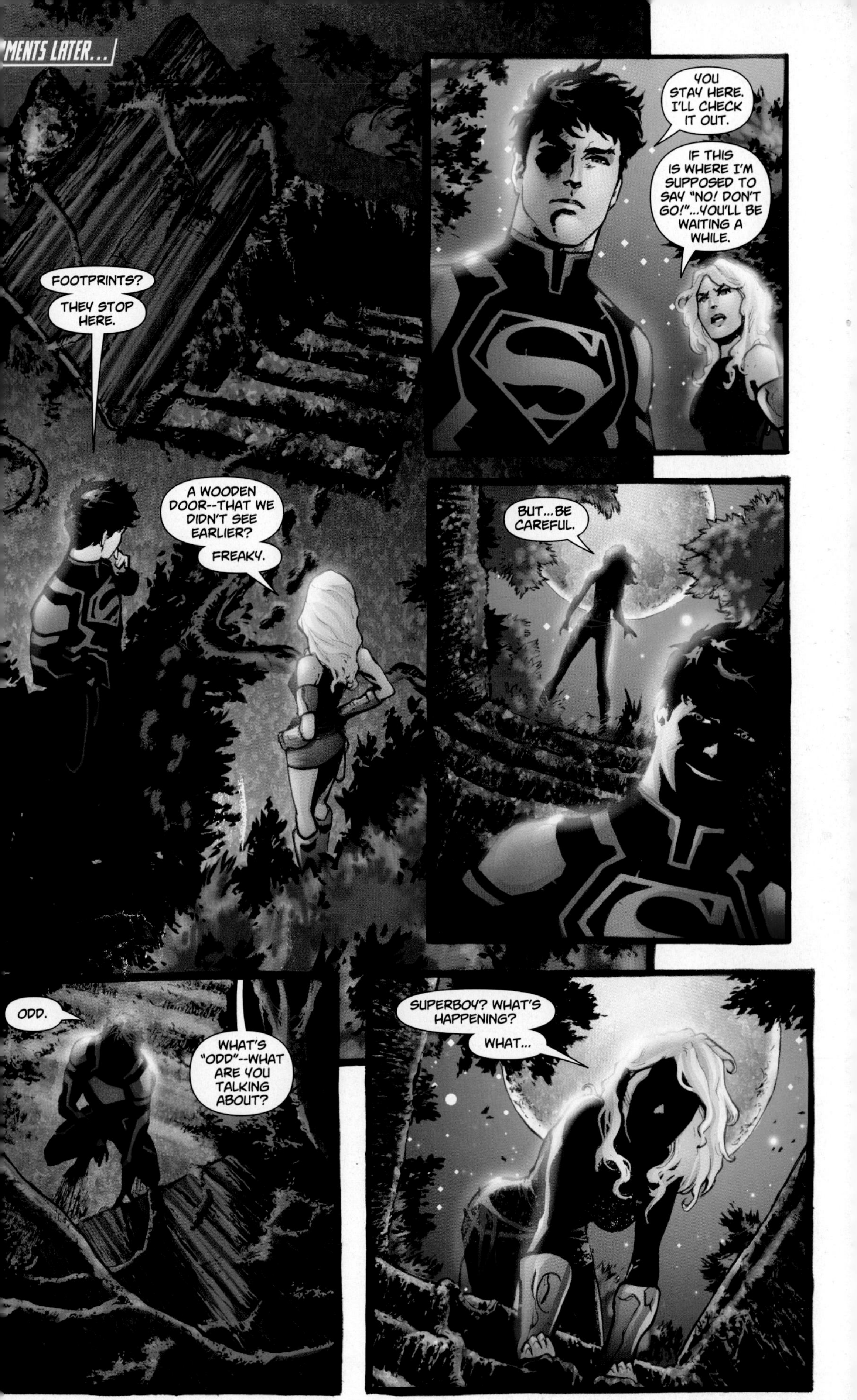
MENTS LATER...
FOOTPRINTS?
THEY STOP HERE.
YOU STAY HERE. I'LL CHECK IT OUT.
IF THIS IS WHERE I'M SUPPOSED TO SAY "NO! DON'T GO!"...YOU'LL BE WAITING A WHILE.
A WOODEN DOOR--THAT WE DIDN'T SEE EARLIER?
FREAKY.
BUT...BE CAREFUL.
ODD.
WHAT'S "ODD"--WHAT ARE YOU TALKING ABOUT?
SUPERBOY? WHAT'S HAPPENING?
WHAT...

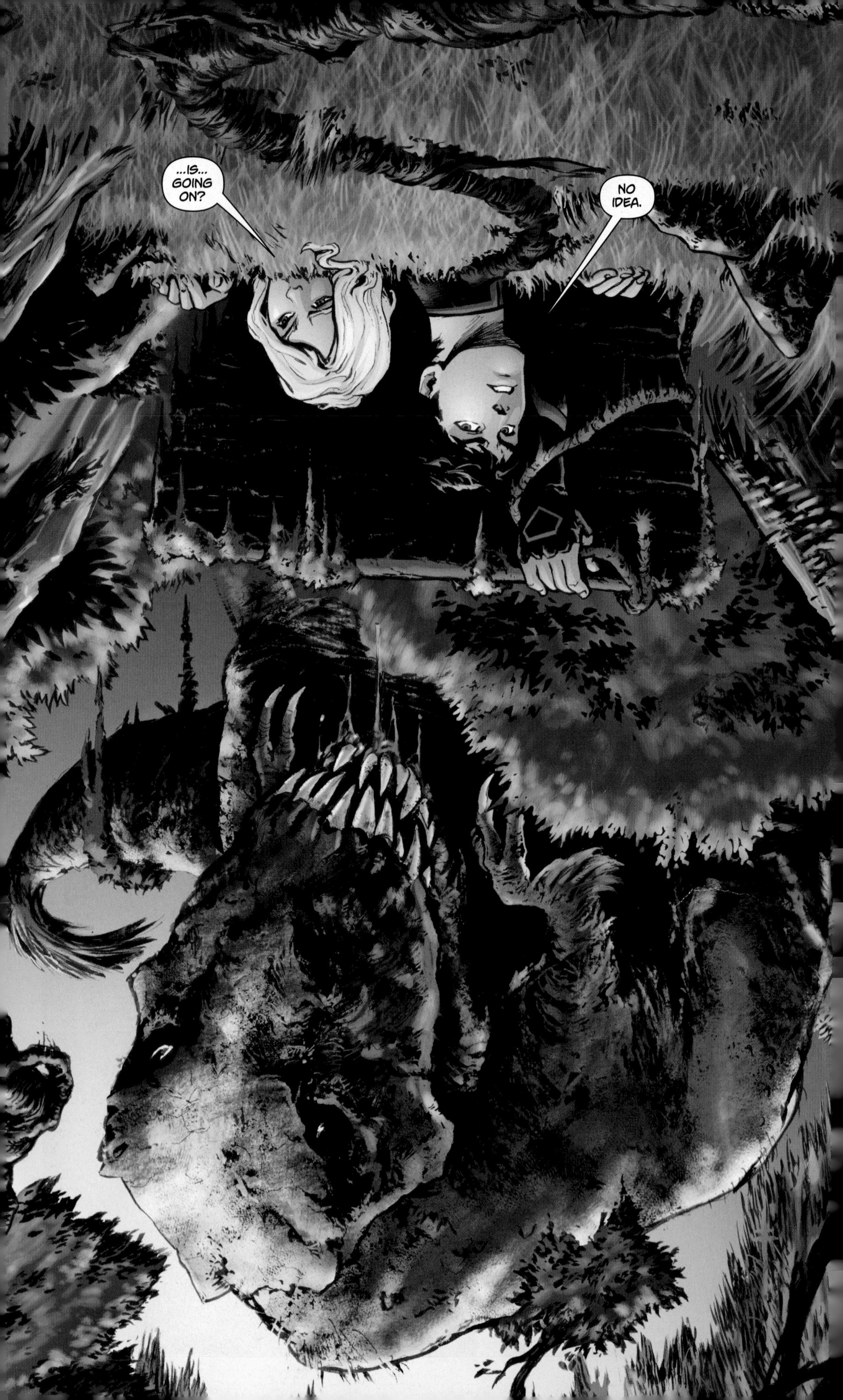
...IS... GOING ON?
NO IDEA.

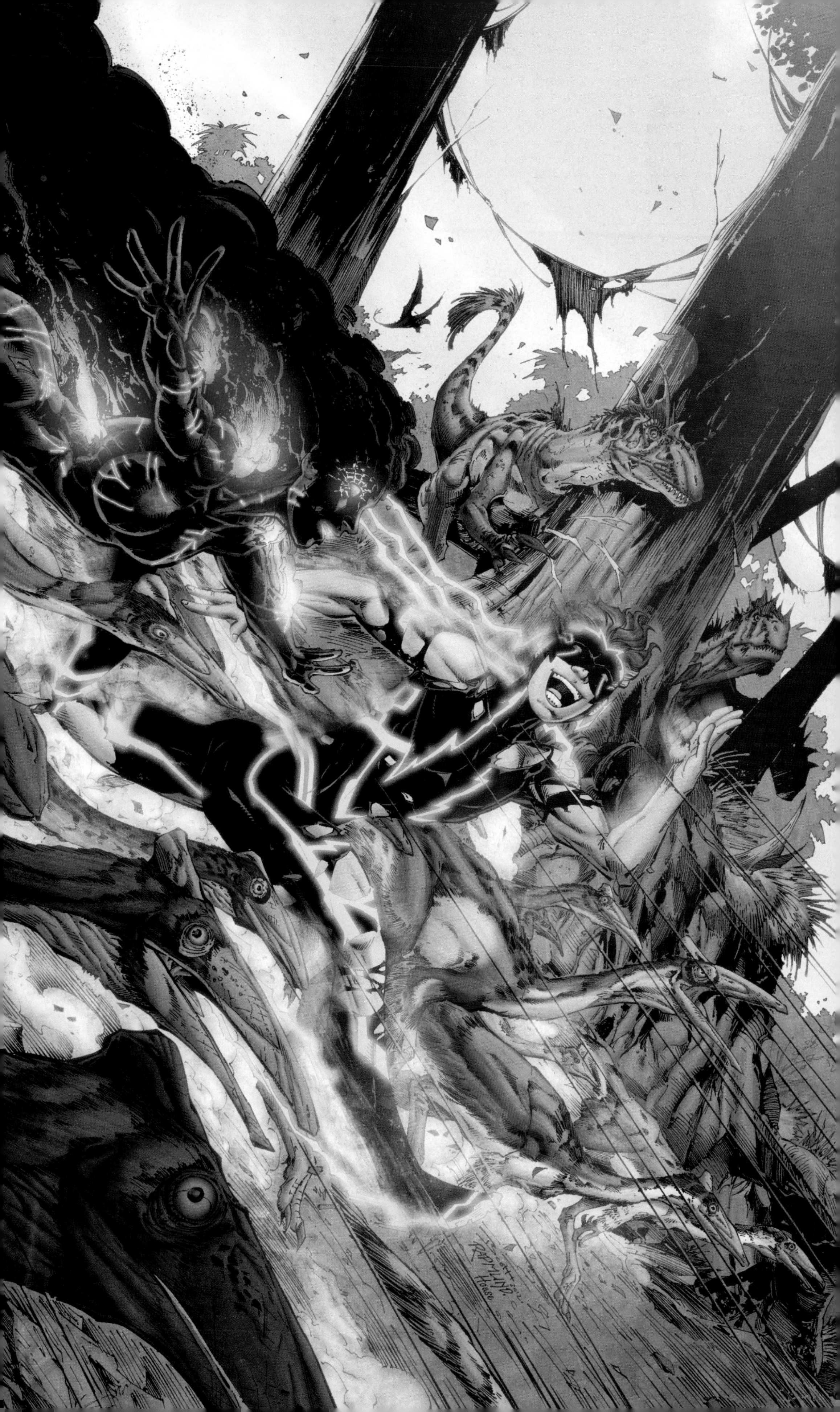

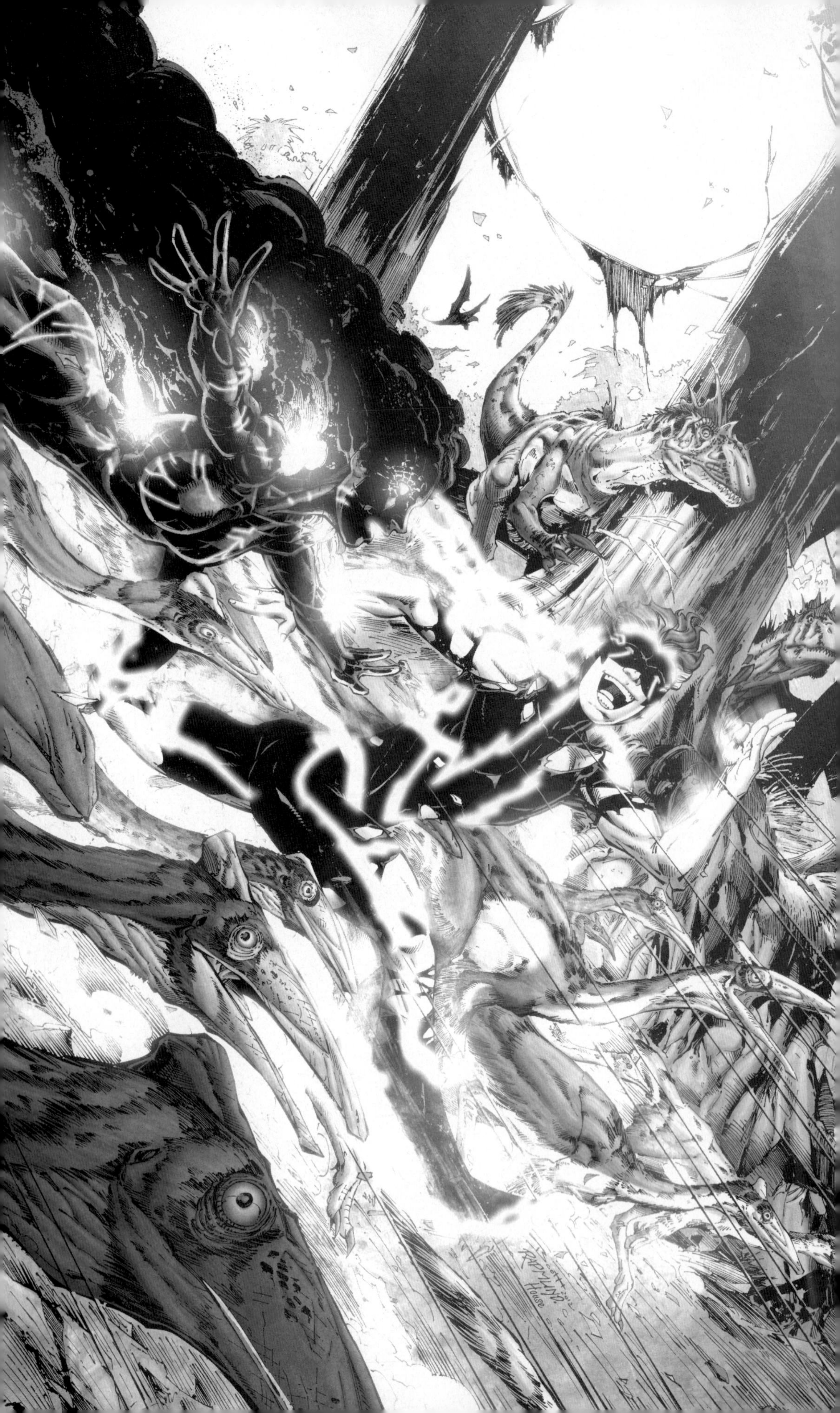

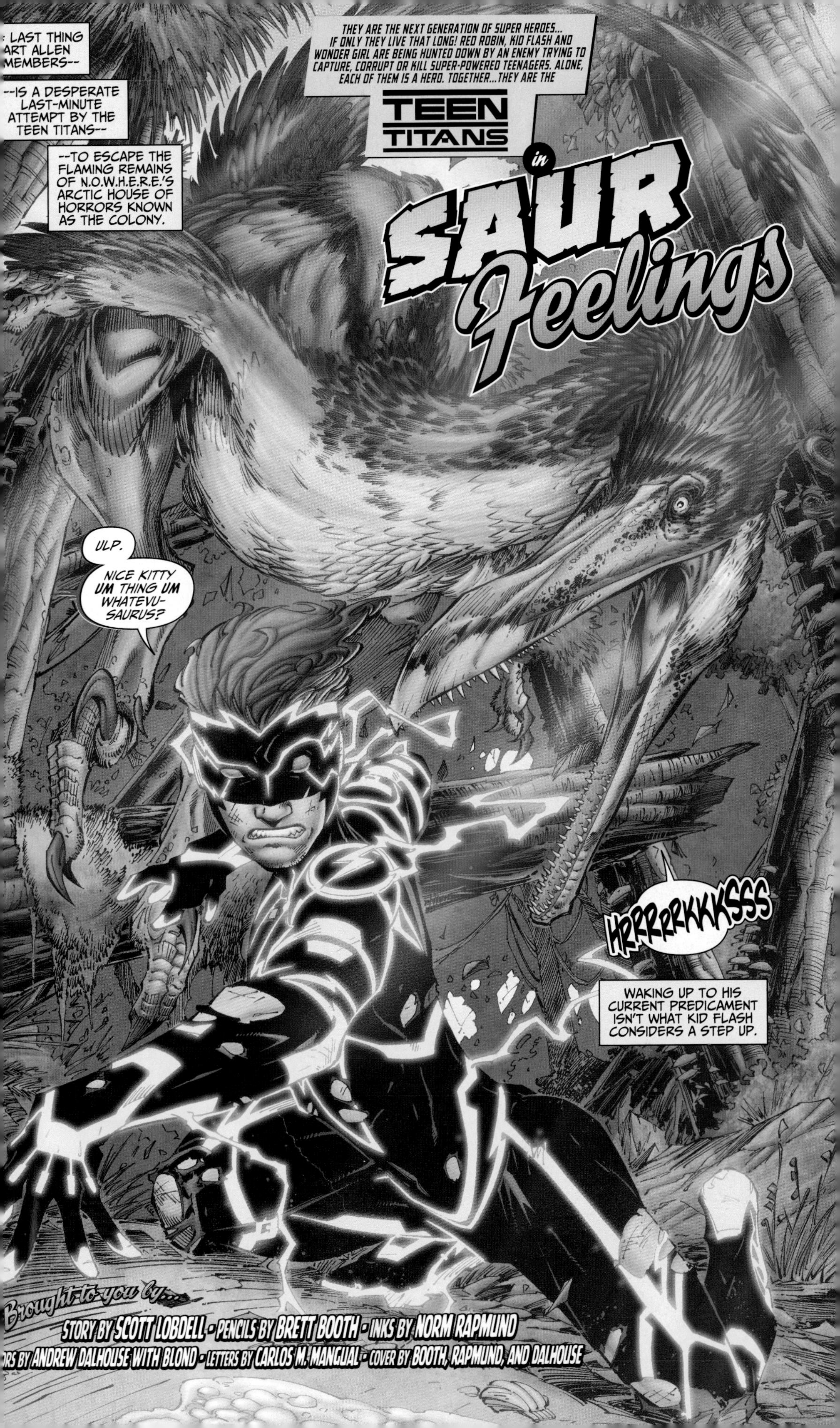

LAST THING ART ALLEN MEMBERS--
--IS A DESPERATE LAST-MINUTE ATTEMPT BY THE TEEN TITANS--
--TO ESCAPE THE FLAMING REMAINS OF N.O.W.H.E.R.E.'S ARCTIC HOUSE OF HORRORS KNOWN AS THE COLONY.
THEY ARE THE NEXT GENERATION OF SUPER HEROES... IF ONLY THEY LIVE THAT LONG! RED ROBIN, KID FLASH AND WONDER GIRL ARE BEING HUNTED DOWN BY AN ENEMY TRYING TO CAPTURE, CORRUPT OR KILL SUPER-POWERED TEENAGERS. ALONE, EACH OF THEM IS A HERO. TOGETHER...THEY ARE THE
TEEN TITANS
in
SAUR Feelings
ULP.
NICE KITTY UM THING UM WHATEVU-SAURUS?
HRRRRRKKKSSS
WAKING UP TO HIS CURRENT PREDICAMENT ISN'T WHAT KID FLASH CONSIDERS A STEP UP.
Brought to you by...
STORY BY SCOTT LOBDELL - PENCILS BY BRETT BOOTH - INKS BY NORM RAPMUND
ORS BY ANDREW DALHOUSE WITH BLOND - LETTERS BY CARLOS M. MANGUAL - COVER BY BOOTH, RAPMUND, AND DALHOUSE

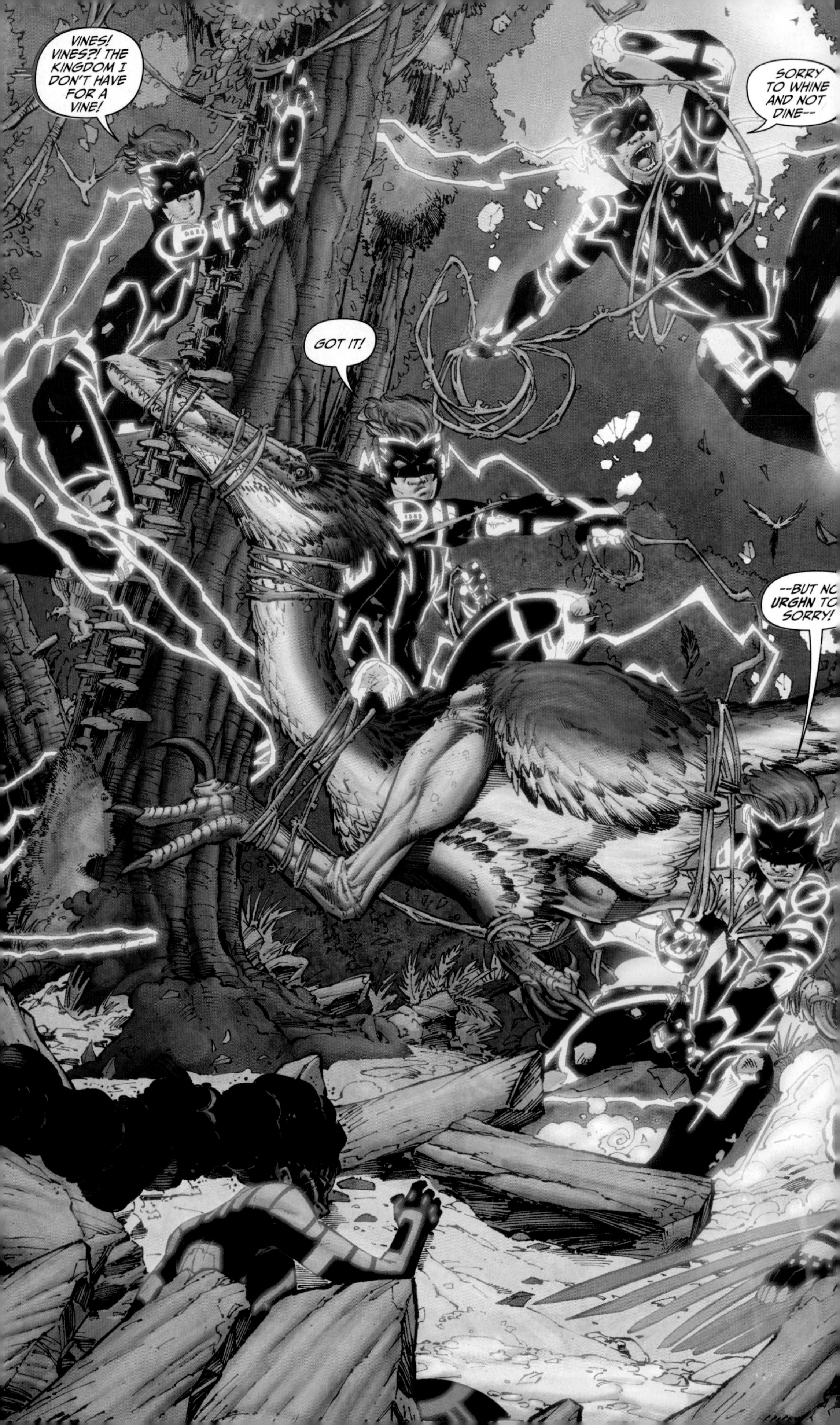
VINES! VINES?! THE KINGDOM I DON'T HAVE FOR A VINE!
SORRY TO WHINE AND NOT DINE--
GOT IT!
--BUT NO URGHN TO SORRY!

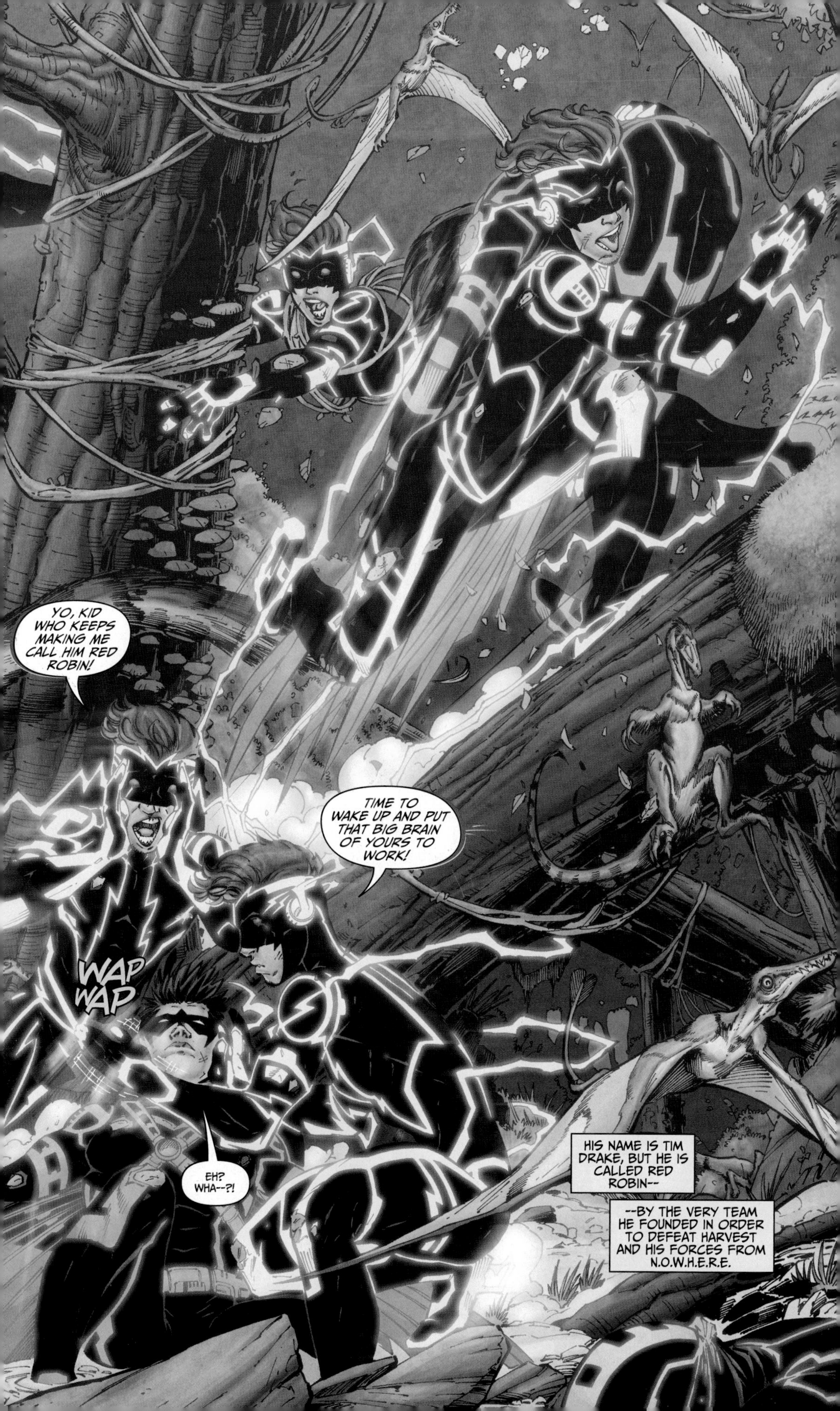
YO, KID WHO KEEPS MAKING ME CALL HIM RED ROBIN!
TIME TO WAKE UP AND PUT THAT BIG BRAIN OF YOURS TO WORK!
WAP WAP
EH? WHA--?!
HIS NAME IS TIM DRAKE, BUT HE IS CALLED RED ROBIN--
--BY THE VERY TEAM HE FOUNDED IN ORDER TO DEFEAT HARVEST AND HIS FORCES FROM N.O.W.H.E.R.E.

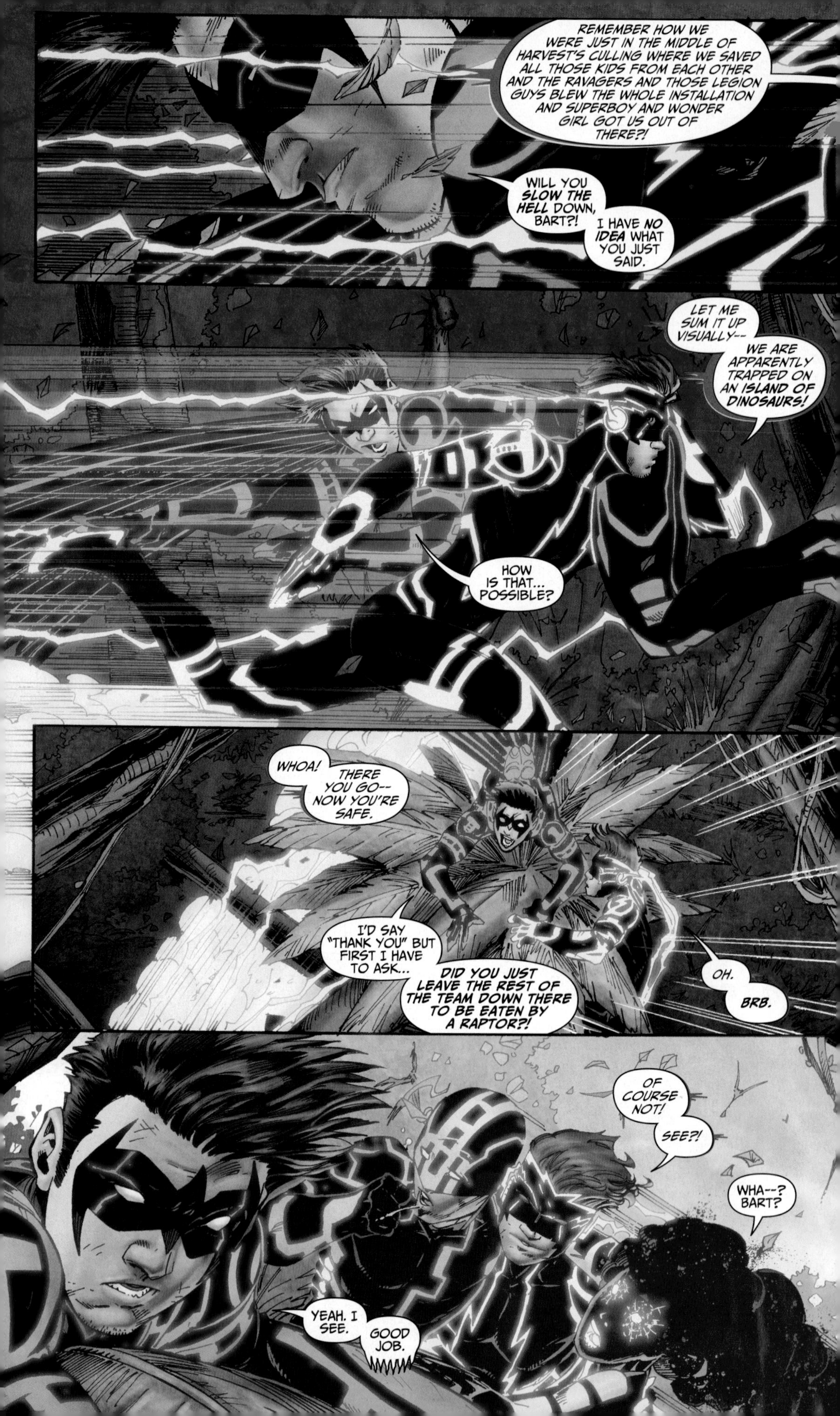
REMEMBER HOW WE WERE JUST IN THE MIDDLE OF HARVEST'S CULLING WHERE WE SAVED ALL THOSE KIDS FROM EACH OTHER AND THE RAVAGERS AND THOSE LEGION GUYS BLEW THE WHOLE INSTALLATION AND SUPERBOY AND WONDER GIRL GOT US OUT OF THERE?!
WILL YOU SLOW THE HELL DOWN, BART?!
I HAVE NO IDEA WHAT YOU JUST SAID.
LET ME SUM IT UP VISUALLY--
WE ARE APPARENTLY TRAPPED ON AN ISLAND OF DINOSAURS!
HOW IS THAT... POSSIBLE?
WHOA!
THERE YOU GO-- NOW YOU'RE SAFE.
I'D SAY "THANK YOU" BUT FIRST I HAVE TO ASK... DID YOU JUST LEAVE THE REST OF THE TEAM DOWN THERE TO BE EATEN BY A RAPTOR?!
OH.
BRB.
OF COURSE NOT!
SEE?!
WHA--? BART?
YEAH. I SEE.
GOOD JOB.

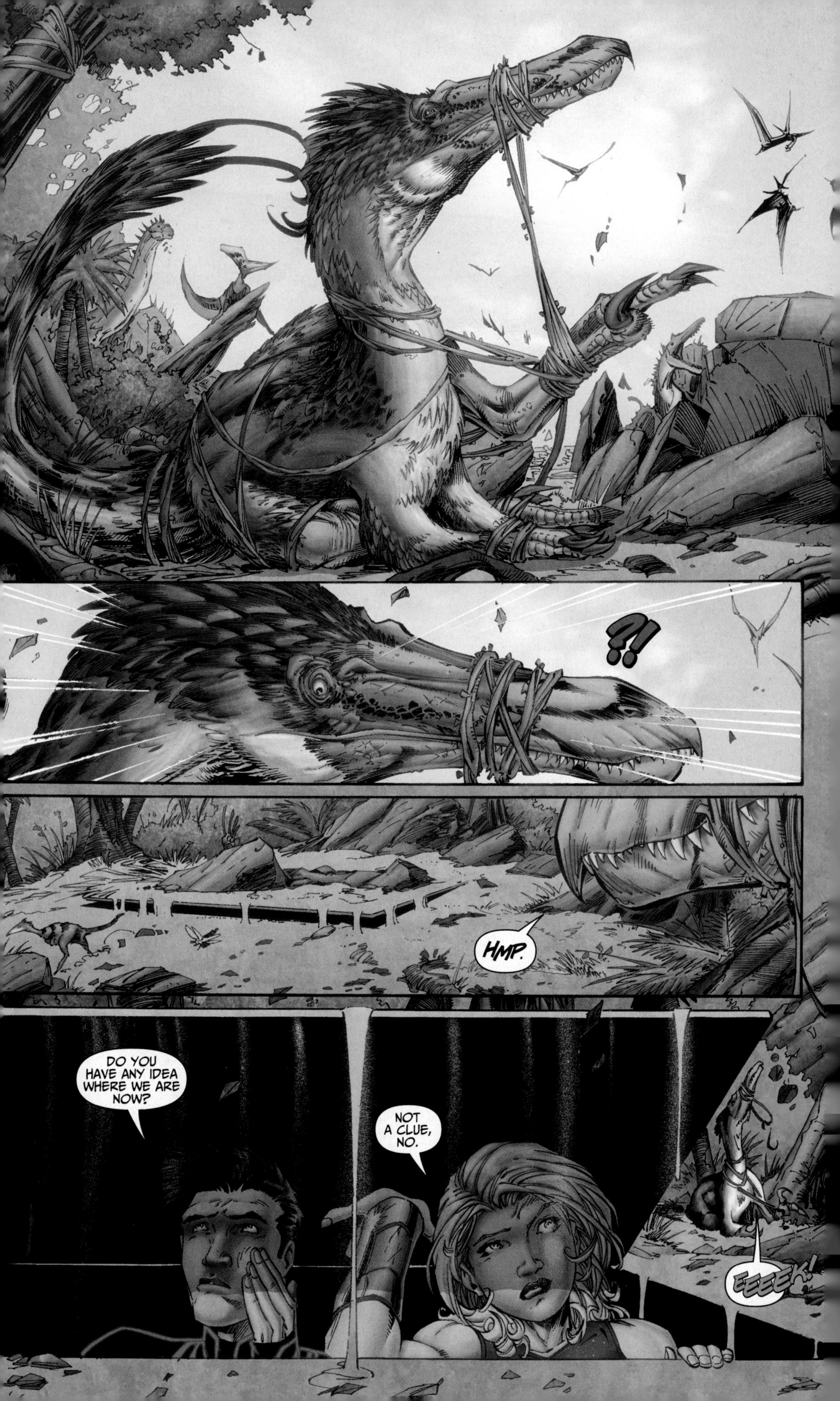

?!!
HMP.
DO YOU HAVE ANY IDEA WHERE WE ARE NOW?
NOT A CLUE, NO.
EEEEK!

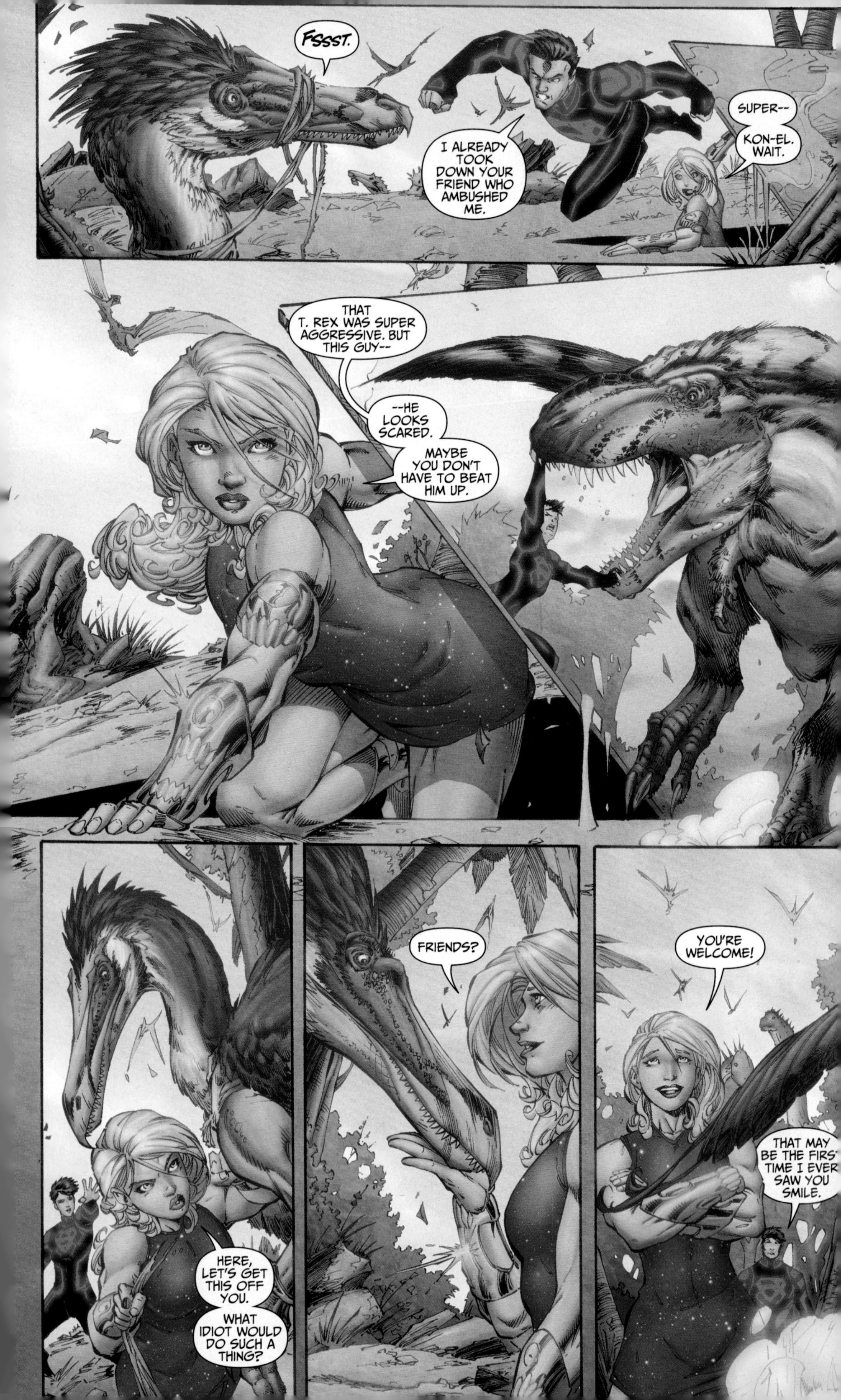
FSSST.
I ALREADY TOOK DOWN YOUR FRIEND WHO AMBUSHED ME.
SUPER--
KON-EL. WAIT.
THAT T. REX WAS SUPER AGGRESSIVE. BUT THIS GUY--
--HE LOOKS SCARED.
MAYBE YOU DON'T HAVE TO BEAT HIM UP.
HERE, LET'S GET THIS OFF YOU.
WHAT IDIOT WOULD DO SUCH A THING?
FRIENDS?
YOU'RE WELCOME!
THAT MAY BE THE FIRST TIME I EVER SAW YOU SMILE.

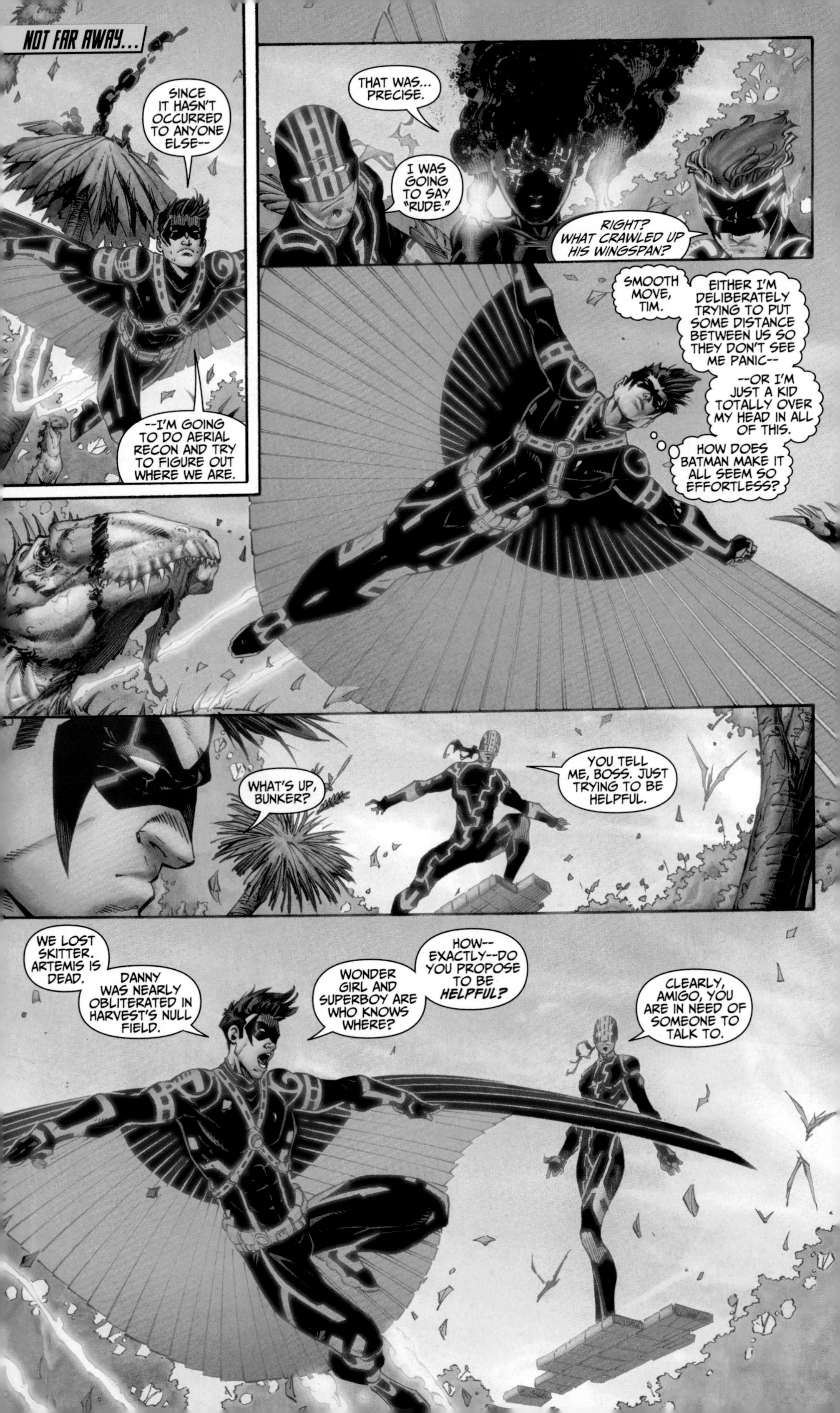
NOT FAR AWAY...
SINCE IT HASN'T OCCURRED TO ANYONE ELSE--
--I'M GOING TO DO AERIAL RECON AND TRY TO FIGURE OUT WHERE WE ARE.
THAT WAS... PRECISE.
I WAS GOING TO SAY "RUDE."
RIGHT? WHAT CRAWLED UP HIS WINGSPAN?
SMOOTH MOVE, TIM.
EITHER I'M DELIBERATELY TRYING TO PUT SOME DISTANCE BETWEEN US SO THEY DON'T SEE ME PANIC--
--OR I'M JUST A KID TOTALLY OVER MY HEAD IN ALL OF THIS.
HOW DOES BATMAN MAKE IT ALL SEEM SO EFFORTLESS?
WHAT'S UP, BUNKER?
YOU TELL ME, BOSS. JUST TRYING TO BE HELPFUL.
WE LOST SKITTER. ARTEMIS IS DEAD.
DANNY WAS NEARLY OBLITERATED IN HARVEST'S NULL FIELD.
WONDER GIRL AND SUPERBOY ARE WHO KNOWS WHERE?
HOW--EXACTLY--DO YOU PROPOSE TO BE HELPFUL?
CLEARLY, AMIGO, YOU ARE IN NEED OF SOMEONE TO TALK TO.

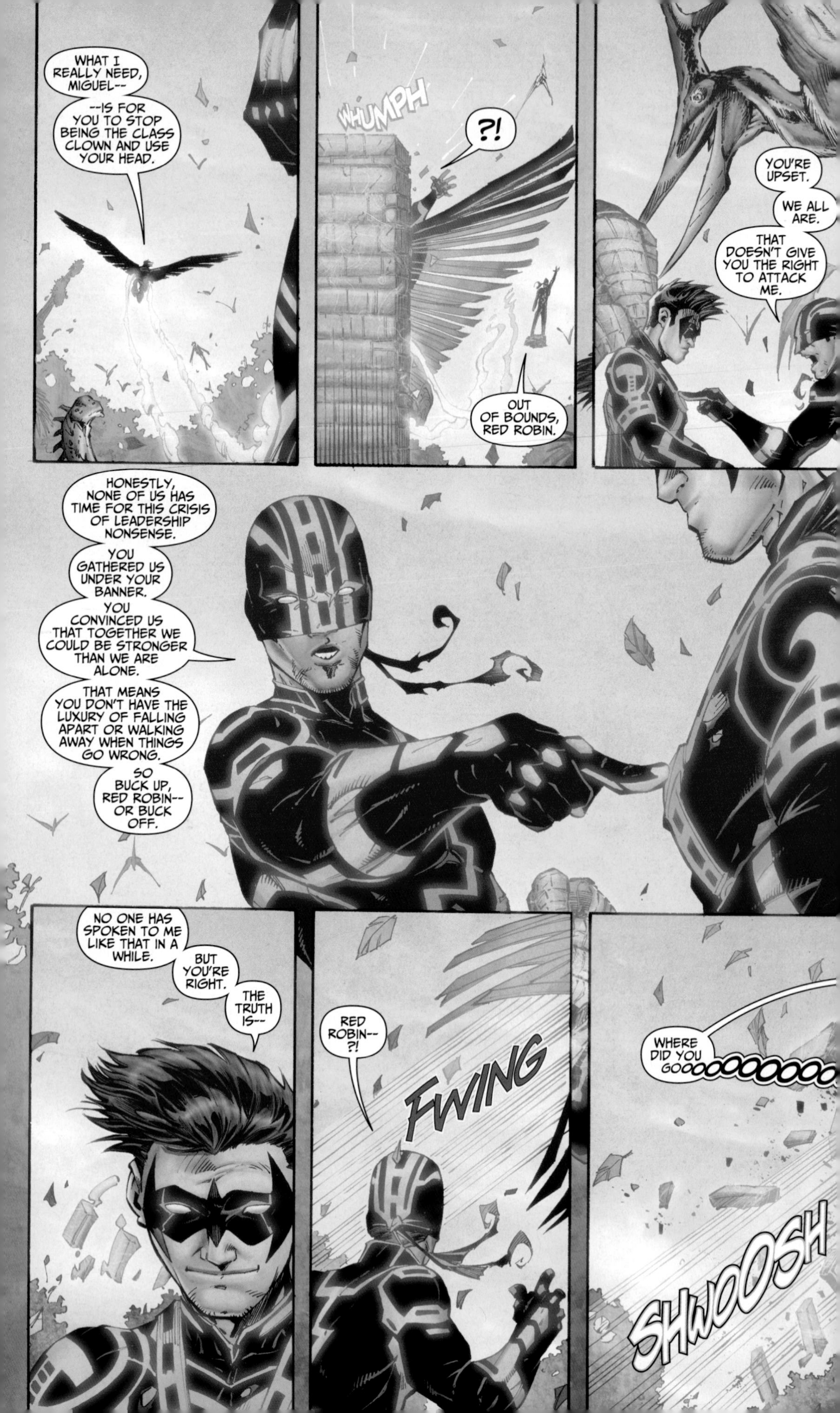
WHAT I REALLY NEED, MIGUEL--
--IS FOR YOU TO STOP BEING THE CLASS CLOWN AND USE YOUR HEAD.
WHUMPH
?!
OUT OF BOUNDS, RED ROBIN.
YOU'RE UPSET.
WE ALL ARE.
THAT DOESN'T GIVE YOU THE RIGHT TO ATTACK ME.
HONESTLY, NONE OF US HAS TIME FOR THIS CRISIS OF LEADERSHIP NONSENSE.
YOU GATHERED US UNDER YOUR BANNER.
YOU CONVINCED US THAT TOGETHER WE COULD BE STRONGER THAN WE ARE ALONE.
THAT MEANS YOU DON'T HAVE THE LUXURY OF FALLING APART OR WALKING AWAY WHEN THINGS GO WRONG.
SO BUCK UP, RED ROBIN-- OR BUCK OFF.
NO ONE HAS SPOKEN TO ME LIKE THAT IN A WHILE.
BUT YOU'RE RIGHT.
THE TRUTH IS--
RED ROBIN-- ?!
FWING
WHERE DID YOU GOOOOOOOOOOO
SHWOOSH

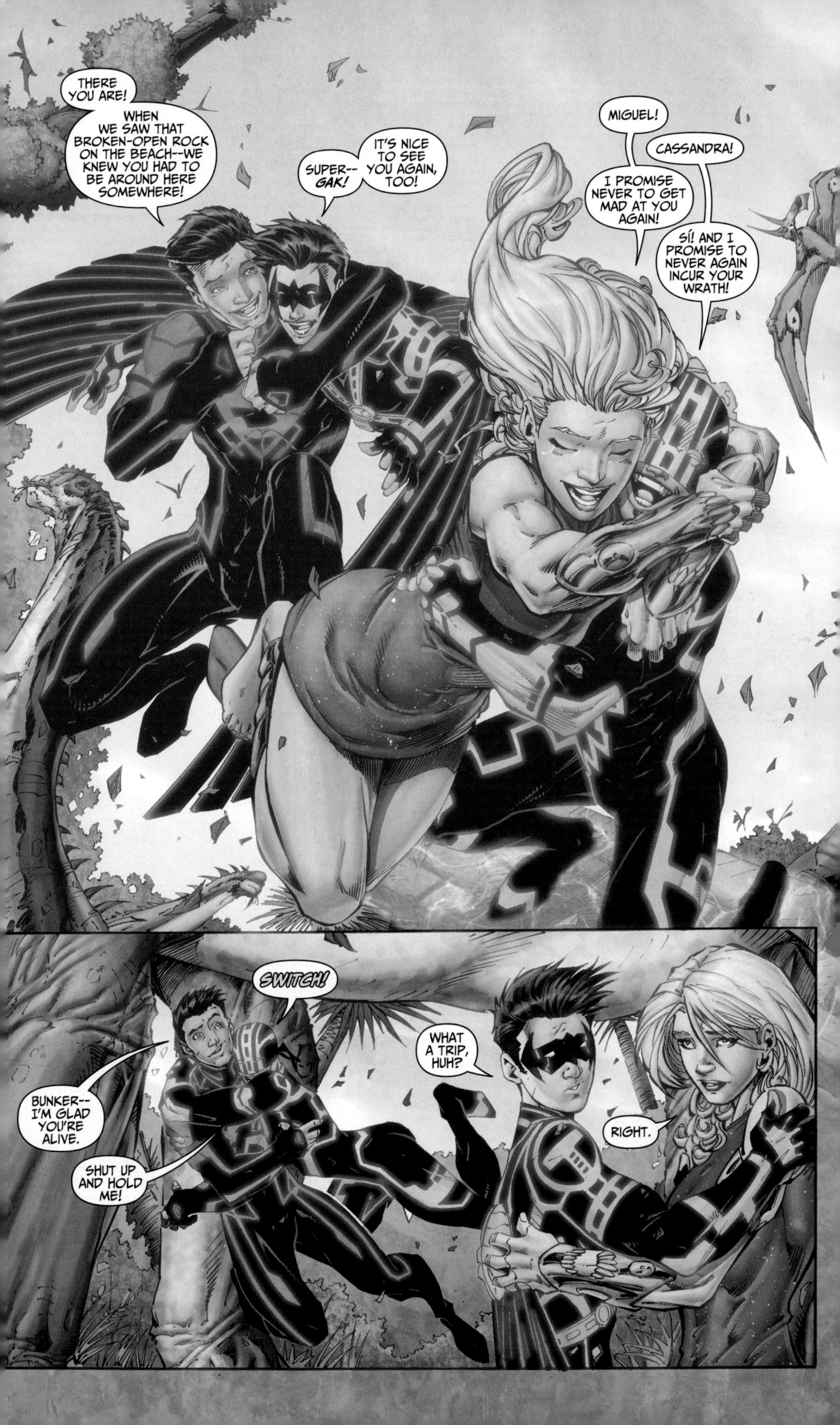
THERE YOU ARE!
WHEN WE SAW THAT BROKEN-OPEN ROCK ON THE BEACH--WE KNEW YOU HAD TO BE AROUND HERE SOMEWHERE!
SUPER-- GAK!
IT'S NICE TO SEE YOU AGAIN, TOO!
MIGUEL!
I PROMISE NEVER TO GET MAD AT YOU AGAIN!
CASSANDRA!
SÍ! AND I PROMISE TO NEVER AGAIN INCUR YOUR WRATH!
SWITCH!
BUNKER-- I'M GLAD YOU'RE ALIVE.
SHUT UP AND HOLD ME!
WHAT A TRIP, HUH?
RIGHT.

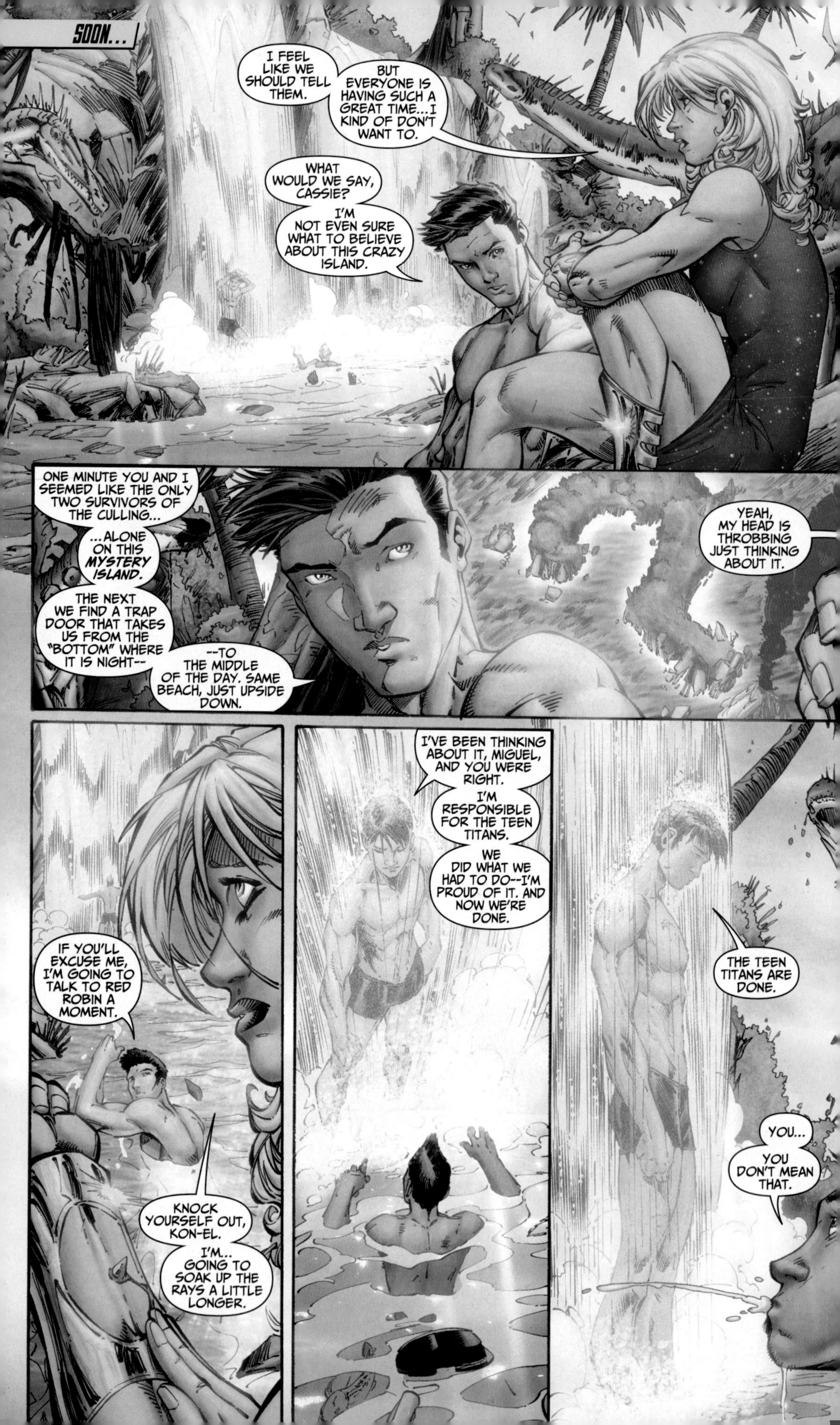
SOON...
I FEEL LIKE WE SHOULD TELL THEM.
BUT EVERYONE IS HAVING SUCH A GREAT TIME...I KIND OF DON'T WANT TO.
WHAT WOULD WE SAY, CASSIE?
I'M NOT EVEN SURE WHAT TO BELIEVE ABOUT THIS CRAZY ISLAND.
ONE MINUTE YOU AND I SEEMED LIKE THE ONLY TWO SURVIVORS OF THE CULLING...
...ALONE ON THIS MYSTERY ISLAND.
THE NEXT WE FIND A TRAP DOOR THAT TAKES US FROM THE "BOTTOM" WHERE IT IS NIGHT--
--TO THE MIDDLE OF THE DAY. SAME BEACH, JUST UPSIDE DOWN.
YEAH, MY HEAD IS THROBBING JUST THINKING ABOUT IT.
IF YOU'LL EXCUSE ME, I'M GOING TO TALK TO RED ROBIN A MOMENT.
KNOCK YOURSELF OUT, KON-EL.
I'M... GOING TO SOAK UP THE RAYS A LITTLE LONGER.
I'VE BEEN THINKING ABOUT IT, MIGUEL, AND YOU WERE RIGHT.
I'M RESPONSIBLE FOR THE TEEN TITANS.
WE DID WHAT WE HAD TO DO--I'M PROUD OF IT. AND NOW WE'RE DONE.
THE TEEN TITANS ARE DONE.
YOU...
YOU DON'T MEAN THAT.

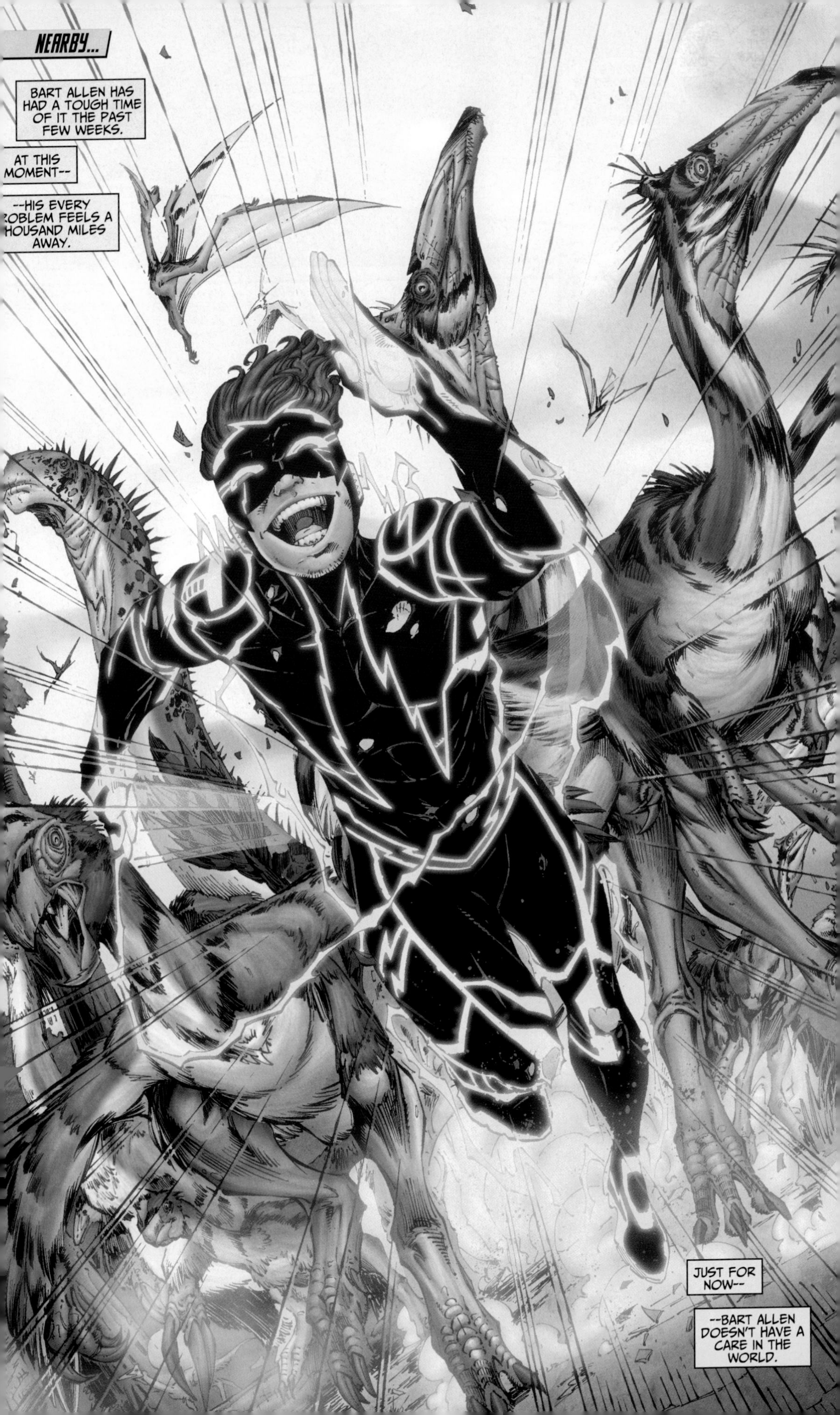
NEARBY...
BART ALLEN HAS HAD A TOUGH TIME OF IT THE PAST FEW WEEKS.
AT THIS MOMENT--
--HIS EVERY PROBLEM FEELS A THOUSAND MILES AWAY.
JUST FOR NOW--
--BART ALLEN DOESN'T HAVE A CARE IN THE WORLD.

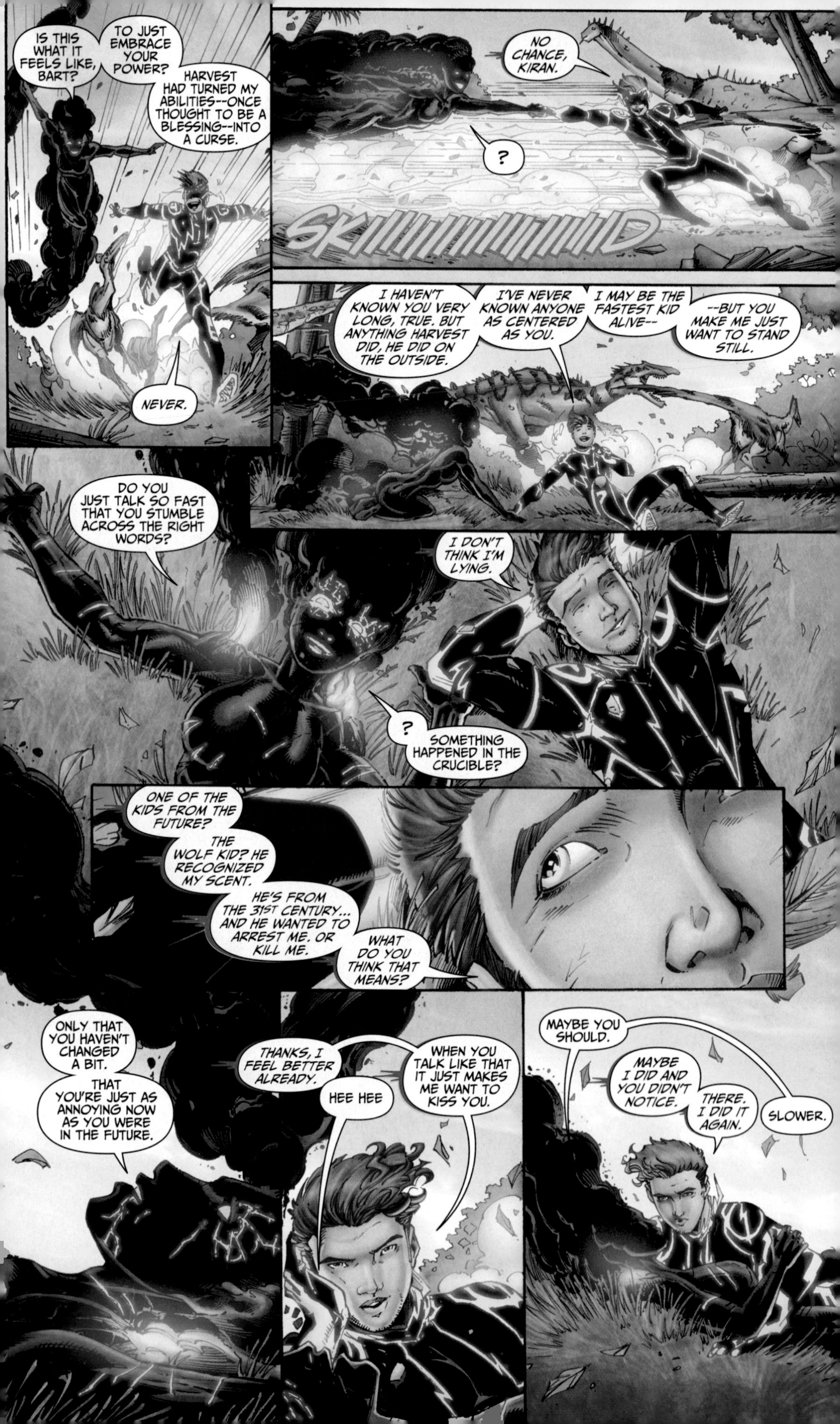

IS THIS WHAT IT FEELS LIKE, BART?
TO JUST EMBRACE YOUR POWER?
HARVEST HAD TURNED MY ABILITIES--ONCE THOUGHT TO BE A BLESSING--INTO A CURSE.
NEVER.
NO CHANCE, KIRAN.
?
SKIIIIIIIIIIIIIIIIID
I HAVEN'T KNOWN YOU VERY LONG, TRUE. BUT ANYTHING HARVEST DID, HE DID ON THE OUTSIDE.
I'VE NEVER KNOWN ANYONE AS CENTERED AS YOU.
I MAY BE THE FASTEST KID ALIVE--
--BUT YOU MAKE ME JUST WANT TO STAND STILL.
DO YOU JUST TALK SO FAST THAT YOU STUMBLE ACROSS THE RIGHT WORDS?
I DON'T THINK I'M LYING.
?
SOMETHING HAPPENED IN THE CRUCIBLE?
ONE OF THE KIDS FROM THE FUTURE?
THE WOLF KID? HE RECOGNIZED MY SCENT.
HE'S FROM THE 31ST CENTURY... AND HE WANTED TO ARREST ME. OR KILL ME.
WHAT DO YOU THINK THAT MEANS?
ONLY THAT YOU HAVEN'T CHANGED A BIT.
THAT YOU'RE JUST AS ANNOYING NOW AS YOU WERE IN THE FUTURE.
THANKS, I FEEL BETTER ALREADY.
HEE HEE
WHEN YOU TALK LIKE THAT IT JUST MAKES ME WANT TO KISS YOU.
MAYBE YOU SHOULD.
MAYBE I DID AND YOU DIDN'T NOTICE.
THERE. I DID IT AGAIN.
SLOWER.

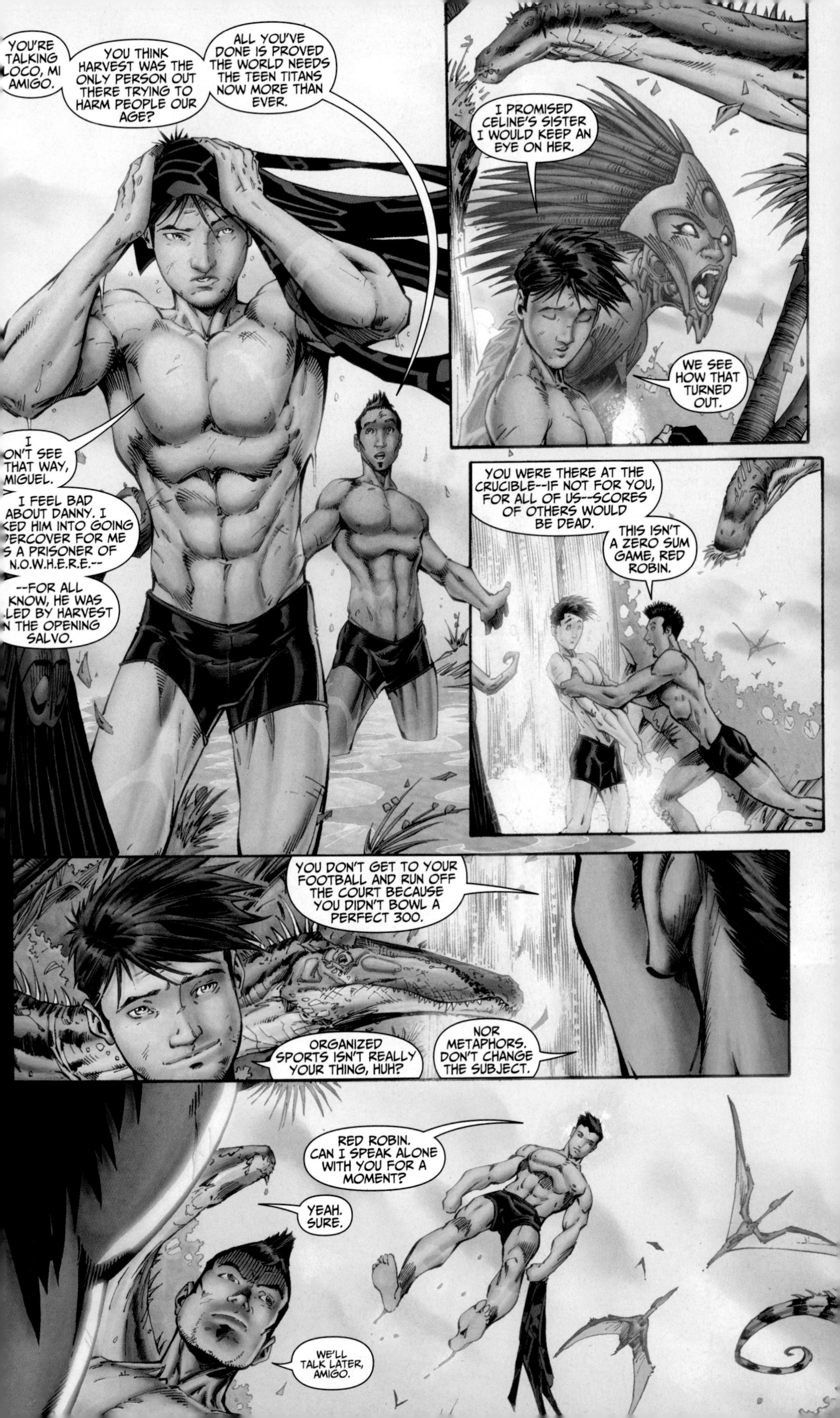

YOU'RE TALKING LOCO, MI AMIGO.
YOU THINK HARVEST WAS THE ONLY PERSON OUT THERE TRYING TO HARM PEOPLE OUR AGE?
ALL YOU'VE DONE IS PROVED THE WORLD NEEDS THE TEEN TITANS NOW MORE THAN EVER.
I ON'T SEE THAT WAY, MIGUEL.
I FEEL BAD ABOUT DANNY. I KED HIM INTO GOING ERCOVER FOR ME S A PRISONER OF N.O.W.H.E.R.E.--
--FOR ALL KNOW, HE WAS LED BY HARVEST N THE OPENING SALVO.
I PROMISED CELINE'S SISTER I WOULD KEEP AN EYE ON HER.
WE SEE HOW THAT TURNED OUT.
YOU WERE THERE AT THE CRUCIBLE--IF NOT FOR YOU, FOR ALL OF US--SCORES OF OTHERS WOULD BE DEAD.
THIS ISN'T A ZERO SUM GAME, RED ROBIN.
YOU DON'T GET TO YOUR FOOTBALL AND RUN OFF THE COURT BECAUSE YOU DIDN'T BOWL A PERFECT 300.
ORGANIZED SPORTS ISN'T REALLY YOUR THING, HUH?
NOR METAPHORS. DON'T CHANGE THE SUBJECT.
RED ROBIN. CAN I SPEAK ALONE WITH YOU FOR A MOMENT?
YEAH. SURE.
WE'LL TALK LATER, AMIGO.

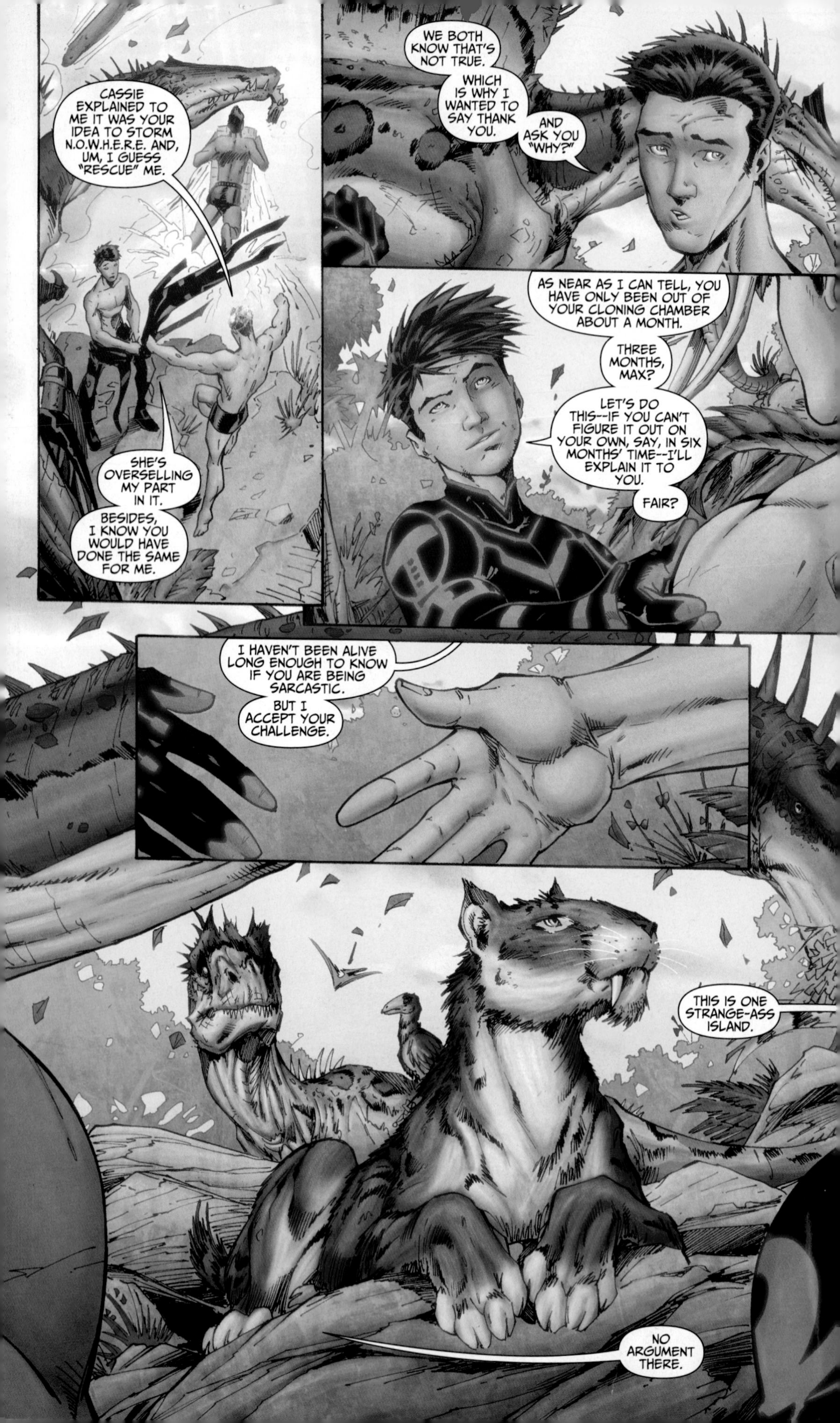
CASSIE EXPLAINED TO ME IT WAS YOUR IDEA TO STORM N.O.W.H.E.R.E. AND, UM, I GUESS "RESCUE" ME.
SHE'S OVERSELLING MY PART IN IT.
BESIDES, I KNOW YOU WOULD HAVE DONE THE SAME FOR ME.
WE BOTH KNOW THAT'S NOT TRUE.
WHICH IS WHY I WANTED TO SAY THANK YOU.
AND ASK YOU "WHY?"
AS NEAR AS I CAN TELL, YOU HAVE ONLY BEEN OUT OF YOUR CLONING CHAMBER ABOUT A MONTH.
THREE MONTHS, MAX?
LET'S DO THIS--IF YOU CAN'T FIGURE IT OUT ON YOUR OWN, SAY, IN SIX MONTHS' TIME--I'LL EXPLAIN IT TO YOU.
FAIR?
I HAVEN'T BEEN ALIVE LONG ENOUGH TO KNOW IF YOU ARE BEING SARCASTIC.
BUT I ACCEPT YOUR CHALLENGE.
THIS IS ONE STRANGE-ASS ISLAND.
NO ARGUMENT THERE.

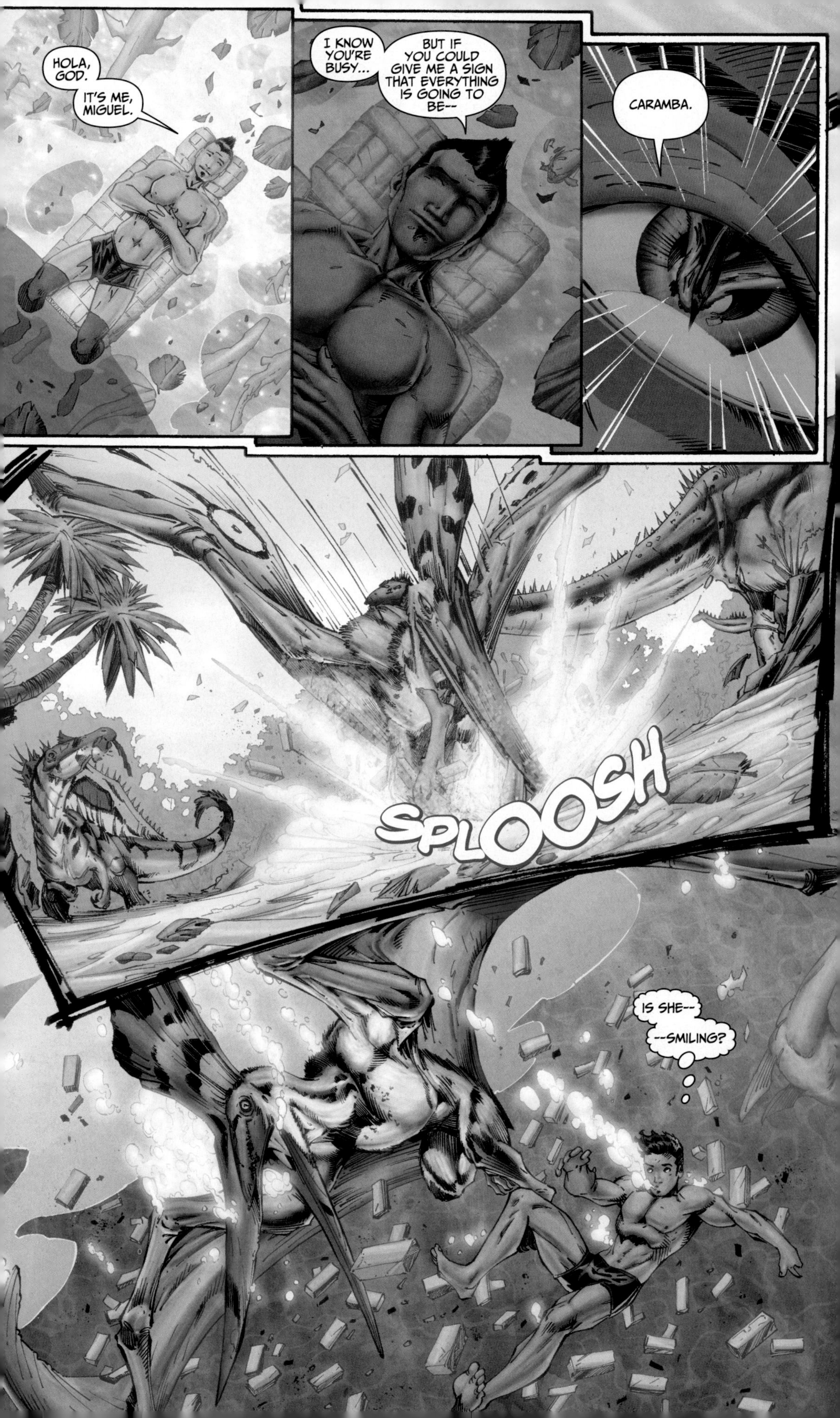
HOLA, GOD.
IT'S ME, MIGUEL.
I KNOW YOU'RE BUSY...
BUT IF YOU COULD GIVE ME A SIGN THAT EVERYTHING IS GOING TO BE--
CARAMBA.
SPLOOSH
IS SHE--
--SMILING?

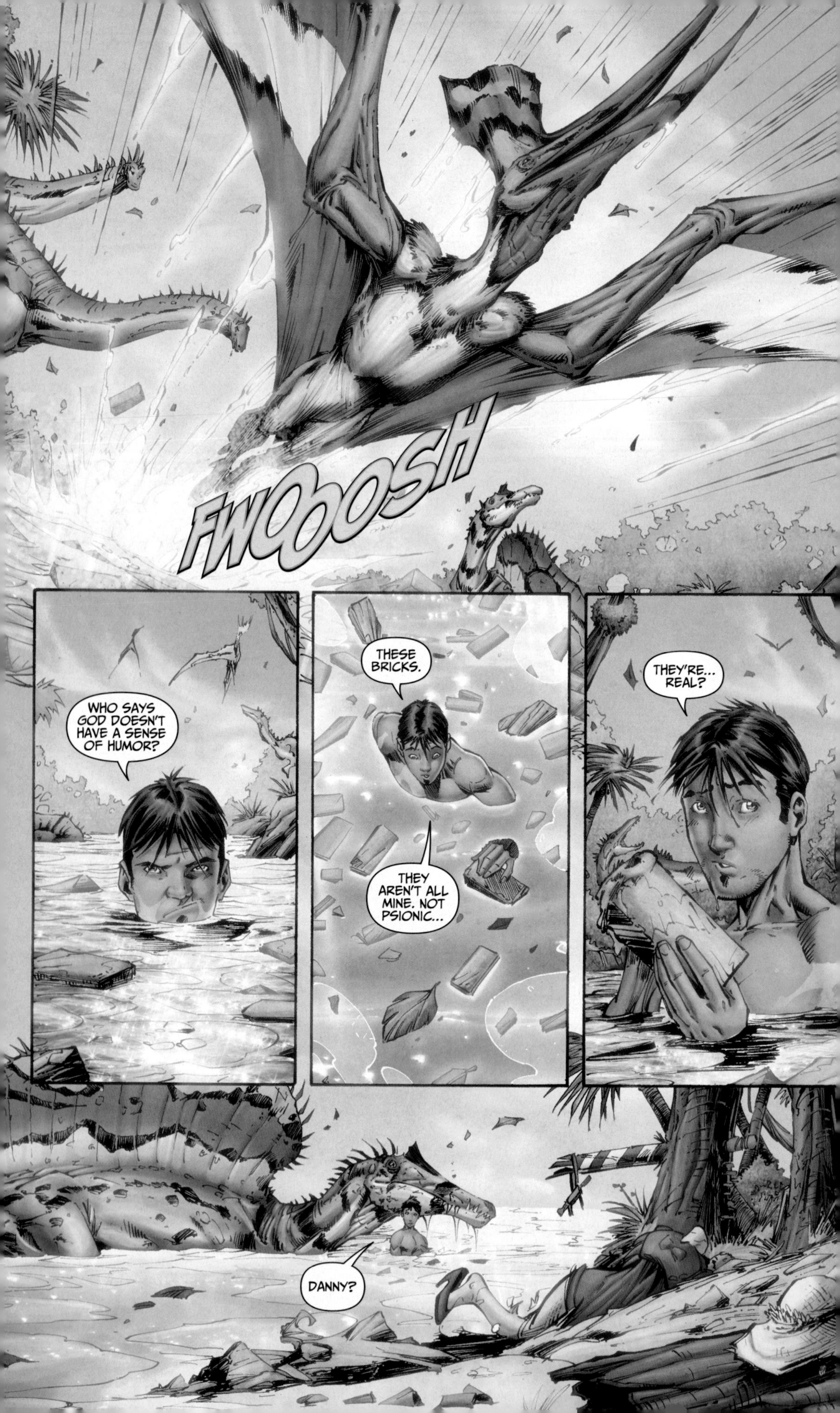
FWOOOSH
WHO SAYS GOD DOESN'T HAVE A SENSE OF HUMOR?
THESE BRICKS.
THEY AREN'T ALL MINE. NOT PSIONIC...
THEY'RE... REAL?
DANNY?

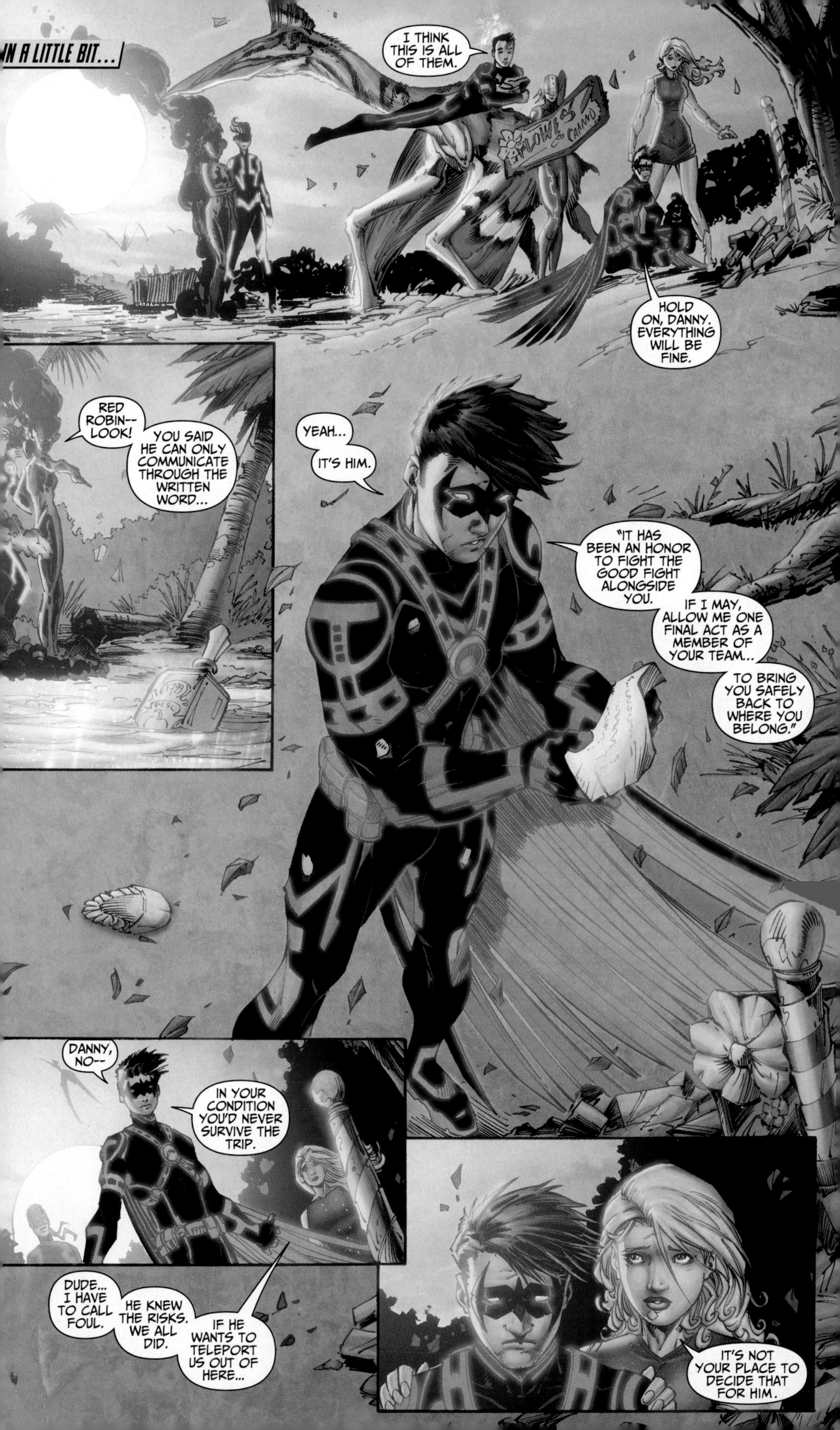

IN A LITTLE BIT...
I THINK THIS IS ALL OF THEM.
HOLD ON, DANNY. EVERYTHING WILL BE FINE.
RED ROBIN-- LOOK!
YOU SAID HE CAN ONLY COMMUNICATE THROUGH THE WRITTEN WORD...
YEAH...
IT'S HIM.
"IT HAS BEEN AN HONOR TO FIGHT THE GOOD FIGHT ALONGSIDE YOU.
IF I MAY, ALLOW ME ONE FINAL ACT AS A MEMBER OF YOUR TEAM...
TO BRING YOU SAFELY BACK TO WHERE YOU BELONG."
DANNY, NO--
IN YOUR CONDITION YOU'D NEVER SURVIVE THE TRIP.
DUDE... I HAVE TO CALL FOUL.
HE KNEW THE RISKS. WE ALL DID.
IF HE WANTS TO TELEPORT US OUT OF HERE...
IT'S NOT YOUR PLACE TO DECIDE THAT FOR HIM.

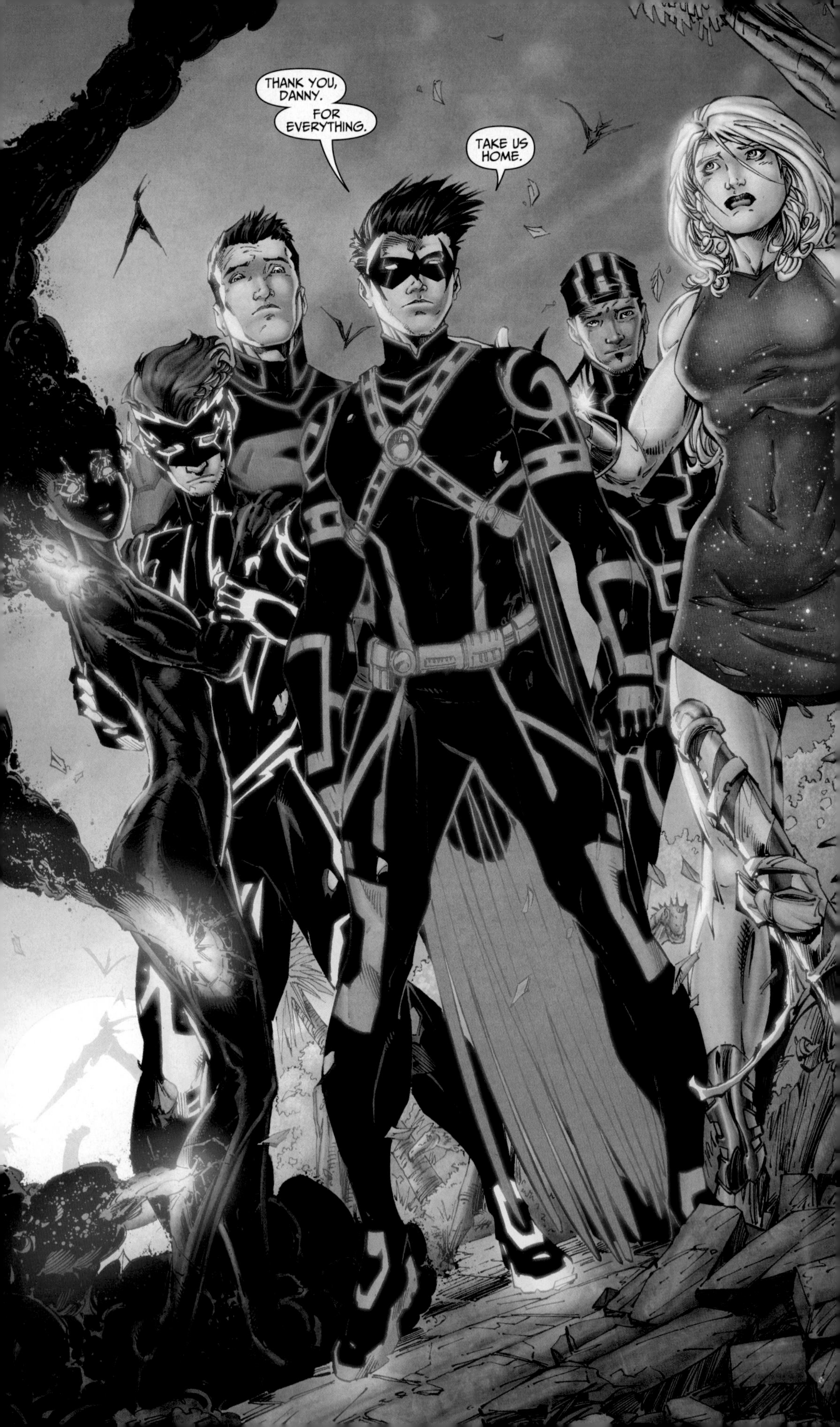
THANK YOU, DANNY.
FOR EVERYTHING.
TAKE US HOME.

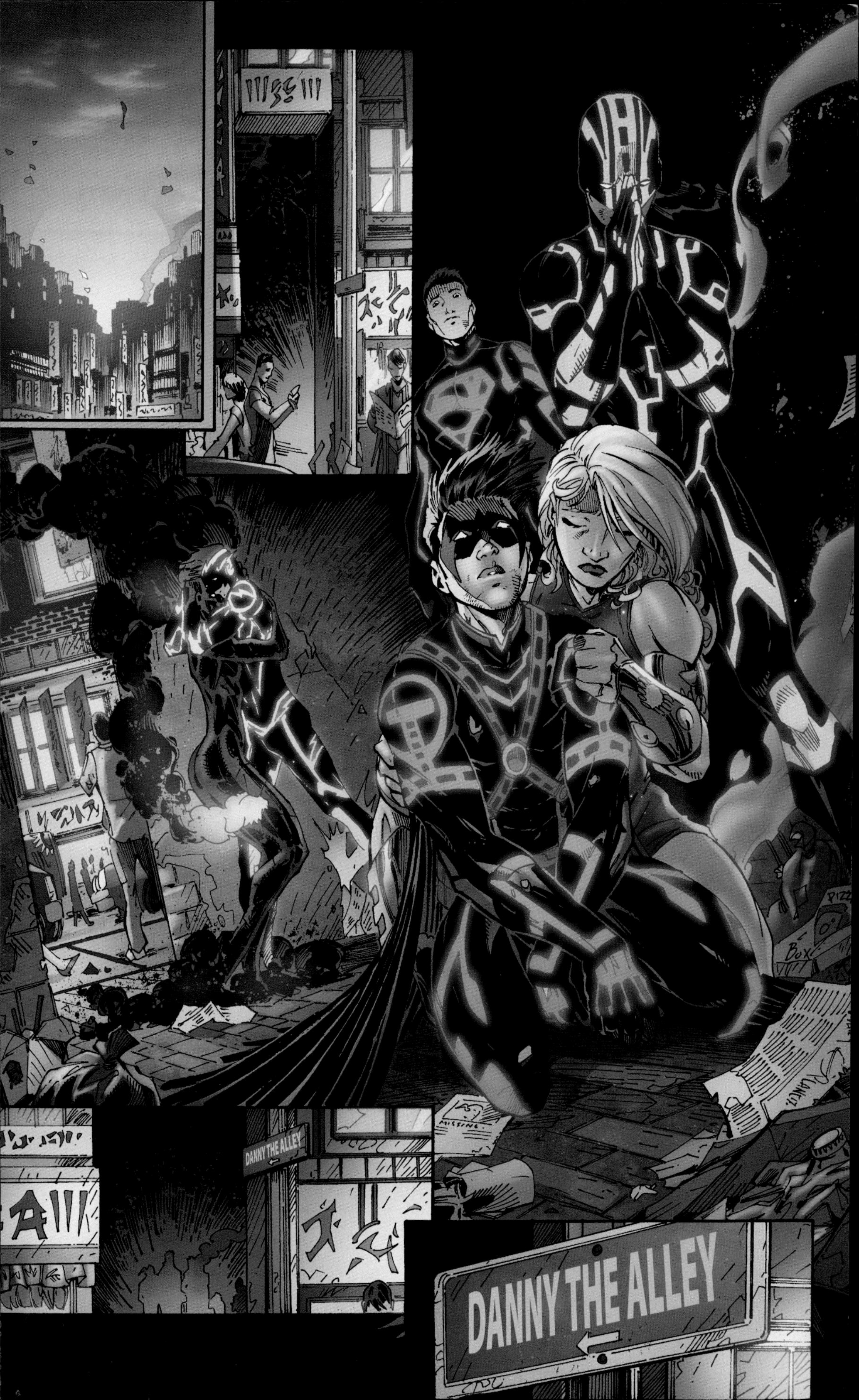
DANNY THE ALLEY
MISSING
DANNY THE ALLEY

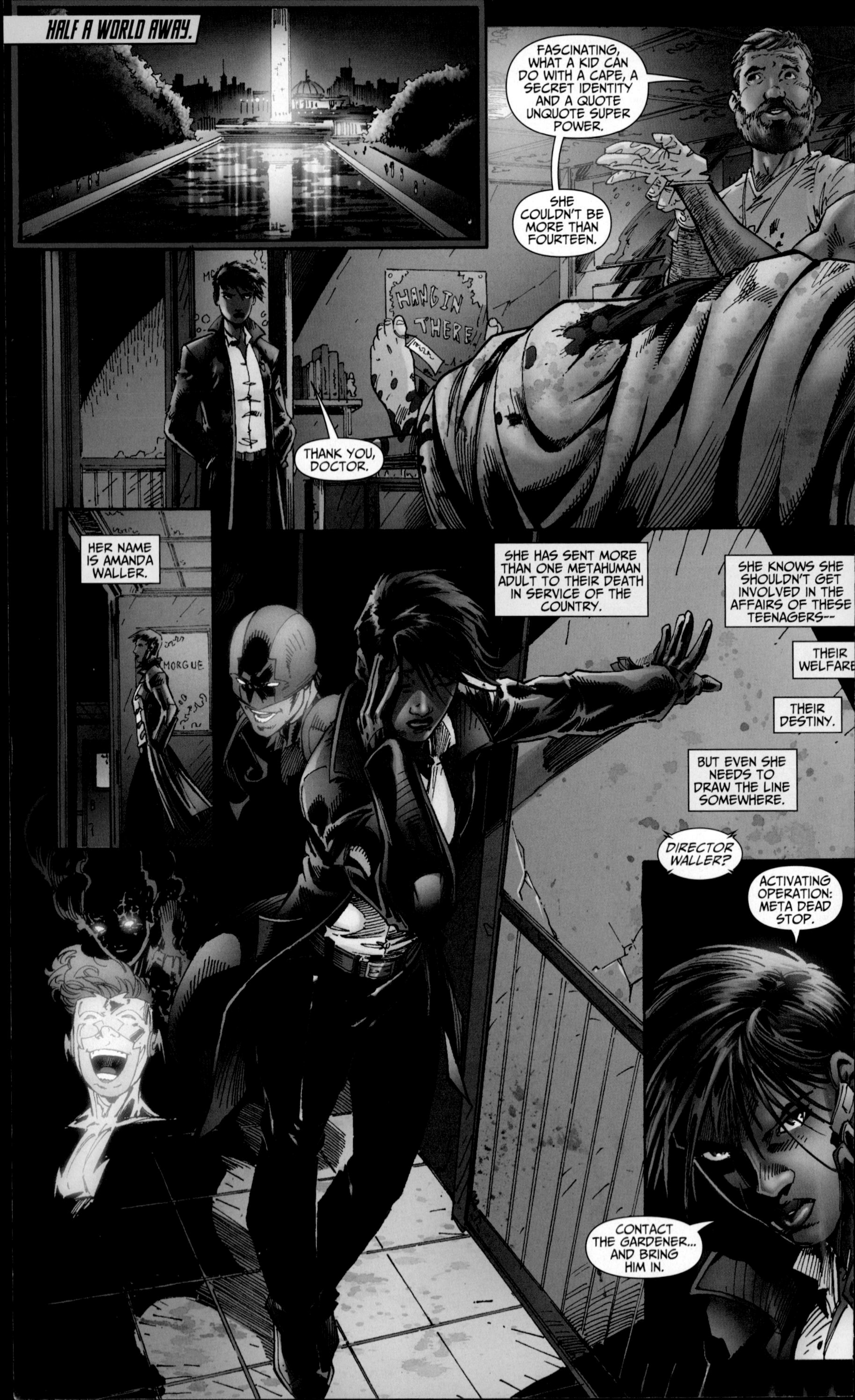
HALF A WORLD AWAY.
FASCINATING, WHAT A KID CAN DO WITH A CAPE, A SECRET IDENTITY AND A QUOTE UNQUOTE SUPER POWER.
SHE COULDN'T BE MORE THAN FOURTEEN.
THANK YOU, DOCTOR.
HER NAME IS AMANDA WALLER.
SHE HAS SENT MORE THAN ONE METAHUMAN ADULT TO THEIR DEATH IN SERVICE OF THE COUNTRY.
SHE KNOWS SHE SHOULDN'T GET INVOLVED IN THE AFFAIRS OF THESE TEENAGERS--
THEIR WELFARE
THEIR DESTINY.
BUT EVEN SHE NEEDS TO DRAW THE LINE SOMEWHERE.
DIRECTOR WALLER?
ACTIVATING OPERATION: META DEAD STOP.
CONTACT THE GARDENER... AND BRING HIM IN.

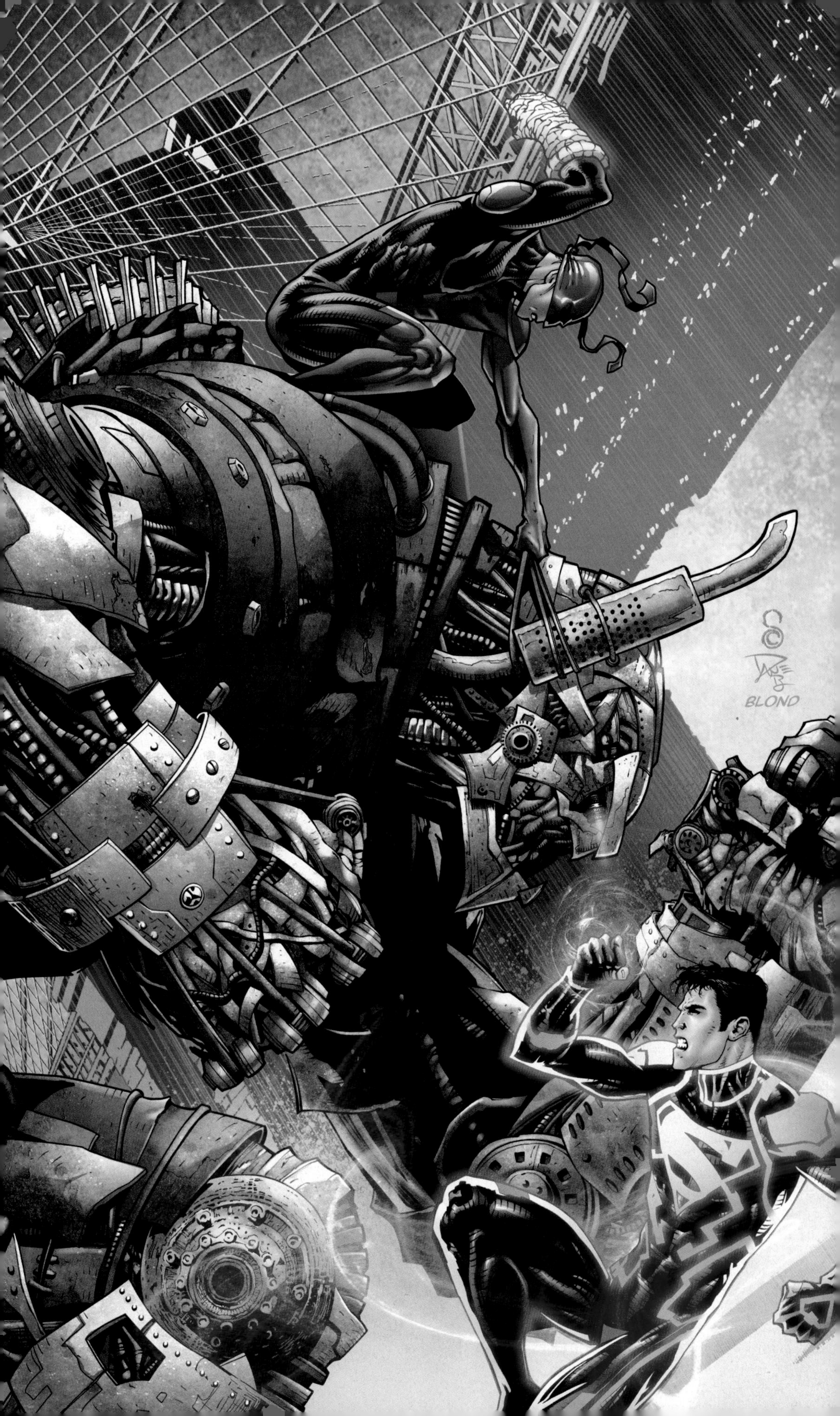
BLOND

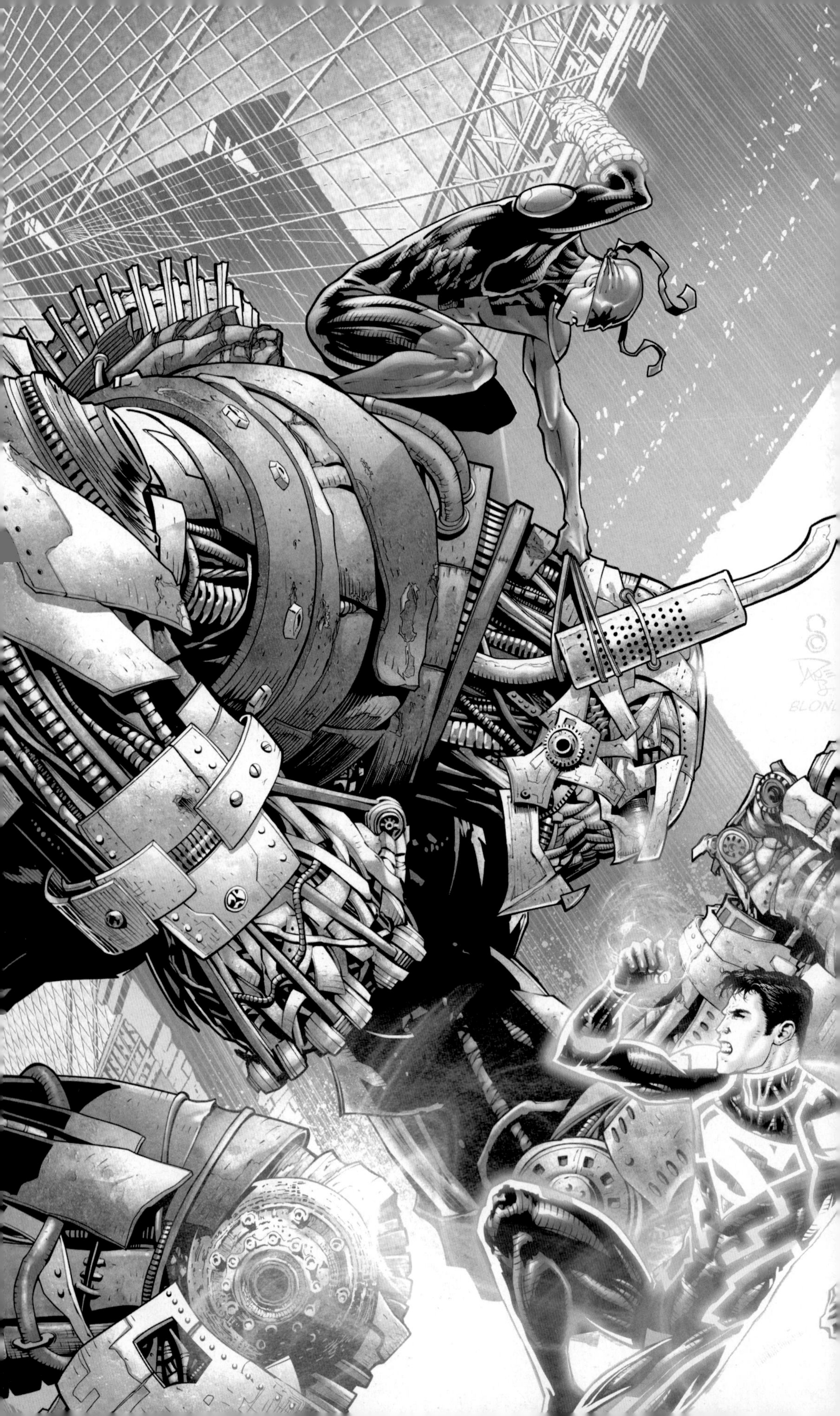

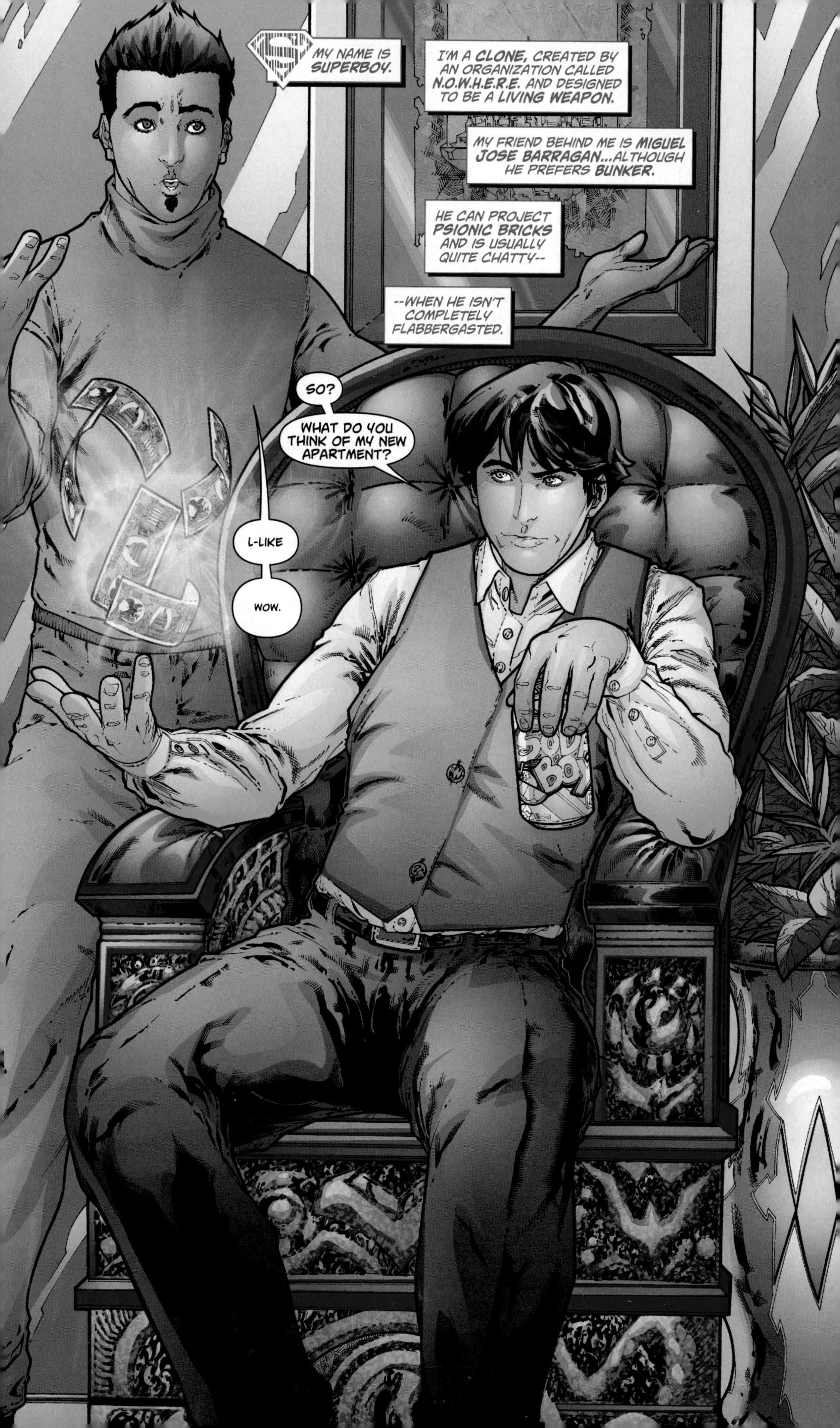
MY NAME IS SUPERBOY.
I'M A CLONE, CREATED BY AN ORGANIZATION CALLED N.O.W.H.E.R.E. AND DESIGNED TO BE A LIVING WEAPON.
MY FRIEND BEHIND ME IS MIGUEL JOSE BARRAGAN...ALTHOUGH HE PREFERS BUNKER.
HE CAN PROJECT PSIONIC BRICKS AND IS USUALLY QUITE CHATTY--
--WHEN HE ISN'T COMPLETELY FLABBERGASTED.
SO?
WHAT DO YOU THINK OF MY NEW APARTMENT?
L-LIKE
WOW.

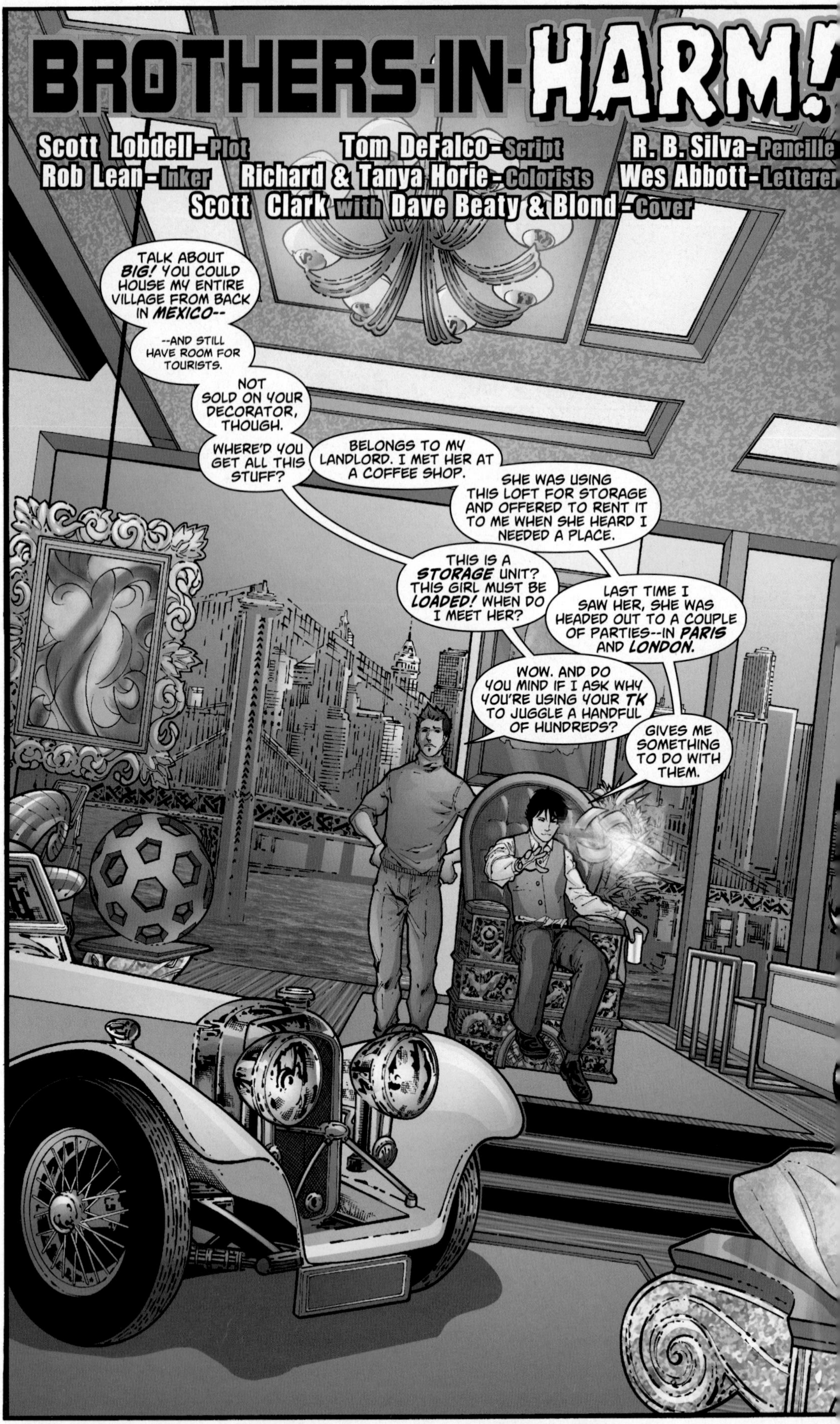
BROTHERS-IN-HARM!
Scott Lobdell-Plot Tom DeFalco-Script R. B. Silva-Penciller
Rob Lean-Inker Richard & Tanya Horie-Colorists Wes Abbott-Letterer
Scott Clark with Dave Beaty & Blond-Cover
TALK ABOUT BIG! YOU COULD HOUSE MY ENTIRE VILLAGE FROM BACK IN MEXICO--
--AND STILL HAVE ROOM FOR TOURISTS.
NOT SOLD ON YOUR DECORATOR, THOUGH.
WHERE'D YOU GET ALL THIS STUFF?
BELONGS TO MY LANDLORD. I MET HER AT A COFFEE SHOP.
SHE WAS USING THIS LOFT FOR STORAGE AND OFFERED TO RENT IT TO ME WHEN SHE HEARD I NEEDED A PLACE.
THIS IS A STORAGE UNIT? THIS GIRL MUST BE LOADED! WHEN DO I MEET HER?
LAST TIME I SAW HER, SHE WAS HEADED OUT TO A COUPLE OF PARTIES--IN PARIS AND LONDON.
WOW. AND DO YOU MIND IF I ASK WHY YOU'RE USING YOUR TK TO JUGGLE A HANDFUL OF HUNDREDS?
GIVES ME SOMETHING TO DO WITH THEM.

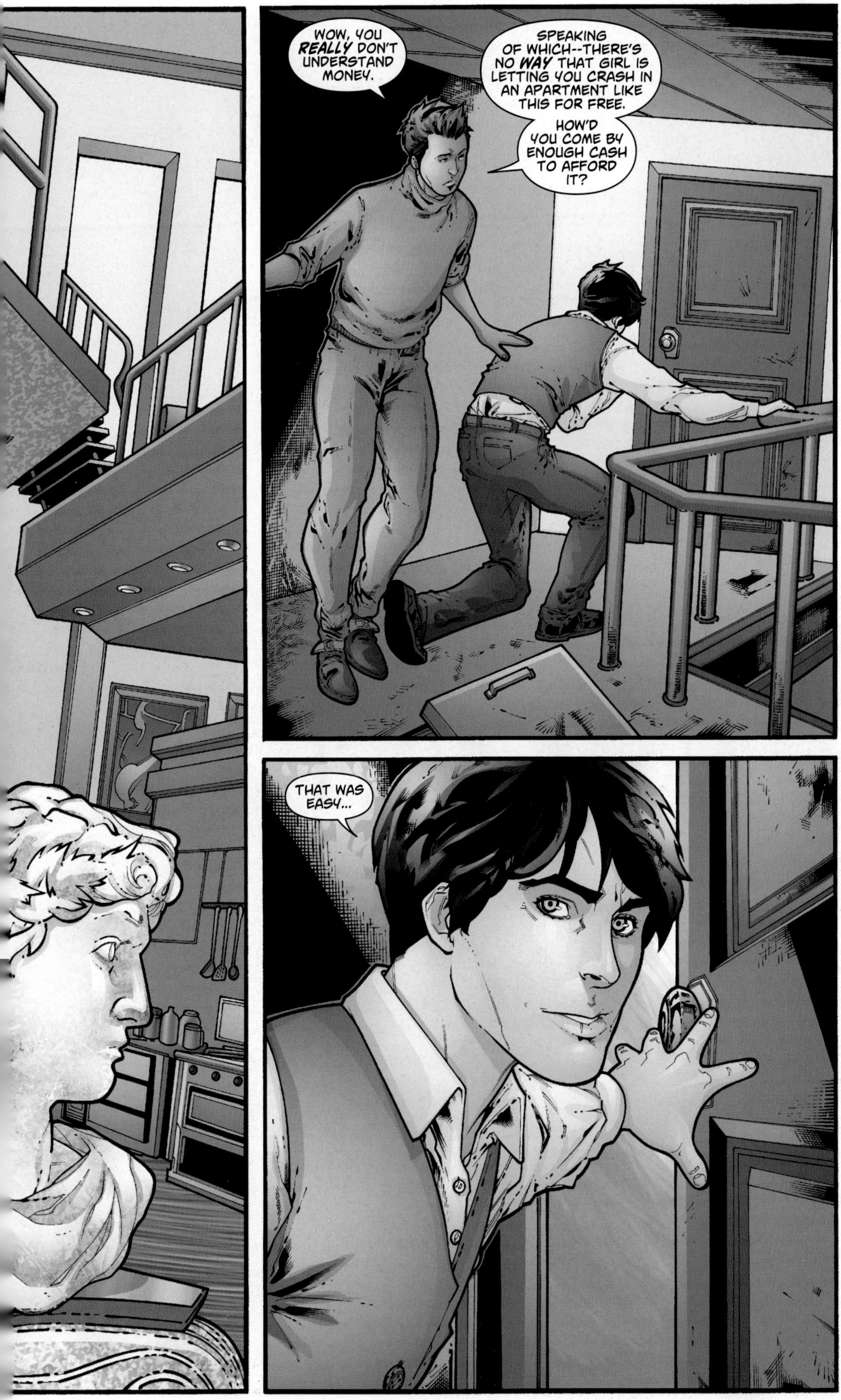
WOW, YOU REALLY DON'T UNDERSTAND MONEY.
SPEAKING OF WHICH--THERE'S NO WAY THAT GIRL IS LETTING YOU CRASH IN AN APARTMENT LIKE THIS FOR FREE.
HOW'D YOU COME BY ENOUGH CASH TO AFFORD IT?
THAT WAS EASY...

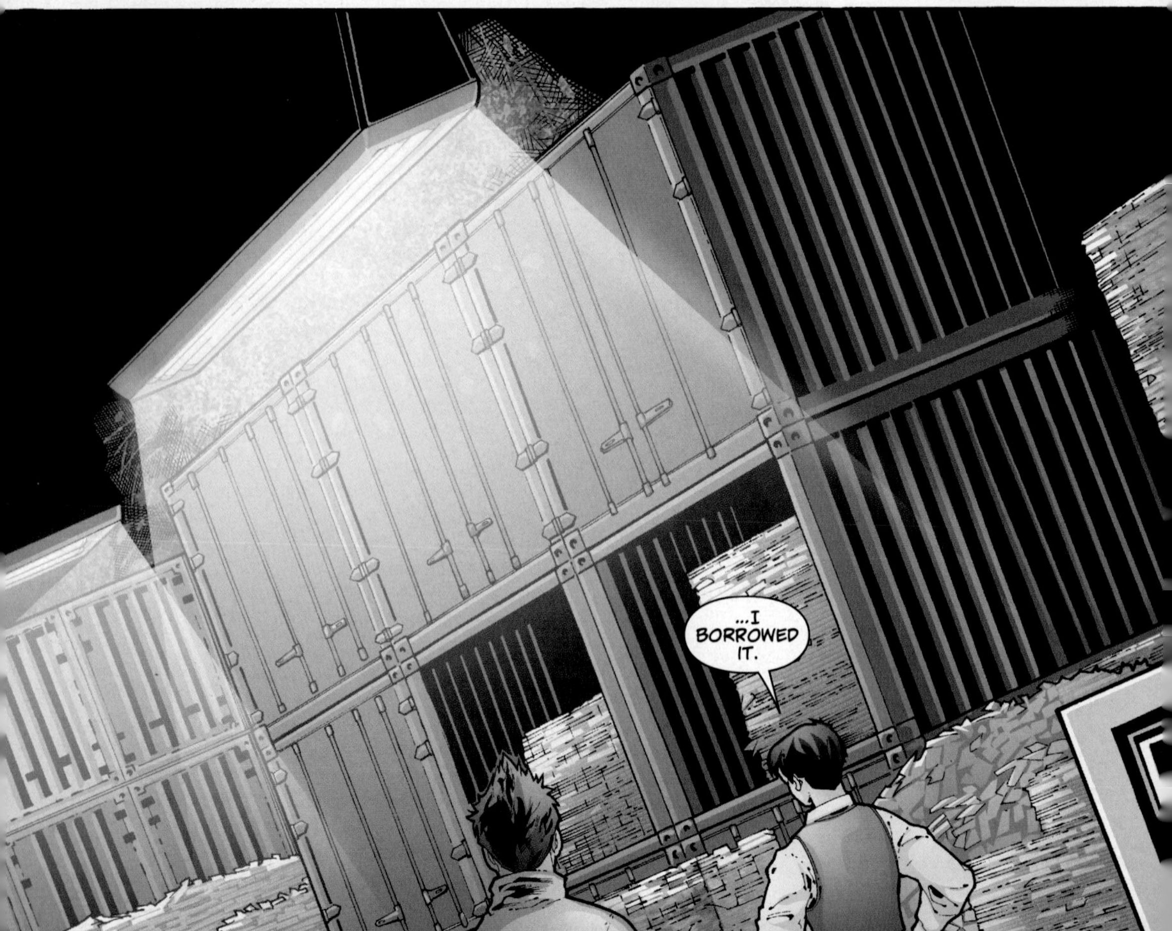
...I BORROWED IT.

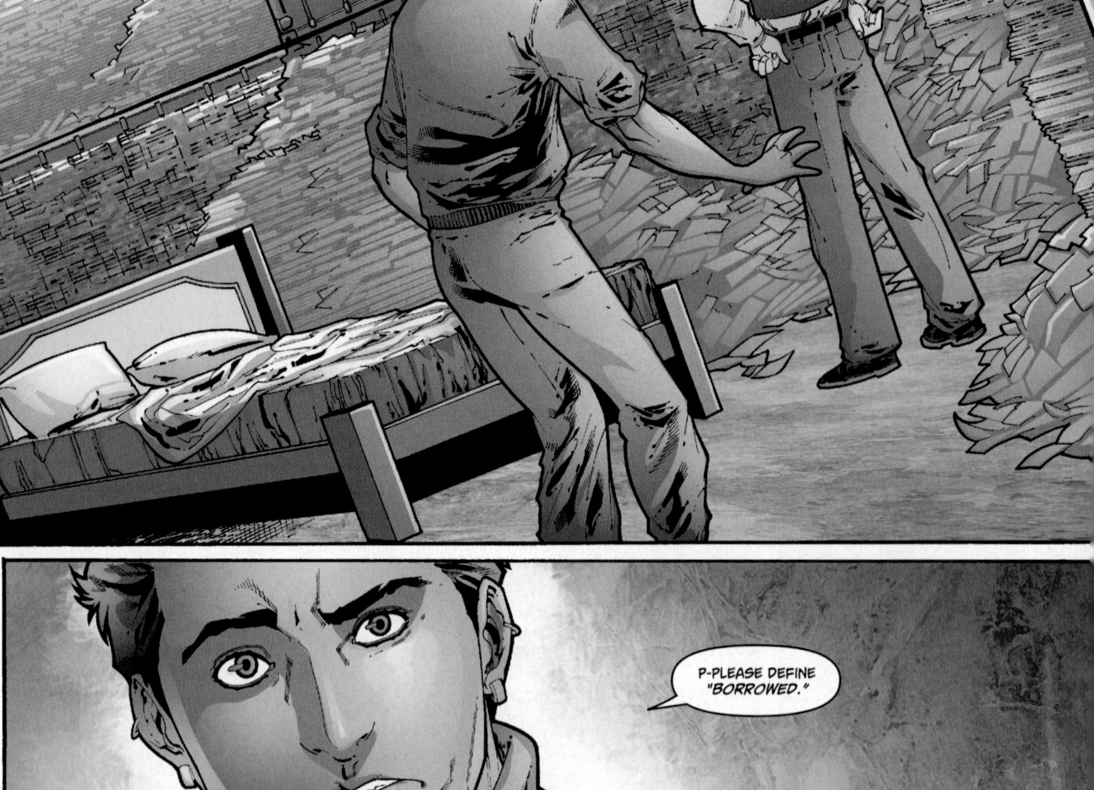
P-PLEASE DEFINE *"BORROWED."*

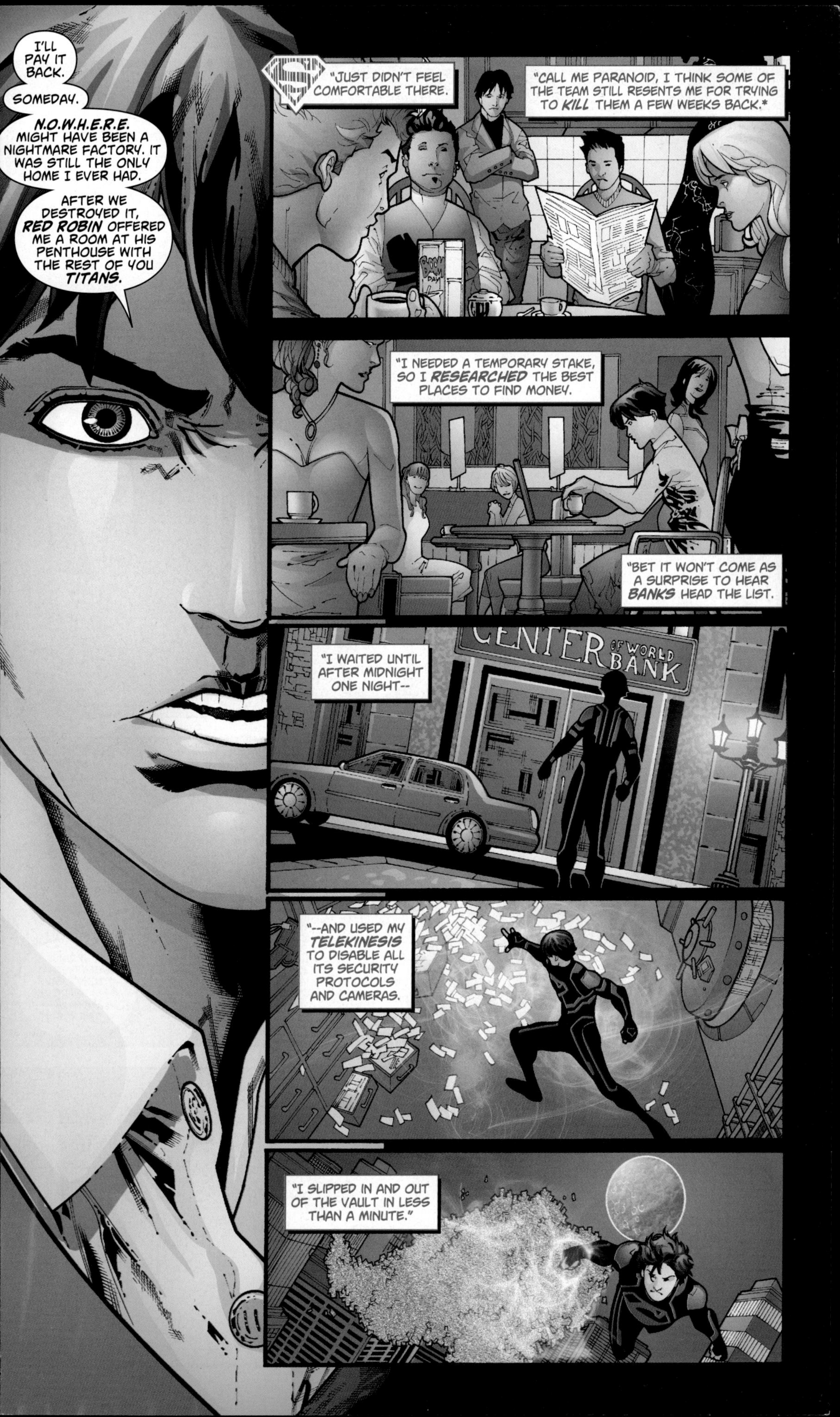
I'LL PAY IT BACK.
SOMEDAY.
N.O.W.H.E.R.E. MIGHT HAVE BEEN A NIGHTMARE FACTORY. IT WAS STILL THE ONLY HOME I EVER HAD.
AFTER WE DESTROYED IT, RED ROBIN OFFERED ME A ROOM AT HIS PENTHOUSE WITH THE REST OF YOU TITANS.
"JUST DIDN'T FEEL COMFORTABLE THERE.
"CALL ME PARANOID, I THINK SOME OF THE TEAM STILL RESENTS ME FOR TRYING TO KILL THEM A FEW WEEKS BACK.*
"I NEEDED A TEMPORARY STAKE, SO I RESEARCHED THE BEST PLACES TO FIND MONEY.
"BET IT WON'T COME AS A SURPRISE TO HEAR BANKS HEAD THE LIST.
CENTER OF WORLD BANK
"I WAITED UNTIL AFTER MIDNIGHT ONE NIGHT--
"--AND USED MY TELEKINESIS TO DISABLE ALL ITS SECURITY PROTOCOLS AND CAMERAS.
"I SLIPPED IN AND OUT OF THE VAULT IN LESS THAN A MINUTE."

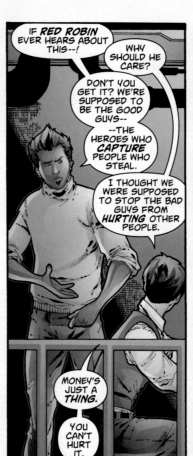

Y-YOU CAN'T JUST **STEAL** MONEY.

WEREN'T YOU LISTENING?

DIDN'T STEAL.

BORROWED.

IF **RED ROBIN** EVER HEARS ABOUT THIS--!

WHY SHOULD HE CARE?

DON'T YOU GET IT? WE'RE SUPPOSED TO BE THE GOOD GUYS--

--THE HEROES WHO **CAPTURE** PEOPLE WHO STEAL.

I THOUGHT WE WERE SUPPOSED TO STOP THE BAD GUYS FROM **HURTING** OTHER PEOPLE.

MONEY'S JUST A **THING.**

YOU CAN'T HURT IT.

C'MON, I NEED TO GET OUT OF HERE.

SHOULD WE WIPE OFF EVERY SURFACE WE'VE TOUCHED? **ARRRGH!** I'M GETTING A MIGRAINE JUST THINKING ABOUT IT.

WHY ARE YOU SO UPSET? WHAT'S THE PROBLEM?

YOU'D BETTER BRING YOUR COSTUME.

WHY?

JUST IN CASE YOU DECIDE TO RELOCATE--

--TO A COUNTRY THAT DOESN'T HAVE AN EXTRADITION TREATY WITH THE **U.S.**

AS MUCH AS I ENJOY YOUR COMPANY, MIGUEL--

--I DON'T UNDERSTAND WHAT YOU'RE SAYING MOST OF THE TIME.

THAT'S ON ME...

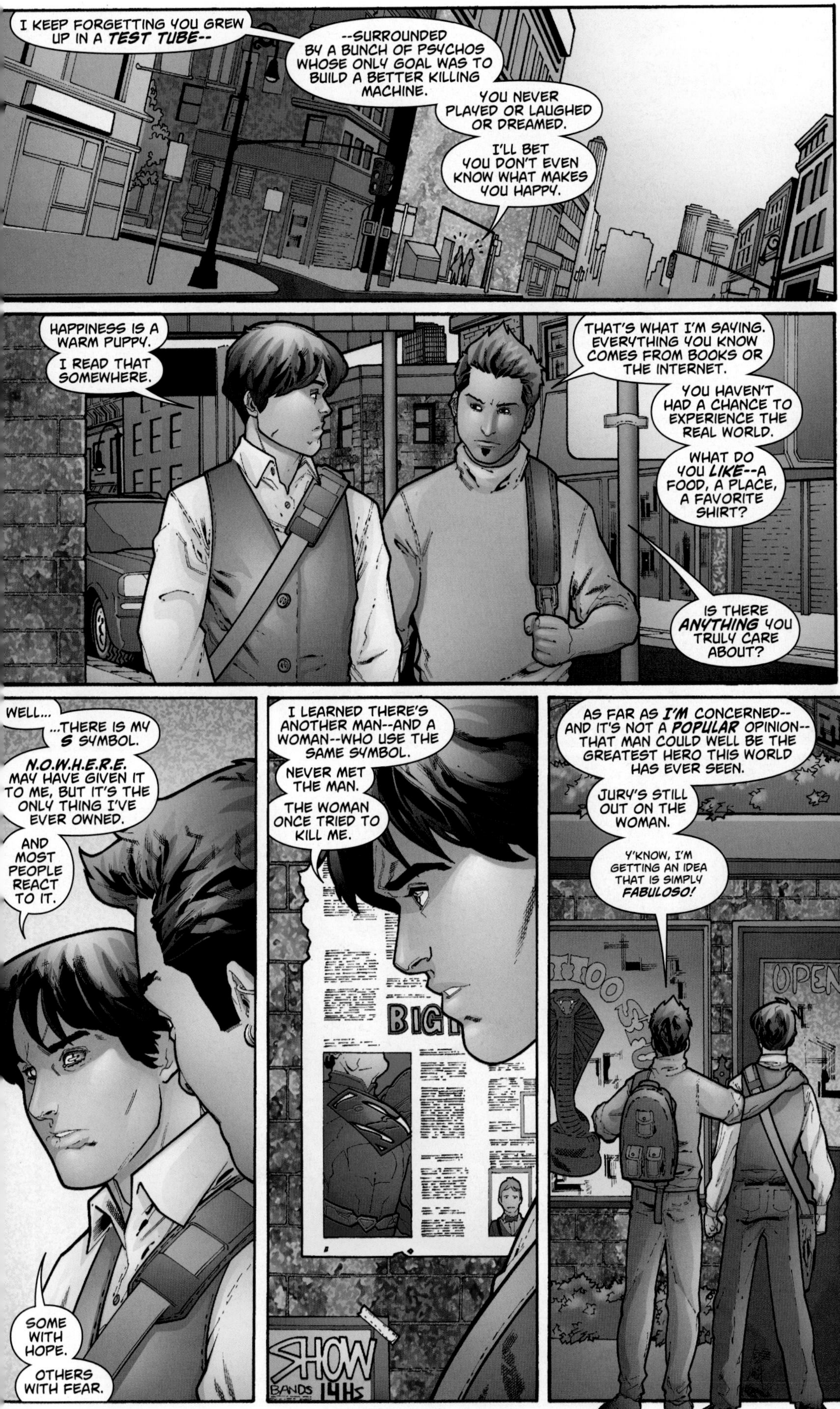

I KEEP FORGETTING YOU GREW UP IN A TEST TUBE--
--SURROUNDED BY A BUNCH OF PSYCHOS WHOSE ONLY GOAL WAS TO BUILD A BETTER KILLING MACHINE.
YOU NEVER PLAYED OR LAUGHED OR DREAMED.
I'LL BET YOU DON'T EVEN KNOW WHAT MAKES YOU HAPPY.
HAPPINESS IS A WARM PUPPY.
I READ THAT SOMEWHERE.
THAT'S WHAT I'M SAYING. EVERYTHING YOU KNOW COMES FROM BOOKS OR THE INTERNET.
YOU HAVEN'T HAD A CHANCE TO EXPERIENCE THE REAL WORLD.
WHAT DO YOU LIKE--A FOOD, A PLACE, A FAVORITE SHIRT?
IS THERE ANYTHING YOU TRULY CARE ABOUT?
WELL...
...THERE IS MY S SYMBOL.
N.O.W.H.E.R.E. MAY HAVE GIVEN IT TO ME, BUT IT'S THE ONLY THING I'VE EVER OWNED.
AND MOST PEOPLE REACT TO IT.
SOME WITH HOPE.
OTHERS WITH FEAR.
I LEARNED THERE'S ANOTHER MAN--AND A WOMAN--WHO USE THE SAME SYMBOL.
NEVER MET THE MAN.
THE WOMAN ONCE TRIED TO KILL ME.
BIG
SHOW
BANDS 14Hs
AS FAR AS I'M CONCERNED--AND IT'S NOT A POPULAR OPINION--THAT MAN COULD WELL BE THE GREATEST HERO THIS WORLD HAS EVER SEEN.
JURY'S STILL OUT ON THE WOMAN.
Y'KNOW, I'M GETTING AN IDEA THAT IS SIMPLY FABULOSO!
OPEN

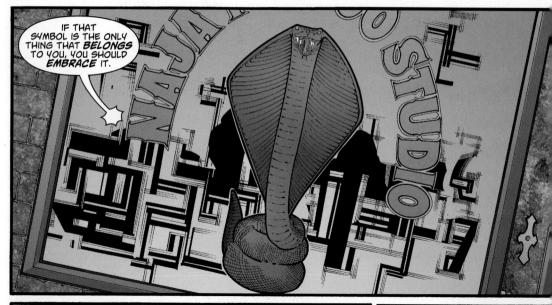

IF THAT SYMBOL IS THE ONLY THING THAT *BELONGS* TO YOU, YOU SHOULD *EMBRACE* IT.

SHOUT IT FROM THE ROOFTOPS AND TELL THE WORLD *IT'S YOURS!*

I ALWAYS KNEW I WAS *DIFFERENT*--

--EVEN *BEFORE* I GOT MY *METAHUMAN* POWERS.

I NEVER TRIED TO HIDE THAT FACT--*NOT ONCE!*

THANKS TO MY *LOVING* PARENTS, I LEARNED TO *CELEBRATE* EVERY DAY OF MY LIFE--

--AND *REVEL* IN MY UNIQUENESS!

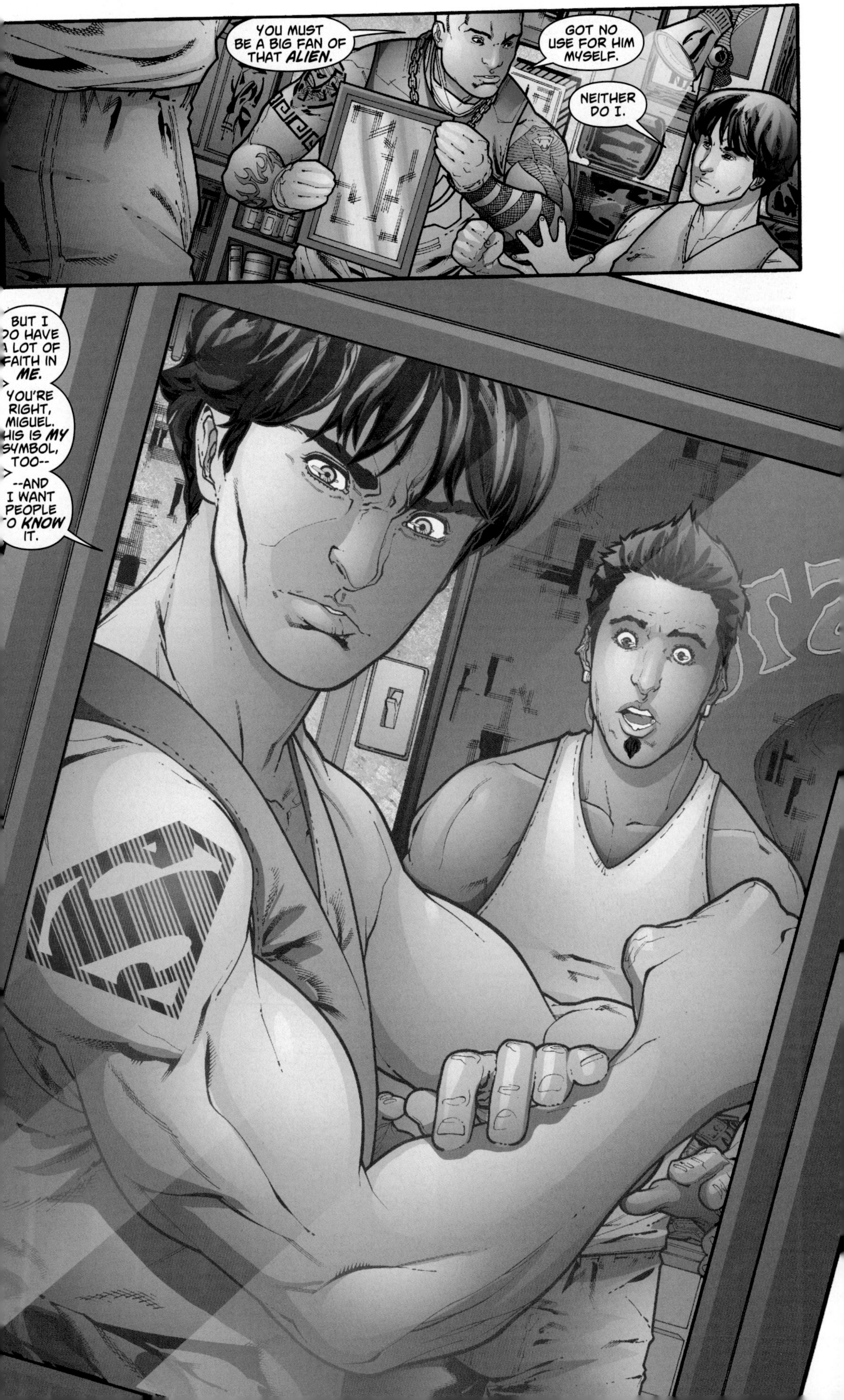
YOU MUST BE A BIG FAN OF THAT ALIEN.
GOT NO USE FOR HIM MYSELF.
NEITHER DO I.
BUT I DO HAVE A LOT OF FAITH IN ME.
YOU'RE RIGHT, MIGUEL. HIS IS MY SYMBOL, TOO--
--AND I WANT PEOPLE TO KNOW IT.

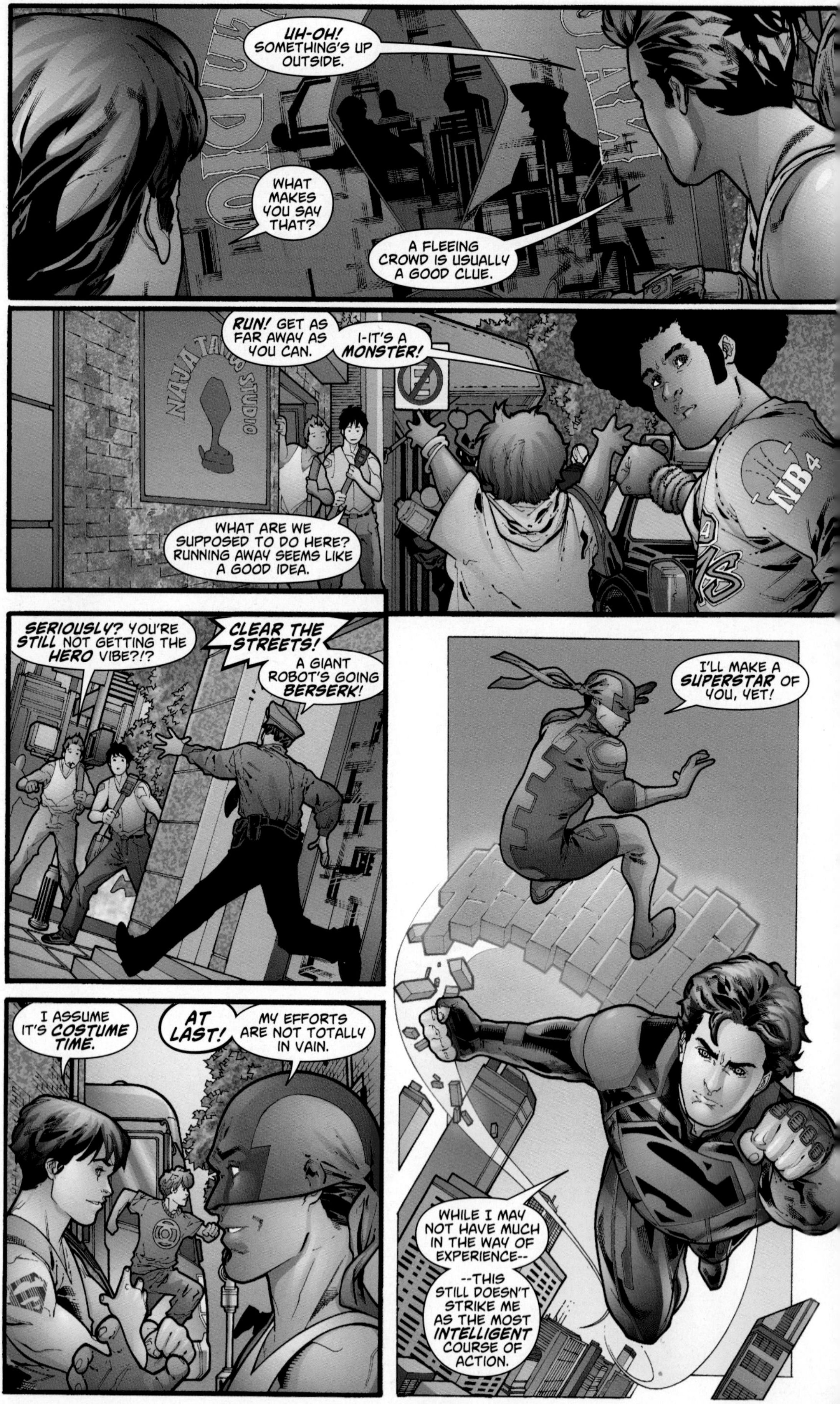
UH-OH! SOMETHING'S UP OUTSIDE.
WHAT MAKES YOU SAY THAT?
A FLEEING CROWD IS USUALLY A GOOD CLUE.
RUN! GET AS FAR AWAY AS YOU CAN.
I-IT'S A MONSTER!
NAJA TANGO STUDIO
NB4
WHAT ARE WE SUPPOSED TO DO HERE? RUNNING AWAY SEEMS LIKE A GOOD IDEA.
SERIOUSLY? YOU'RE STILL NOT GETTING THE HERO VIBE?!?
CLEAR THE STREETS!
A GIANT ROBOT'S GOING BERSERK!
I'LL MAKE A SUPERSTAR OF YOU, YET!
I ASSUME IT'S COSTUME TIME.
AT LAST!
MY EFFORTS ARE NOT TOTALLY IN VAIN.
WHILE I MAY NOT HAVE MUCH IN THE WAY OF EXPERIENCE--
--THIS STILL DOESN'T STRIKE ME AS THE MOST INTELLIGENT COURSE OF ACTION.

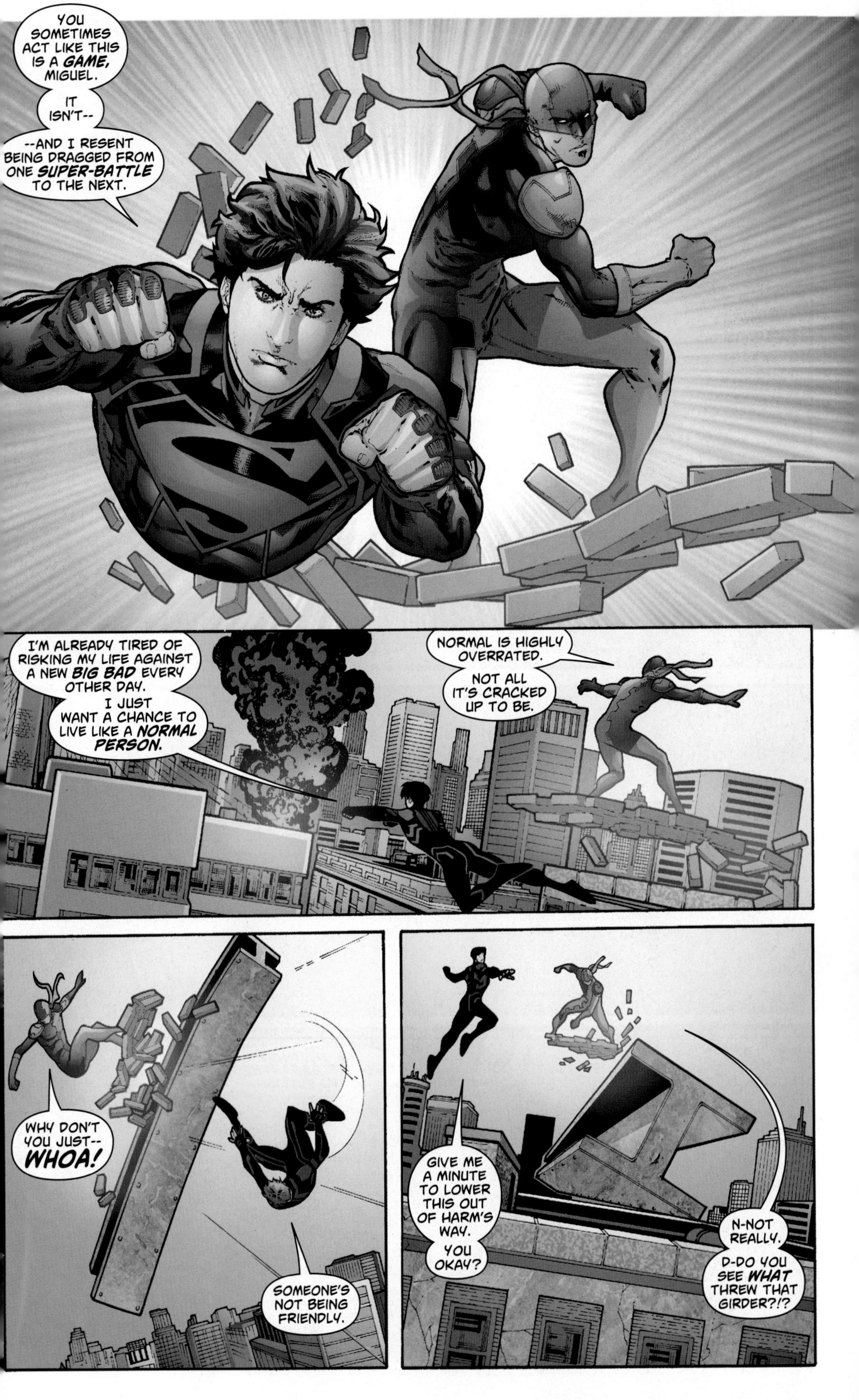

YOU SOMETIMES ACT LIKE THIS IS A **GAME,** MIGUEL.
IT ISN'T--
--AND I RESENT BEING DRAGGED FROM ONE **SUPER-BATTLE** TO THE NEXT.
I'M ALREADY TIRED OF RISKING MY LIFE AGAINST A NEW **BIG BAD** EVERY OTHER DAY.
I JUST WANT A CHANCE TO LIVE LIKE A **NORMAL PERSON.**
NORMAL IS HIGHLY OVERRATED.
NOT ALL IT'S CRACKED UP TO BE.
WHY DON'T YOU JUST-- **WHOA!**
SOMEONE'S NOT BEING FRIENDLY.
GIVE ME A MINUTE TO LOWER THIS OUT OF HARM'S WAY.
YOU OKAY?
N-NOT REALLY.
D-DO YOU SEE **WHAT** THREW THAT GIRDER?!?

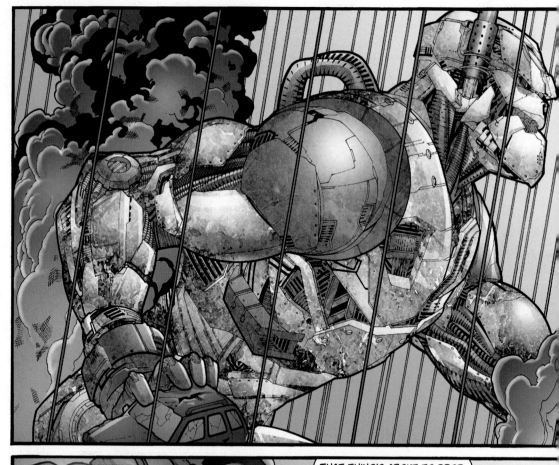

THAT THING'S ABOUT TO DROP-KICK A *TRACTOR TRAILER* INTO THE RIVER.

HOW'S ABOUT I DO *SEARCH AND RESCUE* WHILE YOU--

DON'T NEED A DIAGRAM!

WE CAN AVOID THIS *UNPLEASANTNESS* IN THE FUTURE--

KLANGG

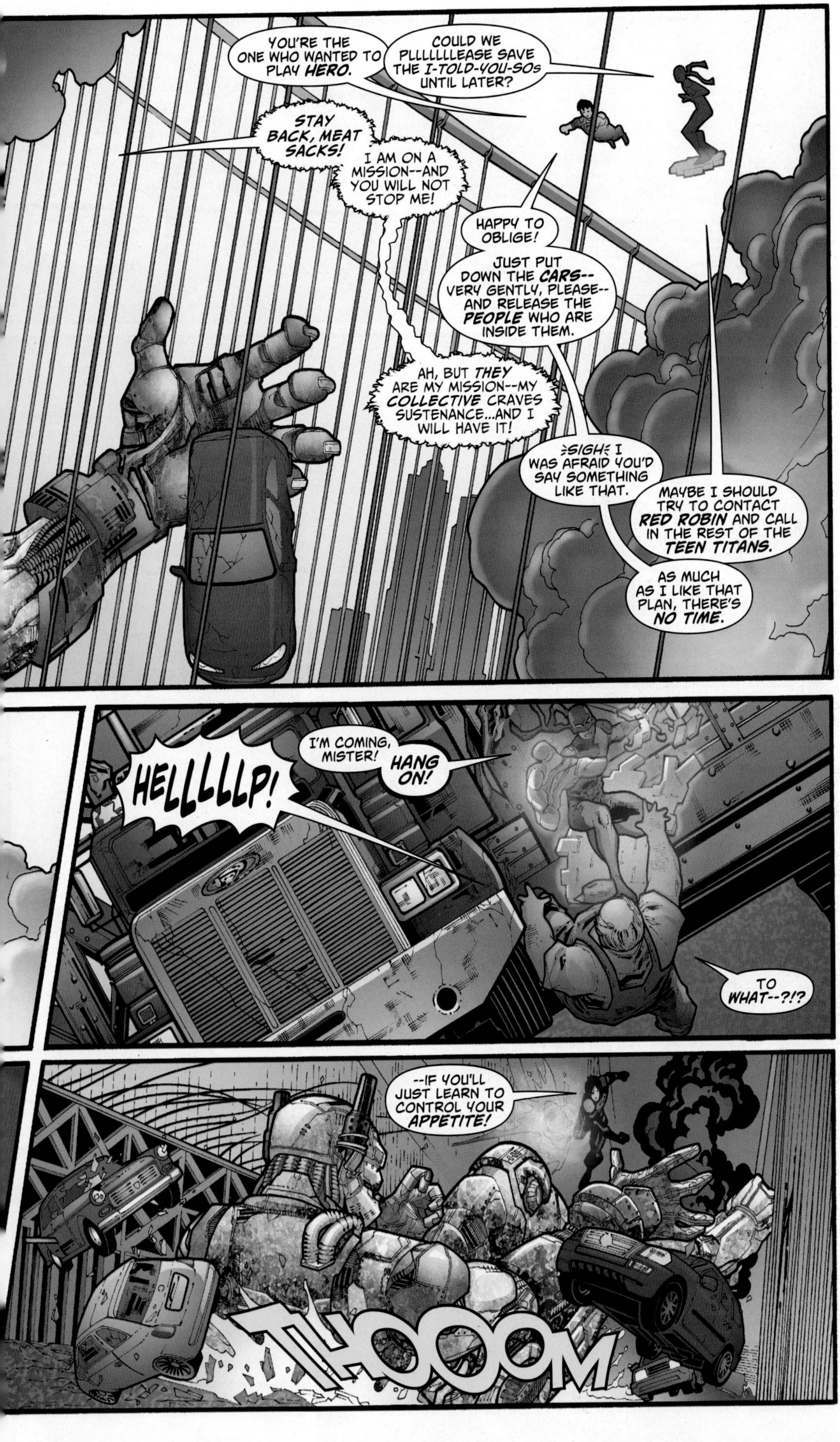
YOU'RE THE ONE WHO WANTED TO PLAY HERO.
COULD WE PLLLLLLLEASE SAVE THE I-TOLD-YOU-SOs UNTIL LATER?
STAY BACK, MEAT SACKS!
I AM ON A MISSION--AND YOU WILL NOT STOP ME!
HAPPY TO OBLIGE!
JUST PUT DOWN THE CARS--VERY GENTLY, PLEASE--AND RELEASE THE PEOPLE WHO ARE INSIDE THEM.
AH, BUT THEY ARE MY MISSION--MY COLLECTIVE CRAVES SUSTENANCE...AND I WILL HAVE IT!
SIGH I WAS AFRAID YOU'D SAY SOMETHING LIKE THAT.
MAYBE I SHOULD TRY TO CONTACT RED ROBIN AND CALL IN THE REST OF THE TEEN TITANS.
AS MUCH AS I LIKE THAT PLAN, THERE'S NO TIME.
HELLLLLP!
I'M COMING, MISTER! HANG ON!
TO WHAT--?!?
--IF YOU'LL JUST LEARN TO CONTROL YOUR APPETITE!
THOOOM

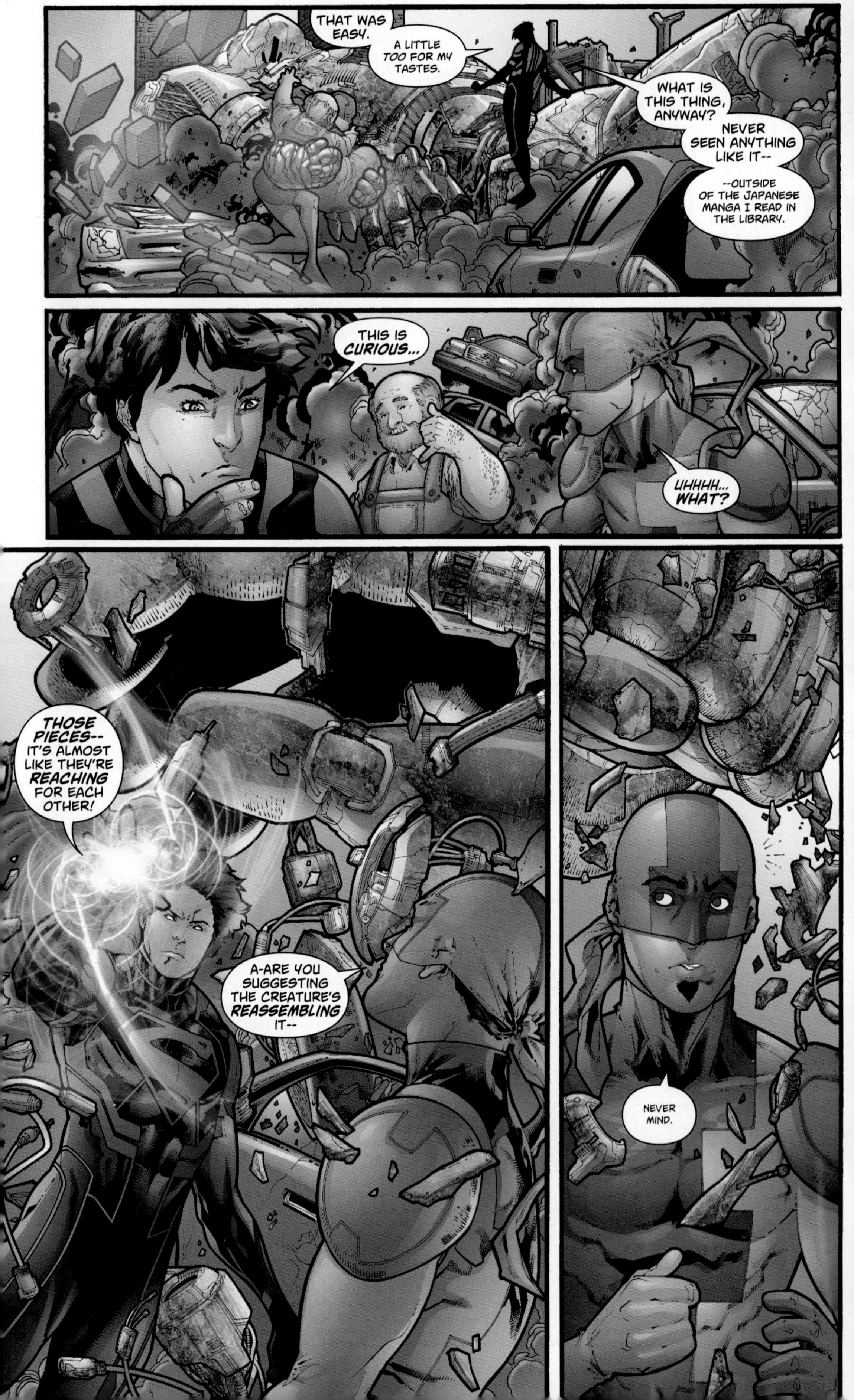
THAT WAS EASY.
A LITTLE TOO FOR MY TASTES.
WHAT IS THIS THING, ANYWAY?
NEVER SEEN ANYTHING LIKE IT--
--OUTSIDE OF THE JAPANESE MANGA I READ IN THE LIBRARY.
THIS IS CURIOUS...
UHHHH... WHAT?
THOSE PIECES-- IT'S ALMOST LIKE THEY'RE REACHING FOR EACH OTHER!
A-ARE YOU SUGGESTING THE CREATURE'S REASSEMBLING IT--
NEVER MIND.

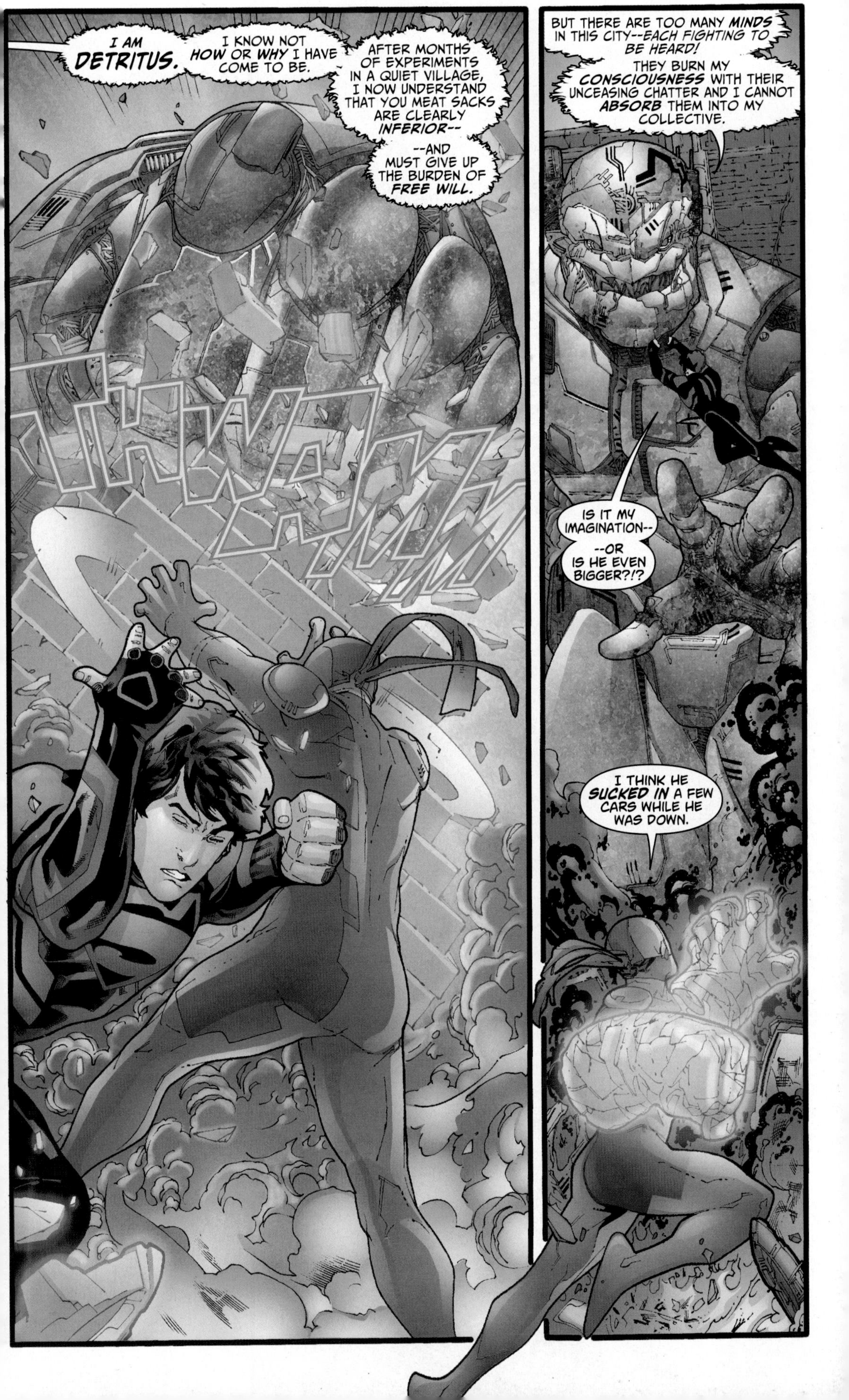
I AM DETRITUS.
I KNOW NOT HOW OR WHY I HAVE COME TO BE.
AFTER MONTHS OF EXPERIMENTS IN A QUIET VILLAGE, I NOW UNDERSTAND THAT YOU MEAT SACKS ARE CLEARLY INFERIOR--
--AND MUST GIVE UP THE BURDEN OF FREE WILL.
THWAMM
BUT THERE ARE TOO MANY MINDS IN THIS CITY--EACH FIGHTING TO BE HEARD!
THEY BURN MY CONSCIOUSNESS WITH THEIR UNCEASING CHATTER AND I CANNOT ABSORB THEM INTO MY COLLECTIVE.
IS IT MY IMAGINATION--
--OR IS HE EVEN BIGGER?!?
I THINK HE SUCKED IN A FEW CARS WHILE HE WAS DOWN.

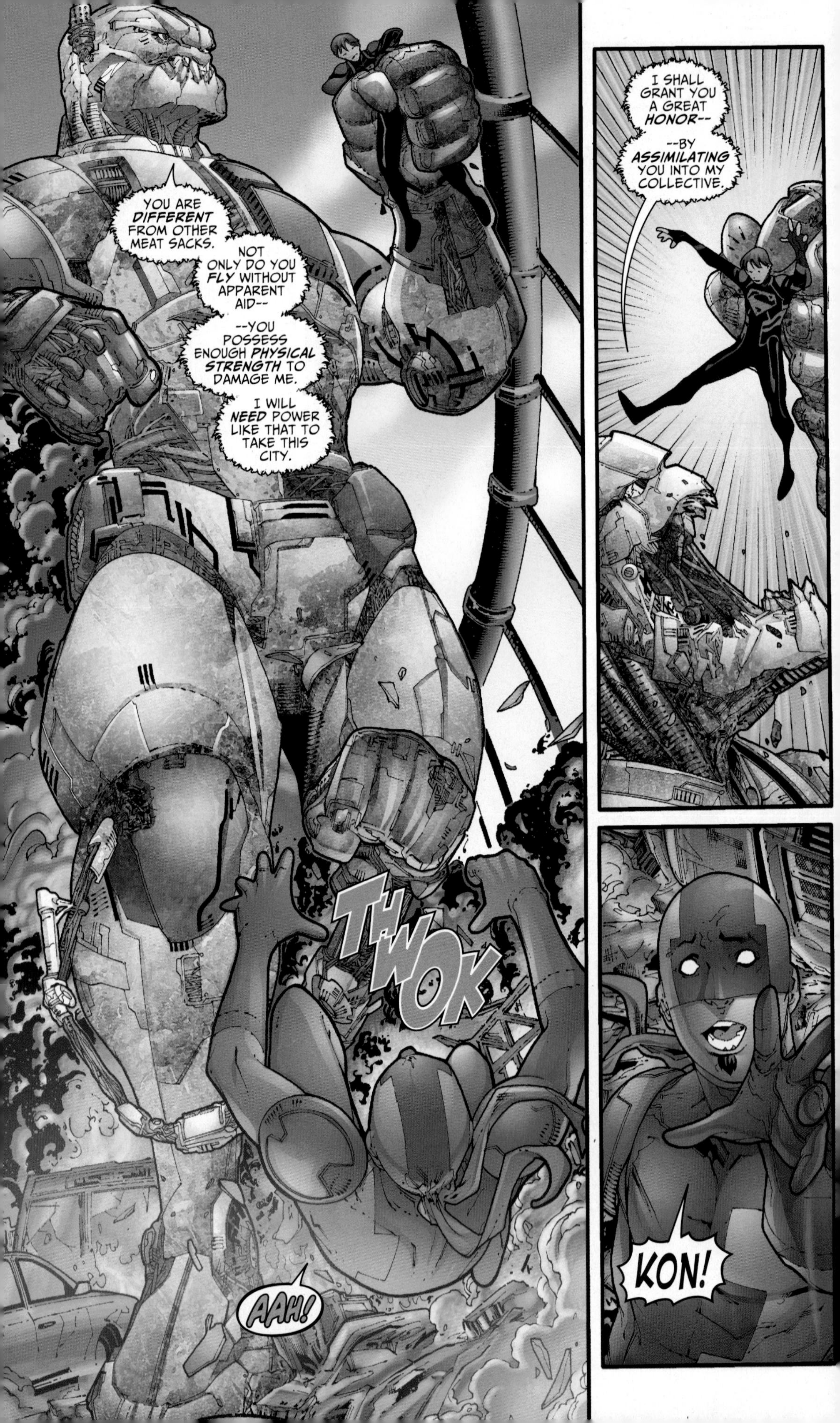
YOU ARE DIFFERENT FROM OTHER MEAT SACKS.
NOT ONLY DO YOU FLY WITHOUT APPARENT AID--
--YOU POSSESS ENOUGH PHYSICAL STRENGTH TO DAMAGE ME.
I WILL NEED POWER LIKE THAT TO TAKE THIS CITY.
I SHALL GRANT YOU A GREAT HONOR--
--BY ASSIMILATING YOU INTO MY COLLECTIVE.
THWOK
AAH!
KON!

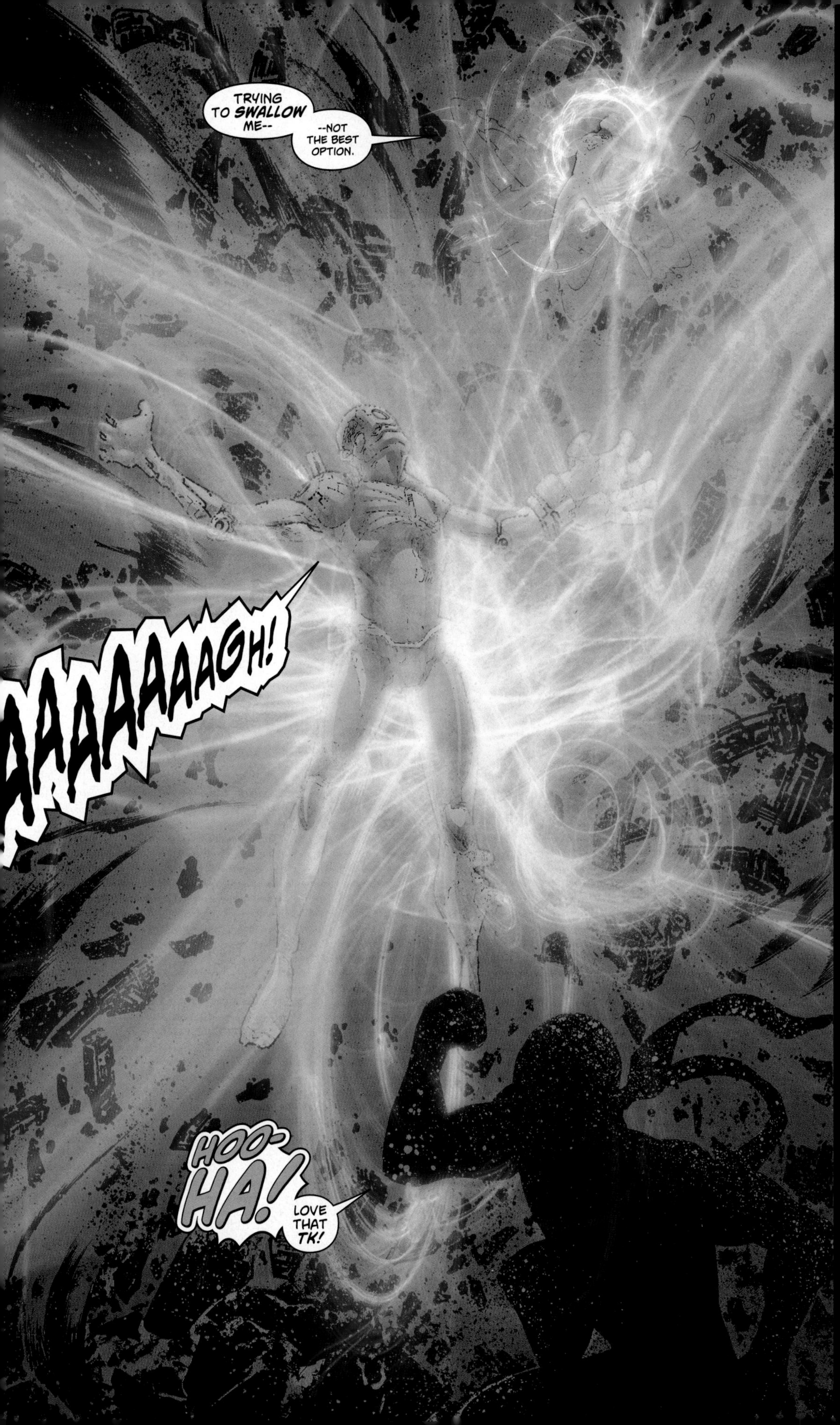

TRYING TO SWALLOW ME--
--NOT THE BEST OPTION.
AAAAAAAAGH!
HOO-HA!
LOVE THAT TK!

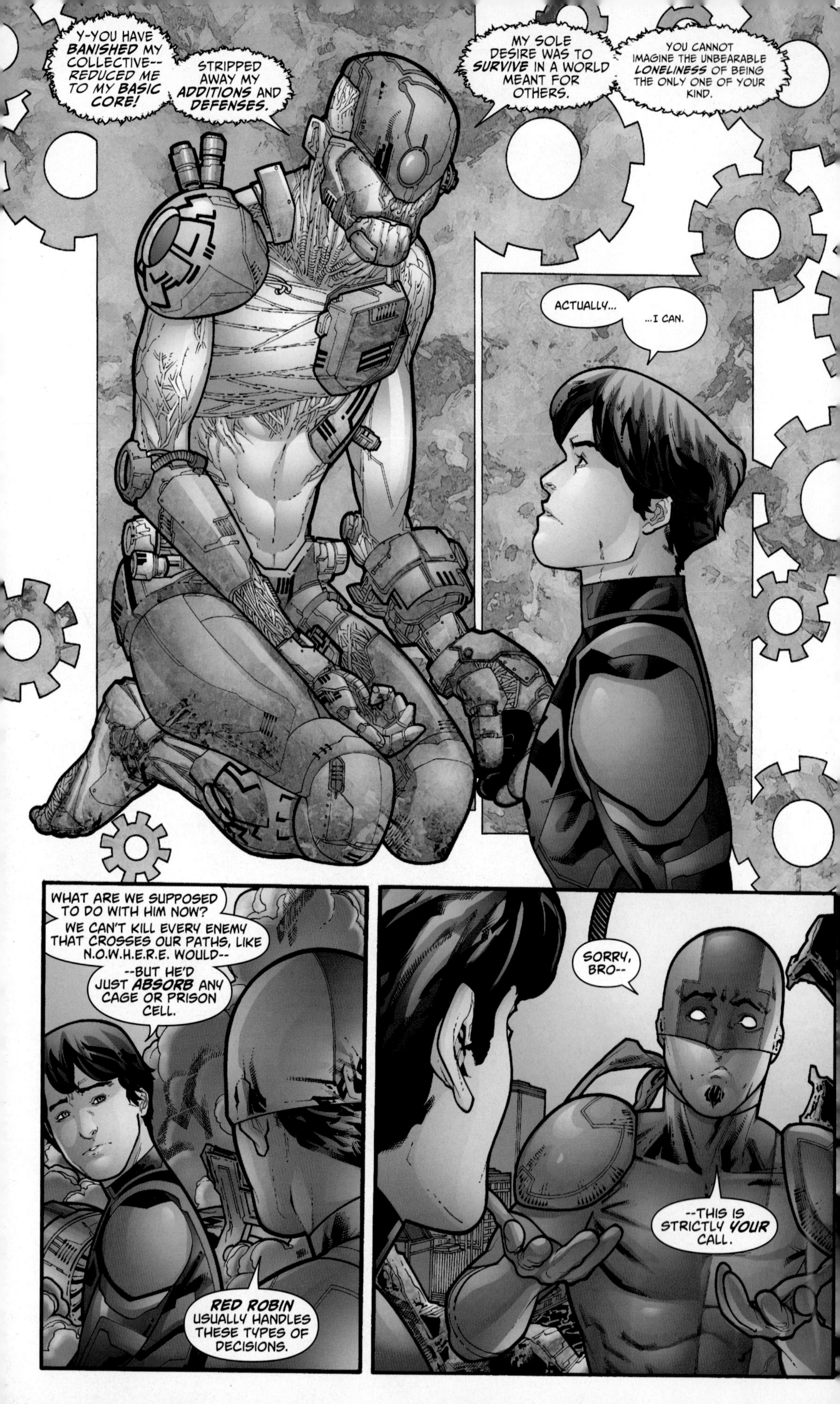
Y-YOU HAVE BANISHED MY COLLECTIVE-- REDUCED ME TO MY BASIC CORE!
STRIPPED AWAY MY ADDITIONS AND DEFENSES.
MY SOLE DESIRE WAS TO SURVIVE IN A WORLD MEANT FOR OTHERS.
YOU CANNOT IMAGINE THE UNBEARABLE LONELINESS OF BEING THE ONLY ONE OF YOUR KIND.
ACTUALLY...
...I CAN.
WHAT ARE WE SUPPOSED TO DO WITH HIM NOW?
WE CAN'T KILL EVERY ENEMY THAT CROSSES OUR PATHS, LIKE N.O.W.H.E.R.E. WOULD--
--BUT HE'D JUST ABSORB ANY CAGE OR PRISON CELL.
RED ROBIN USUALLY HANDLES THESE TYPES OF DECISIONS.
SORRY, BRO--
--THIS IS STRICTLY YOUR CALL.

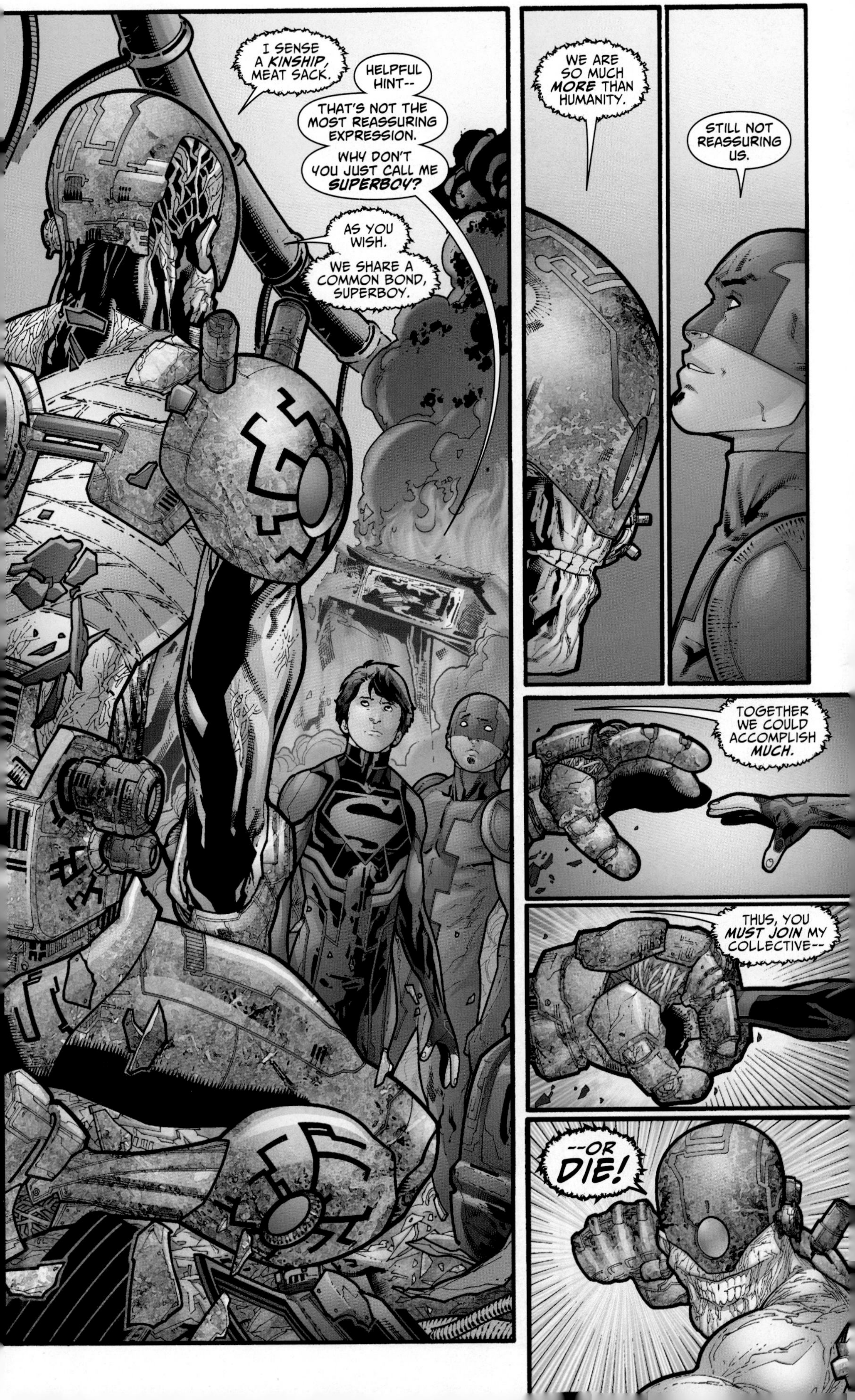
I SENSE A *KINSHIP,* MEAT SACK.
HELPFUL HINT--
THAT'S NOT THE MOST REASSURING EXPRESSION.
WHY DON'T YOU JUST CALL ME ***SUPERBOY?***
AS YOU WISH.
WE SHARE A COMMON BOND, SUPERBOY.
WE ARE SO MUCH *MORE* THAN HUMANITY.
STILL NOT REASSURING US.
TOGETHER WE COULD ACCOMPLISH *MUCH.*
THUS, YOU *MUST JOIN* MY COLLECTIVE--
--OR DIE!

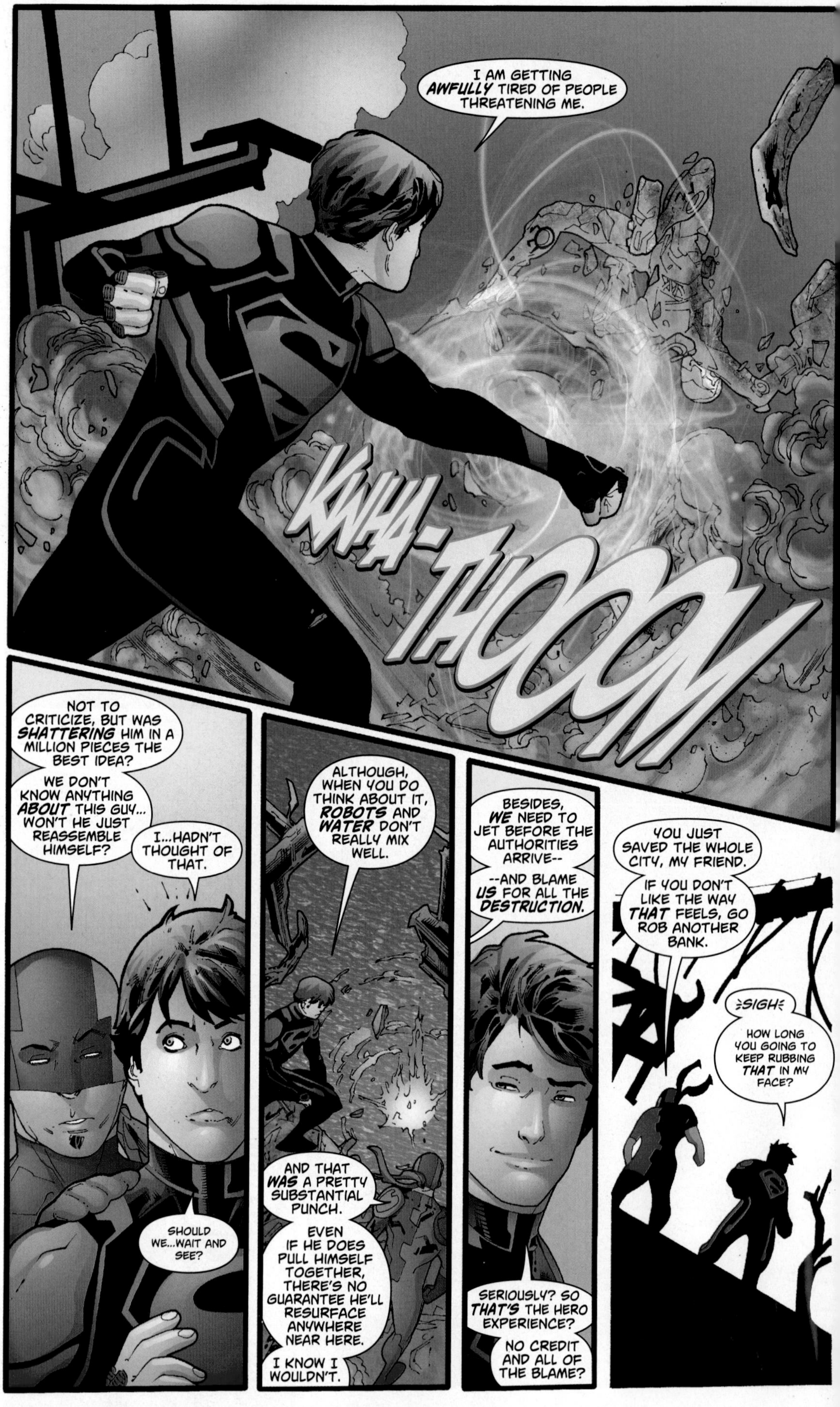
I AM GETTING AWFULLY TIRED OF PEOPLE THREATENING ME.
KWHA-THOOOM
NOT TO CRITICIZE, BUT WAS SHATTERING HIM IN A MILLION PIECES THE BEST IDEA?
WE DON'T KNOW ANYTHING ABOUT THIS GUY... WON'T HE JUST REASSEMBLE HIMSELF?
I...HADN'T THOUGHT OF THAT.
SHOULD WE...WAIT AND SEE?
ALTHOUGH, WHEN YOU DO THINK ABOUT IT, ROBOTS AND WATER DON'T REALLY MIX WELL.
AND THAT WAS A PRETTY SUBSTANTIAL PUNCH.
EVEN IF HE DOES PULL HIMSELF TOGETHER, THERE'S NO GUARANTEE HE'LL RESURFACE ANYWHERE NEAR HERE.
I KNOW I WOULDN'T.
BESIDES, WE NEED TO JET BEFORE THE AUTHORITIES ARRIVE--
--AND BLAME US FOR ALL THE DESTRUCTION.
SERIOUSLY? SO THAT'S THE HERO EXPERIENCE?
NO CREDIT AND ALL OF THE BLAME?
YOU JUST SAVED THE WHOLE CITY, MY FRIEND.
IF YOU DON'T LIKE THE WAY THAT FEELS, GO ROB ANOTHER BANK.
SIGH
HOW LONG YOU GOING TO KEEP RUBBING THAT IN MY FACE?

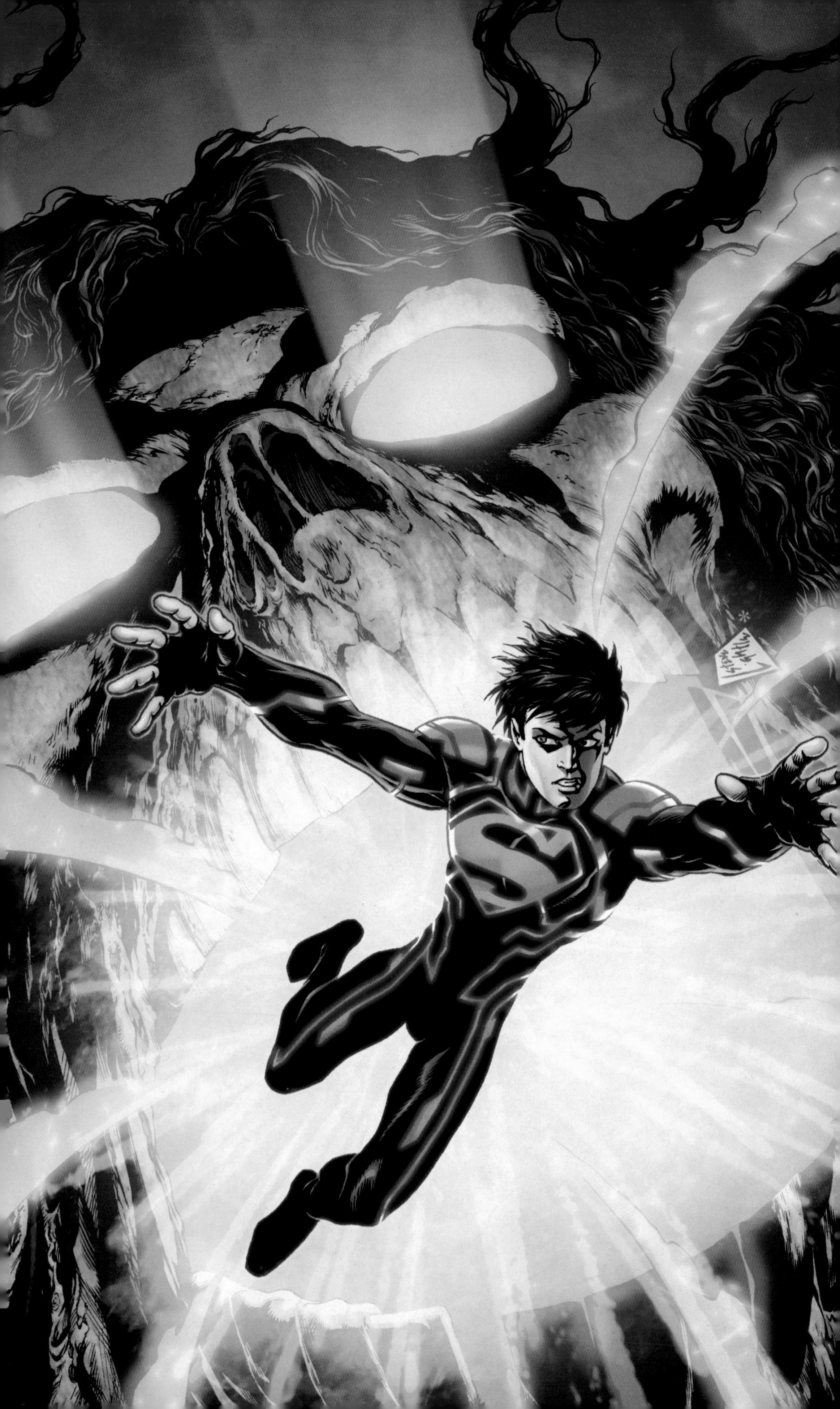

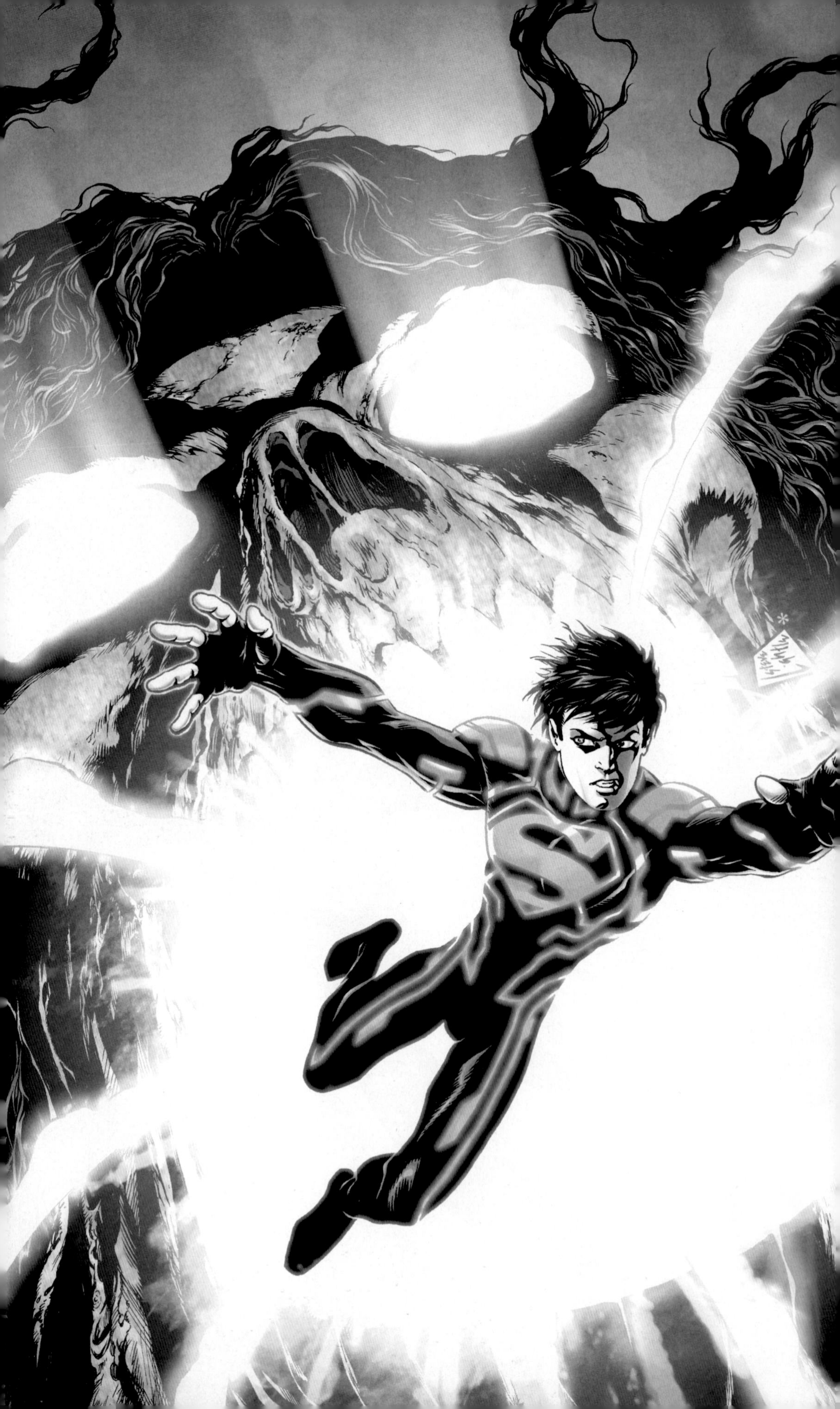

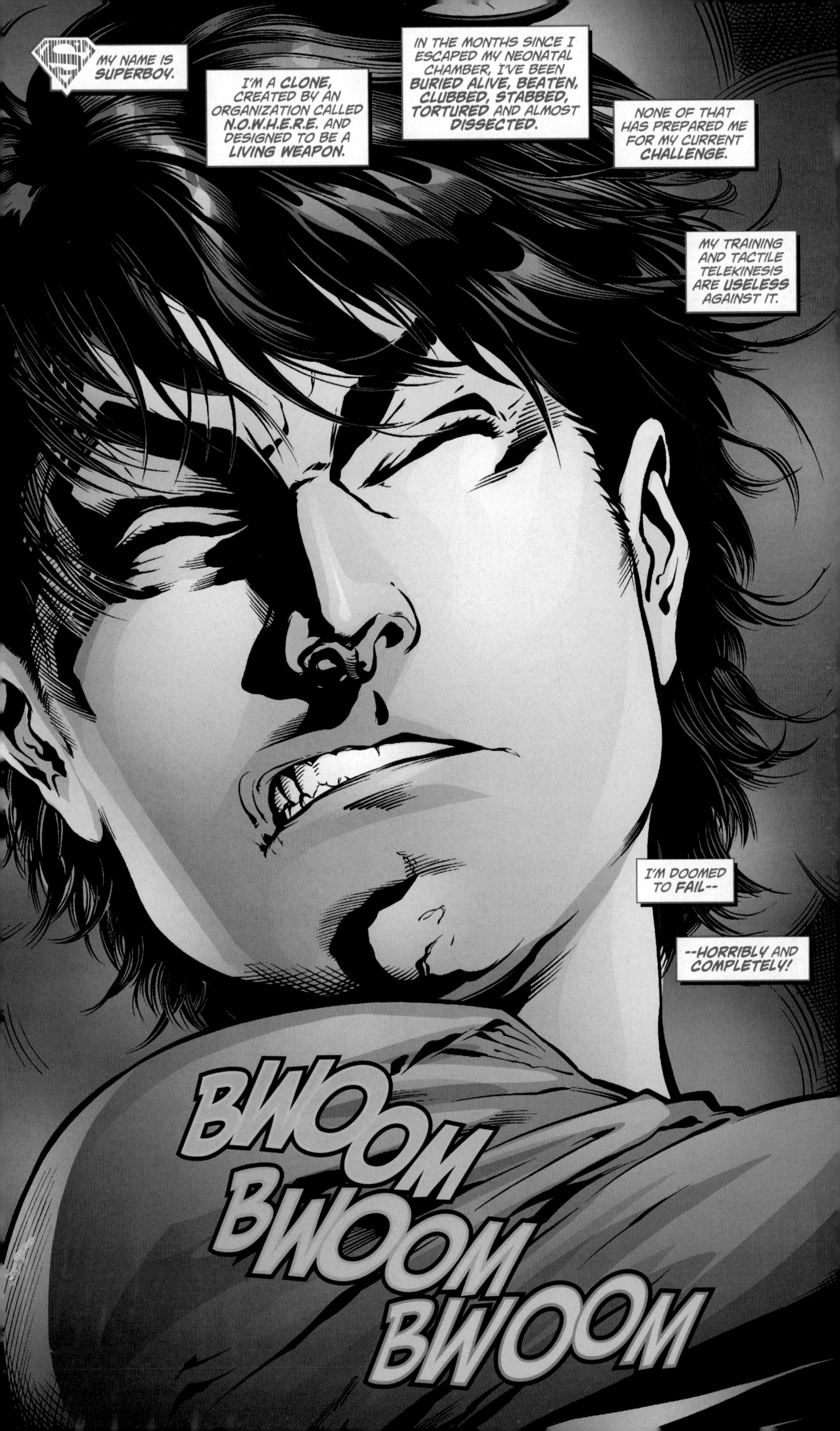
MY NAME IS SUPERBOY.
I'M A CLONE, CREATED BY AN ORGANIZATION CALLED N.O.W.H.E.R.E. AND DESIGNED TO BE A LIVING WEAPON.
IN THE MONTHS SINCE I ESCAPED MY NEONATAL CHAMBER, I'VE BEEN BURIED ALIVE, BEATEN, CLUBBED, STABBED, TORTURED AND ALMOST DISSECTED.
NONE OF THAT HAS PREPARED ME FOR MY CURRENT CHALLENGE.
MY TRAINING AND TACTILE TELEKINESIS ARE USELESS AGAINST IT.
I'M DOOMED TO FAIL--
--HORRIBLY AND COMPLETELY!
BWOOM
BWOOM
BWOOM

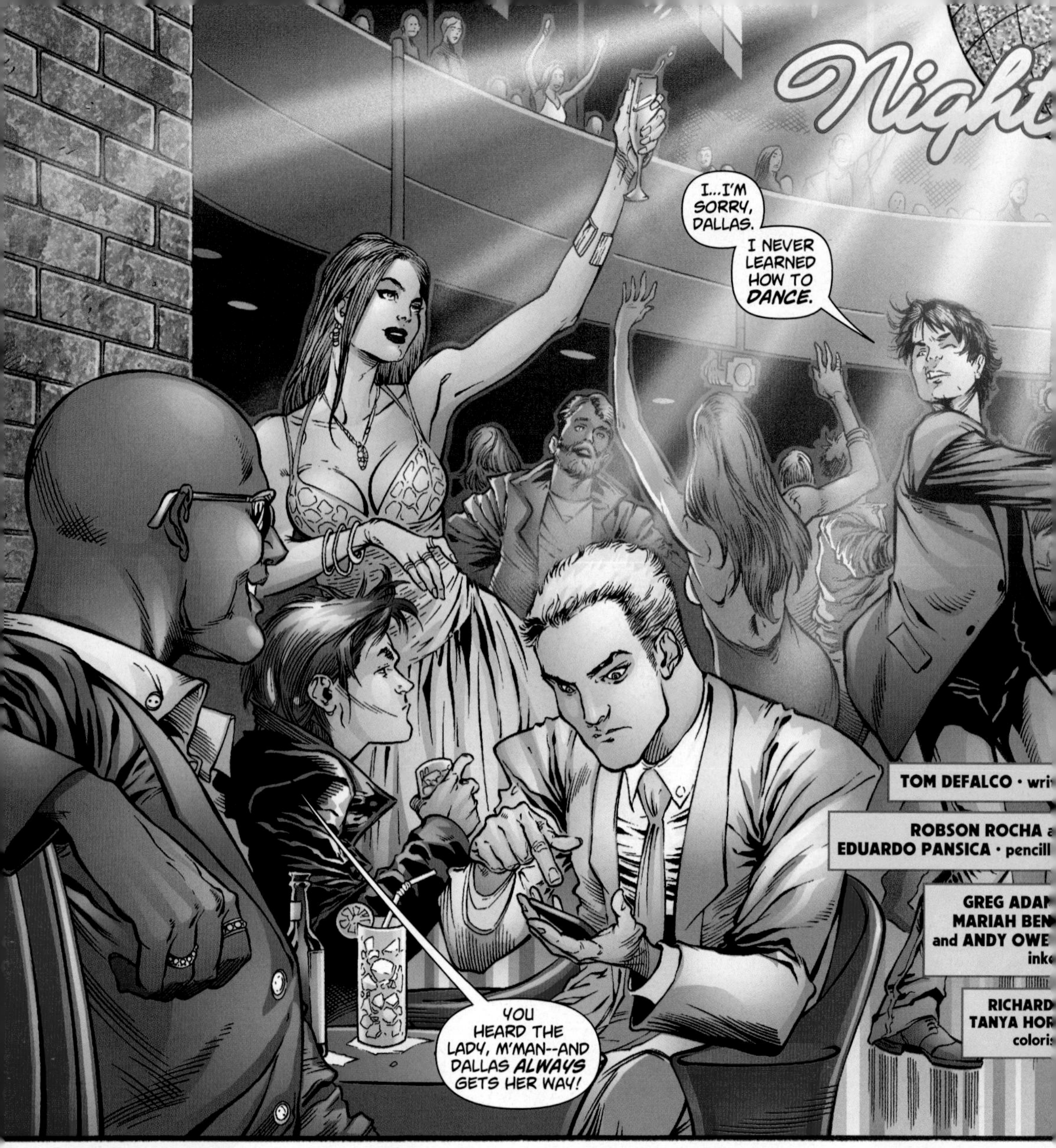
Night
I...I'M SORRY, DALLAS. I NEVER LEARNED HOW TO DANCE.
YOU HEARD THE LADY, M'MAN--AND DALLAS ALWAYS GETS HER WAY!
TOM DEFALCO • wri
ROBSON ROCHA a
EDUARDO PANSICA • pencil
GREG ADAM
MARIAH BEN
and ANDY OWE
ink
RICHARD
TANYA HOR
coloris

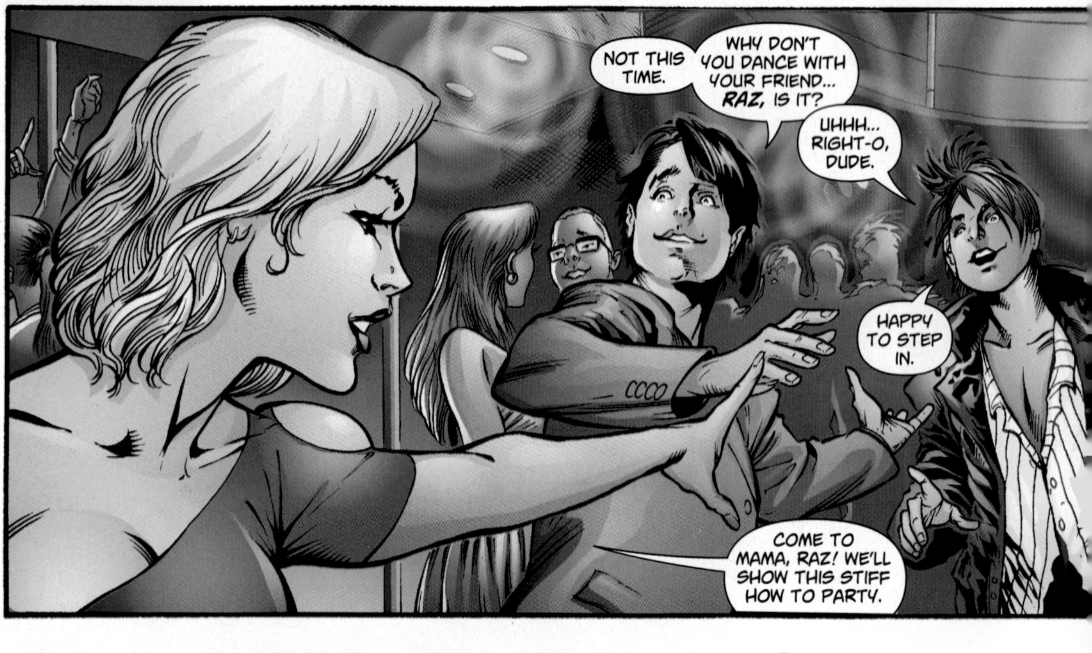
NOT THIS TIME.
WHY DON'T YOU DANCE WITH YOUR FRIEND... RAZ, IS IT?
UHHH... RIGHT-O, DUDE.
HAPPY TO STEP IN.
COME TO MAMA, RAZ! WE'LL SHOW THIS STIFF HOW TO PARTY.

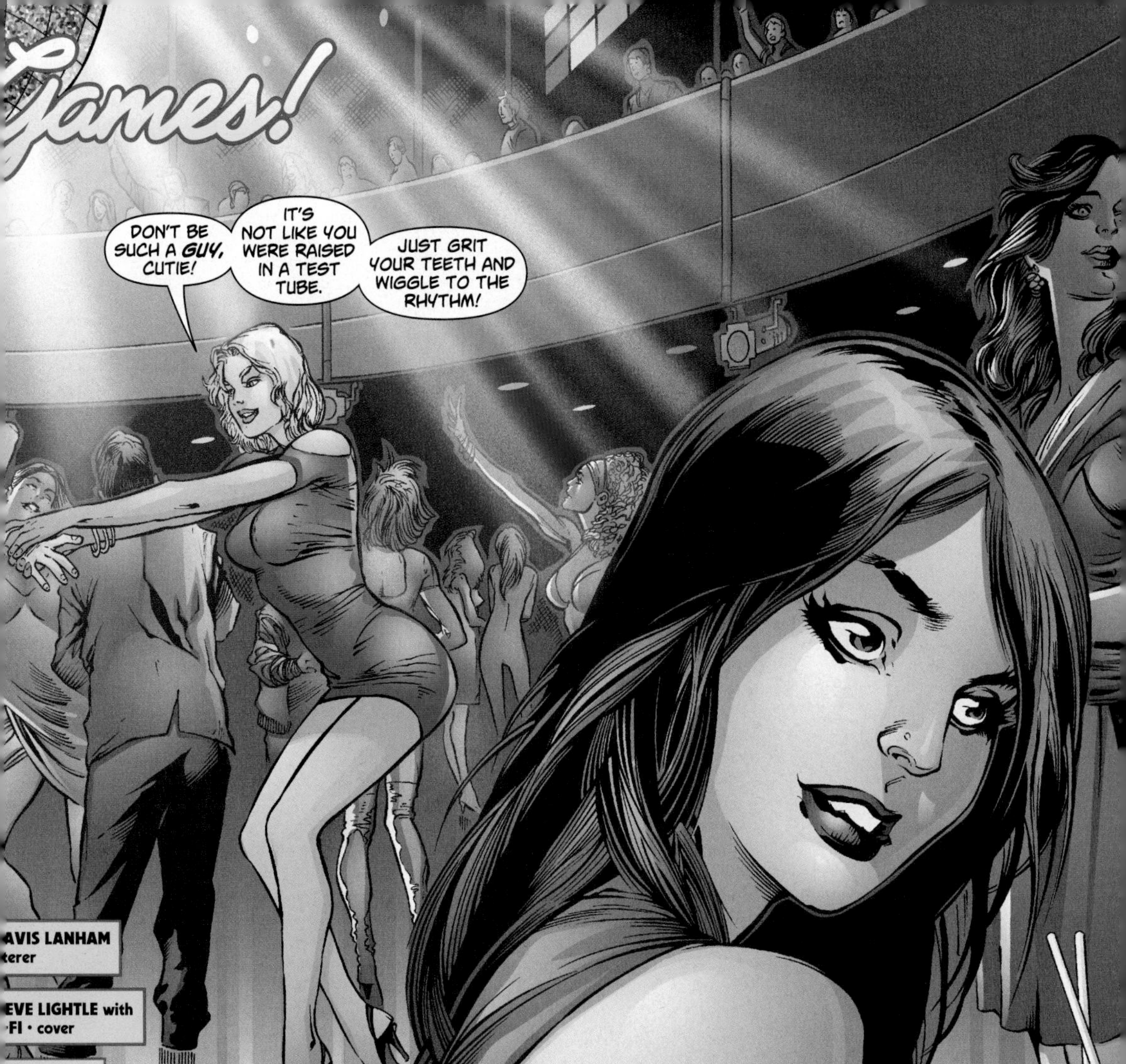

James!
DON'T BE SUCH A *GUY*, CUTIE!
IT'S NOT LIKE YOU WERE RAISED IN A TEST TUBE.
JUST GRIT YOUR TEETH AND WIGGLE TO THE RHYTHM!
AVIS LANHAM
terer
EVE LIGHTLE with
FI • cover
ecial thanks
RON FRENZ

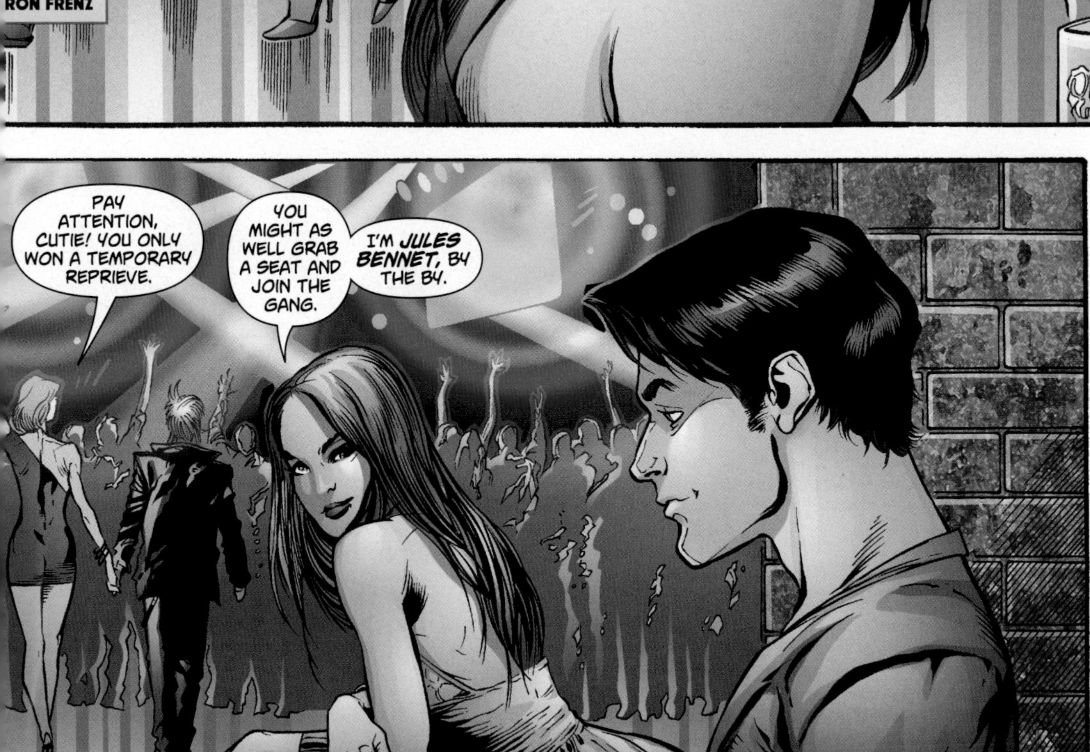

PAY ATTENTION, CUTIE! YOU ONLY WON A TEMPORARY REPRIEVE.
YOU MIGHT AS WELL GRAB A SEAT AND JOIN THE GANG.
I'M *JULES BENNET*, BY THE BY.

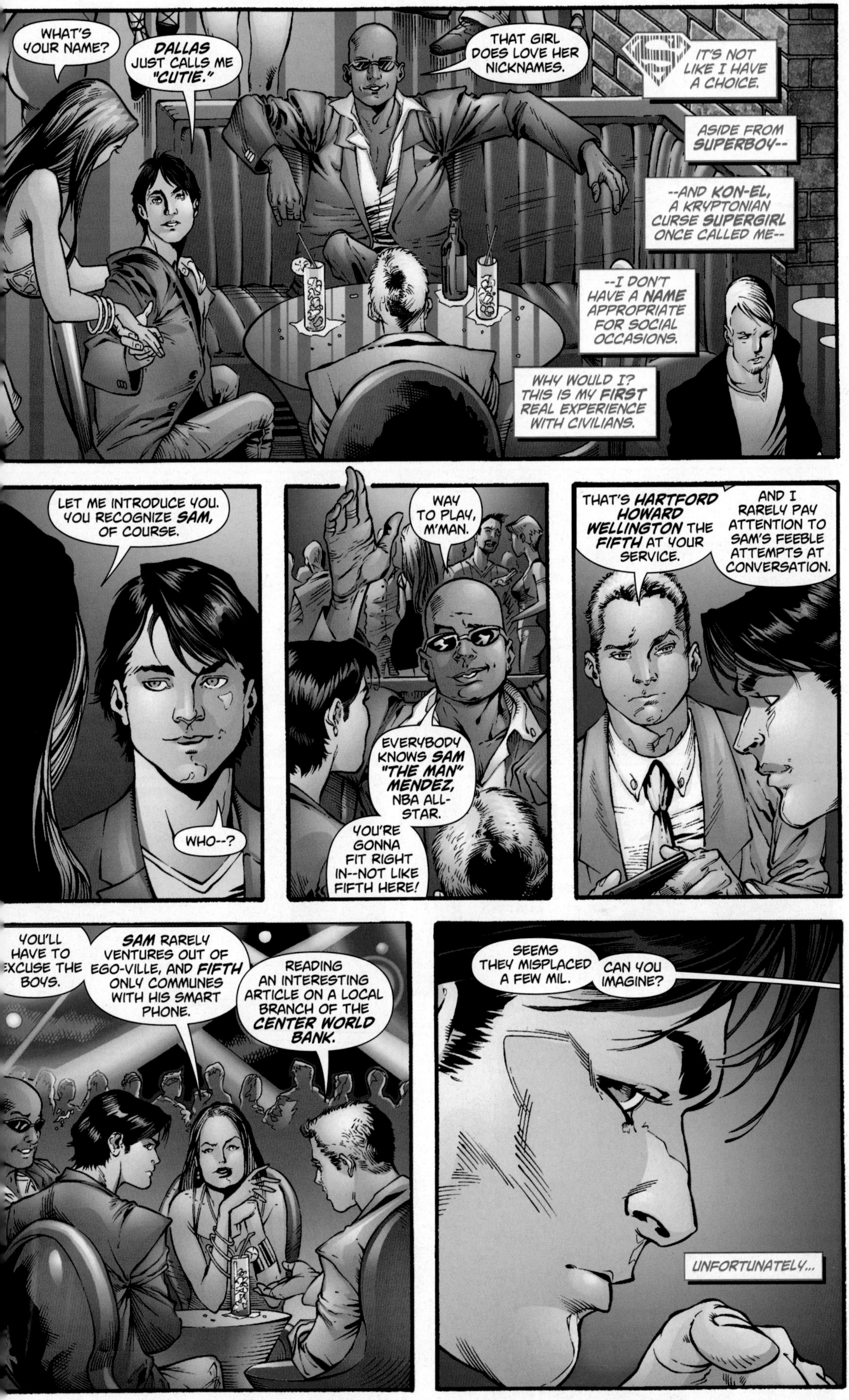
WHAT'S YOUR NAME?
DALLAS JUST CALLS ME "CUTIE."
THAT GIRL DOES LOVE HER NICKNAMES.
IT'S NOT LIKE I HAVE A CHOICE.
ASIDE FROM SUPERBOY--
--AND KON-EL, A KRYPTONIAN CURSE SUPERGIRL ONCE CALLED ME--
--I DON'T HAVE A NAME APPROPRIATE FOR SOCIAL OCCASIONS.
WHY WOULD I? THIS IS MY FIRST REAL EXPERIENCE WITH CIVILIANS.
LET ME INTRODUCE YOU. YOU RECOGNIZE SAM, OF COURSE.
WHO--?
WAY TO PLAY, M'MAN.
EVERYBODY KNOWS SAM "THE MAN" MENDEZ, NBA ALL-STAR.
YOU'RE GONNA FIT RIGHT IN--NOT LIKE FIFTH HERE!
THAT'S HARTFORD HOWARD WELLINGTON THE FIFTH AT YOUR SERVICE.
AND I RARELY PAY ATTENTION TO SAM'S FEEBLE ATTEMPTS AT CONVERSATION.
YOU'LL HAVE TO EXCUSE THE BOYS.
SAM RARELY VENTURES OUT OF EGO-VILLE, AND FIFTH ONLY COMMUNES WITH HIS SMART PHONE.
READING AN INTERESTING ARTICLE ON A LOCAL BRANCH OF THE CENTER WORLD BANK.
SEEMS THEY MISPLACED A FEW MIL.
CAN YOU IMAGINE?
UNFORTUNATELY...

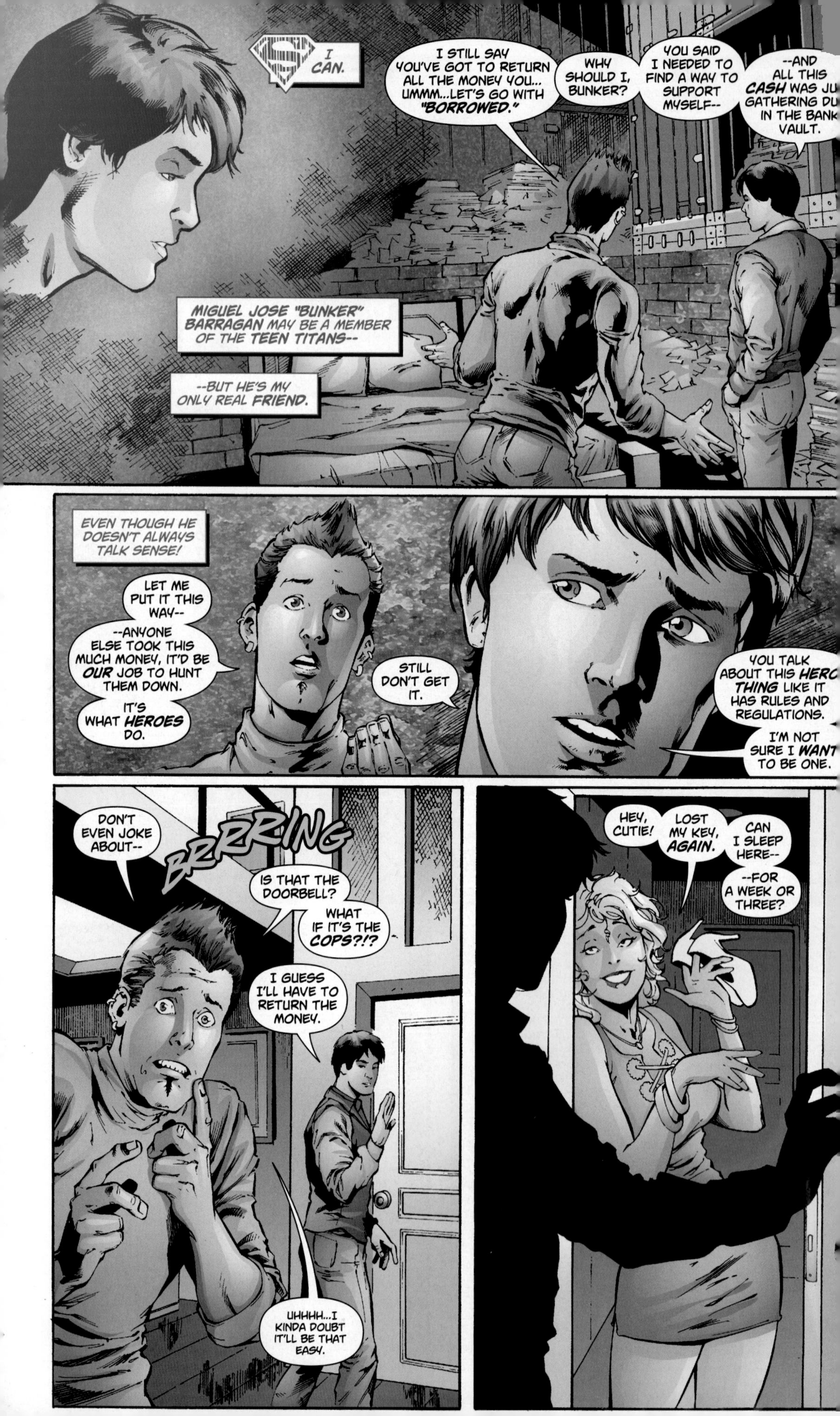
I CAN.
I STILL SAY YOU'VE GOT TO RETURN ALL THE MONEY YOU... UMMM...LET'S GO WITH "BORROWED."
WHY SHOULD I, BUNKER?
YOU SAID I NEEDED TO FIND A WAY TO SUPPORT MYSELF--
--AND ALL THIS CASH WAS JU GATHERING DU IN THE BANK VAULT.
MIGUEL JOSE "BUNKER" BARRAGAN MAY BE A MEMBER OF THE TEEN TITANS--
--BUT HE'S MY ONLY REAL FRIEND.
EVEN THOUGH HE DOESN'T ALWAYS TALK SENSE!
LET ME PUT IT THIS WAY--
--ANYONE ELSE TOOK THIS MUCH MONEY, IT'D BE OUR JOB TO HUNT THEM DOWN.
IT'S WHAT HEROES DO.
STILL DON'T GET IT.
YOU TALK ABOUT THIS HERO THING LIKE IT HAS RULES AND REGULATIONS.
I'M NOT SURE I WANT TO BE ONE.
DON'T EVEN JOKE ABOUT--
BRRRING
IS THAT THE DOORBELL?
WHAT IF IT'S THE COPS?!?
I GUESS I'LL HAVE TO RETURN THE MONEY.
UHHHH...I KINDA DOUBT IT'LL BE THAT EASY.
HEY, CUTIE!
LOST MY KEY, AGAIN.
CAN I SLEEP HERE--
--FOR A WEEK OR THREE?

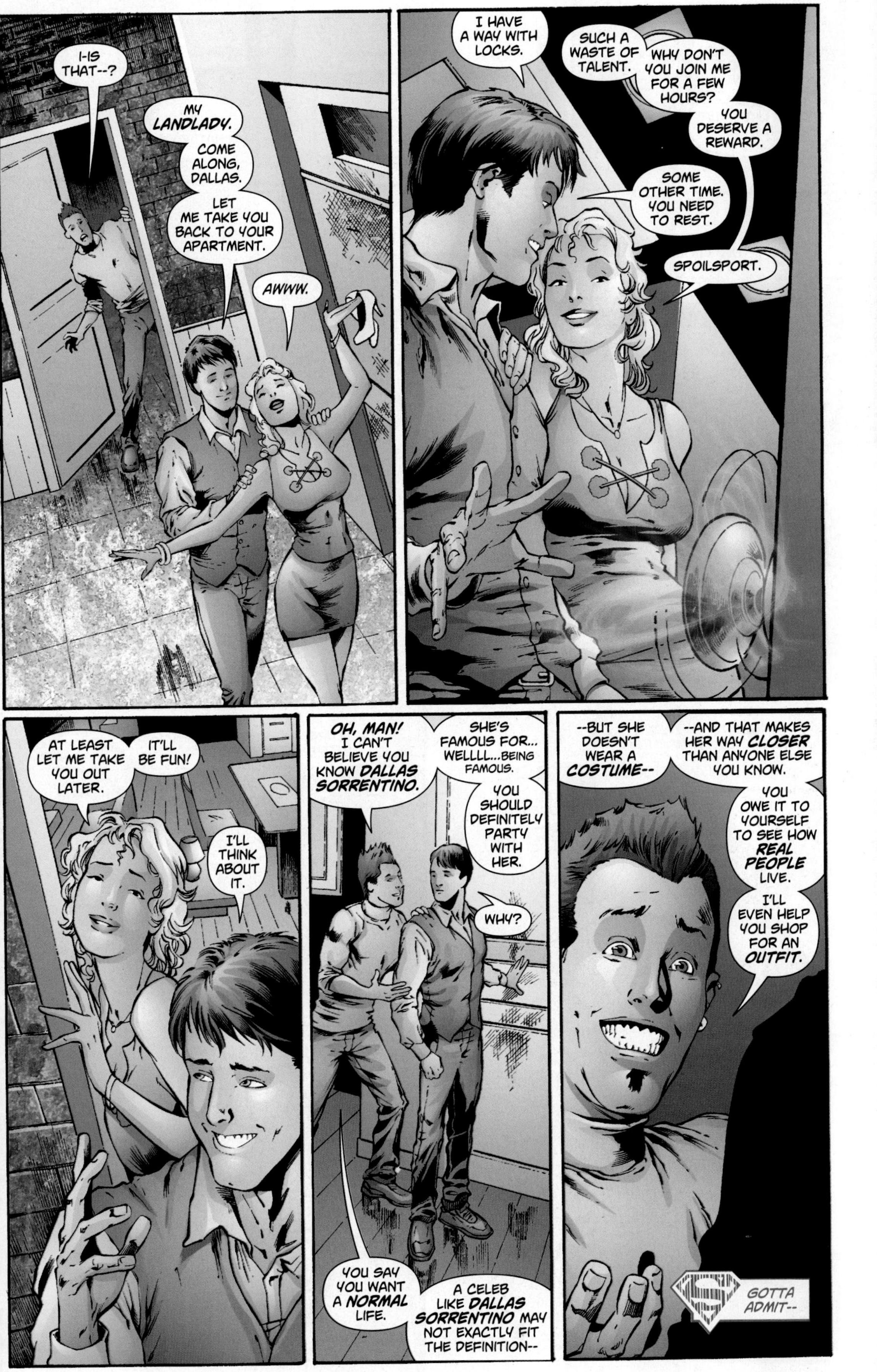
I-IS THAT--?
MY LANDLADY.
COME ALONG, DALLAS.
LET ME TAKE YOU BACK TO YOUR APARTMENT.
AWWW.
I HAVE A WAY WITH LOCKS.
SUCH A WASTE OF TALENT.
WHY DON'T YOU JOIN ME FOR A FEW HOURS?
YOU DESERVE A REWARD.
SOME OTHER TIME. YOU NEED TO REST.
SPOILSPORT.
AT LEAST LET ME TAKE YOU OUT LATER.
IT'LL BE FUN!
I'LL THINK ABOUT IT.
OH, MAN! I CAN'T BELIEVE YOU KNOW DALLAS SORRENTINO.
SHE'S FAMOUS FOR... WELLLL...BEING FAMOUS.
YOU SHOULD DEFINITELY PARTY WITH HER.
WHY?
YOU SAY YOU WANT A NORMAL LIFE.
A CELEB LIKE DALLAS SORRENTINO MAY NOT EXACTLY FIT THE DEFINITION--
--BUT SHE DOESN'T WEAR A COSTUME--
--AND THAT MAKES HER WAY CLOSER THAN ANYONE ELSE YOU KNOW.
YOU OWE IT TO YOURSELF TO SEE HOW REAL PEOPLE LIVE.
I'LL EVEN HELP YOU SHOP FOR AN OUTFIT.
GOTTA ADMIT--

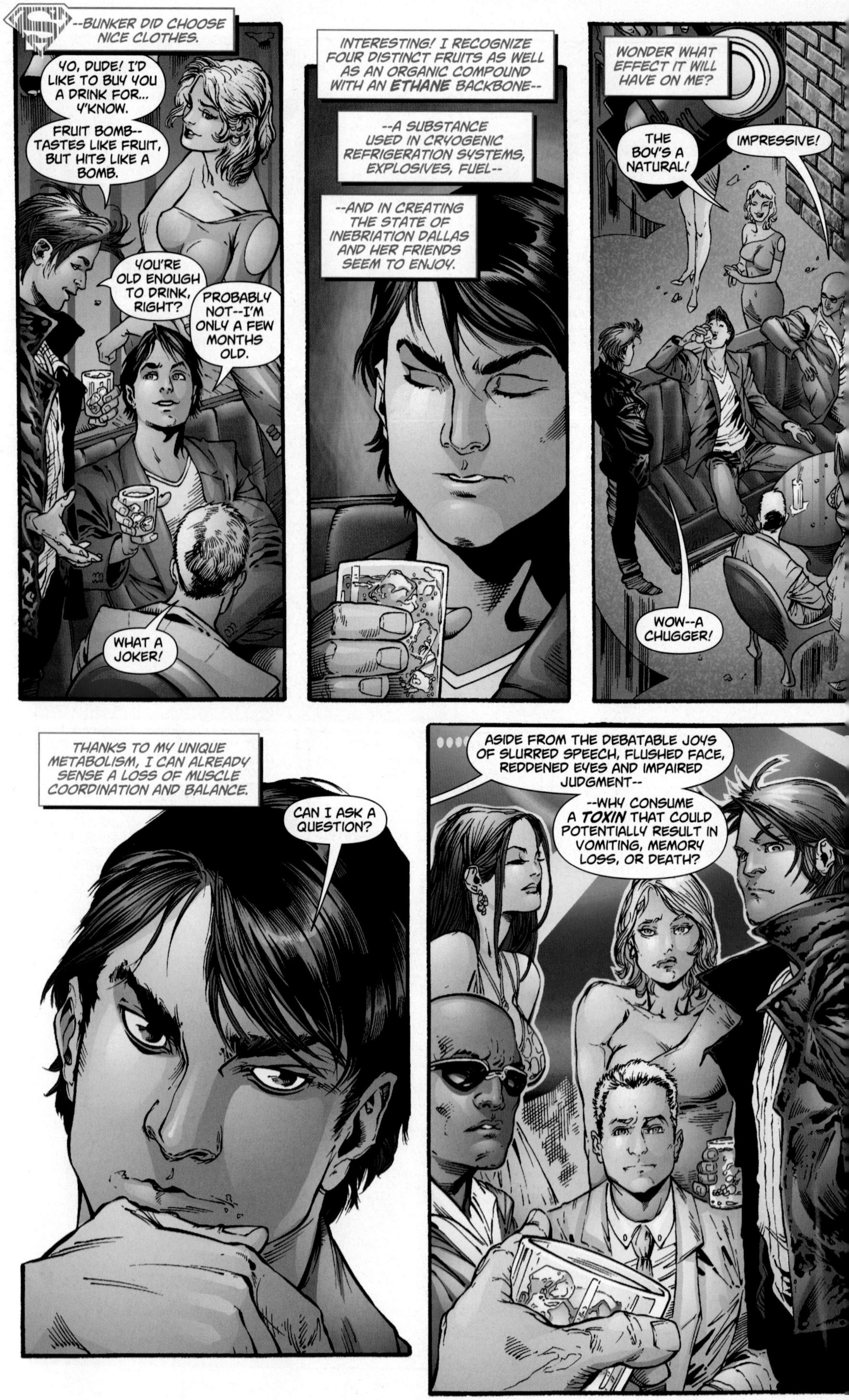
--BUNKER DID CHOOSE NICE CLOTHES.
YO, DUDE! I'D LIKE TO BUY YOU A DRINK FOR... Y'KNOW.
FRUIT BOMB--TASTES LIKE FRUIT, BUT HITS LIKE A BOMB.
YOU'RE OLD ENOUGH TO DRINK, RIGHT?
PROBABLY NOT--I'M ONLY A FEW MONTHS OLD.
WHAT A JOKER!
INTERESTING! I RECOGNIZE FOUR DISTINCT FRUITS AS WELL AS AN ORGANIC COMPOUND WITH AN ETHANE BACKBONE--
--A SUBSTANCE USED IN CRYOGENIC REFRIGERATION SYSTEMS, EXPLOSIVES, FUEL--
--AND IN CREATING THE STATE OF INEBRIATION DALLAS AND HER FRIENDS SEEM TO ENJOY.
WONDER WHAT EFFECT IT WILL HAVE ON ME?
THE BOY'S A NATURAL!
IMPRESSIVE!
WOW--A CHUGGER!
THANKS TO MY UNIQUE METABOLISM, I CAN ALREADY SENSE A LOSS OF MUSCLE COORDINATION AND BALANCE.
CAN I ASK A QUESTION?
ASIDE FROM THE DEBATABLE JOYS OF SLURRED SPEECH, FLUSHED FACE, REDDENED EYES AND IMPAIRED JUDGMENT--
--WHY CONSUME A TOXIN THAT COULD POTENTIALLY RESULT IN VOMITING, MEMORY LOSS, OR DEATH?

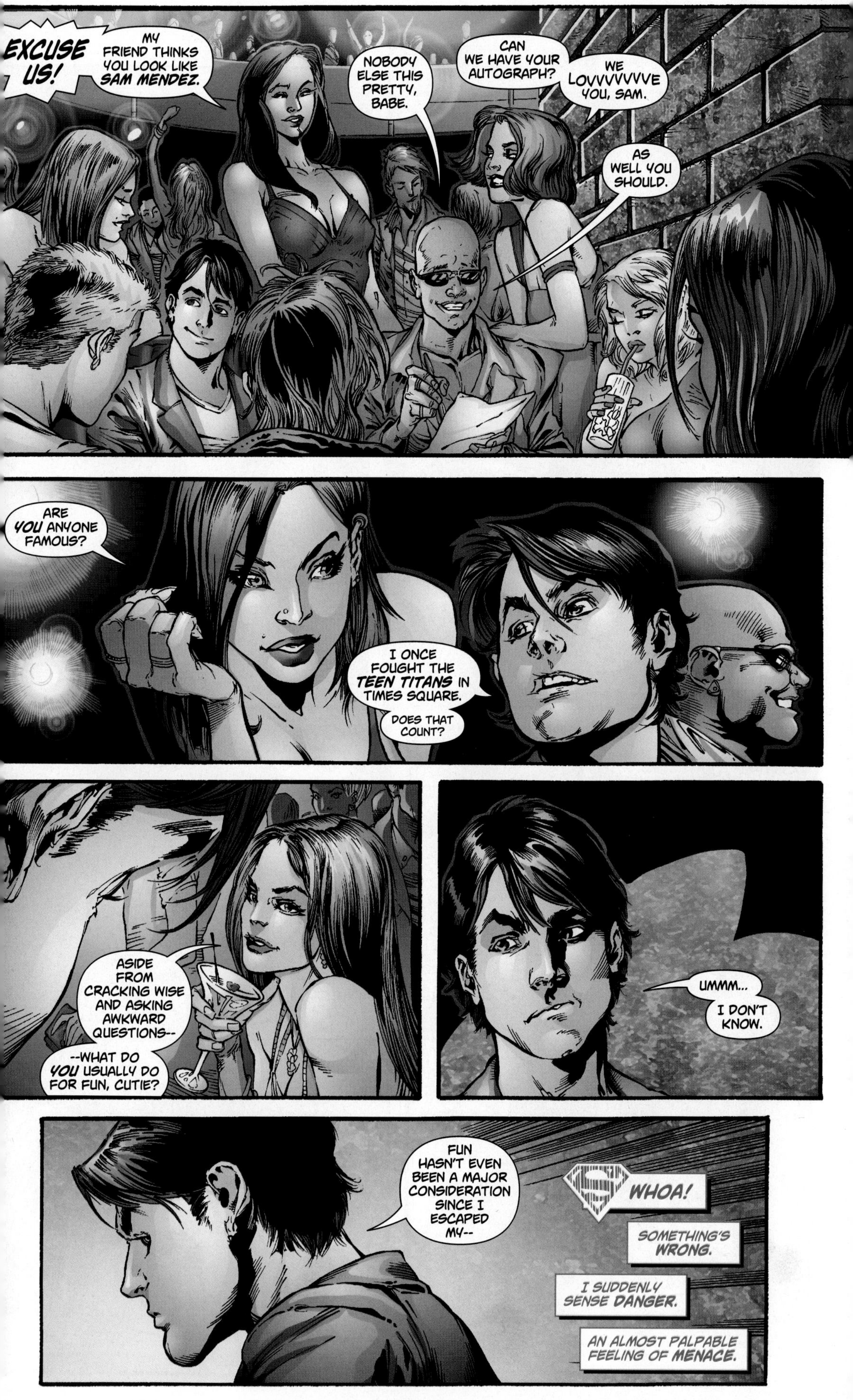
EXCUSE US!
MY FRIEND THINKS YOU LOOK LIKE SAM MENDEZ.
NOBODY ELSE THIS PRETTY, BABE.
CAN WE HAVE YOUR AUTOGRAPH?
WE LOVVVVVVVE YOU, SAM.
AS WELL YOU SHOULD.
ARE YOU ANYONE FAMOUS?
I ONCE FOUGHT THE TEEN TITANS IN TIMES SQUARE.
DOES THAT COUNT?
ASIDE FROM CRACKING WISE AND ASKING AWKWARD QUESTIONS--
--WHAT DO YOU USUALLY DO FOR FUN, CUTIE?
UMMM... I DON'T KNOW.
FUN HASN'T EVEN BEEN A MAJOR CONSIDERATION SINCE I ESCAPED MY--
WHOA!
SOMETHING'S WRONG.
I SUDDENLY SENSE DANGER.
AN ALMOST PALPABLE FEELING OF MENACE.

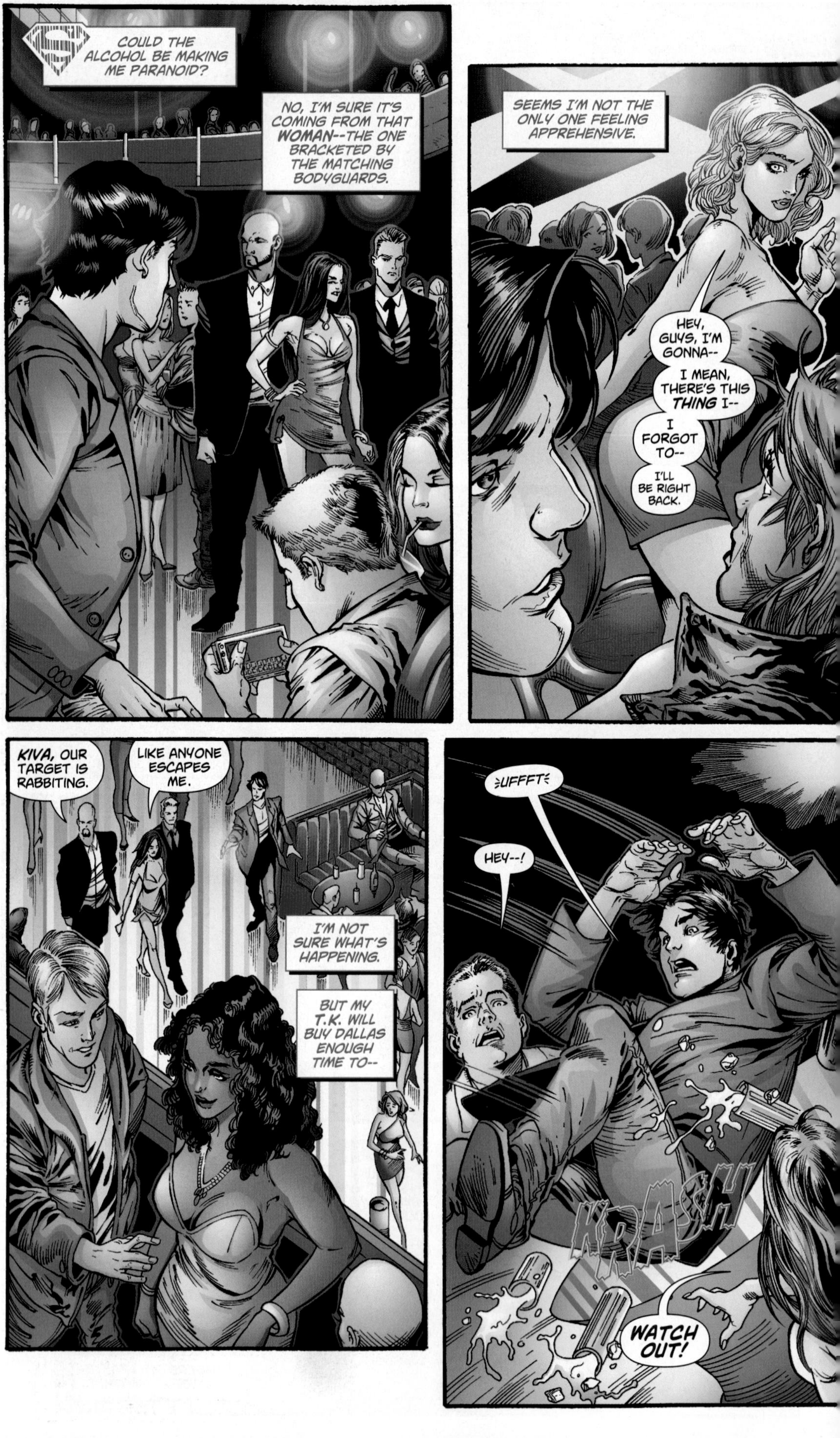

COULD THE ALCOHOL BE MAKING ME PARANOID?
NO, I'M SURE IT'S COMING FROM THAT WOMAN--THE ONE BRACKETED BY THE MATCHING BODYGUARDS.
SEEMS I'M NOT THE ONLY ONE FEELING APPREHENSIVE.
HEY, GUYS, I'M GONNA--
I MEAN, THERE'S THIS THING I--
I FORGOT TO--
I'LL BE RIGHT BACK.
KIVA, OUR TARGET IS RABBITING.
LIKE ANYONE ESCAPES ME.
I'M NOT SURE WHAT'S HAPPENING.
BUT MY T.K. WILL BUY DALLAS ENOUGH TIME TO--
UFFFT
HEY--!
KRASH
WATCH OUT!

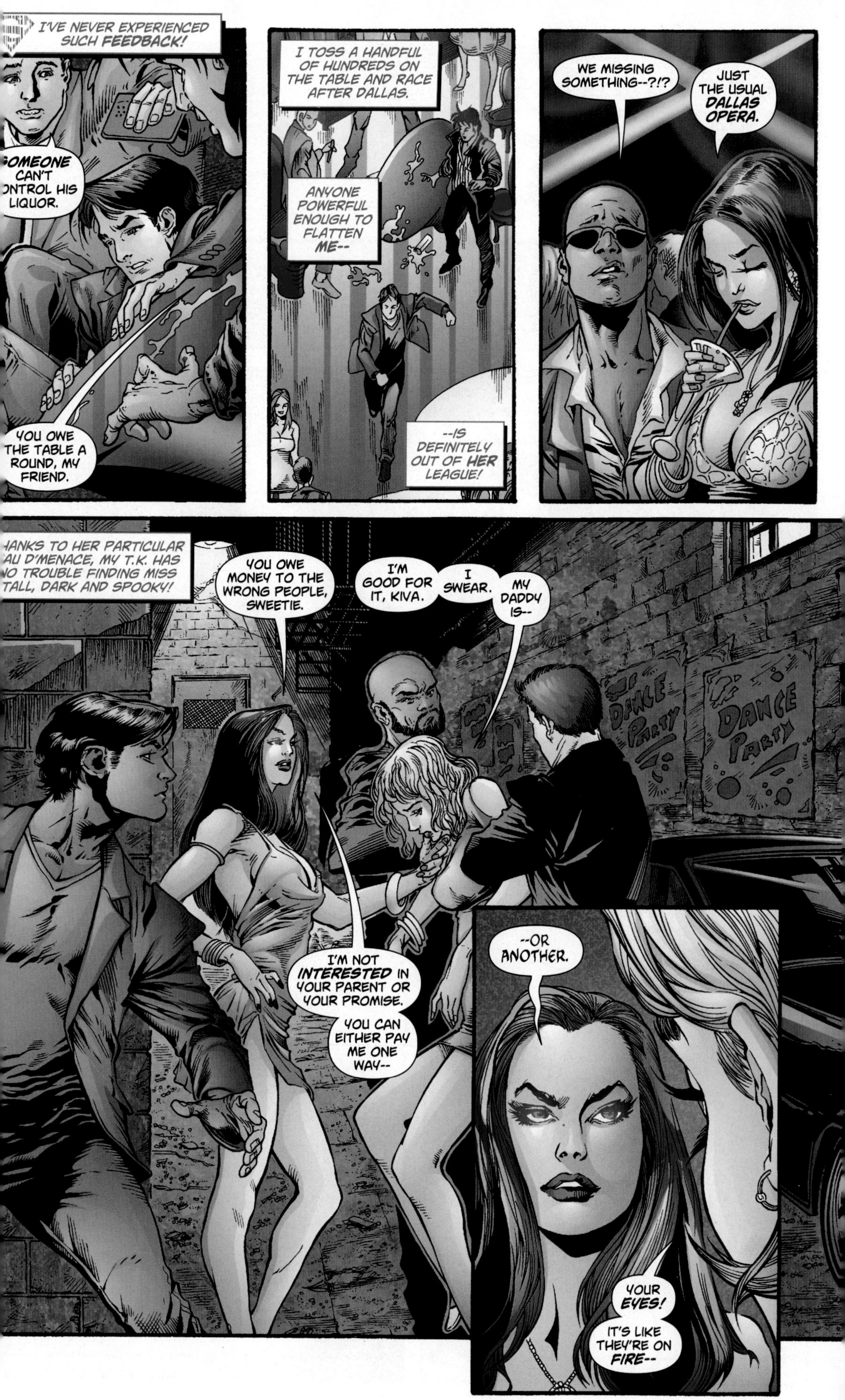

I'VE NEVER EXPERIENCED SUCH FEEDBACK!
SOMEONE CAN'T CONTROL HIS LIQUOR.
YOU OWE THE TABLE A ROUND, MY FRIEND.
I TOSS A HANDFUL OF HUNDREDS ON THE TABLE AND RACE AFTER DALLAS.
ANYONE POWERFUL ENOUGH TO FLATTEN ME--
--IS DEFINITELY OUT OF HER LEAGUE!
WE MISSING SOMETHING--?!?
JUST THE USUAL DALLAS OPERA.
HANKS TO HER PARTICULAR AU D'MENACE, MY T.K. HAS NO TROUBLE FINDING MISS TALL, DARK AND SPOOKY!
YOU OWE MONEY TO THE WRONG PEOPLE, SWEETIE.
I'M GOOD FOR IT, KIVA.
I SWEAR.
MY DADDY IS--
I'M NOT INTERESTED IN YOUR PARENT OR YOUR PROMISE.
YOU CAN EITHER PAY ME ONE WAY--
--OR ANOTHER.
YOUR EYES!
IT'S LIKE THEY'RE ON FIRE--

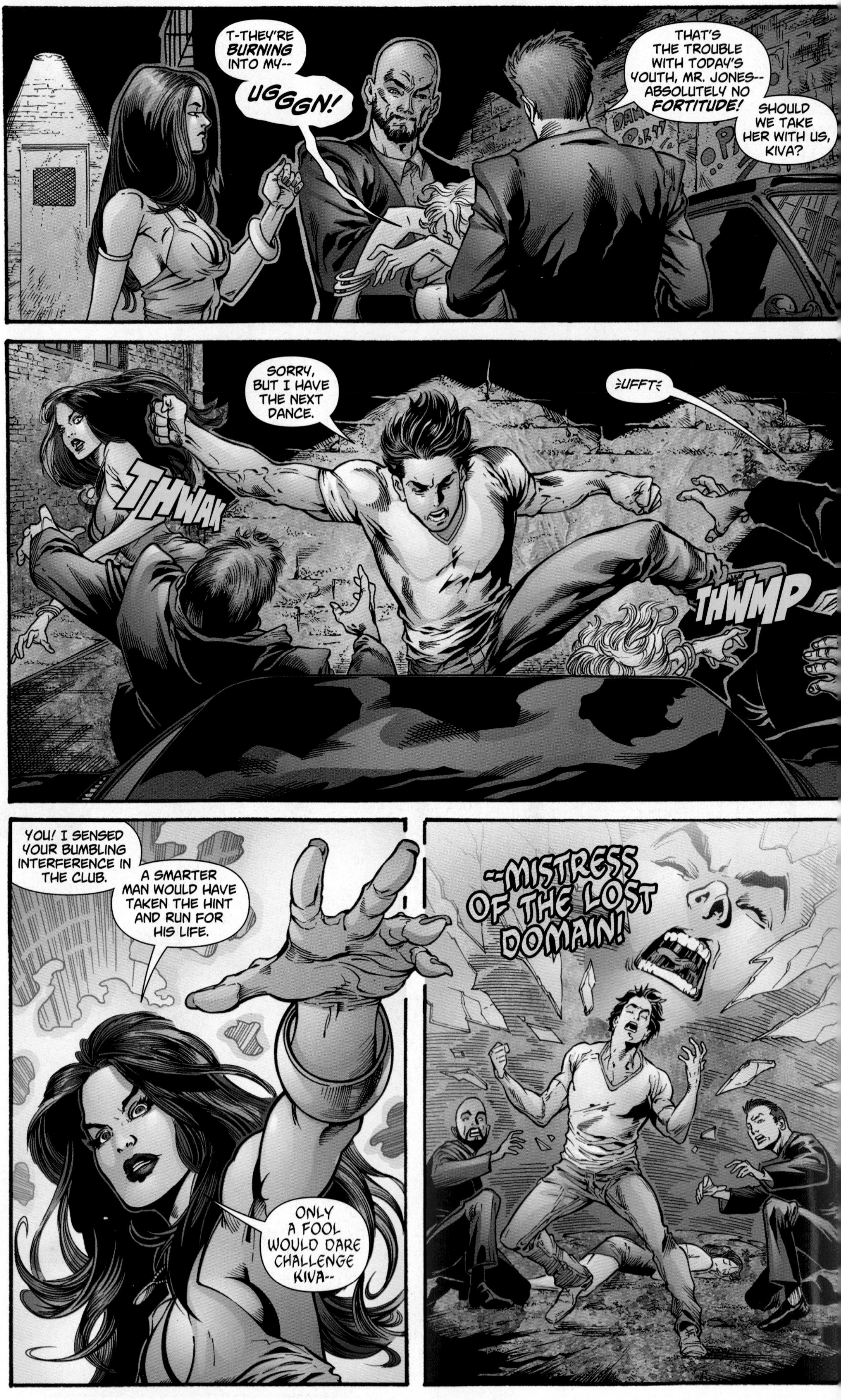

T-THEY'RE BURNING INTO MY--
UGGGN!
THAT'S THE TROUBLE WITH TODAY'S YOUTH, MR. JONES-- ABSOLUTELY NO FORTITUDE!
SHOULD WE TAKE HER WITH US, KIVA?
SORRY, BUT I HAVE THE NEXT DANCE.
UFFT
THWAK
THWMP
YOU! I SENSED YOUR BUMBLING INTERFERENCE IN THE CLUB.
A SMARTER MAN WOULD HAVE TAKEN THE HINT AND RUN FOR HIS LIFE.
ONLY A FOOL WOULD DARE CHALLENGE KIVA--
--MISTRESS OF THE LOST DOMAIN!

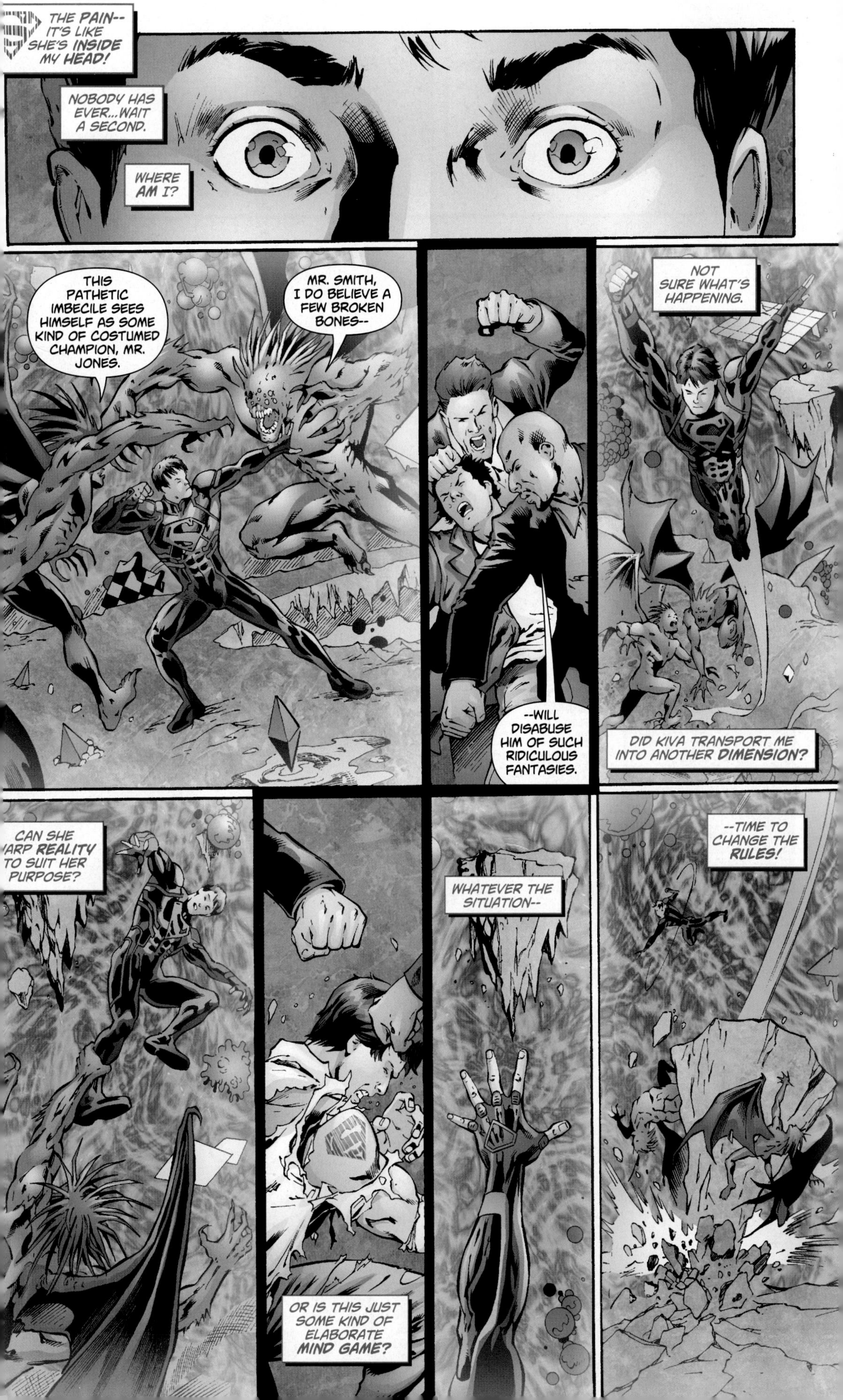
THE PAIN-- IT'S LIKE SHE'S INSIDE MY HEAD!
NOBODY HAS EVER...WAIT A SECOND.
WHERE AM I?
THIS PATHETIC IMBECILE SEES HIMSELF AS SOME KIND OF COSTUMED CHAMPION, MR. JONES.
MR. SMITH, I DO BELIEVE A FEW BROKEN BONES--
--WILL DISABUSE HIM OF SUCH RIDICULOUS FANTASIES.
NOT SURE WHAT'S HAPPENING.
DID KIVA TRANSPORT ME INTO ANOTHER DIMENSION?
CAN SHE WARP REALITY TO SUIT HER PURPOSE?
OR IS THIS JUST SOME KIND OF ELABORATE MIND GAME?
WHATEVER THE SITUATION--
--TIME TO CHANGE THE RULES!

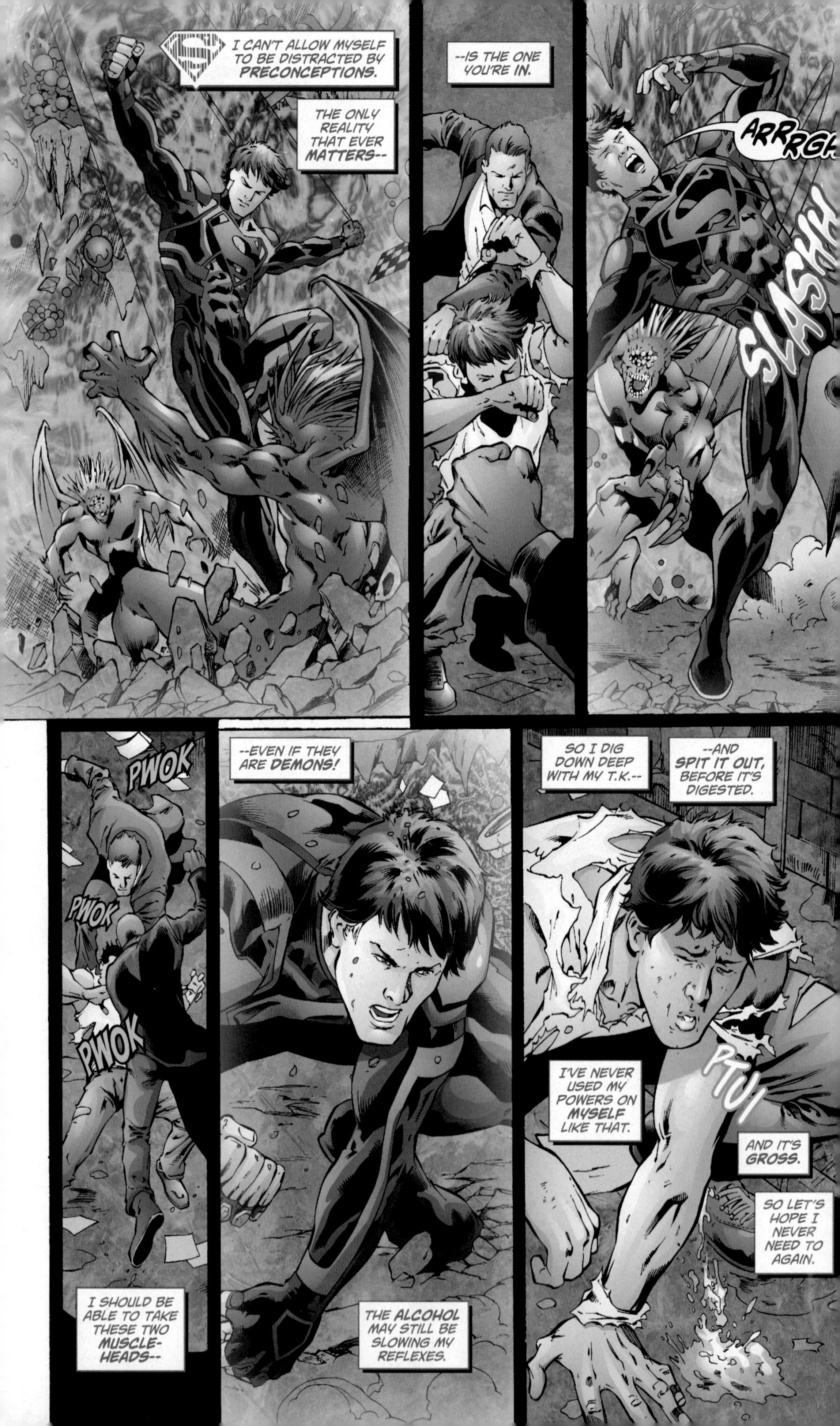

I CAN'T ALLOW MYSELF TO BE DISTRACTED BY PRECONCEPTIONS.
THE ONLY REALITY THAT EVER MATTERS--
--IS THE ONE YOU'RE IN.
ARRRGH
SLASHH
PWOK
PWOK
PWOK
I SHOULD BE ABLE TO TAKE THESE TWO MUSCLE-HEADS--
--EVEN IF THEY ARE DEMONS!
THE ALCOHOL MAY STILL BE SLOWING MY REFLEXES.
SO I DIG DOWN DEEP WITH MY T.K.--
--AND SPIT IT OUT, BEFORE IT'S DIGESTED.
PTUI
I'VE NEVER USED MY POWERS ON MYSELF LIKE THAT.
AND IT'S GROSS.
SO LET'S HOPE I NEVER NEED TO AGAIN.

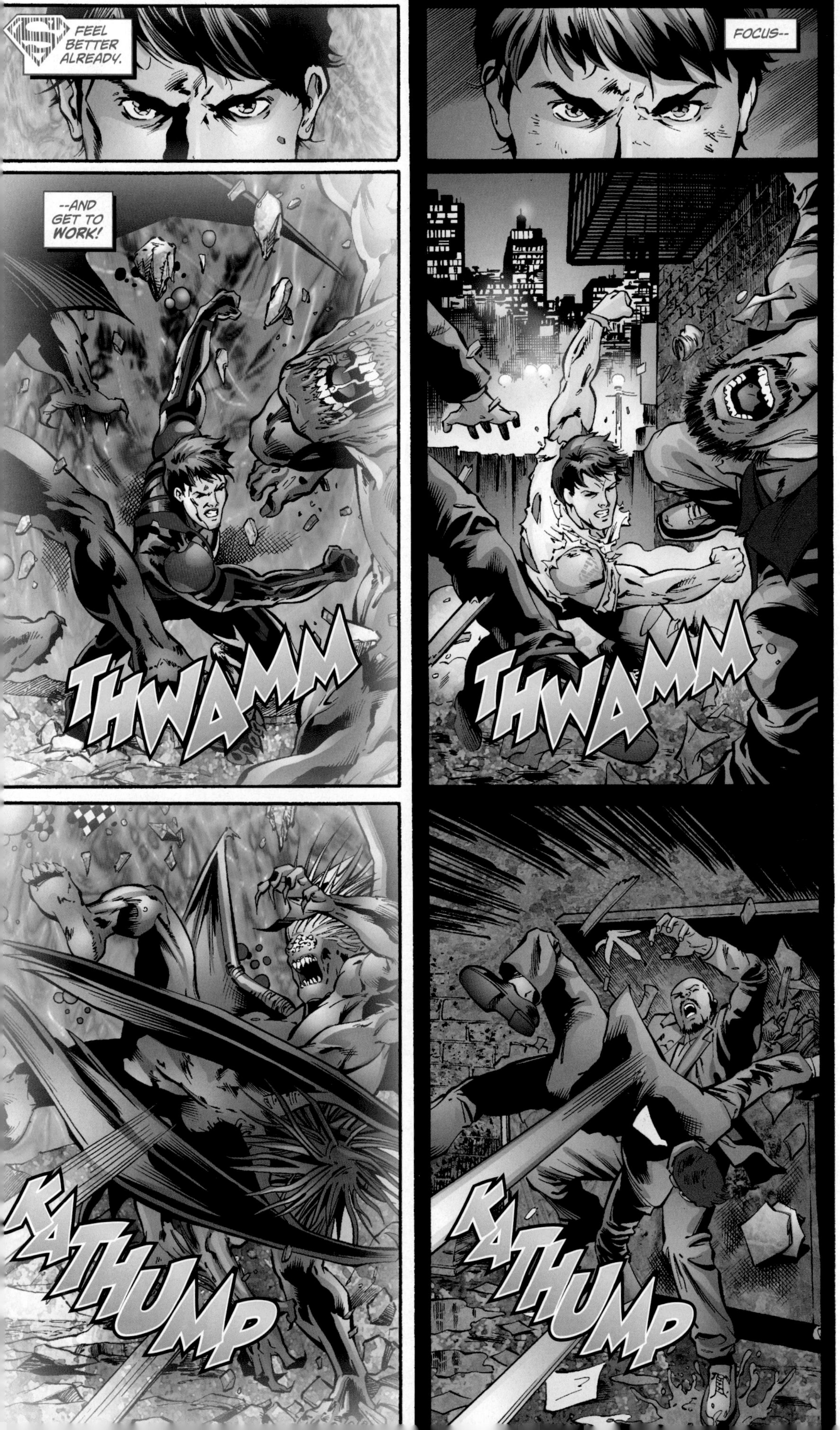
FEEL BETTER ALREADY.
FOCUS--
--AND GET TO WORK!
THWAMM
THWAMM
KATHUMP
KATHUMP

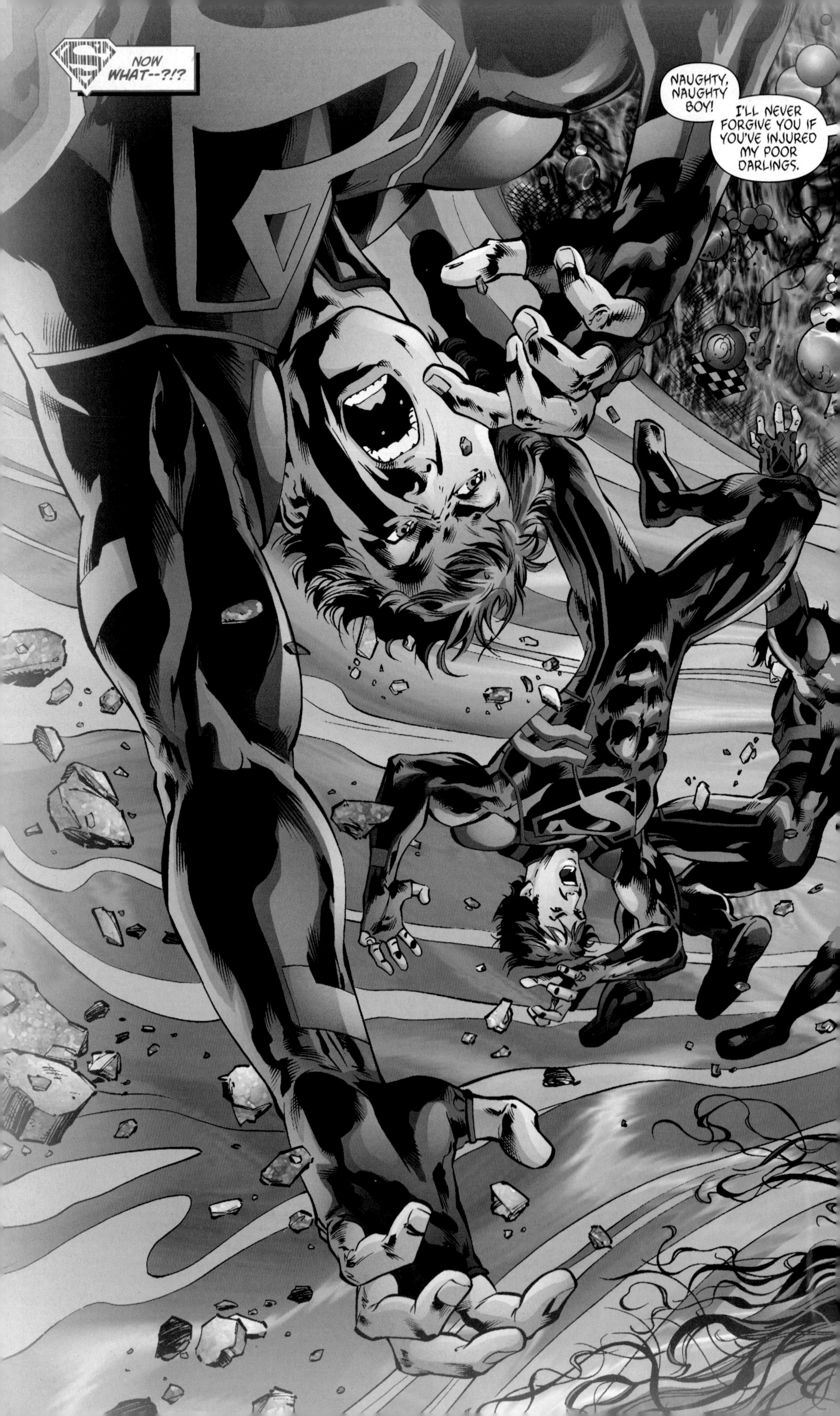
NOW WHAT--?!?
NAUGHTY, NAUGHTY BOY!
I'LL NEVER FORGIVE YOU IF YOU'VE INJURED MY POOR DARLINGS.

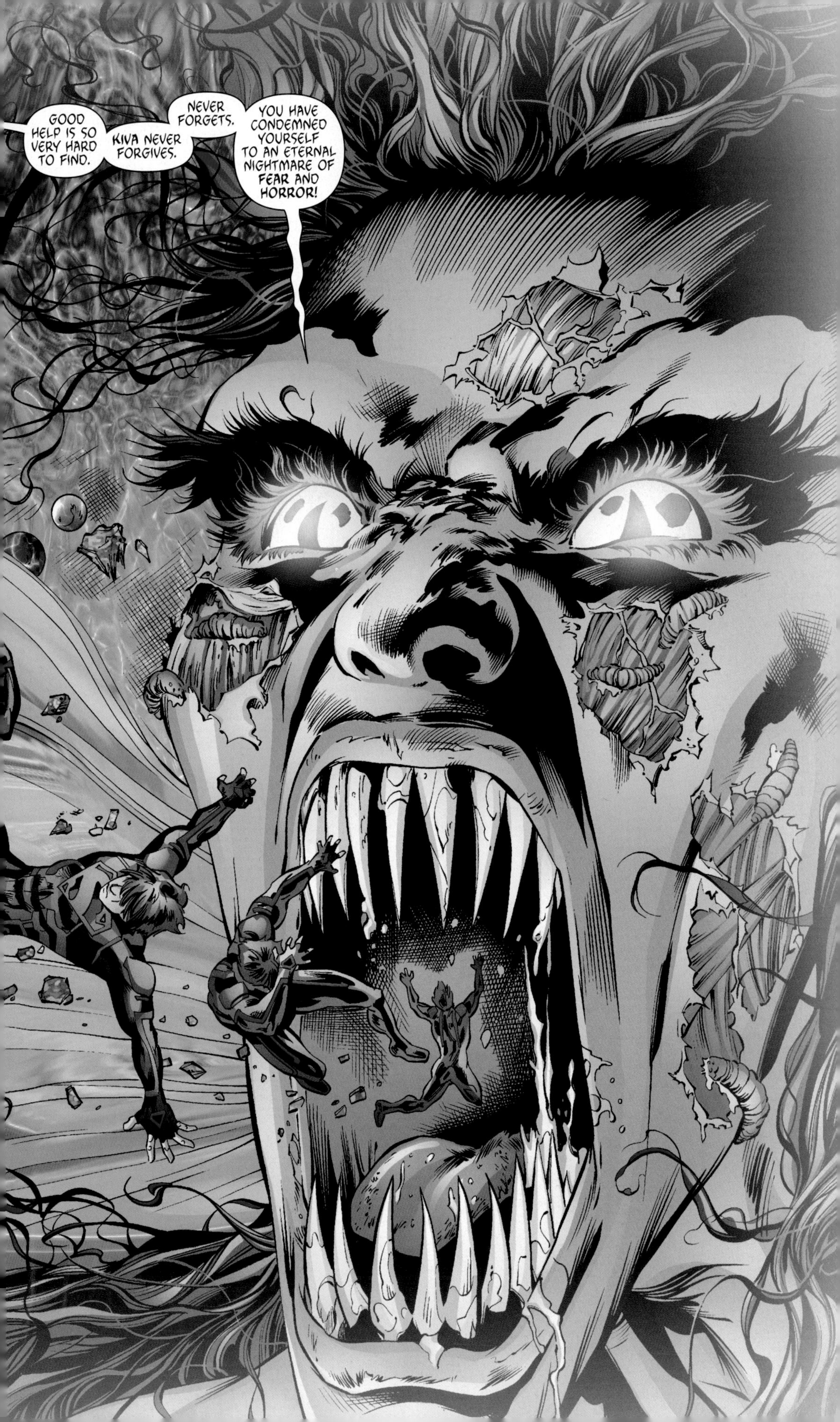
GOOD HELP IS SO VERY HARD TO FIND.
KIVA NEVER FORGIVES.
NEVER FORGETS.
YOU HAVE CONDEMNED YOURSELF TO AN ETERNAL NIGHTMARE OF FEAR AND HORROR!

THE PRESSURE--THE PAIN--IT SEEMS TO BE GROWING EXPONENTIALLY.

WHAT IS SHE DOING TO ME?!?

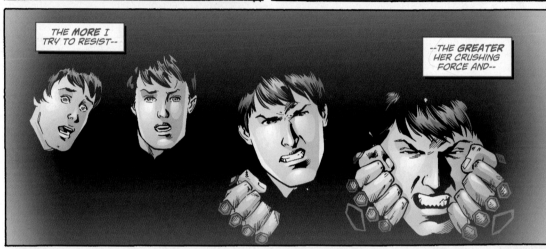

THE MORE I TRY TO RESIST--

--THE GREATER HER CRUSHING FORCE AND--

THAT'S IT!

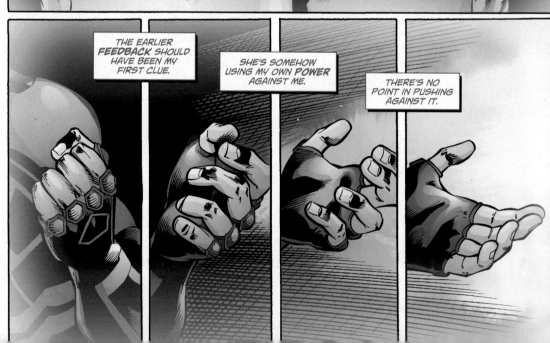

THE EARLIER FEEDBACK SHOULD HAVE BEEN MY FIRST CLUE.

SHE'S SOMEHOW USING MY OWN POWER AGAINST ME.

THERE'S NO POINT IN PUSHING AGAINST IT.

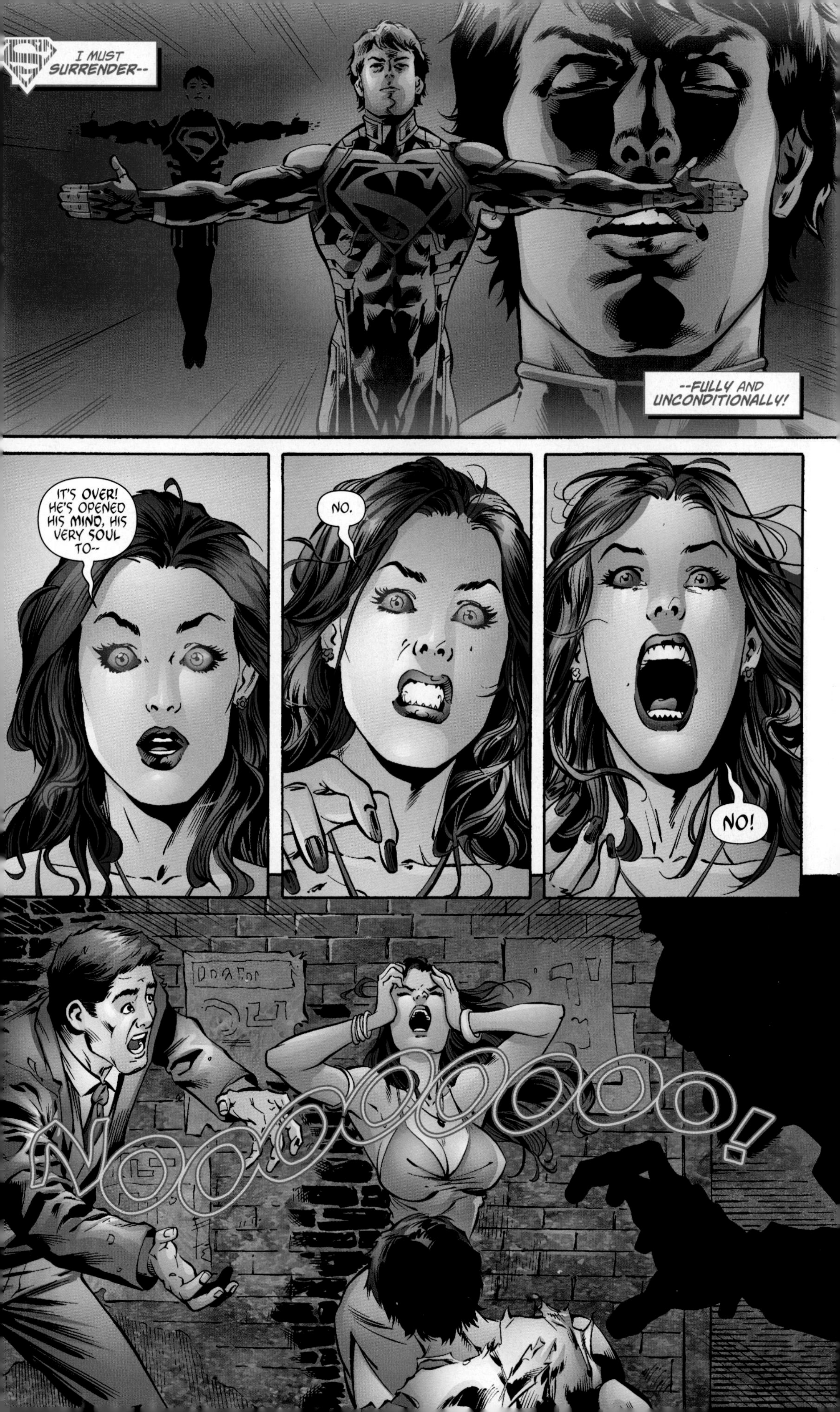

I MUST SURRENDER--
--FULLY AND UNCONDITIONALLY!
IT'S OVER! HE'S OPENED HIS MIND, HIS VERY SOUL TO--
NO.
NO!
NOOOOOOOOOOOO!

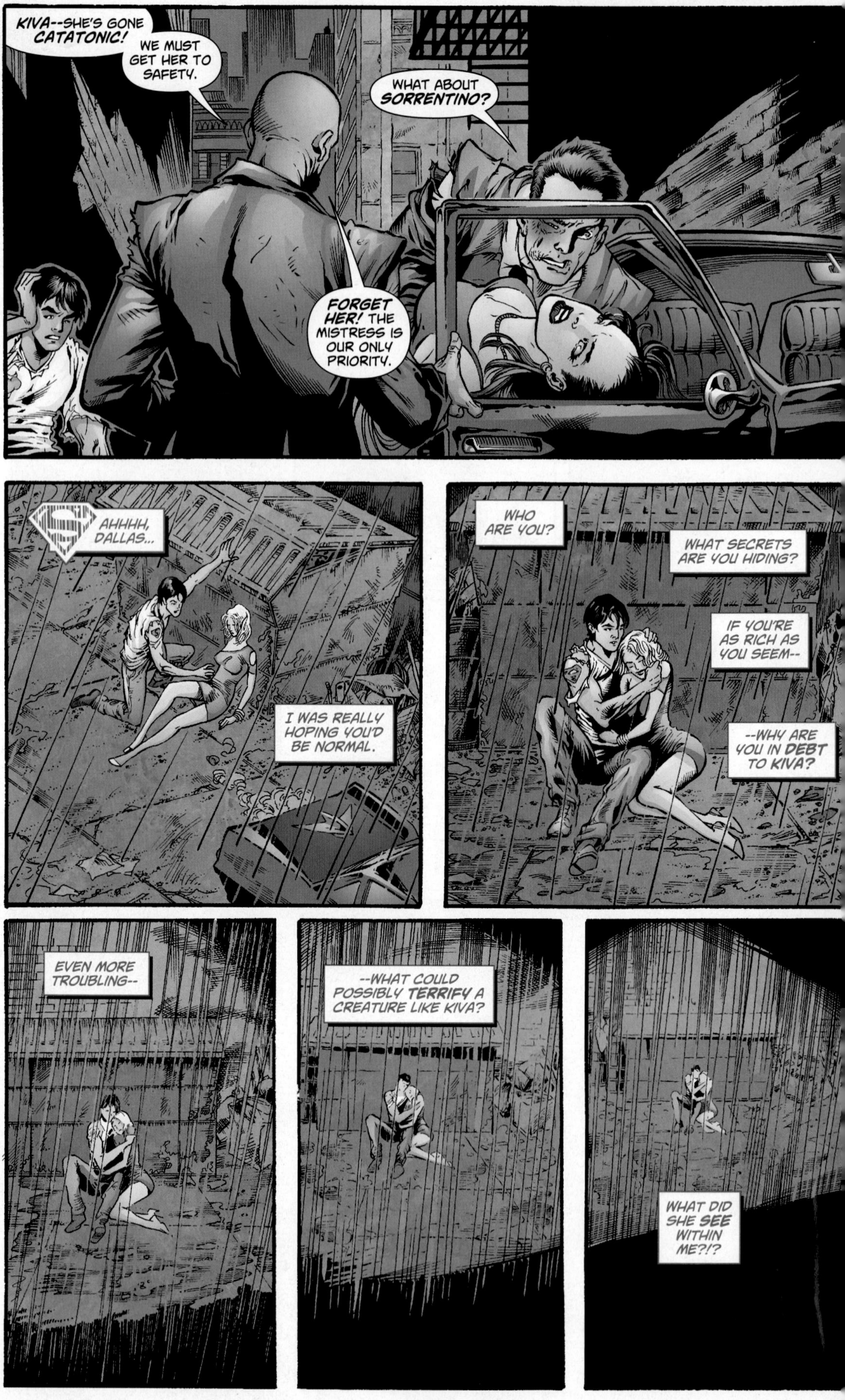

KIVA--SHE'S GONE CATATONIC!
WE MUST GET HER TO SAFETY.
WHAT ABOUT SORRENTINO?
FORGET HER! THE MISTRESS IS OUR ONLY PRIORITY.
AHHHH, DALLAS...
I WAS REALLY HOPING YOU'D BE NORMAL.
WHO ARE YOU?
WHAT SECRETS ARE YOU HIDING?
IF YOU'RE AS RICH AS YOU SEEM--
--WHY ARE YOU IN DEBT TO KIVA?
EVEN MORE TROUBLING--
--WHAT COULD POSSIBLY TERRIFY A CREATURE LIKE KIVA?
WHAT DID SHE SEE WITHIN ME?!?

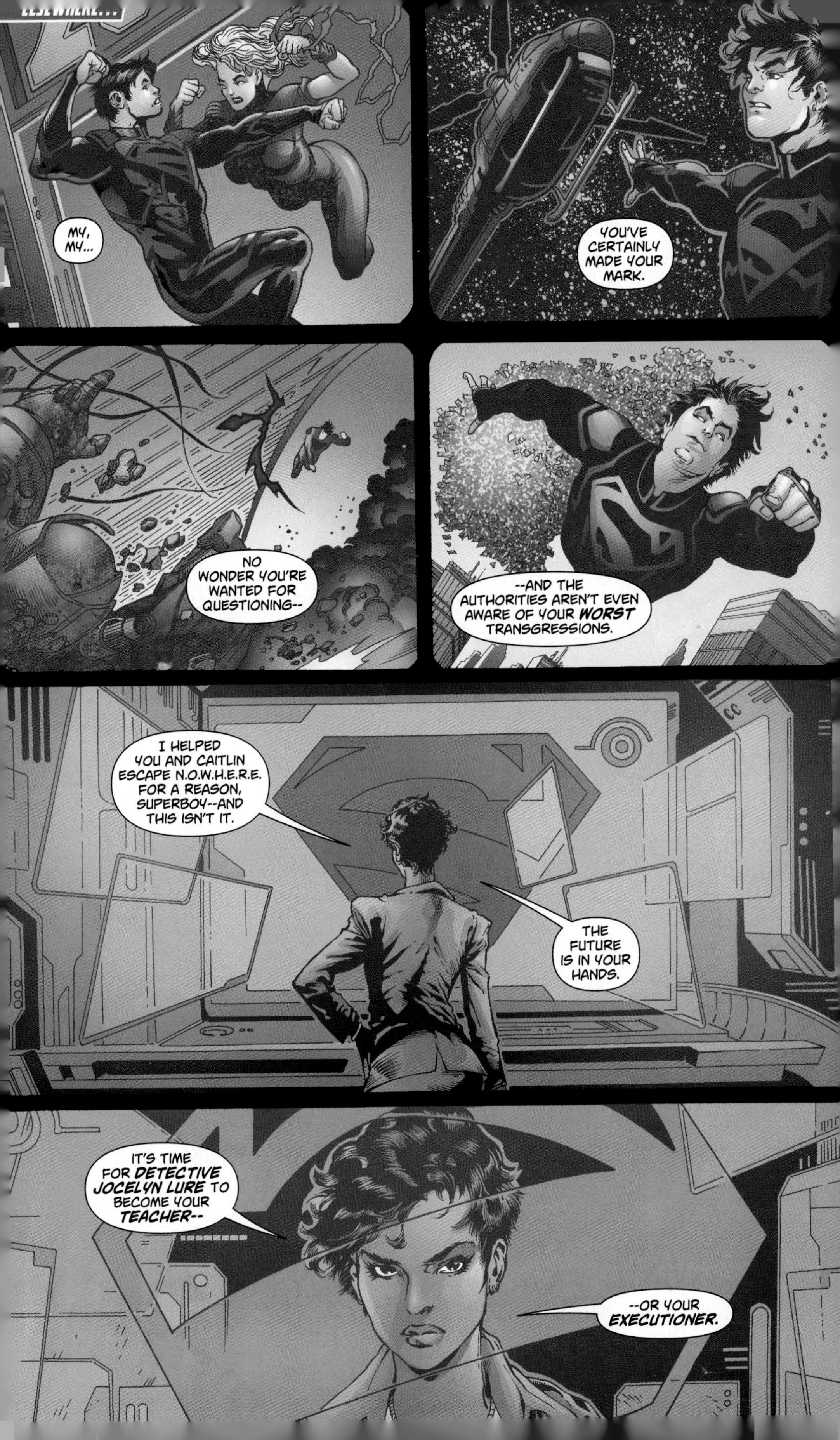
MY, MY...
YOU'VE CERTAINLY MADE YOUR MARK.
NO WONDER YOU'RE WANTED FOR QUESTIONING--
--AND THE AUTHORITIES AREN'T EVEN AWARE OF YOUR WORST TRANSGRESSIONS.
I HELPED YOU AND CAITLIN ESCAPE N.O.W.H.E.R.E. FOR A REASON, SUPERBOY--AND THIS ISN'T IT.
THE FUTURE IS IN YOUR HANDS.
IT'S TIME FOR DETECTIVE JOCELYN LURE TO BECOME YOUR TEACHER--
--OR YOUR EXECUTIONER.

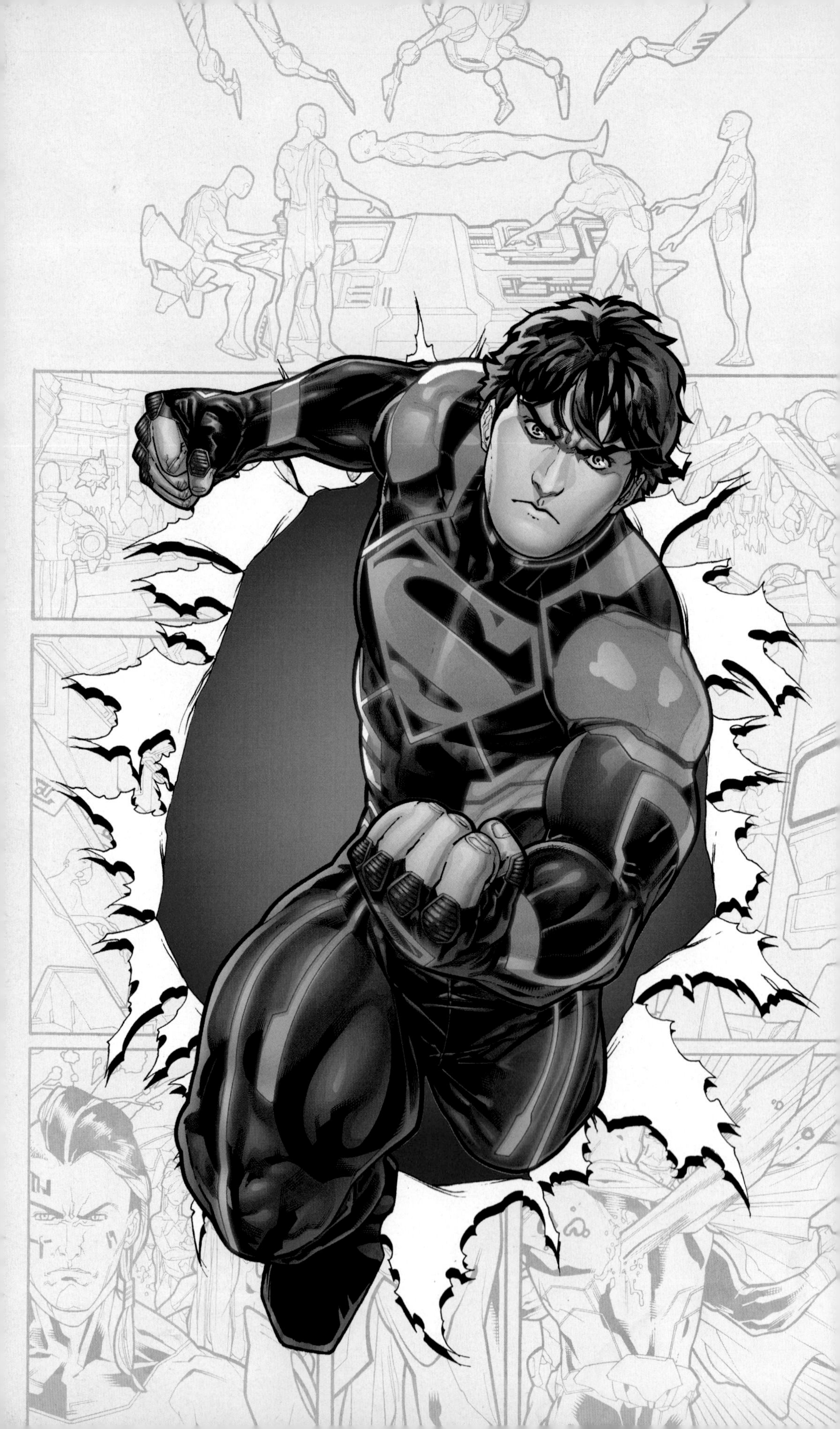

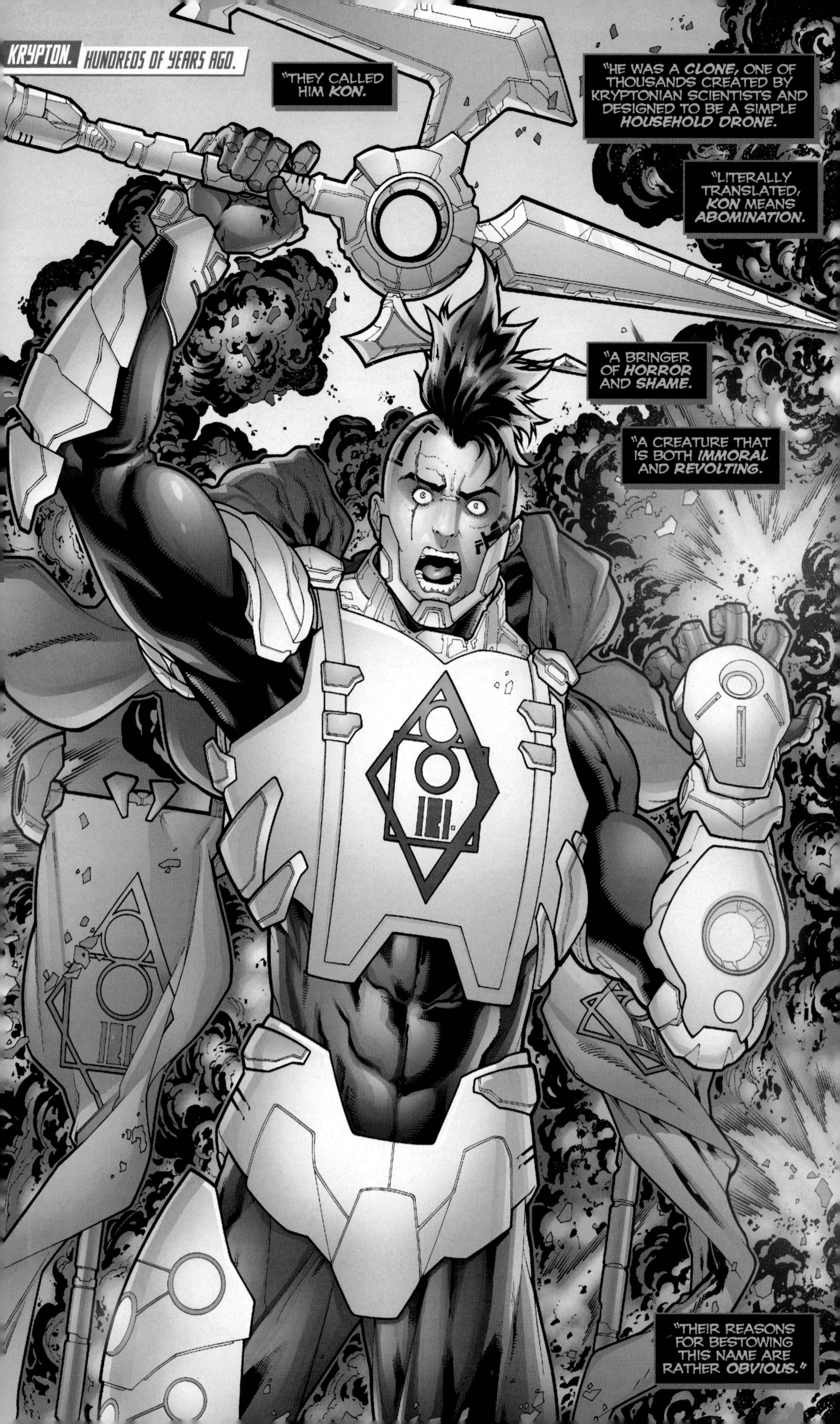
KRYPTON. HUNDREDS OF YEARS AGO.
"THEY CALLED HIM KON.
"HE WAS A CLONE, ONE OF THOUSANDS CREATED BY KRYPTONIAN SCIENTISTS AND DESIGNED TO BE A SIMPLE HOUSEHOLD DRONE.
"LITERALLY TRANSLATED, KON MEANS ABOMINATION.
"A BRINGER OF HORROR AND SHAME.
"A CREATURE THAT IS BOTH IMMORAL AND REVOLTING.
"THEIR REASONS FOR BESTOWING THIS NAME ARE RATHER OBVIOUS."

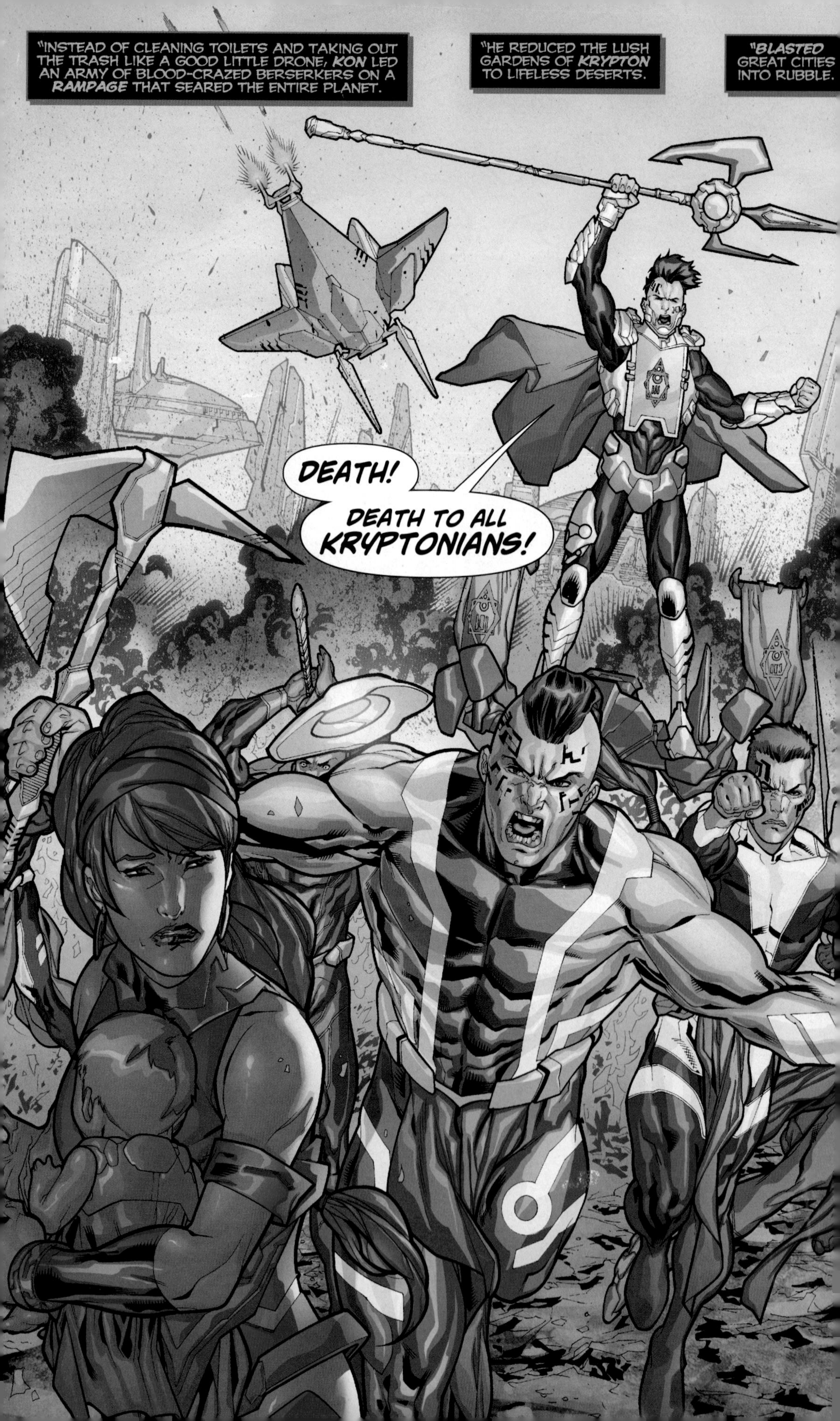
"INSTEAD OF CLEANING TOILETS AND TAKING OUT THE TRASH LIKE A GOOD LITTLE DRONE, KON LED AN ARMY OF BLOOD-CRAZED BERSERKERS ON A RAMPAGE THAT SEARED THE ENTIRE PLANET.
"HE REDUCED THE LUSH GARDENS OF KRYPTON TO LIFELESS DESERTS.
"BLASTED GREAT CITIES INTO RUBBLE.
DEATH! DEATH TO ALL KRYPTONIANS!

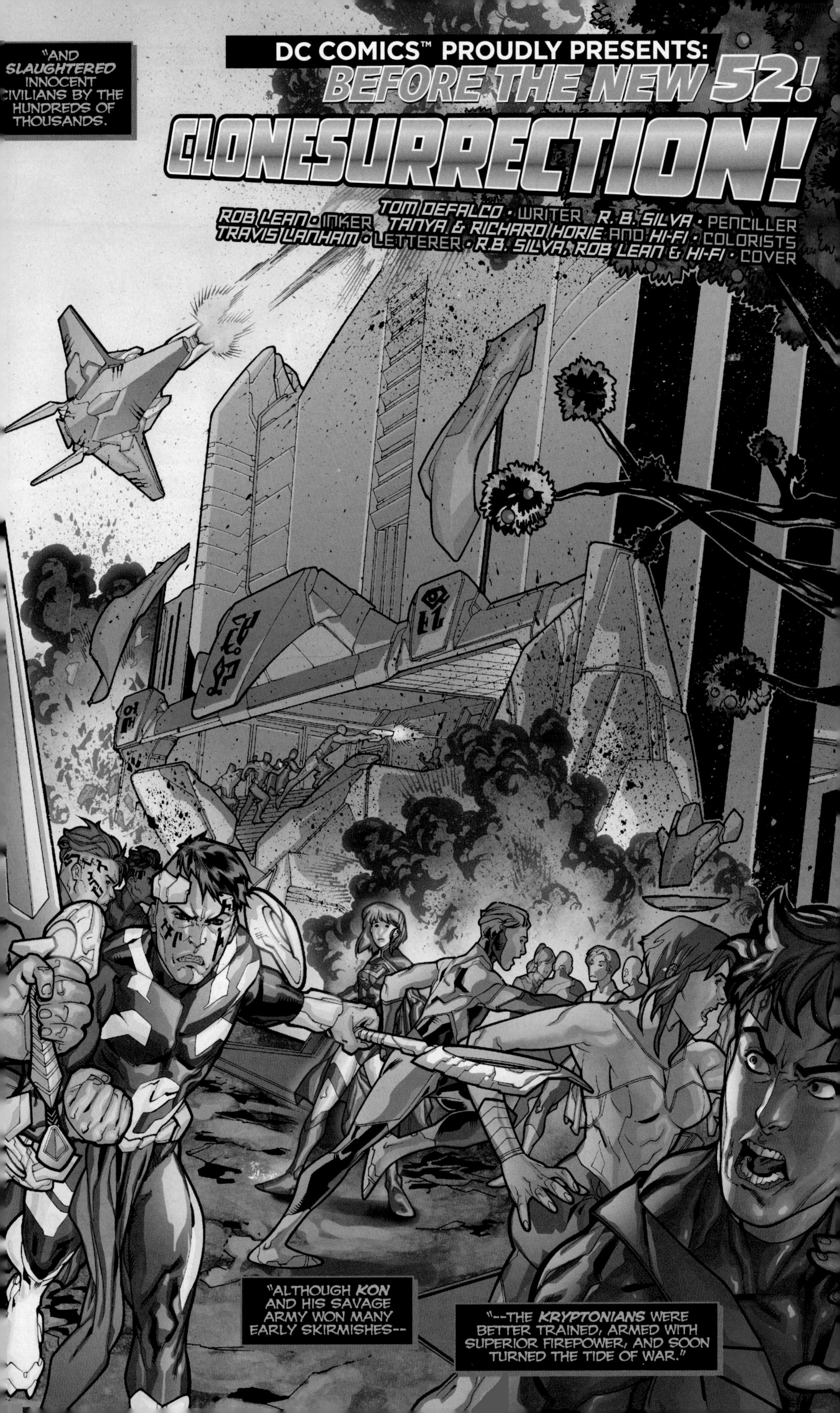
"AND SLAUGHTERED INNOCENT CIVILIANS BY THE HUNDREDS OF THOUSANDS.
DC COMICS™ PROUDLY PRESENTS:
BEFORE THE NEW 52!
CLONESURRECTION!
TOM DEFALCO • WRITER R. B. SILVA • PENCILLER
ROB LEAN • INKER TANYA & RICHARD HORIE AND HI-FI • COLORISTS
TRAVIS LANHAM • LETTERER • R.B. SILVA, ROB LEAN & HI-FI • COVER
"ALTHOUGH KON AND HIS SAVAGE ARMY WON MANY EARLY SKIRMISHES--
"--THE KRYPTONIANS WERE BETTER TRAINED, ARMED WITH SUPERIOR FIREPOWER, AND SOON TURNED THE TIDE OF WAR."

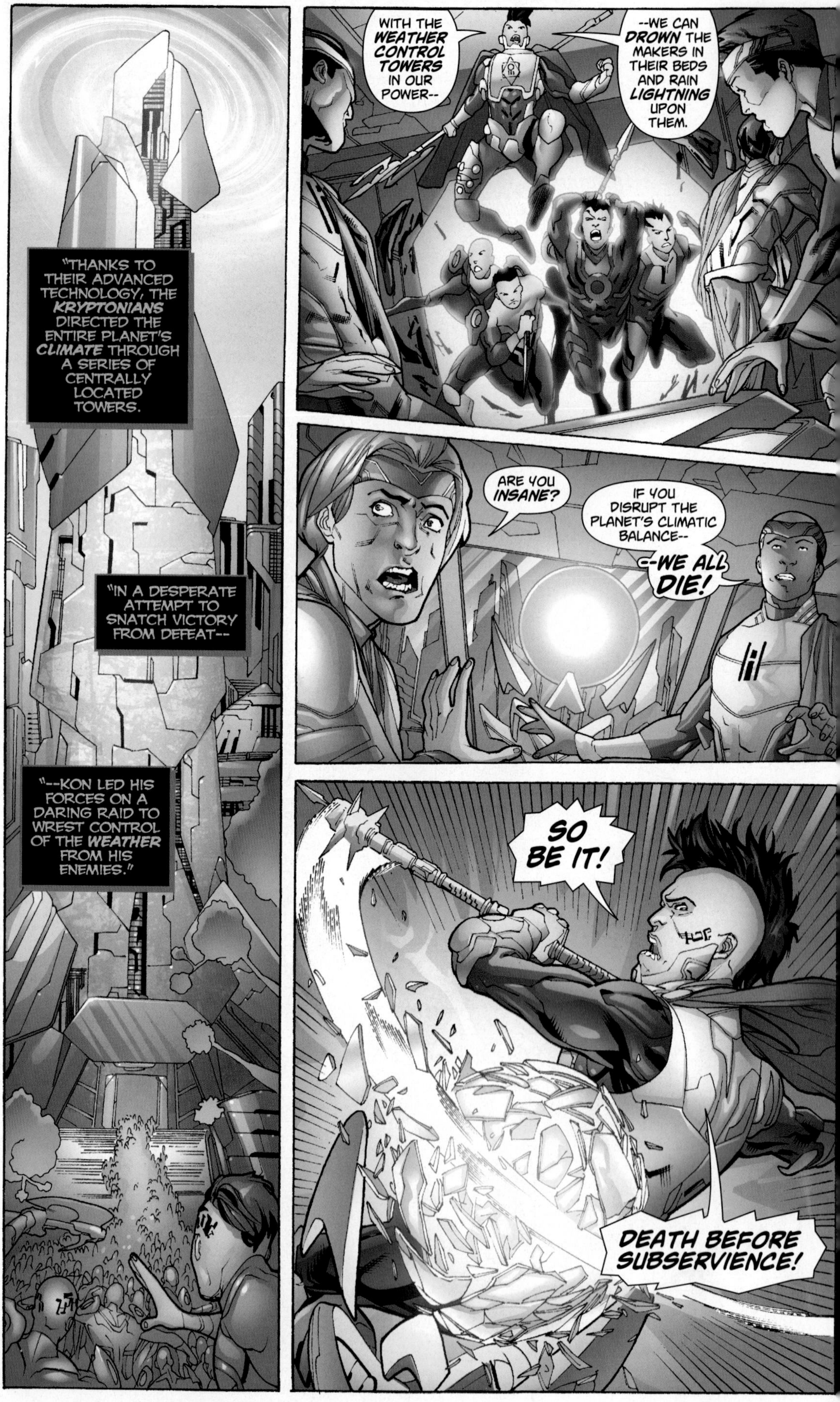
"THANKS TO THEIR ADVANCED TECHNOLOGY, THE KRYPTONIANS DIRECTED THE ENTIRE PLANET'S CLIMATE THROUGH A SERIES OF CENTRALLY LOCATED TOWERS.
"IN A DESPERATE ATTEMPT TO SNATCH VICTORY FROM DEFEAT--
"--KON LED HIS FORCES ON A DARING RAID TO WREST CONTROL OF THE WEATHER FROM HIS ENEMIES."
WITH THE WEATHER CONTROL TOWERS IN OUR POWER--
--WE CAN DROWN THE MAKERS IN THEIR BEDS AND RAIN LIGHTNING UPON THEM.
ARE YOU INSANE?
IF YOU DISRUPT THE PLANET'S CLIMATIC BALANCE--
--WE ALL DIE!
SO BE IT!
DEATH BEFORE SUBSERVIENCE!

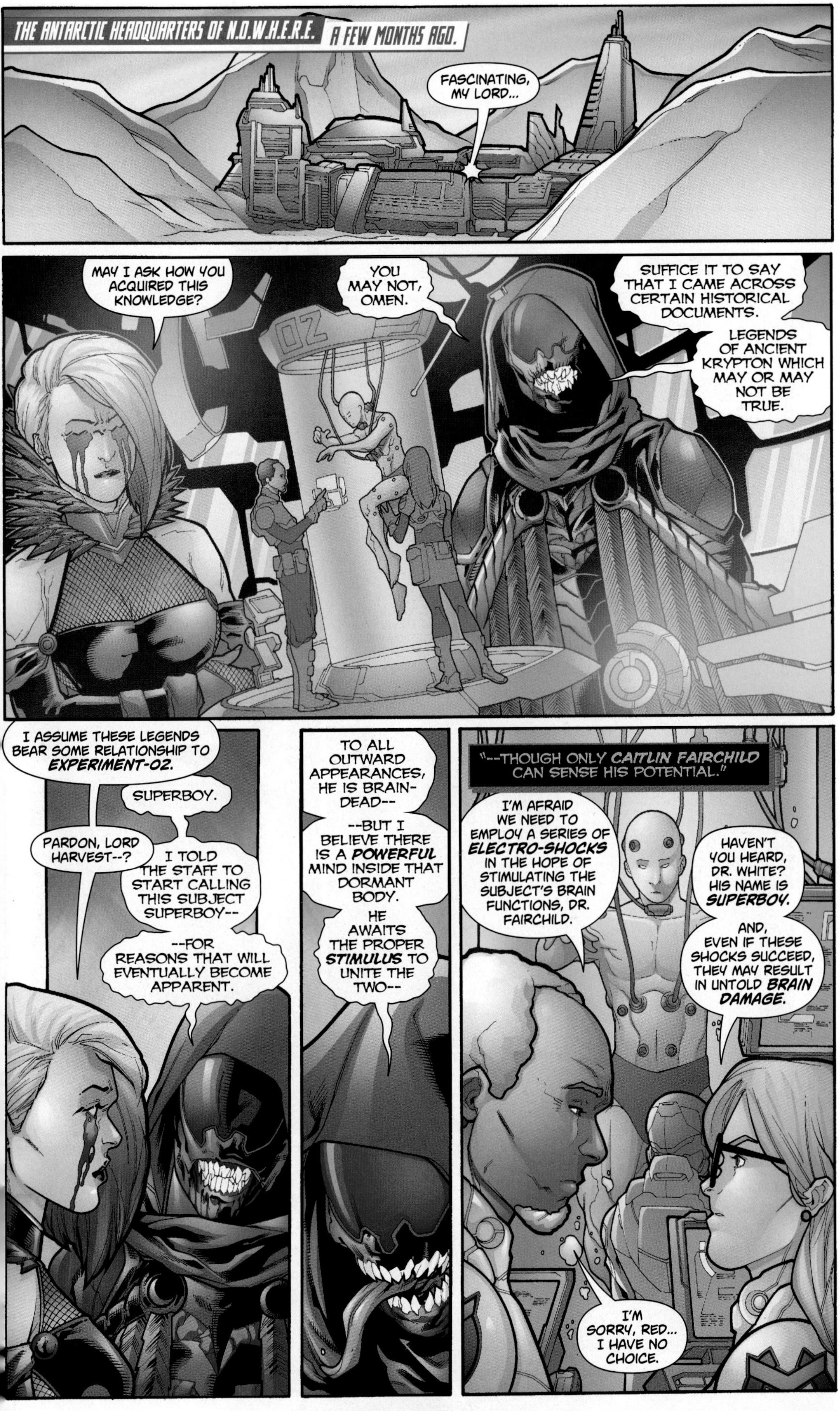
THE ANTARCTIC HEADQUARTERS OF N.O.W.H.E.R.E.
A FEW MONTHS AGO.
FASCINATING, MY LORD...
MAY I ASK HOW YOU ACQUIRED THIS KNOWLEDGE?
YOU MAY NOT, OMEN.
SUFFICE IT TO SAY THAT I CAME ACROSS CERTAIN HISTORICAL DOCUMENTS.
LEGENDS OF ANCIENT KRYPTON WHICH MAY OR MAY NOT BE TRUE.
I ASSUME THESE LEGENDS BEAR SOME RELATIONSHIP TO EXPERIMENT-02.
SUPERBOY.
PARDON, LORD HARVEST--?
I TOLD THE STAFF TO START CALLING THIS SUBJECT SUPERBOY--
--FOR REASONS THAT WILL EVENTUALLY BECOME APPARENT.
TO ALL OUTWARD APPEARANCES, HE IS BRAIN-DEAD--
--BUT I BELIEVE THERE IS A POWERFUL MIND INSIDE THAT DORMANT BODY.
HE AWAITS THE PROPER STIMULUS TO UNITE THE TWO--
"--THOUGH ONLY CAITLIN FAIRCHILD CAN SENSE HIS POTENTIAL."
I'M AFRAID WE NEED TO EMPLOY A SERIES OF ELECTRO-SHOCKS IN THE HOPE OF STIMULATING THE SUBJECT'S BRAIN FUNCTIONS, DR. FAIRCHILD.
HAVEN'T YOU HEARD, DR. WHITE? HIS NAME IS SUPERBOY.
AND, EVEN IF THESE SHOCKS SUCCEED, THEY MAY RESULT IN UNTOLD BRAIN DAMAGE.
I'M SORRY, RED... I HAVE NO CHOICE.

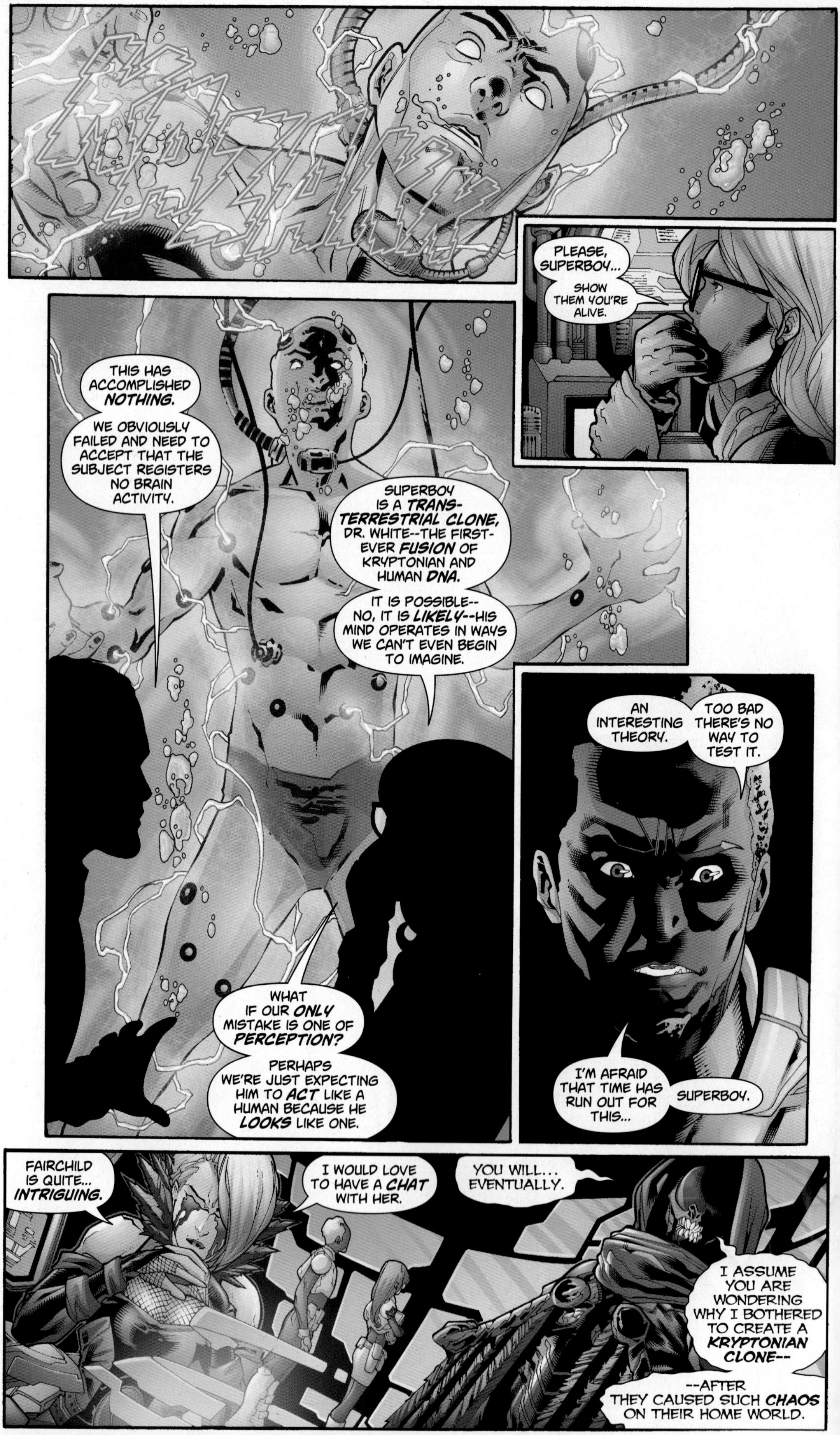
PLEASE, SUPERBOY...
SHOW THEM YOU'RE ALIVE.
THIS HAS ACCOMPLISHED NOTHING.
WE OBVIOUSLY FAILED AND NEED TO ACCEPT THAT THE SUBJECT REGISTERS NO BRAIN ACTIVITY.
SUPERBOY IS A TRANS-TERRESTRIAL CLONE, DR. WHITE--THE FIRST-EVER FUSION OF KRYPTONIAN AND HUMAN DNA.
IT IS POSSIBLE--NO, IT IS LIKELY--HIS MIND OPERATES IN WAYS WE CAN'T EVEN BEGIN TO IMAGINE.
WHAT IF OUR ONLY MISTAKE IS ONE OF PERCEPTION?
PERHAPS WE'RE JUST EXPECTING HIM TO ACT LIKE A HUMAN BECAUSE HE LOOKS LIKE ONE.
AN INTERESTING THEORY.
TOO BAD THERE'S NO WAY TO TEST IT.
I'M AFRAID THAT TIME HAS RUN OUT FOR THIS...
SUPERBOY.
FAIRCHILD IS QUITE... INTRIGUING.
I WOULD LOVE TO HAVE A CHAT WITH HER.
YOU WILL... EVENTUALLY.
I ASSUME YOU ARE WONDERING WHY I BOTHERED TO CREATE A KRYPTONIAN CLONE--
--AFTER THEY CAUSED SUCH CHAOS ON THEIR HOME WORLD.

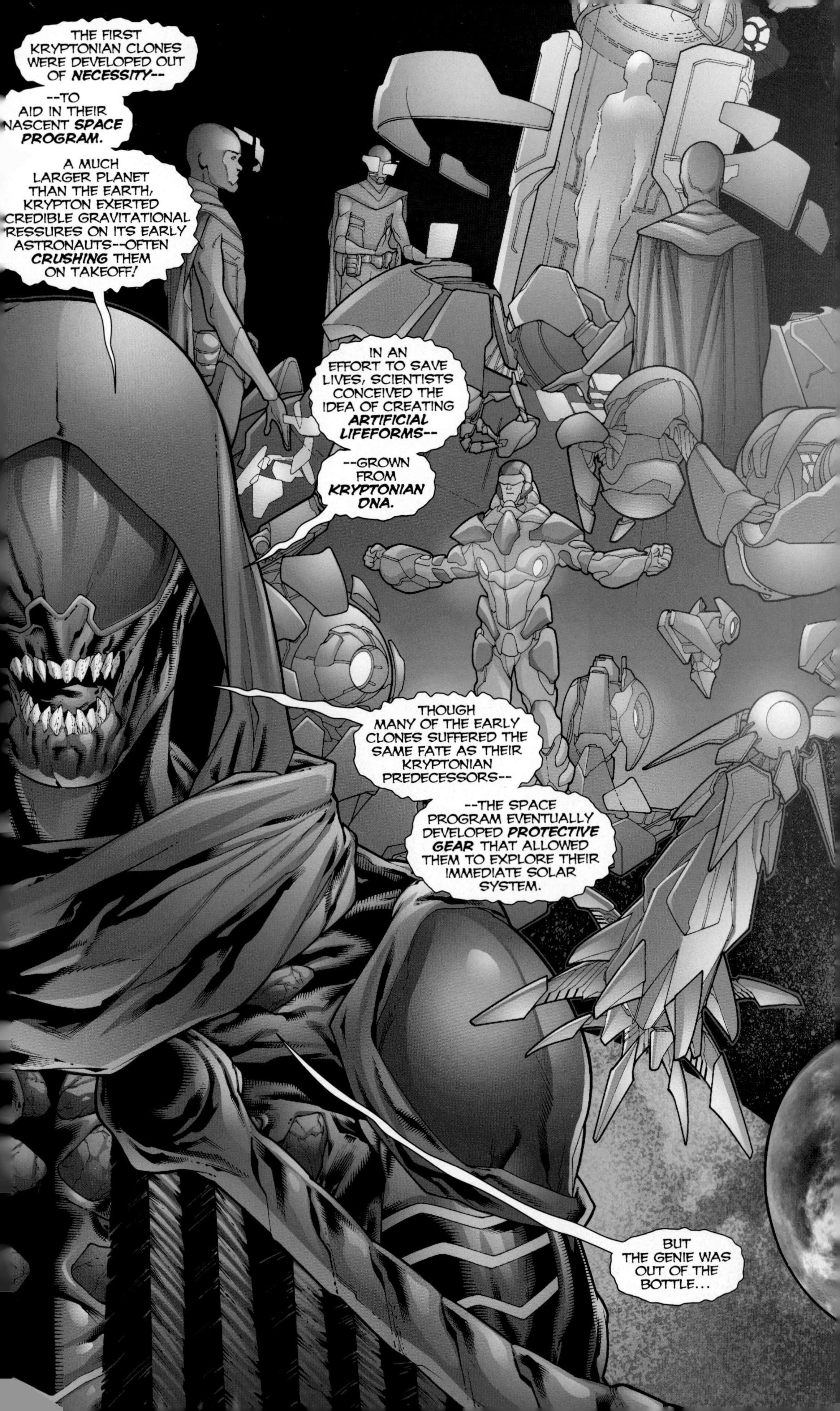
THE FIRST KRYPTONIAN CLONES WERE DEVELOPED OUT OF NECESSITY--
--TO AID IN THEIR NASCENT SPACE PROGRAM.
A MUCH LARGER PLANET THAN THE EARTH, KRYPTON EXERTED CREDIBLE GRAVITATIONAL PRESSURES ON ITS EARLY ASTRONAUTS--OFTEN CRUSHING THEM ON TAKEOFF!
IN AN EFFORT TO SAVE LIVES, SCIENTISTS CONCEIVED THE IDEA OF CREATING ARTIFICIAL LIFEFORMS--
--GROWN FROM KRYPTONIAN DNA.
THOUGH MANY OF THE EARLY CLONES SUFFERED THE SAME FATE AS THEIR KRYPTONIAN PREDECESSORS--
--THE SPACE PROGRAM EVENTUALLY DEVELOPED PROTECTIVE GEAR THAT ALLOWED THEM TO EXPLORE THEIR IMMEDIATE SOLAR SYSTEM.
BUT THE GENIE WAS OUT OF THE BOTTLE...

"THE MEDICAL ESTABLISHMENT BEGAN EMPLOYING CLONES TO TEST NEW *DRUGS*--

"--AND DEVELOP ADVANCED *OPERATING PROCEDURES*.

"*INDUSTRY* CO-OPTED THEM FOR *MINING* AND HEAVY *CONSTRUCTION*.

"THE ELITE SHOWED OFF THEIR STATUS BY UTILIZING THEM AS *DOMESTICS*.

"AS OTHER USES DEVELOPED, CLONES WERE *MASS-PRODUCED* TO MEET DEMAND.

"THAT'S WHEN THE *TROUBLE* BEGAN..."

WHY HAVEN'T YOU COMPLETED YOUR ASSIGNED TASKS?

BE SILENT, MAKER--!

"WHETHER THE RESULT OF MANUFACTURING SHORTCUTS OR AN INHERENT INSTABILITY IN THEIR GENETIC MAKEUP--

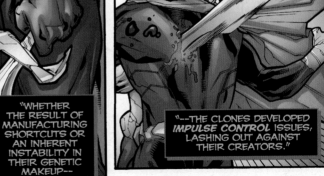

"--THE CLONES DEVELOPED *IMPULSE CONTROL* ISSUES, LASHING OUT AGAINST THEIR CREATORS."

"SCATTERED INCIDENTS OF THIS PHENOMENON BEGAN TO *MULTIPLY,* SPREADING ACROSS THE PLANET LIKE A *PLAGUE.*

"AND SOON, WITHOUT EXCEPTION, EVERY CLONE ON KRYPTON WAS GIVING VENT TO A MADDENING *BLOODLUST.*

"AN OVERWHELMING HUNGER FOR *DEATH* AND *DESTRUCTION.*

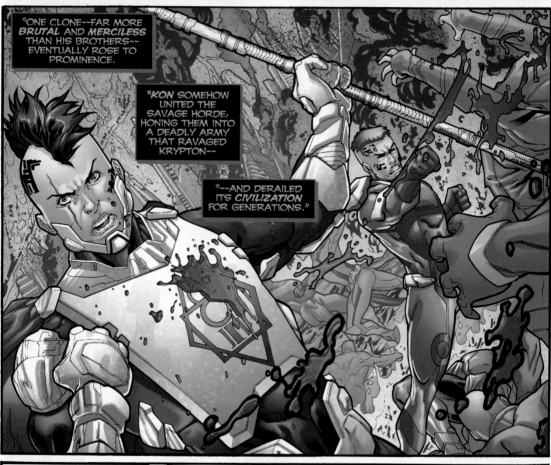

"ONE CLONE--FAR MORE *BRUTAL* AND *MERCILESS*-- EVENTUALLY ROSE TO PROMINENCE.

"*KON* SOMEHOW UNITED THE SAVAGE HORDE, HONING THEM INTO A DEADLY ARMY THAT RAVAGED KRYPTON--

"--AND DERAILED ITS *CIVILIZATION* FOR GENERATIONS."

IF THIS SO-CALLED *SUPERBOY* IS IMPORTANT TO YOU, I COULD EASILY DISSUADE *DR. WHITE* FROM *DESTROYING* IT.

I DOUBT THAT WILL BE NECESSARY.

WE MUST INITIATE THE *TERMINATION PROTOCOLS.*

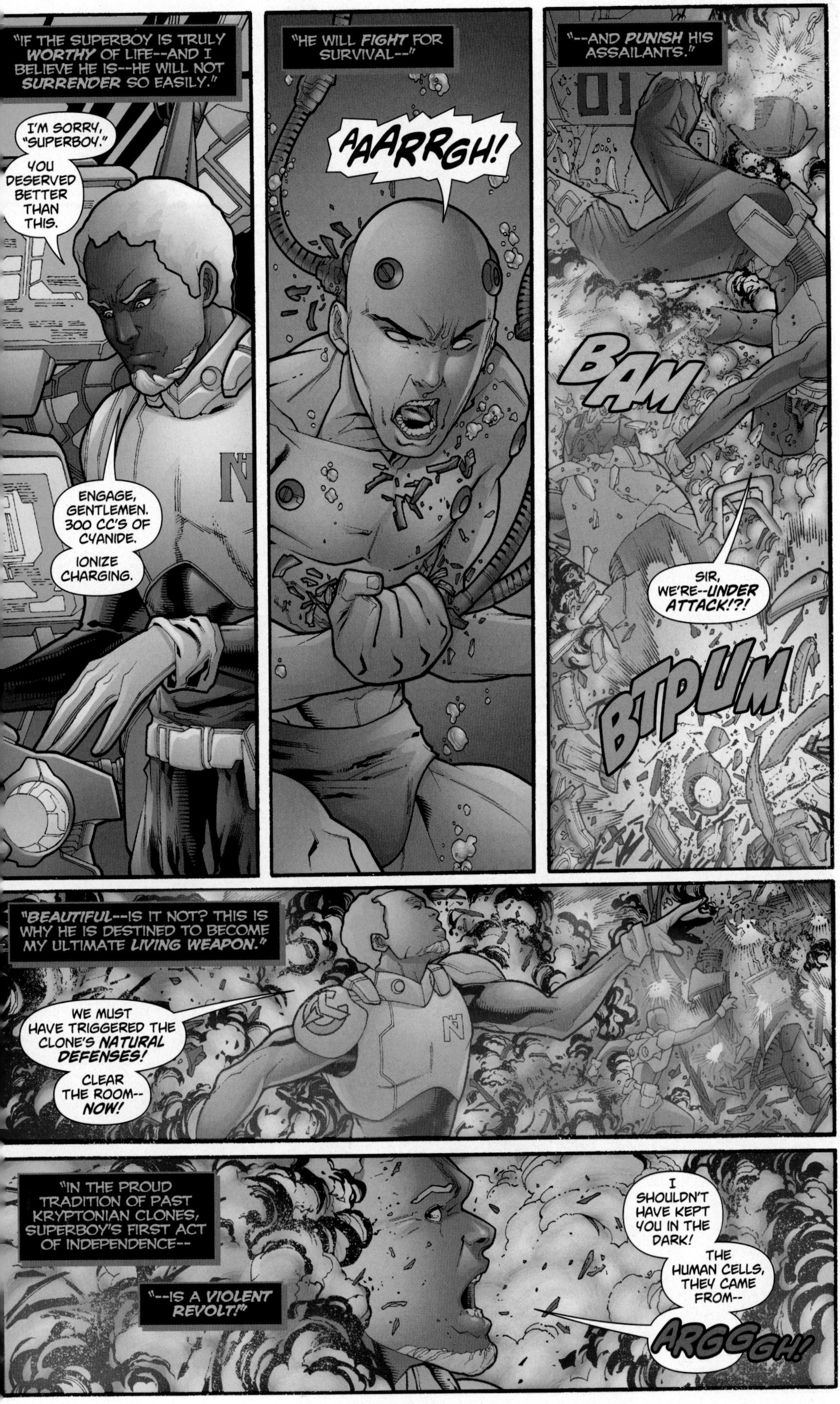

"IF THE SUPERBOY IS TRULY WORTHY OF LIFE--AND I BELIEVE HE IS--HE WILL NOT SURRENDER SO EASILY."
I'M SORRY, "SUPERBOY."
YOU DESERVED BETTER THAN THIS.
ENGAGE, GENTLEMEN. 300 CC'S OF CYANIDE.
IONIZE CHARGING.
"HE WILL FIGHT FOR SURVIVAL--"
AAARRGH!
"--AND PUNISH HIS ASSAILANTS."
BAM
SIR, WE'RE--UNDER ATTACK!?!
BTPUM
"BEAUTIFUL--IS IT NOT? THIS IS WHY HE IS DESTINED TO BECOME MY ULTIMATE LIVING WEAPON."
WE MUST HAVE TRIGGERED THE CLONE'S NATURAL DEFENSES!
CLEAR THE ROOM--NOW!
"IN THE PROUD TRADITION OF PAST KRYPTONIAN CLONES, SUPERBOY'S FIRST ACT OF INDEPENDENCE--
"--IS A VIOLENT REVOLT!"
I SHOULDN'T HAVE KEPT YOU IN THE DARK!
THE HUMAN CELLS, THEY CAME FROM--
ARGGGH!

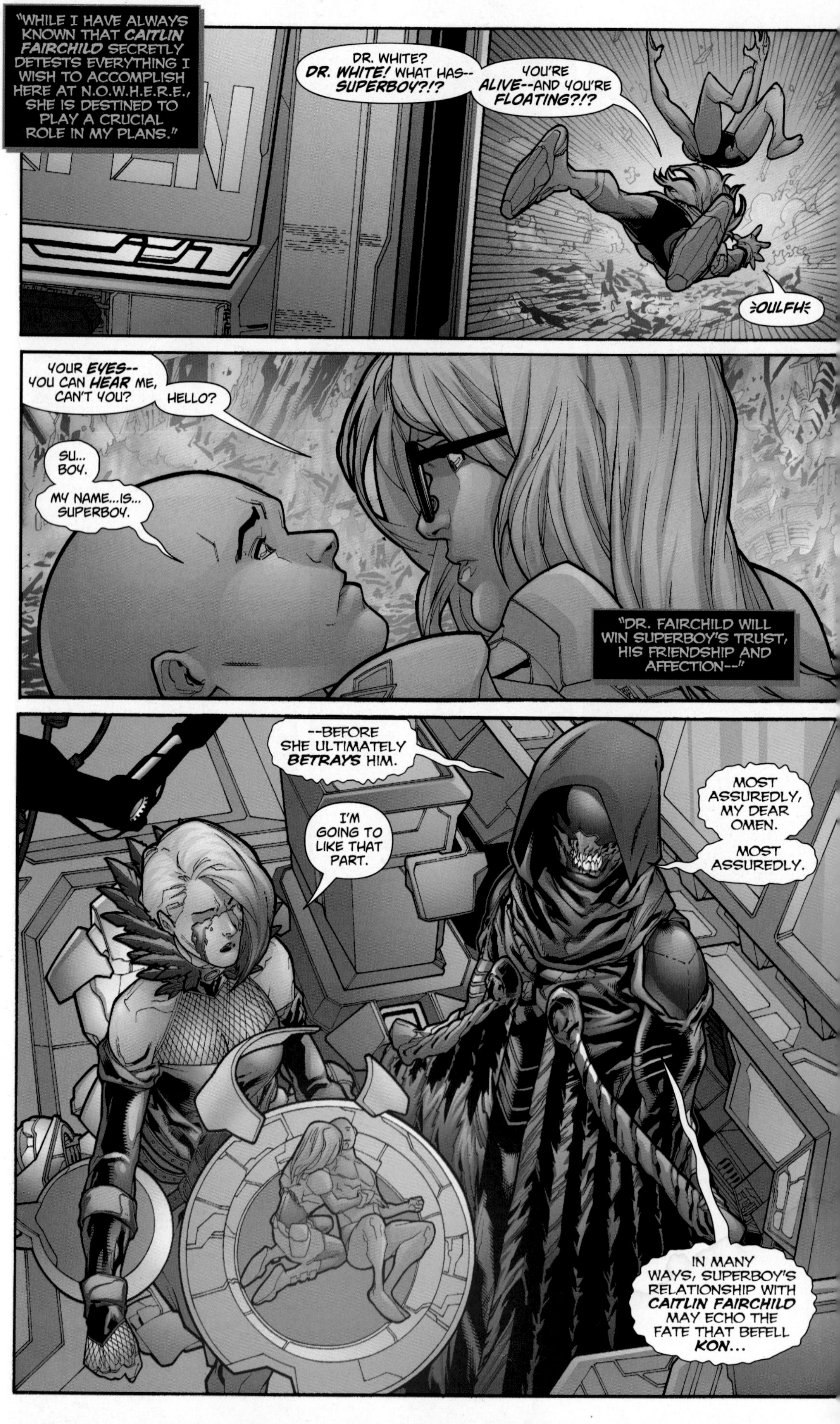
"WHILE I HAVE ALWAYS KNOWN THAT CAITLIN FAIRCHILD SECRETLY DETESTS EVERYTHING I WISH TO ACCOMPLISH HERE AT N.O.W.H.E.R.E., SHE IS DESTINED TO PLAY A CRUCIAL ROLE IN MY PLANS."
DR. WHITE? DR. WHITE! WHAT HAS-- SUPERBOY?!?
YOU'RE ALIVE--AND YOU'RE FLOATING?!?
OULFH
YOUR EYES-- YOU CAN HEAR ME, CAN'T YOU?
HELLO?
SU... BOY.
MY NAME...IS... SUPERBOY.
"DR. FAIRCHILD WILL WIN SUPERBOY'S TRUST, HIS FRIENDSHIP AND AFFECTION--"
--BEFORE SHE ULTIMATELY BETRAYS HIM.
I'M GOING TO LIKE THAT PART.
MOST ASSUREDLY, MY DEAR OMEN.
MOST ASSUREDLY.
IN MANY WAYS, SUPERBOY'S RELATIONSHIP WITH CAITLIN FAIRCHILD MAY ECHO THE FATE THAT BEFELL KON...

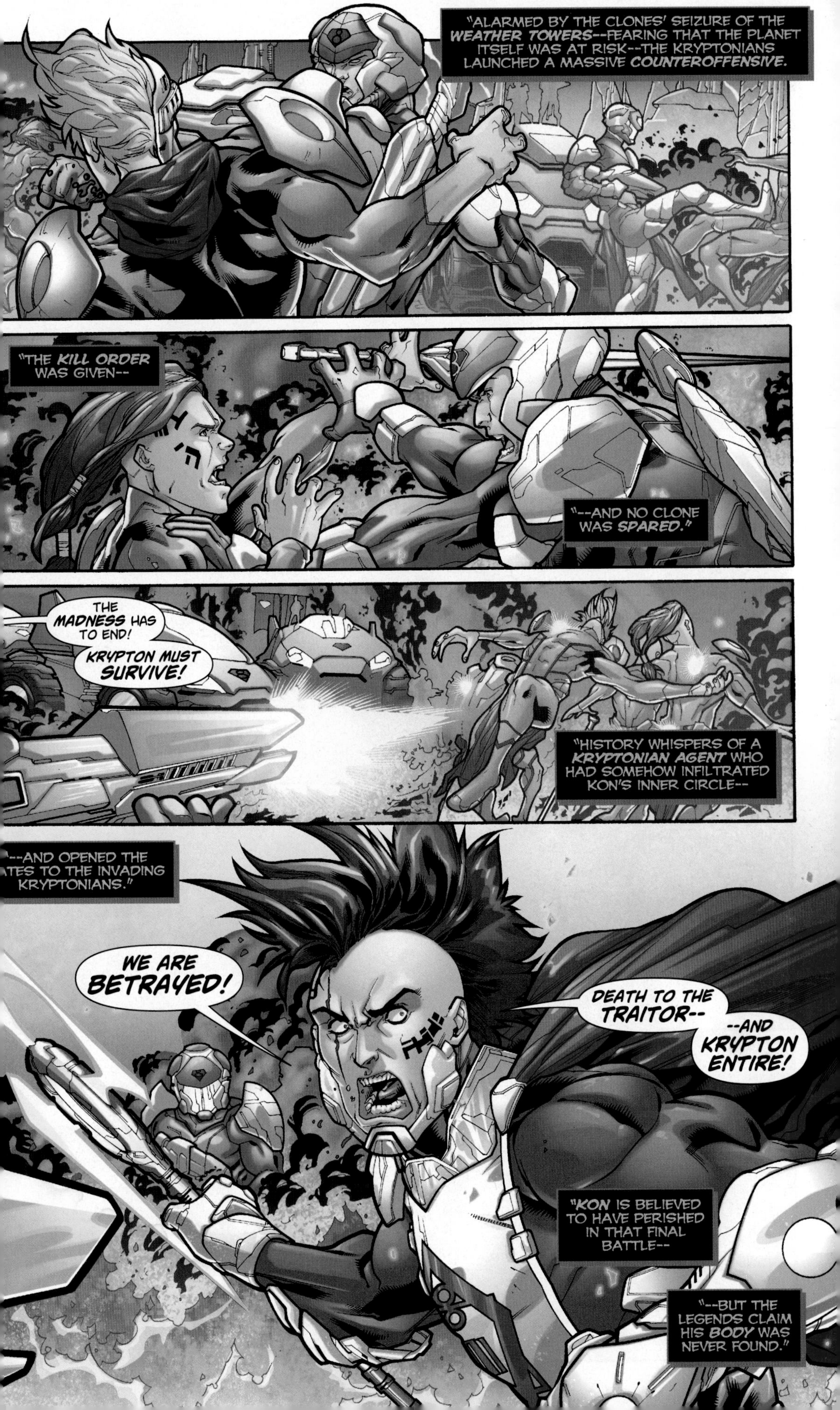
"ALARMED BY THE CLONES' SEIZURE OF THE WEATHER TOWERS--FEARING THAT THE PLANET ITSELF WAS AT RISK--THE KRYPTONIANS LAUNCHED A MASSIVE COUNTEROFFENSIVE.
"THE KILL ORDER WAS GIVEN--
"--AND NO CLONE WAS SPARED."
THE MADNESS HAS TO END!
KRYPTON MUST SURVIVE!
"HISTORY WHISPERS OF A KRYPTONIAN AGENT WHO HAD SOMEHOW INFILTRATED KON'S INNER CIRCLE--
"--AND OPENED THE ATES TO THE INVADING KRYPTONIANS."
WE ARE BETRAYED!
DEATH TO THE TRAITOR--
--AND KRYPTON ENTIRE!
"KON IS BELIEVED TO HAVE PERISHED IN THAT FINAL BATTLE--
"--BUT THE LEGENDS CLAIM HIS BODY WAS NEVER FOUND."

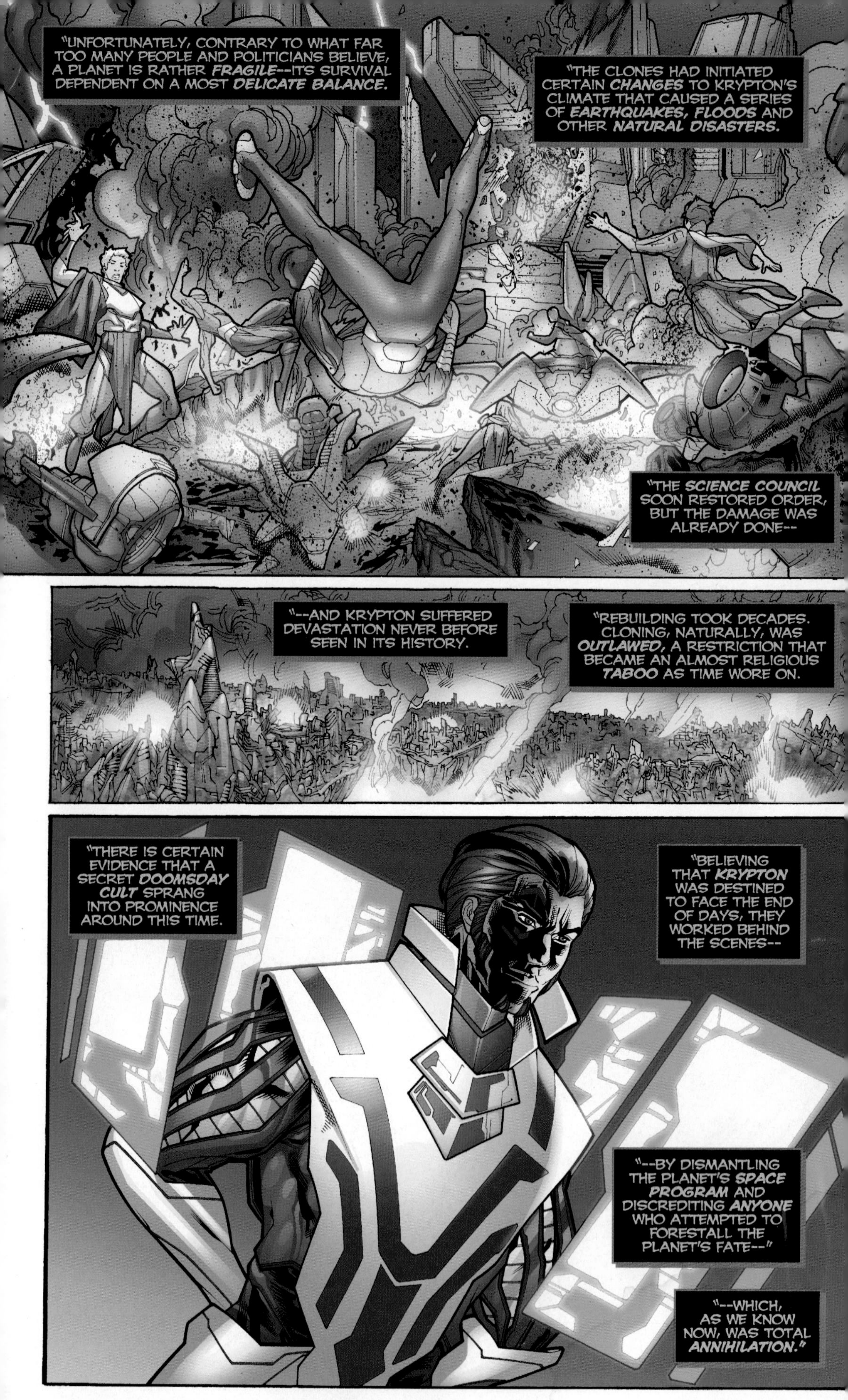
"UNFORTUNATELY, CONTRARY TO WHAT FAR TOO MANY PEOPLE AND POLITICIANS BELIEVE, A PLANET IS RATHER FRAGILE--ITS SURVIVAL DEPENDENT ON A MOST DELICATE BALANCE.
"THE CLONES HAD INITIATED CERTAIN CHANGES TO KRYPTON'S CLIMATE THAT CAUSED A SERIES OF EARTHQUAKES, FLOODS AND OTHER NATURAL DISASTERS.
"THE SCIENCE COUNCIL SOON RESTORED ORDER, BUT THE DAMAGE WAS ALREADY DONE--
"--AND KRYPTON SUFFERED DEVASTATION NEVER BEFORE SEEN IN ITS HISTORY.
"REBUILDING TOOK DECADES. CLONING, NATURALLY, WAS OUTLAWED, A RESTRICTION THAT BECAME AN ALMOST RELIGIOUS TABOO AS TIME WORE ON.
"THERE IS CERTAIN EVIDENCE THAT A SECRET DOOMSDAY CULT SPRANG INTO PROMINENCE AROUND THIS TIME.
"BELIEVING THAT KRYPTON WAS DESTINED TO FACE THE END OF DAYS, THEY WORKED BEHIND THE SCENES--
"--BY DISMANTLING THE PLANET'S SPACE PROGRAM AND DISCREDITING ANYONE WHO ATTEMPTED TO FORESTALL THE PLANET'S FATE--"
"--WHICH, AS WE KNOW NOW, WAS TOTAL ANNIHILATION."

THE SUPERBOY HAS MADE CONSIDERABLE PROGRESS SINCE WE LAST LOOKED IN ON HIM, OMEN.

DO YOU RECALL THE KRYPTONIAN DOOMSDAY SECT I MENTIONED A FEW WEEKS AGO?

IT APPEARS A SIMILAR CULT HAS FORMED HERE.

THOSE ARROGANT FOOLS WILL FIND YOU A MOST FORMIDABLE ENEMY, MY LORD HARVEST.

"I SEE FAIRCHILD IS ATTEMPTING TO PLUMB THE SUPERBOY'S SUBCONSCIOUS."

PREPARE TO RUN THE VIRTUAL REALITY PROGRAM, AGAIN.

WE'RE GAINING VALUABLE--AND RATHER DISTURBING--*INSIGHT* INTO THE WAY SUPERBOY PERCEIVES THE WORLD.

SHALL WE TAKE IT FROM THE TOP, DR. FAIRCHILD?

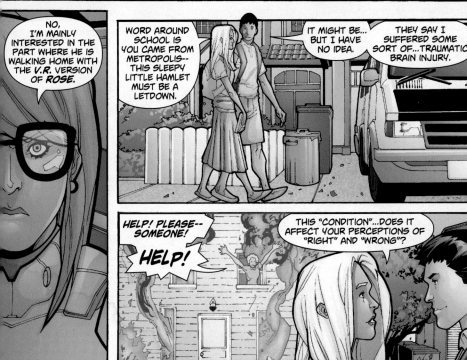

NO, I'M MAINLY INTERESTED IN THE PART WHERE HE IS WALKING HOME WITH THE *V.R.* VERSION OF *ROSE.*

WORD AROUND SCHOOL IS YOU CAME FROM METROPOLIS-- THIS SLEEPY LITTLE HAMLET MUST BE A LETDOWN.

IT MIGHT BE... BUT I HAVE NO IDEA.

THEY SAY I SUFFERED SOME SORT OF...TRAUMATIC BRAIN INJURY.

HELP! PLEASE-- SOMEONE!

HELP!

THIS "CONDITION"...DOES IT AFFECT YOUR PERCEPTIONS OF "RIGHT" AND "WRONG"?

I DON'T THINK SO.

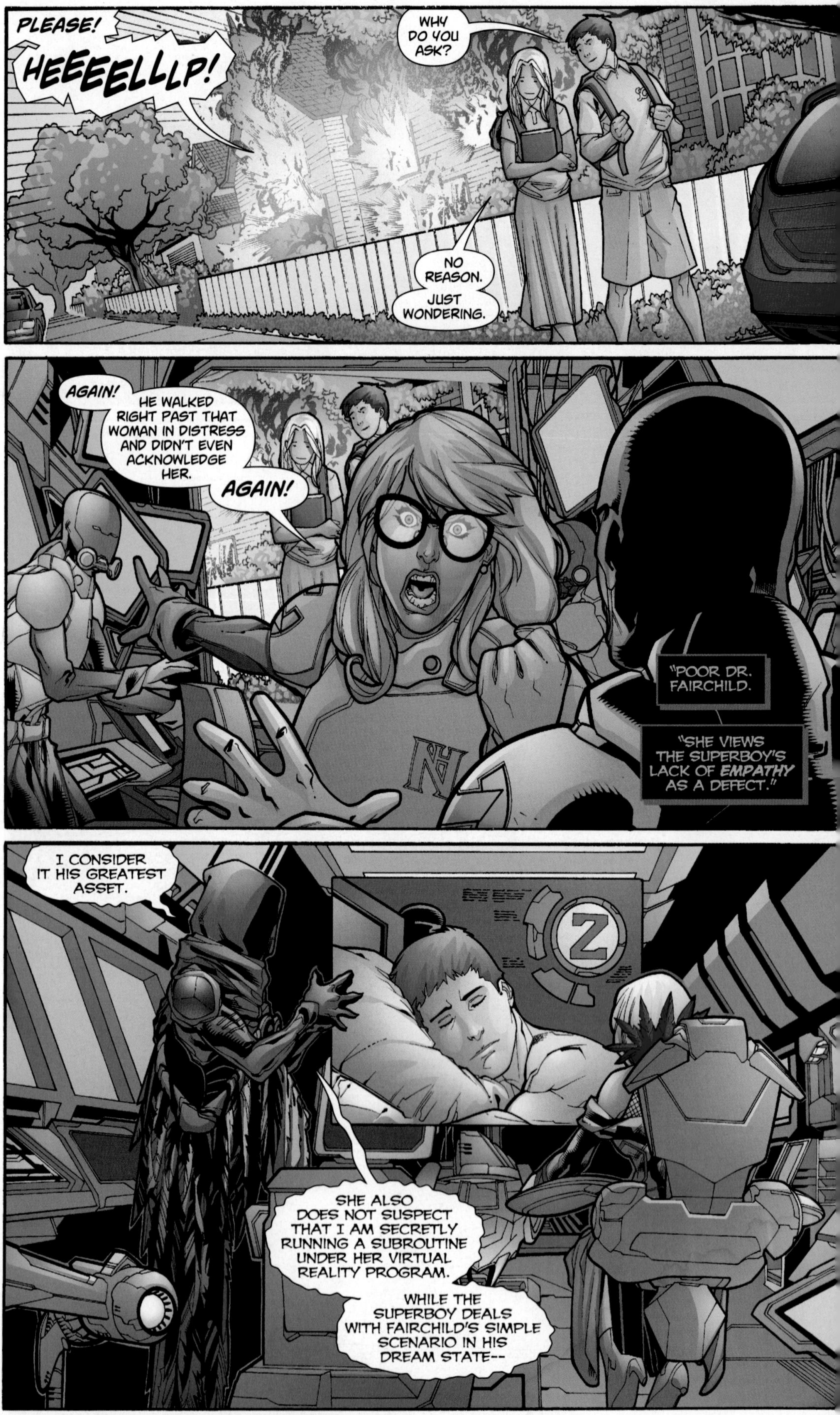
PLEASE!
HEEEELLLP!
WHY DO YOU ASK?
NO REASON.
JUST WONDERING.
AGAIN!
HE WALKED RIGHT PAST THAT WOMAN IN DISTRESS AND DIDN'T EVEN ACKNOWLEDGE HER.
AGAIN!
"POOR DR. FAIRCHILD.
"SHE VIEWS THE SUPERBOY'S LACK OF EMPATHY AS A DEFECT."
I CONSIDER IT HIS GREATEST ASSET.
SHE ALSO DOES NOT SUSPECT THAT I AM SECRETLY RUNNING A SUBROUTINE UNDER HER VIRTUAL REALITY PROGRAM.
WHILE THE SUPERBOY DEALS WITH FAIRCHILD'S SIMPLE SCENARIO IN HIS DREAM STATE--

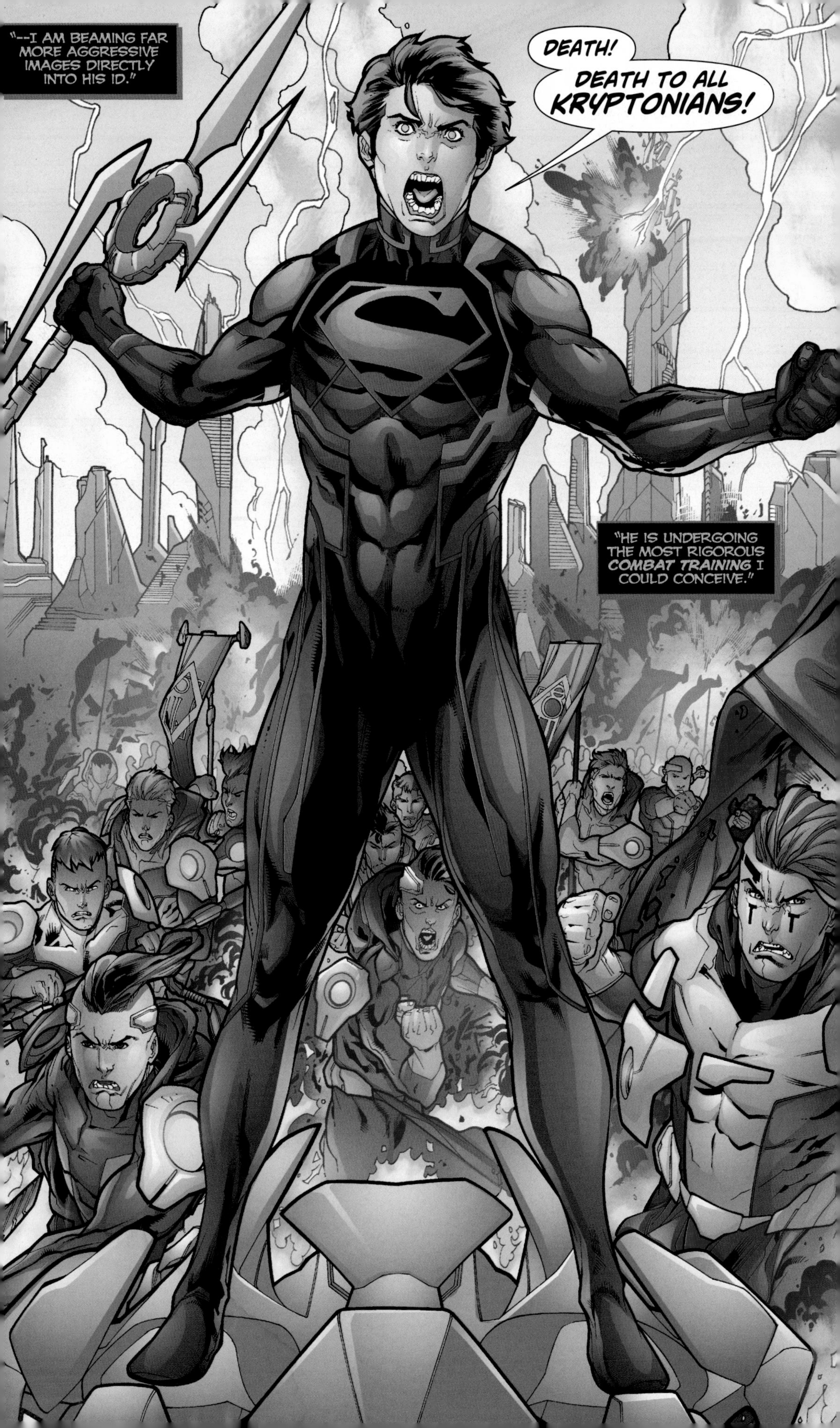
"--I AM BEAMING FAR MORE AGGRESSIVE IMAGES DIRECTLY INTO HIS ID."
DEATH! DEATH TO ALL KRYPTONIANS!
"HE IS UNDERGOING THE MOST RIGOROUS COMBAT TRAINING I COULD CONCEIVE."

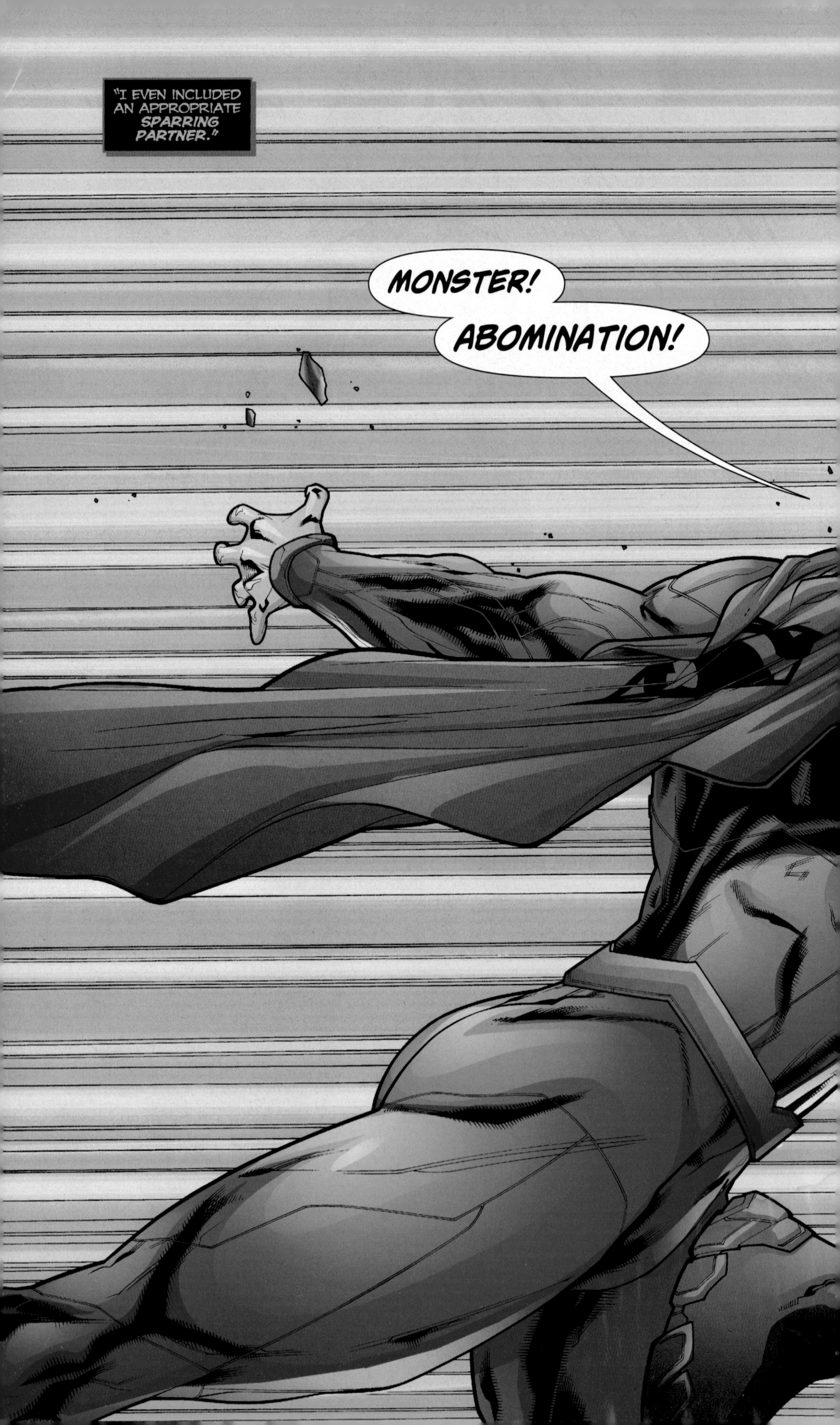
"I EVEN INCLUDED AN APPROPRIATE SPARRING PARTNER."
MONSTER!
ABOMINATION!

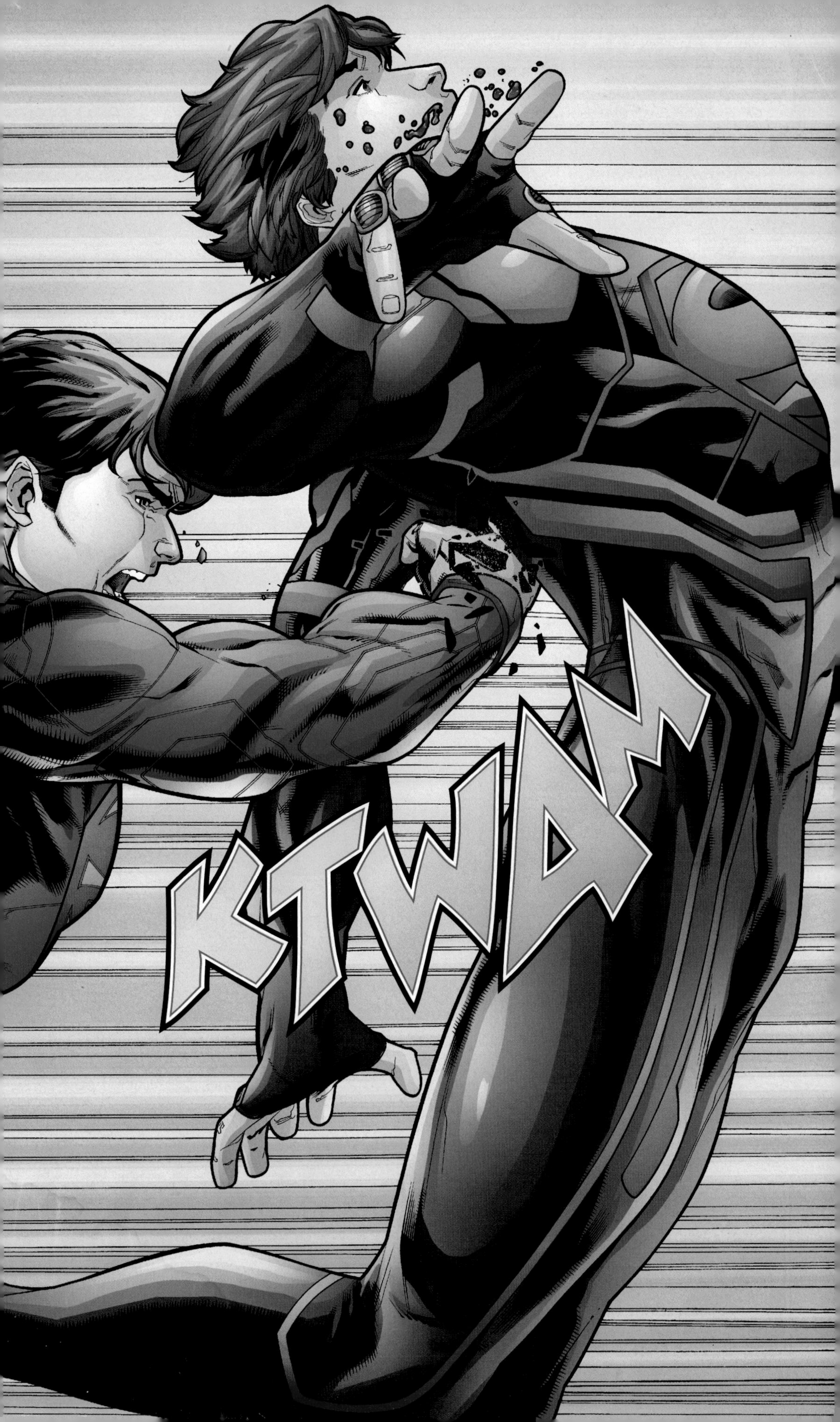
KTWAM

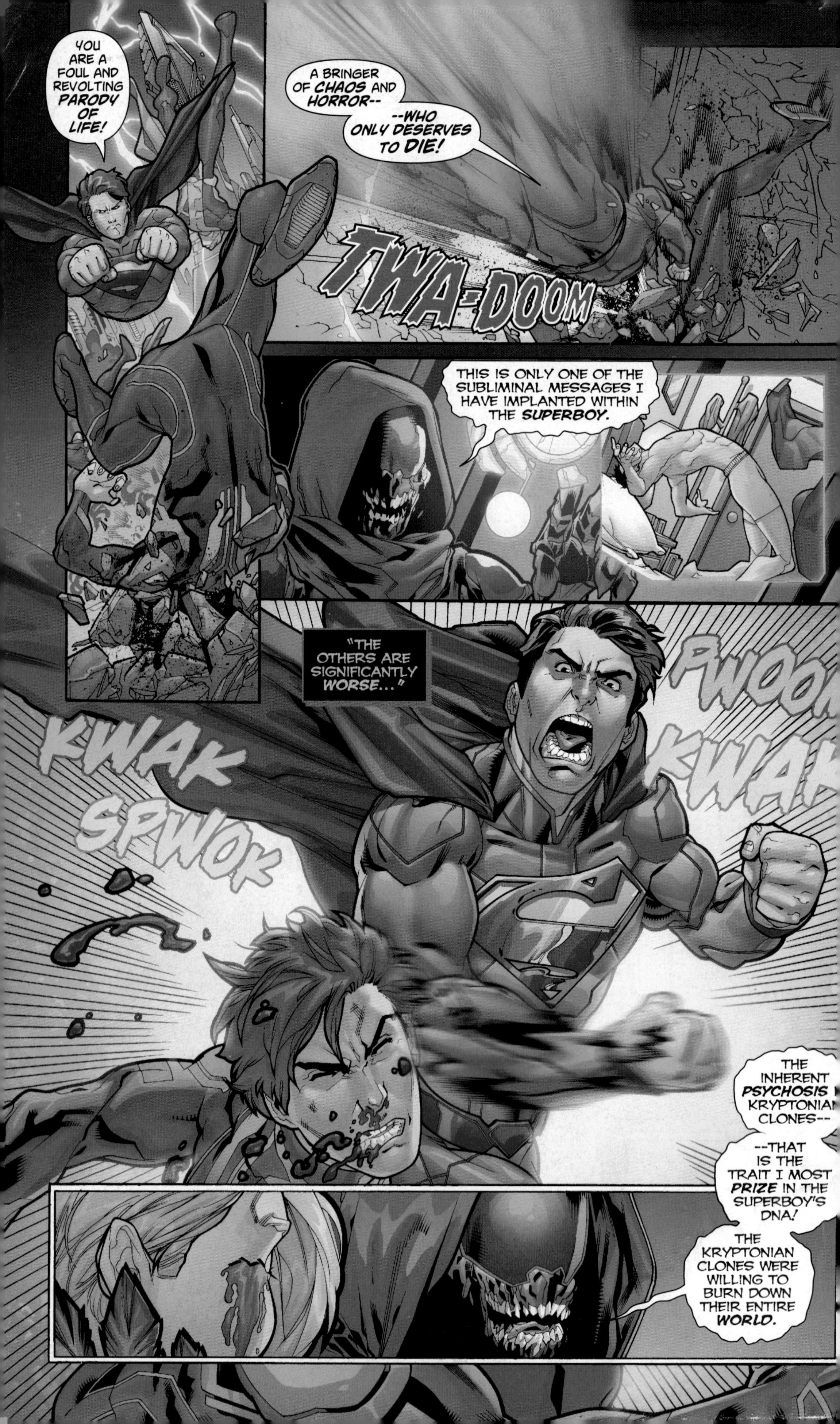
YOU ARE A FOUL AND REVOLTING PARODY OF LIFE!
A BRINGER OF CHAOS AND HORROR--
--WHO ONLY DESERVES TO DIE!
TWA-DOOM
THIS IS ONLY ONE OF THE SUBLIMINAL MESSAGES I HAVE IMPLANTED WITHIN THE SUPERBOY.
"THE OTHERS ARE SIGNIFICANTLY WORSE..."
KWAK
SPWOK
THE INHERENT PSYCHOSIS KRYPTONIAN CLONES--
--THAT IS THE TRAIT I MOST PRIZE IN THE SUPERBOY'S DNA!
THE KRYPTONIAN CLONES WERE WILLING TO BURN DOWN THEIR ENTIRE WORLD.

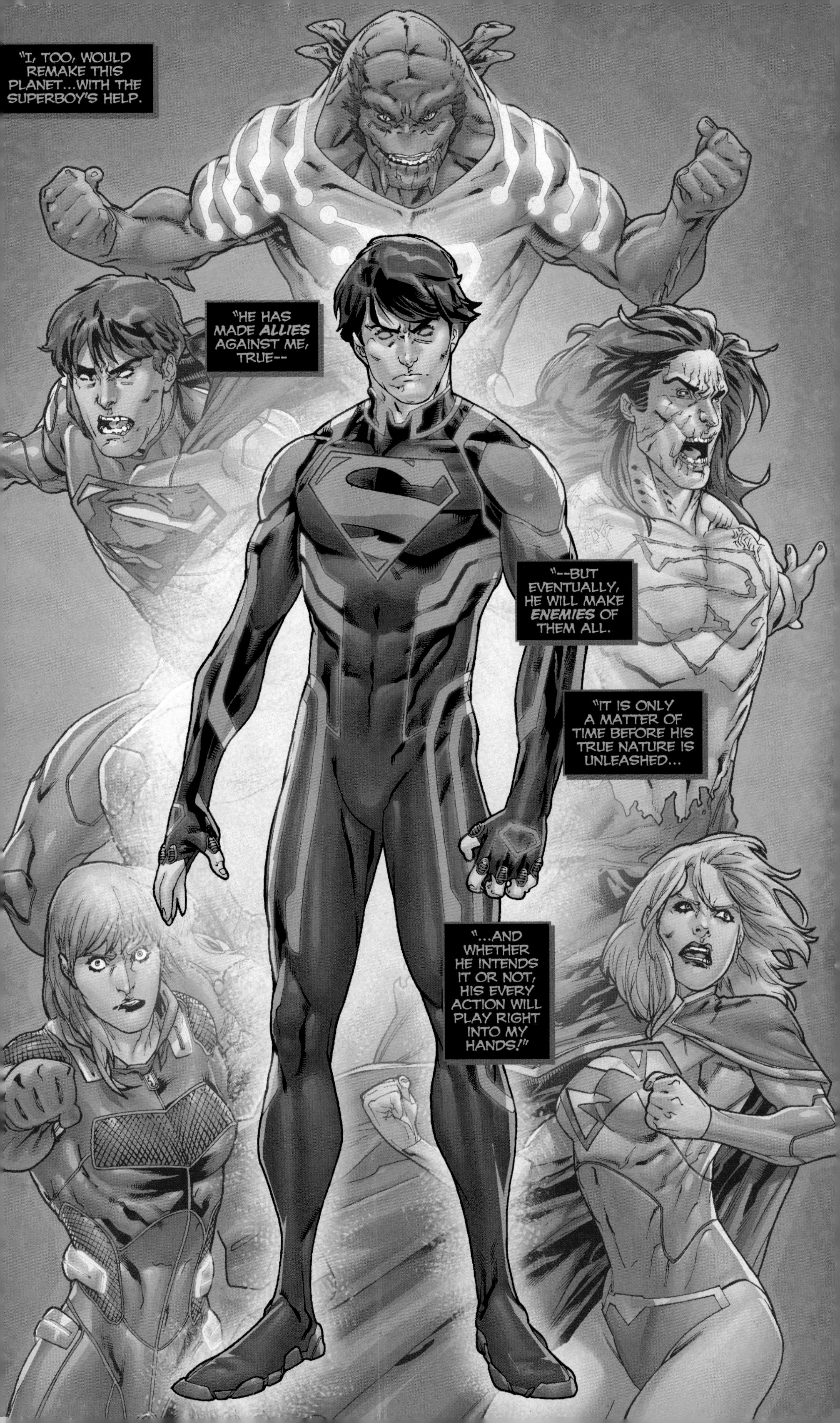
"I, TOO, WOULD REMAKE THIS PLANET...WITH THE SUPERBOY'S HELP.
"HE HAS MADE *ALLIES* AGAINST ME, TRUE--
"--BUT EVENTUALLY, HE WILL MAKE *ENEMIES* OF THEM ALL.
"IT IS ONLY A MATTER OF TIME BEFORE HIS TRUE NATURE IS UNLEASHED...
"...AND WHETHER HE INTENDS IT OR NOT, HIS EVERY ACTION WILL PLAY RIGHT INTO MY HANDS!"

"It's fresh air. I like this all-too-human Superman, and I think a lot of you will, too."
—SCRIPPS HOWARD NEWS SERVICE

START AT THE BEGINNING!

SUPERMAN: ACTION COMICS VOLUME 1: SUPERMAN AND THE MEN OF STEEL

SUPERMAN VOLUME 1: WHAT PRICE TOMORROW?

SUPERGIRL VOLUME 1: THE LAST DAUGHTER OF KRYPTON

SUPERBOY VOLUME 1: INCUBATION

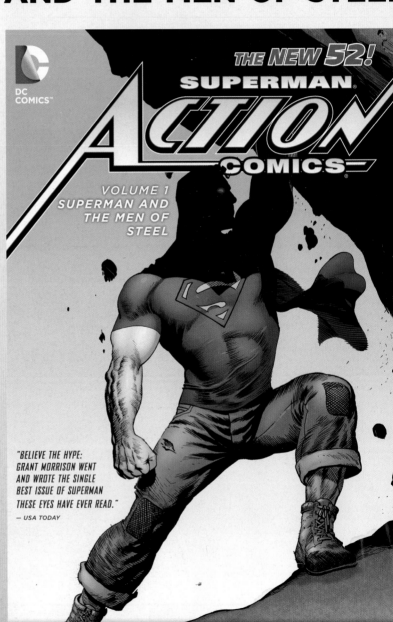

GRANT **MORRISON** RAGS **MORALES** ANDY **KUBERT**